Why Mary Matters

WHY MARY MATTERS

PROTESTANTS AND THE VIRGIN MARY

4th Edition

Kristofer Carlson

Dormition Publishing
Norfolk, Virginia

Copyright

ISBN-13 978-0692273197

ISBN-10 0692273190

Scripture quotations, unless otherwise noted, are from the Authorized King James Version.

Back cover photograph by Kim Bentz.

Dedication

This book is dedicated to my wife Susanna, who has had to put up with my various enthusiasms, my many moods, and my incomprehensible gibberish for the past thirty plus years. Thanks for hanging in there.

Epigraph

Let my will stand for the reason

On what grounds of principle do the denominations around us vindicate their right to exist? To some of the sects this question would come like a thunderbolt. They have never raised it. They never knew that such a question could be raised. In the Sectarian Declaration of Independence, among the certain inalienable rights are sectarian life, sectarian liberty, and sectarian pursuit of happiness. They may deny a man's right to wear a coat or a hat not fashioned after the sacred pattern shown them in the mount of their private hallucination, but as to a man's right to join himself to any sect he thinks good, or to make another sect if the existing sects do not suit him, of that they never doubted. In the Popery of Sect, "*Stat pro ratione voluntas*" — their best reason is, they wish it so.

Yet this question is a great question. It is the question. The denomination which has not raised it is a self-convicted sect. The denomination which cannot return such an answer to it as at least shows sincere conviction that it has such reasons, should be shunned by all Christians who would not have the guilt of other men's sins.[1]

Charles Porterfield Krauth (1823 – 1883), D. D., LL. D., Norton Professor of Systematic Theology and Ecclesiastical Polity in the Evangelical Lutheran Theological Seminary, Philadelphia.

Preface to the Fourth Edition

The benefits of self-publishing are many; likewise the perils. The first edition of this book was a Kindle edition, and fell victim to a Digital Millennium Copyright Act (DMCA) takedown notice from a copyright troll. The second Kindle edition removed the offending material, after which I published the third edition in print.

This fourth edition is the result of another year's worth of research. I also changed the citation style, choosing to use endnotes instead of in-line citations. I make an attempt to define a word the first time I use it; I realize that when next encountered in a different context, that definition may be forgotten. Therefore, at the request of one of my readers, I added a glossary.

I remain firmly convinced of the need for a book like this, a book that addresses the theological and historical rationale for the veneration of the Virgin Mary. This book is intended as an apologetic for rather than a theological treatise on the Virgin Mary. It is not enough, as many do, to simply state our beliefs; we must be able to defend them in a spirit of humility, and let the Holy Spirit do His work.

I intended this book for the curious Protestant, not for the Orthodox. Yet I have discovered that its best use may be as an aid to Catechesis in the Orthodox Church. The reason is that most Protestants are incurious about the Virgin Mary; it is not until they begin exploring the apostolic church that they come face to face with the Virgin Mary.

The Blessed Virgin is a great comfort to those Christians who know her, but also a stone of stumbling and a rock of offense to those who do not. A priest who is not an American convert may not understand the visceral distaste of Protestant catechumens for the ways in which we speak of her, and the instinctual manner in which Protestants recoil from her. A Protestant catechumen will not understand the difference between veneration and worship, nor the important place the Blessed Virgin plays in the Incarnation of the Son of God.

It is my prayer that those who read this book will, if nothing else, come away with an appreciation of the scriptural, theological, and historical basis for the veneration of the Virgin Mary.

In that spirit, let us pray with all the saints:

It is truly meet to bless you, O Theotokos, ever blessed and most pure and the Mother of our God! More honorable than the cherubim and more glorious beyond compare than the seraphim: in virginity you gave birth to God the Word, True Theotokos, we magnify you!

Glory to the Father and to the Son and to the Holy Spirit, now and ever and unto the ages of ages. Amen.

LORD have mercy! LORD have mercy! LORD have mercy!

Through the prayers of our brothers and sisters, LORD Jesus Christ our God, have mercy on us and save us. Amen.

Table of Contents

DEDICATION   III

EPIGRAPH   IV

PREFACE TO THE FOURTH EDITION   V

TABLE OF CONTENTS   VII

TABLE OF FIGURES   X

ACKNOWLEDGEMENTS   XI

PART I: PROTESTANTS AND THE VIRGIN MARY   1

    1: FROM FUNDAMENTALISM TO ORTHODOXY   2

    2: CATHOLIPHOBIA   7

    3: THE CHARACTER OF PROTESTANTISM   10

PART II: WHY MARY MATTERS   15

    4: THE VIRGIN MARY AND THE INCARNATION   16

    5: THE NECESSITY OF THE VIRGIN BIRTH   29

    6: MARIOLOGY AND CHRISTOLOGY   34

    7: THE TRINITY AND THE INCARNATION   47

    8: THE ABANDONMENT OF MARIAN THEOLOGY   49

PART III: COSMOLOGY AND ANTHROPOLOGY   53

    9: CHRISTIAN COSMOLOGY, CHRISTIAN ANTHROPOLOGY   54

    10: A COMMUNITARIAN ANTHROPOLOGY   61

    11: COSMOLOGY AND THE CHRISTIANIZATION OF ANTHROPOLOGY   64

    12: THE MEANING OF GOD'S IMAGE AND LIKENESS   71

        The Protestant Argument   76

        The Creation Accounts   77

    13: THE ECUMENICAL COUNCILS   81

    14: HERESY AND CHRISTIAN ANTHROPOLOGY   87

    15: THE THEOLOGY OF THE BODY   93

    16: THE COMMUNION OF PERSONS AND THE GIFT OF SELF   97

    17: THE PRIEST OF CREATION   104

    18: CLOTHED WITH THE GLORY OF GOD   111

    19: THE MARIAN BRIDGE   115

PART IV: MARIOLOGY IN THE LIFE OF THE CHURCH   121

  20: THE HISTORICAL DEVELOPMENT OF MARIOLOGY   122

  21: MARIOLOGY AND THE CHURCH   127

  22: MARIOLOGY AND CATHOLICITY   133

  23: MARIOLOGY AND PRAYER TO THE SAINTS   136

    The Scriptural Witness   137

    Prayer to the Queen of Heaven   145

PART V: THE PERPETUAL VIRGINITY OF THE VIRGIN MARY   147

  24: MARRIAGE AND VIRGINITY   148

  25: VIRGINITY IN CHURCH HISTORY   161

  26: PERSECUTION, SECULARIZATION, AND MONASTICISM   165

  27: THE VIRGIN MARY AS THE PROTOTYPICAL CHRISTIAN   169

  28: VIRGINITY FOR THE SAKE OF THE KINGDOM OF HEAVEN   172

  29: VIRGINITY IN SACRED SCRIPTURE   175

  30: VIRGINITY AS AN ESCHATOLOGICAL SIGN   179

  31: THE SUPPOSED SONS OF THE VIRGIN MARY   184

    Why the Virgin Birth   186

    Perpetual Virginity as Guarantee of the Incarnation   188

    The Modern Protestant and Mary's Virginity   189

    Clans, Tribes, and the Supposed Sons of Mary   194

    The Scriptures and the Supposed Brothers of Jesus   199

    Against Mary's Perpetual Virginity   204

PART VI: THE VIRGIN MARY IN THE NEW TESTAMENT   207

  32: SCRIPTURE ALONE AND THE VIRGIN MARY   208

  33: THE VIRGIN MARY AND THE NEW TESTAMENT   211

  34: THE WITNESS OF PAUL AND THE GOSPEL OF LUKE   213

  35: THE WITNESS OF THE APOSTLE JOHN   218

  36: THE IMPLICIT WITNESS REGARDING MARY   220

    Mary is the Greatest Woman Who Ever Lived.   220

    Mary is our Model for the Christian Life.   221

    Mary is our model of obedience.   221

    Mary is our model of purity and holiness.   222

    Mary is our model of royalty and intercession.   224

    Mary is the Mother of God.   225

We Are to Honor Mary and Call Her Blessed.   226

37: PROTESTANTS ON THE ANNUNCIATION   227

38: THE ANNUNCIATION: THE COURTSHIP OF THE VIRGIN   229

39: HAIL, FULL OF GRACE   237

40: REJOICE, DAUGHTER OF ZION   241

41: HOW SHALL THESE THINGS BE?   247

42: THE FREE CHOICE OF MARY   250

43: THE VISITATION   260

44: THE MAGNIFICAT   262

45: BLESSED ART THOU AMONG WOMEN   267

PART VII: THE VIRGIN MARY IN THE OLD TESTAMENT   269

46: THE TYPOLOGY OF THE BLESSED VIRGIN   270

47: THE VIRGINAL CONCEPTION AND BIRTH   274

48: THE PROTOEVANGELIUM   285

49: THE WOMAN IN TRAVAIL   287

50: THE SEALED GATE   290

PART VIII: MARIAN TYPES, SYMBOLS, AND TITLES   295

51: SYMBOLS AND SCRIPTURAL INTERPRETATION   296

Types and Symbols   297

Symbols and Their Multiple Meanings   298

Specific Marian Prefigurations   300

Other Marian Prefigurations   300

The Temple: its Vessels and Furnishings   301

52: THE BURNING BUSH   302

53: WISDOM HATH BUILT HER HOUSE   307

54: MARY AS THE NEW ARK   311

55: THEOTÓKOS, THE MOTHER OF GOD   317

56: PROTESTANTS AND THE MOTHER OF GOD   320

57: THE HISTORY OF THE TERM THEOTÓKOS   322

The Theotokos and the Creeds   326

The Theotokos and Chalcedonian Christology   329

58: AEIPARTHENOS, OR EVER-VIRGIN   332

59: PANAGIA, OR ALL-HOLY   340

The Panagia and Original Sin   341

The Holiness of Mary and the Fathers of the Church   346

60: MARY AS THE NEW EVE   351

61: QUEEN OF HEAVEN   357

62: MOTHER OF THE CHRISTIAN RACE   363

EPILOGUE: WHY MARY MATTERS   370

GLOSSARY   372

BIBLIOGRAPHY   376

INDEX   401

ENDNOTES   418

Table of Figures

Figure 1: The Tripartite Theology of the Body 98
Figure 2: The Communitarian Triangle......................................100
Figure 3: Mary, the Wife of Clopas...200

Acknowledgements

I gratefully thank the following people and institutions for their insight, access, and assistance:

To the American Lutheran Theological Seminary (ALTS), for providing me with access to the complete set of the Ante-Nicene, Nicene, and Post-Nicene Fathers, as well as the reason and opportunity to begin studying them;

To the Reverend Dr. John Kleinig, former Head of the Biblical Department at Australian Lutheran College, for introducing me to the way the holiness of God is treated in the Old and New Testaments;

To Reverend David Petersen, pastor of Redeemer Lutheran Church (Ft Wayne, IN) for his initial suggestion that Mariology was consistent with Scripture;

To the Walther Library at Concordia Theological Seminary (Ft. Wayne, IN), for allowing me to access a wide variety of theological resources;

To All Saints Religious Goods (Ft. Wayne, IN) for helping me find my initial resources on Mariology and the Church Fathers;

To All Saints of America Orthodox Mission (Alexandria, VA) and The Dormition of the Theotokos Orthodox Church (Norfolk, VA) for allowing me the use of their church libraries;

To the Very Reverend Fr. Michael Koblosh, for encouraging my investigations, loaning me books from his personal library, and pointing me towards the more important Orthodox authors;

And to Fr. John Cox, for his patience and guidance in my spiritual journey.

Part I: Protestants and the Virgin Mary

1: From Fundamentalism to Orthodoxy

In my mid-twenties I grew increasingly uneasy with the fundamentalist/evangelical milieu. I began looking not for something different, and perhaps something more, although I could not have told you what "more" looked like. I briefly flirted with Eastern Orthodoxy (during which I read about it, but never actually attended a service), but soon rejected it out of hand — for I discovered their veneration of Mary, which I judged to be a Roman Catholic doctrine and therefore contemptible. I had a different but related difficulty with Lutheranism; after my first Lutheran worship service, which seemed too Catholic, I vowed never to return. Nevertheless, the pastor dealt with me gently, and almost against my will, I slowly became convinced that the Lutheran understanding of Sacred Scripture was true and faithful to the Word of God. Yet in many ways, I remained firmly fundamentalist. It took my some time to come to grips with sacramental theology; it took me nearly two decades before I rejected dispensationalism as a grievous theological error; and a little longer to finally understand the rationale for infant baptism. During my more than twenty years as a Lutheran, I maintained much of my Protestant hostility to Catholicism, most especially in my open hostility to any hint of Mariology.

My Protestant background convinced me that the Virgin Mary was nothing more than a bit player, a young Jewish girl who made a cameo appearance in the first Christmas pageant, only to quickly fade into the background. I believed Mary was an incidental participant in the Incarnation, and not much more than an incubator for the Christ;[2] I believed Mary was perhaps an example of Christian obedience and womanly submission, but no more than that. I could see no evidence in the scriptures to convince me otherwise.

From Fundamentalism to Orthodoxy

One Sunday during Advent, my pastor mentioned he had no problem believing in the perpetual virginity of Mary, briefly demonstrating that it was theologically consistent with the Old and New Testaments. He also said he had no problem with a variety of other Marian doctrines. He then produced some historical evidence for the bodily Assumption of Mary (what the Orthodox describe as her Dormition), although he said the evidence was too slight to be dogmatic about it. Given my hostility to Roman Catholic theology, this was disturbing, and I began a quest to discover the scriptural foundations of Mariology (the doctrines and beliefs about the Virgin Mary).

The evidence surprised me. The scriptural evidence for Mariology — instead of being slight and easily dismissed — turned out to be quite extensive. My own knowledge was so limited that I did not know enough to ask the most interesting questions; my Protestant background — with its automatic hostility to Catholicism — had ill equipped me for this sort of investigation. Eventually it became clear that the standard arguments against Mariology were weak at best, showing strong evidence of the logical fallacy called "Begging the Question" where the proposition to be proven is assumed in the premise. Most Protestant interpreters of Scripture begin with the premise that Mariology cannot be proven in scripture, and then proceed to demonstrate how correct they are by ignoring or explaining away that which they have already chosen not to see.

I began my formal investigation by trying to discover why Roman Catholics (along with the Eastern Orthodox, and every non-Western, non-Protestant branch of Christianity) believe what they believe about Mary. I asked myself how Catholics can justify their beliefs, and whether they even pretend to have a biblical basis for their doctrines. At first, I confined myself to reading what various Protestants said about Catholicism and Mariology. It quickly became clear that most Protestants authors did not know

3

why Catholics believed as they did; they quoted each other quite extensively and quoted minor or popular Catholic authors, but rarely quoted authoritative Catholic source documents.

Once I read Roman Catholic sources, I quickly discovered many of the Protestant apologists had misquoted and distorted them. If I was to be intellectually honest, if I was going to learn enough to ask the right questions, then I was going to have to leave the Protestant milieu and travel through unfamiliar territory. Eventually I began to read the early church fathers, which was quite startling in itself (because most evangelicals — and dispensationalists in particular — do not read the fathers.) I went to a Lutheran seminary and browsed the stacks for information on Mary; I went to a Catholic bookstore and asked for their more academic books on doctrine and Mariology; I began searching the Internet for various scholarly articles from authors of different denominations and communions.

My investigations startled me. Contrary to what I had been taught, Roman Catholics, Eastern Orthodox, and others based their Mariology on Sacred Scripture; not only that, but their analysis of the relevant scriptural passages was quite profound.[3] I discovered that at its core, Marian doctrine permeates the Old Testament, providing color and depth to the New.[4] I discovered that even amongst Catholics, Marian doctrine does not stand alone, but is profoundly Christological — and that a formal Mariology counters Christological errors.[5] Like the blessed apostle, I had the sensation that someone had touched my eyes; when the scales fell from my eyes, I felt I was seeing scripture clearly for the first time. This was not comfortable for me then, and remains a painful process.

My research taught me something else. I had a rather low standard of proof for things I was convinced of, yet required a higher standard of proof for positions that did not agree with mine. I accepted my doctrinal positions because they were consonant with my existing doctrinal structure; I rejected other positions simply because they were incompatible with that system, because to do otherwise put my entire theological structure at risk. Therefore, for any position that I was unfamiliar with, or that did not fit, I required some form of external proof, while positions that fit into my doctrinal structure were (more or less) accepted solely on that basis. Marian doctrine was one thing that did not fit my existing doctrinal structure, and it took a lot to get me to change my mind. Yet based on Sacred Scripture, I have been forced to accept certain Marian doctrines — doctrines that I had long considered exclusively Catholic, and which ultimately called into question my otherwise internally coherent system of belief.

I could not shake the sense that these explorations were guiding me toward an alternate and perhaps a fuller expression of Christianity. It was this exploration of Marian doctrine — and the reflexive hostility it engendered among my Lutheran fellow travelers — that led me away from the Lutheran communion and into Orthodoxy. I discovered that the more I learned about the Blessed Virgin, the more difficulties I encountered within my own theological communion.

Even though I am Eastern Orthodox[6] today, I still believe a strong Mariology is compatible with Lutheranism and with the Protestantism of the reformers — though perhaps not most modern-day Protestants, who have carried juridical theology to its logical extreme. My hope is that the record of my exploration of Marian doctrine will be interesting, and that my attempt at providing answers to the important Marian questions will be useful to some. I acknowledge that although the Marian questions deserve answers, the attempt to provide the answers is problematic; and, for those whose minds are already made up, the attempt is likely futile.

Of this, Alexander Schmemann writes:

[I]t is no easy task to give such an explanation. As one of the hymns for the Annunciation says, "Let no impure hand touch the living temple of God." The more elevated, the more pure, the more holy, the more beautiful the subject one wants to speak about, the more difficult it is. And to me it seems impossible for words to fully express precisely what, in this singular image of Mother and Child, church consciousness has in all ages seen, understood, and come to love and glorify with such joy and tenderness.[7]

If you, dear reader, are opposed to Marian doctrine, it is possible that no amount of evidence will change your mind. Sacred Scripture is not a systematic theology, nor is it comprised of doctrinal treatises. Any number of people have approached Sacred Scripture in all sincerity and have devised any number of different theological systems, each internally coherent and with great explanatory power.[8] Despite this, one of the unique things about human consciousness is our ability to step outside ourselves, to see things from another perspective, and to change our minds. I ask you to examine the Sacred Scriptures with an open mind, to see them through another person's eyes, and to examine the views of people you might normally discard out of hand. If you do this, even if you remain unconvinced, I still believe you will find the process spiritually rewarding.

2: Catholiphobia

It may seem strange to begin this introduction to Mariology with a description of my anti-Catholic bias, but it is necessary. For many Protestants, an antipathy towards Rome is one of the defining characteristics of their faith. America being a deeply Protestant country, it is no wonder why the historian Arthur Schlesinger Sr. called anti-Catholicism "the deepest-held bias in the history of the American people."[9] Likewise, the historian John Highham described anti-Catholicism as "the most luxuriant, tenacious tradition of paranoiac agitation in American history".[10] While the anti-Catholic bias in the United States has abated as of late, it still exists in popular culture, as well as within the fundamentalist milieu. Therefore, any discussion of Mary must begin by describing this bias, a bias in which I thoroughly luxuriated for over forty years.

David B. Currie writes:

My own feelings for Mary were probably very representative of those of other Evangelicals — I never thought much about her. ...I can definitely say that Evangelicals do not talk about Mary very much. ...Could it be that Evangelicals are afraid of sounding Catholic, so they ignore a major player in the incarnation? Why doesn't it bother Evangelicals that they are failing to fulfill the words of the Holy Spirit through Mary: "From now on all generations will call me blessed" (Lu 1:48)?[11]

I was raised to be a good fundamentalist, which meant I was convinced that the Roman Catholics were my theological enemies (a judgment that included the Orthodox, whom in my ignorance I considered as merely Catholics without the Pope, or Catholic lite).[12] When I was a child, I remember a family once withdrew their membership from our church because a guest preacher quoted St. Augustine.

Even then this seemed to me a bit over the top — but only a little — for our hostility to Catholicism ran deep.

David B. Currie, in his book *Born Fundamentalist, Born Again Catholic*, writes of his childhood memory of President Kennedy's assassination, and his dismay that Kennedy, as a Catholic, would spend eternity in Hell.

A sixth-grader, I was playing on the playground when the rumors started. Just before the dismissal bell at the end of the day, the principle made the announcement of the PA system. JFK had been assassinated. School was dismissed in [eerie] silence. Tears welled up on my eyes as I walked the half mile home that afternoon. My sorrow was almost overwhelming for a sixth-grader, not only because our President was dead, but because in my heart of hearts I knew that he was in hell. He was a Catholic, and I was a Christian fundamentalist. [13]

Former Campus Crusade for Christ staff member Peter Gillquist, in discussing the history of the post-Reformation Protestant churches, mentioned that despite their differences, they had one thing in common.

All seemed to share a dislike for the bishop of Rome and the practice of his church, and most wanted far less centralized forms of leadership. ...To this day, many sincere, professing Christians will reject even the biblical data which speak to the practice of the Christian Church, simply because they think such historic practices are "too Catholic." In its zeal to regain purity, the Protestant movement pursued an agenda of overreaction without even being aware of it. [14]

Kenneth R. Samples, in a monograph entitled "What Think Ye of Rome? An Evangelical Appraisal of Contemporary Catholicism (Part One)", discusses the hostility to the Roman Catholics as expressed by the wing of Protestantism in which I spent my formative years:

8

At the other extreme is a band of Protestant fundamentalists who are literally rabid in their denunciation of Catholicism. This assemblage (usually led by vociferous ex-Catholics) dismisses Catholicism outright as an inherently unbiblical and evil institution. They not only consider the Roman church to be doctrinally deviant, but also the efficient cause of many or most of the social, political, and moral ills evident in the world today. Genuinely "anti-Catholic," this faction views the Catholic church as the "Whore of Babylon," a pseudo-Christian religion or cult. They seem to concentrate exclusively on those various doctrines that sharply divide Protestants and Catholics.[15]

In the same vein, the Lutheran theologian Gustaf Aulén notes that much Evangelical theology is determined to some extent by opposition to Rome.

The attitude of evangelical Christianity has to a very large extent been determined by the opposition to the Roman doctrine of the saints and to Mariology. The opposition has been and continues to be inevitable. But the evangelical attitude has remained purely negative and has therefore lost something of that living and life-giving relationship which unites the faithful in all ages.[16]

There is a question as to the extent of this catholiphobia: is it confined to one extreme of Protestantism, or might it be, as some indicate, Protestantism's defining characteristic?

3: The Character of Protestantism

In light of the reflexive hostility of most Protestant churches towards the Roman Catholic Church, we should take a moment to discuss the general character of the Protestant mind. Russian theologian Aleksei Khomyakov claims that hostility towards "the Church", generally defined as Roman Catholicism, is the defining characteristic of Protestantism. In his essay "On the Western Confessions of Faith", Khomyakov tries to find the central distinctiveness of Protestantism. He does not find it in the "act of protest made on behalf of faith" for central to the development and defense of Christian dogma is the protest against error; nor in "freedom of investigation", which is nothing more than "the beginning of conversion". Khomyakov finally concludes:

Protestantism means the expression of doubt in essential dogma. In other words, the denial of dogma as a living tradition; in short, a denial of the Church. ...Protestantism is one world simply negating another. ...its whole life consists in negation. The body of doctrines it still holds, the work undertaken by the enterprise of a few scholars and later received by the apathetic credulity of several million uneducated people, is surviving only because the need is felt to oppose the Roman confession. As soon as this feeling disappears, Protestantism at once breaks down into private opinion with no common bonds whatever.[17]

Mother Maria Skobtsova defines the essential character of Protestant belief somewhat differently, as a sort of mystical individualism.

The Christian soul has been suffering from a sort of mystical Protestantism. Only the combination of two words carries full weight for it: God and I, God and my soul, and my path, and my salvation. For the modern Christian soul it is

10

easier and more natural to say "My Father" than "Our Father," "deliver me from the evil one," "Give me this day my daily bread," and so on. ...And heavy as it may be, whatever human sufferings it may place on my shoulders, it is all the same my cross, which determines my personal way to God, my personal following in the footsteps of Christ. My illness, my grief, my loss of dear ones, my relations to people, to my vocation, to my work — these are details of my path, not ends in themselves, but a sort of grindstone on which my soul is sharpened, certain — perhaps sometimes burdensome — exercises for my soul, the particularities of my personal path.[18]

Both of these approaches are complementary, and are useful to our discussion. The first approach is a denial of the authority of the church; the second approach suggests the autonomy of the individual conscience in matters of faith has replaced the authority of the church. The most famous example of this change is Martin Luther's final statement before the Imperial Diet of Worms (which was called to force Luther to recant his teachings):

Since your most serene majesty and your high mightinesses require of me a simple, clear and direct answer, I will give one, and it is this: I can not submit my faith either to the pope or to the council, because it is as clear as noonday that they have fallen into error and even into glaring inconsistency with themselves. If, then, I am not convinced by proof from Holy Scripture, or by cogent reasons, if I am not satisfied by the very text I have cited, and if my judgment is not in this way brought into subjection to God's word, I neither can nor will retract anything; for it can not be right for a Christian to speak against his country. I stand here and can say no more. God help me. Amen.[19]

This statement is important because it proposes a tripartite authority: scripture, reason, and judgment (or conscience). This insistence on reason and conscience as authorities on par with the Word of God, and as more important than the witness of the church, has become an essential characteristic of Protestantism.

This reliance upon reason and conscience as guides for the interpretation of Sacred Scripture is a problem: reason can be faulty, and conscience can be betrayed. The Protestant's reasoning faculties prevent the apprehension and acknowledgement of evidence for Mariology that is seemingly right in front of them, for the Protestant's conscience tells them Mariology is a human invention at best, and false religion at worst. Central to some Fundamentalist antipathy towards Catholicism is the belief that it involves the grafting of the ancient pagan worship of Nimrod and his mother/wife onto Christianity — or, in the words of John Cardinal Ratzinger (Benedict XVI), that Roman Catholicism is "a recrudescence[20] of paganism".[21]

Seen in this light, the worship of Jesus and the veneration of his mother is a disguised version of an ancient mystery religion.[22] The fundamentalist site entitled "The Christian Expositor" provides a disturbing example of equating the honor due Mary with the worship given to pagan gods, and then using that to conflate Catholicism and Paganism.

Hinduism happily amalgamates with Rome — what are a few more 'gods' like Mary to a deception that absorbs all other religions? Likewise the deadly spiritist cult of Santeria is a blend of African witchcraft and Catholicism carried on in the name of 'saints' who front for African gods. In Rio de Janeiro the Catholic faithful visit cemeteries to petition the spirits of their ancestors along with the Catholic 'saints' and whichever version of 'Mary' they idolize! Catholicism's paganized Christianity was developed by Constantine to unite his empire and he really was the first 'Pope John Paul' in recognising the value of religious concord in bringing political unity through an ecumenism of his time.[23]

Karl Barth rejects this notion in this manner:

It is not to be recommended that we should base our repudiation on the assertion that there has taken place here an irruption from the heathen sphere, an adoption of the idea, current in many non-Christian religions, of a more or less central and original female or mother deity. In dogmatics you can establish everything or nothing with parallels from the history of religions. The biblical witness to revelation itself worked with 'heathen' ideas and germs of ideas; indeed it had to do so, as the world in which it aimed at getting a hearing was a 'heathen' world. The assertion may be ever so correct in itself; but leave your Catholic opponent at peace in this respect. Such an assertion cannot possibly be a statement of Evangelical belief. It cannot, therefore, be a serious question for Catholicism."[24]

Two things that appear to be similar are not necessarily equivalent. Moreover, just because two things are roughly parallel does not mean we can arbitrarily decide which of the two things is the source of the other. This is especially true in Christian theology: for example, the Incarnation is an event taking place both within and outside time, and whose effects reverberate backwards and forwards through time. Therefore, it is just as easy to say that paganism is the devil's counterfeit of the Christian faith rather than assuming any similarity between paganism and Christianity is simply a recurrence of paganism in Christian garb.

Part II: Why Mary Matters

4: The Virgin Mary and the Incarnation

Mary matters, because the Virgin Mary is the one in whom is best manifest our Lord.[25,26] Or, as a former Presbyterian convert to Eastern Orthodoxy remarked: "[T]he paradigm for bearing Christ to the world is the one who bore Christ to the world!"[27] This is what the church (everywhere, at all times, and in all places) believes, teaches, and confesses about the Virgin Mary.[28]

Mary was, as Sacred Scripture tells us, the one through whom our Lord was incarnate and made manifest to the world. The Blessed Virgin was the one to whom the angel announced the Incarnation, the one upon whom the Holy Ghost came, the one who was overshadowed by the power of the Highest, and the one who is therefore the Mother of God after the flesh, both now and ever and unto ages of ages, amen.

The author known as Pseudo-Dionysius, who wrote under the pseudonym Dionysius the Areopagite, dares not explain the Incarnation of Our Lord, or define its manner of functioning. These things are sacred mysteries beyond all words, beyond all reasonings, beyond the grasp of finite minds. This divine invasion of creation occurred, and its effects reverberate from eternity past to eternity future, despite the fact that the event itself remains ever outside our understanding. Yet the Incarnation did not occur without the participation and consent of the Virgin Mary, for God is not a rapist.

The most evident idea in theology, namely, the sacred incarnation of Jesus for our sakes, is something which cannot be enclosed in words nor grasped by any mind, not even by the leaders among the front ranks of the angels. That he undertook to be a man is, for us, entirely mysterious. We have no way of understanding how, in a fashion at variance with nature, he was formed from a virgin's blood.

The Virgin Mary and the Incarnation

...Out of love he has come down to be at our level of nature and has become a being. He, the transcendent God, has taken on the name of man. (Such things, beyond mind and beyond words, we just praise with all reverence.) In all this he remains what he is---supernatural, transcendent---and he has come to join us in what we are without himself undergoing change or confusion. His fullness was unaffected by that inexpressible emptying of self, and, most novel of all, amid the things or our nature he remained supernatural and amid the things of being he remained beyond being. From us he took what was of us and yet he surpassed us here too.[29]

Maximus the Confessor reminds us of the importance of the Incarnation (and by extension, the one through whom our Lord was incarnate): "The mystery of the incarnation of the Logos is the key to all the arcane symbolism and typology in the Scriptures, and in addition gives us knowledge of created things, both visible and intelligible."[30] Orthodox theologian Paul Evdokimov takes this discussion one step further: "From the beginning, discussion centred on the Incarnation as the means of salvation: *Cur Deus Homo?* — why God-Man? It is the question of life or death, a theology of Salvation as its most dramatic and historical."[31]

The witness of even the earliest church fathers placed the Virgin Mary clearly and deliberately within the Incarnational teachings regarding our Lord. The decrees of the ecumenical councils, in particular their statements concerning the Virgin Mary, were not only Christological, but we are to understand these as part of the larger theological discussion. It is unfortunate that those linkages are misunderstood, and that the role of the Virgin Mary in the history of the Incarnation is unappreciated. Mary herself noted she is to be blessed henceforth to all generations,[32] and Elizabeth is the first person recorded as venerating her; if the Virgin Mary were simply the vessel through whom our

Lord was incarnate, that would be insufficient reason to continue to bless her. Moreover, the fact that Protestants in general do not truly bless and honor Mary is curious and disturbing, and has profound theological consequences.

The theotokian (or hymn to Mary) known as *Axion estin* (or *It is truly meet*), is sung in the Orthodox liturgy, and is part of the daily prayers in most Orthodox prayer books. It reads as follows:

It is truly meet to bless you, O Theotokos,
Ever blessed and most pure and the Mother of our God!
More honorable than the cherubim,
and more glorious beyond compare than the seraphim.
Without corruption you gave birth to God the Word.
True Theotokos, we magnify you!

Protestants would likely be uncomfortable with this hymn; I know I was. Yet as Robert Arakaki demonstrates, the expressions of this hymn are entirely biblical.

Blessed — *"Blessed are you among women, and blessed is the child you will bear!" (Luke 1:42)*

Theotokos *(God-bearer) — "And whence is this to me, that the mother of my Lord should come to me?" (Luke 1:43; see also Isaiah 7:14, Matthew 1:21-25, Luke 2:6-7, Revelation 12:5)*

Ever-blessed — *"From now on all generations will call me blessed...." (Luke 1:48)*

All-holy — *"But just as he who called you is holy, so be holy in all you do; for it is written: 'Be holy, because I am holy.'" (I Peter 1:15-16)*

Utterly pure — *"Blessed are the pure in heart for they will see God." (Matthew 5:8). "Everyone who has this hope in him purifies himself, just as he is pure." (I John 3:3)*

Mother of God — *"The virgin will be with child and will give birth to a son, and will call him Immanuel– which means, 'God with us.'" (Matthew 1:23, cf. Isaiah 7:14)*

The Virgin Mary and the Incarnation

More honorable than — *"You made him a little lower than the heavenly beings the Cherubim and crowned him with glory and honor." (Psalm 8:5) "And God raised us up with Christ and seated us with him in the heavenly realms in Christ." (Ephesians 2:6)[33]*

If we can accept that the various phrases of the *Axion estin* hymn are biblical, what then is the problem? Why would a Protestant find this hymn so troubling? Once again, Robert Arakaki provides the answer. He writes:

Many Protestants are afraid that venerating Mary will eventually lead to worshiping her. Protestants' confusion when Orthodoxy claims that it venerates Mary but does not worship her arises from differences in their understanding of worship. Where the sermon is central to Protestant worship, the center of Orthodox worship is the Eucharist.[34]

The evangelical converts to Catholicism, Scott and Kimberly Hahn, describe their difficulties with these different definitions of worship.

I could not figure out why it was that it seemed to be that Catholics worshiped Mary, even though I knew worship of Mary was clearly condemned by the Church. Then I got an insight: Protestants defined worship as songs, prayers and a sermon. So when Catholics sang songs to Mary, petitioned Mary in prayer and preached about her, Protestants concluded she was being worshiped. But Catholics defined worship as the sacrifice of the body and Blood of Jesus, and Catholics would never have offered a sacrifice of Mary nor to Mary on the altar.[35]

Moreover, the Virgin Mary matters not only because she was the Birthgiver of God, but for her place in the preservation and transmission of the Gospel. Father John

Why Mary Matters

Anthony McGuckin, of the Romanian Orthodox Church, writes:

> *There can be little doubt that the Blessed Virgin was one who actively shaped the transmission of the Gospel traditions after the death of her son. Modern biblical exegesis has been strangely reluctant to admit anything of this, despite Luke's repeated insistence that it was Mary who treasured the significance of the story of her Son's birth, Mary who initiated his education in the understanding of the Torah and the Prophets, and Mary who was one of the towering figures in the first organization of the church of Jerusalem in the time of James the brother of the Lord. The silence about her role in contemporary Western biblical criticism is positively deafening.[36]*

Mary matters for her hearing of the word of God, for keeping all these things, for pondering them in her heart, and ultimately for keeping His word (Lu 11:27-28). To put it another way, and in accord with the words of our Lord, the Virgin Mary was the least among women and therefore the greatest of His disciples (Mt 11:11; Lu 9:48). Hieromartyr Hilarion (Troitsky) (1886–1929) quotes the first stanza of the hymns for the Forefeast of the Nativity, a hymn which describes the effect of the Incarnation upon the Virgin Mary: "Marvel not this day, O Mother, seeing the Infant, Who was born of the Father before the world: Who has come manifestly to raise and glorify fallen human nature, with faith and love magnifying Thee."[37,38] The Son of God magnified the Virgin Mary by means of the Incarnation, and on account of the Incarnation.

The Blessed Virgin Mary is the nexus between the human and the divine, and between the Old and New Testaments. Armenian theologian Vigen Guroian notes: "Mary is the bridge from Old Testament righteousness to its fulfillment in the New Covenant."[39] She is, as Hilda Graef

20

notes, "a kind of chiaroscuro"[40]; both hidden in shadow and blazing like the sun.[41] Mary occupies the foreground in Luke's account of the Incarnation, receding into the background as Jesus grows and begins His ministry. What John the Baptist said of himself could just as well have said of the Virgin Mary: "He must increase, but I must decrease" (John 3:30).

Additionally, the Virgin Mary is both Israel in a person, and is the Mother of the Christian Race. The Mother of Our Lord is Jesus' first catechumen, His first disciple, and the archetype of His virgin bride, which is the church. As a member of His church, we are also the seed of the woman, who is the last Eve (Ge 3:15; Rev 12:17). But most of all, Mary is the greatest and most holy of all the saints, the one who is most like him, the one in whom is best manifest our Lord.

We honor (venerate) Moses as the lawgiver, and we honor Mary as the one through whom the Word became incarnate. Enoch and Elijah are honored because they walked with God, and were taken up into heaven; we honor Mary because she too walked with God. We honor John the Baptist as the forerunner; we honor Mary as the first disciple and catechumen of our Lord. We honor Lazarus for being resurrected from the dead prior to Christ's conquering of sin, death, and the devil, just as we honor Mary in her Dormition (her death and translation into heaven). We honor the prophets who announced the Word of God just as we honor Mary, the mother of the divine Word.

If you are Protestant, you will no doubt find the majority of these statements rather offensive; you will think them papist, probably heretical, and quite likely derived from pagan religion. At the very least, to quote the Dominican theologian Eric Mascall, you will find all this to be "either an extravagance or an inessential luxury in theology."[42] I know this about you, because I have been one of you. I grew up in a fundamentalist milieu;[43] for me,

Christian fundamentalism is foundational, and remains a large part of how I relate to the world. I do not regret my upbringing as a fundamentalist, for it was through that means that I came to saving faith, and came to love both our Sacred Scriptures and our Lord Jesus Christ.

Yet what Thomas Howard wrote in his book *Evangelical is Not Enough* is still relevant today, and describes my relationship to Protestantism in general.

My own nurture took place in a particularly earnest and, to my mind, admirable sector of Protestantism, namely, evangelicalism. I have never come upon Christian believers of any ilk who exhibit more clearly than do the evangelicals the simplicity, earnestness, and purity of heart that the gospel asks of us.[44]

Thomas Howard, professor of English at St. John's Seminary, notes that although the faith he was raised in would have accepted the creedal formulations of the ancient church, it was curiously non-creedal.

At bottom, though, one cannot distinguish evangelical teaching from traditional Christian orthodoxy. We could be counted on to embrace wholeheartedly all that is spelled out in the ancient creeds of the Church. There is nothing in the Apostles', Nicene, Chalcedonian, or Athanasian creeds that we would have jibbed at. ...But there is something peculiar in this way of talking about evangelicalism. Our imagination did not run to creeds, fathers, doctors, tradition, or catholic orthodoxy. When it came to anchoring our faith, we cited texts from the New Testament and nothing else.[45]

Thomas Howard notes that in leaving Evangelicalism, he has "left nothing behind", something I find to be mostly true. Howard demonstrates this through Evangelical teaching on the Incarnation.

The Virgin Mary and the Incarnation

I was taught, for example, that Jesus was born of a virgin. This meant that He did not have a human father. At the Annunciation the Holy Ghost brought about what ordinarily occurs at human conception. Something gynecological occurred. Evangelicalism teaches this; ancient catholic orthodoxy teaches this. ...My own passage from childhood to adolescence to adulthood, and thence to approaching old age, has not obliged me to shift ground from what my Sunday school teachers taught me. They agreed with the fathers and doctors of the Church that the Virgin Birth happened in the real world before any early Christian piety went to work on the notion. Similarly, the Resurrection happened before any "Easter Faith" existed.[46]

Yet despite our basic agreement concerning the bare facts of the Incarnation, I spent very little time meditating upon the Incarnation. As a Protestant, I was little concerned with what it means for man that God is one of us; what it means for God to have been born of a woman; what it means for Mary to have been in physical contact with her Maker, and for her Maker to have built for Himself a body from and of her flesh. Protestants will spill gallons of ink defending justification by faith and substitutionary atonement, but for most Protestants, their interest in the Incarnation is little more than a sentimental attachment, seemingly no deeper than the annual Christmas pageant. Thomas Howard describes the reason for this: for most Protestants, Christianity is spiritual rather than physical; that "worship in spirit and in truth" is taken to mean a divorce between matter and spirit. Thus, the physicality of the Virgin Birth is disturbing.[47]

There came an end to those gory altars and all that slaughter. But it was not a tissue of elevated thoughts that replaced them. Rather, an angel appeared to a woman and said, "Hail!" What we now had, far from the summons away

23

from the physical realm that highminded men might have wished, was gynecology, obstetrics, and a birth. Whatever we may imagine about the spiritual rhapsody that might have attended this angelic visitation to the Virgin, the one thing we know to have occurred was a conception. The Virgin's womb teemed.

It was embarrassing to the religious mind. It proved a scandal. The whole ensuing story bothered and even enraged religious men, and it has continued to do so. Christian history is littered not only with the bones of martyrs who have died at the hands of enemies who hated this story but also with the confused and heretical attempts of Christians themselves to skirt it. Seizing on Saint Paul's vocabulary and wrenching it about, they have tried to pit the spiritual against the physical and have tried to make Christianity like Buddhism, a religion that summons us away from earthly, earthy life.[48]

The physicality of the Incarnation is difficult for the modern mind to grasp. We clean it up, and make of the story something pious and sentimental. But the very earthiness of the story is what provides us with the deepest meaning of the Incarnation of our Lord. Our Lord became man not in a palace, not in the home of a wealthy merchant, and not in the home of one of the religious authorities. Instead, our Lord was born to a peasant girl and her betrothed, and not even in a house. Our Lord was born in a stable, surrounded by filthy animals and their excrement. Foul odors filled our Lord's nostrils as He took His first breath; he was first clothed in rags like those used to wrap dead bodies. Thus our Lord took upon himself the form of a servant, lived as a peasant laborer, and died a criminal's death. St. John of Kronstadt notes how this close association with humanity — and the created order — is the point of the Incarnation.

The Virgin Mary and the Incarnation

Through His incarnation the Lord has entered into the closest relation with man. It is marvellous! God Himself is united in one person with man. God became flesh--"the Word was made flesh." [390] God Himself partook of our carnal food and drink, was laid in a manger, lived in a house. He Who cannot be contained by the heavens walked upon the earth, upon the waters, upon the air. 'He went up," it is said, "toward heaven." [391] He was nailed to the tree, "He Who hangeth the earth upon nothing by His command." [392] The whole earth, the waters, and the air--all are sanctified by the incarnate Son of God; therefore the earth is dear to Him--this temporary abode of men, this inn of the human race, this place of His habitation amongst men. But especially dear to Him are men themselves, whose souls and bodies He has received into unity with His own Person, and especially with true Christians. He is in them, and they in Him.[49]

The Reformation began in 1517 when an Augustinian monk named Martin Luther nailed his 95 Theses to the Wittenberg door. The actions of Pope Leo X and the reactions of Martin Luther and the German princes gave rise to what is termed the Magisterial Reformation. Historically, the Magisterial Reformation was followed by Pietism and the Radical Reformation. This, in turn gave way to Revivalism in the 18th century, through a succession of "Awakenings", the most recent of which is the Azusa Street Revival in the early 20th century, from which arose the modern Charismatic movement and the various Pentecostal denominations. Besides being based on a radical individualism and a rejection of the sacramental importance of community (replacing the sacramental understanding with an ordinance, in that we are commanded not to reject the coming together on the Lord's day), the Radical Reformation, Pietism, and Revivalism emphasize the spiritual over the physical in a manner that is dualistic, and therefore an implicit denial of the Incarnation.

Why Mary Matters

Fr. Andrew Stephen Damick writes:

At its heart, the Radical Reformation is a rejection of the Incarnation. Most of the Radicals would of course adhere conceptually to the traditional dogmas about the Son of God becoming a man, but their theology and practice fail to reflect all the implications of the Incarnation. For the Orthodox, because God became a physical, material man, the Church has a concrete, historical reality. Ordination requires a physical act of laying on of hands. The Eucharist has a physical component to its spiritual reality. The physical act of baptism really accomplishes something spiritual. Icons are a witness to the Incarnation and an integral part of church life. All of these material elements in the ongoing salvation life of the Christian are rejected by the Radicals, and so we can only conclude that their theology of the Incarnation is lacking something at its heart. What was rejected in the Radical Reformation was the physical side of being spiritual.[50]

But the Radical Reformation had a curious Mariological side effect. The heirs of the Radical Reformation rejected Mariology and all its attendant theological implication, claiming to base their faith on "Scripture Alone." Yet the Mariological positions they arrived at have more in common with those of the theological liberals who reject the historicity of the scriptures than with the ancient Christian church. Witness, if you will, the conclusions of Hilda Graef in her book *Mary: A History of Doctrine and Devotion*.[51] The first chapter of this book (entitled "Mary in the Scriptures") consists of a series of polemics regarding Mary that, despite coming from a theological liberal, nevertheless sound somewhat similar in form to those I heard as a fundamentalist and as a confessional Lutheran. Hilda Graef writes: "There are many other Old Testament texts, especially from the Wisdom books and the Canticle, which have been applied to Mary throughout the centuries,

26

both in the Liturgy and by individual authors; but they refer to her only in an "accommodated sense," that is to say, they do not envisage her directly, as does the Isaiah passage. [Isa 7:14]"[52] It is this reference to the various O.T. passages regarding Mary as the "accommodated sense" which allows for another point of view; including an outright dismissal of them as having anything to do with Mary.

I contrast Graef's comments with these by Bishop Hilarion, commenting on the writings of St. Isaac of Syria.

The Incarnation of the Son of God is, according to Isaac, the new revelation about God. In the Old Testament times, before the Incarnation, people were unable to contemplate God and to hear His voice, but after the Incarnation this became possible: 'Creation could not look upon Him unless He took part of it to Himself and thus conversed with it, and neither could it hear the words of His mouth face to face. The sons of Israel were not even able to hear His voice when He spoke with them from the cloud... The sons of Israel made ready and prepared themselves, keeping themselves chaste for three days according to the command of Moses, that they might be made worthy of hearing the voice of God, and of the vision of His revelation. And when the time was come, they could not receive the vision of His light and the fierceness of the voice of His thunder. But now, when He poured out His grace upon the world through His own coming, He has descended not in an earthquake, not in a fire, not in a terrible and mighty sound, but "as the rain upon a fleece, and rain-drops that fall upon the earth" softly, and He was seen conversing with us after another fashion. This came to pass when, as though in a treasury, He concealed His majesty with the veil of His flesh, and among us spoke with us in that body which His own bidding wrought for Him out of the womb of the Virgin'. Not only for human beings, but also for angels the door of contemplation and vision was opened in Jesus, when the

27

Word became flesh, as before the Incarnation they could not penetrate into these mysteries, Isaac claims.[53]

5: The Necessity of the Virgin Birth

As we have seen, the Incarnation is foundational to our understanding of Christianity, and the Virgin Birth is inextricably intertwined with the Incarnation, such that it is difficult to speak of the one without mentioning the other. Karl Barth notes: "No one can dispute the existence of a biblical testimony to the Virgin Birth."[54] Yet is the Virgin Birth necessary to the Incarnation of our Lord, or is it "theologically superfluous"?[55] If we accept that Jesus was born of a Virgin, and if we understand that the Virgin Birth was somehow an essential component of the Incarnation, can we explain the reason why the Virgin Birth was necessary? What is our apologetic? Can we construct some sort of rationale for it, one that seems satisfactory, one that can pass muster?

The first explanation I remember regarding the necessity of the Virgin Birth was that the sin nature was passed on through the male. Therefore Jesus, being born without the agency of a human father, did not inherit the guilt of original sin. Since He was Himself sinless (being the God/man), and absent the guilt of Adam's sin, he could substitute his death for ours, bearing the penalty for our sins by his substitutionary death.

So if sin is passed on through the male line, is sin then genetic? Of course not. But if the guilt of original sin is not passed genetically, in what way is it passed from the father to the children? Without getting too deep into it, there are any number of problems with a purely materialistic understanding of the virgin birth, especially for the necessity of the virgin birth.[56]

A more satisfactory explanation for the necessity of the virgin birth is provided by Romanian Orthodox author Fr. Dumitru Staniloae, who clearly expresses the necessity of the Virgin Birth in Incarnational terms.

He [the Son of God] wants to make the transition in the dialogue with human beings from the position of partner outside their order to that within their order. For this purpose He can no longer make use of human persons, who are born from one another. He produces for Himself from the Virgin Mary a human nature of His own, as human subject. He Himself is born as man. This is not only a new act, but also a totally new beginning that is produced in the history of humankind. This new beginning could not have been produced by the human initiative, but only by the divine initiative.

Another human subject, born the natural way of a man and a woman, would not have fulfilled the Son of God's plan to become himself a human subject in dialogue with human beings, without ceasing to remain the Son of God at the same time. A birth as a result of human autonomy, namely out of a human pair capable of bringing into existence by inherently human powers another human person, would not have introduced — into the line of human persons — a human Person that would be at the same time a divine Person. The birth of the Son of God from the Virgin took into consideration the inability of humanity to be saved by its own power, to break through the closed horizon of humanity subjected to repetition and death, and to include all who are born of Christ according to grace within the line of those "born" of God.[57]

There are a number of things we learn from this explanation. First, this argument neatly connects the necessity of the Virgin Birth with the Incarnation. Second, this argument does away with any tendency towards the Adoptionist heresy, the idea that God adopted the man Jesus as the Son of God at some later date; typically it is thought this happened at his baptism, his resurrection, or his ascension, but could have taken place even earlier. Adoptionism has the consequence of making Christ's divinity something added to His humanity, which eliminates the possibility for the divine and human natures being united in the one person of the Christ.

But the connection between the Virgin Birth and the Incarnation can be carried too far. Anthony Lane, Professor of Historical Theology at the London School of Theology, notes the following:

> *In the popular mind the virgin birth is often confused with the Incarnation. This has led to the belief that Jesus is the Son of God because God was His Father instead of Joseph. ... But this involves a fallacious view of the virgin birth as a biological explanation of the Incarnation. Jesus is seen as human on his mother's side and divine on his Father's side. A position similar to this has been given scholarly expression recently by J. Stafford Wright in a paper entitled, significantly, 'The Virgin Birth as a Biological Necessity'. He argues that one set of chromosomes was provided by Mary while the other set was created 'to be the vehicle of the divine personality'. Thus we have 'a single person, both human and divine'. He 'was both human through his mother's chromosomes, and could be divine through the newly-formed chromosomes'.*[58]

Anthony Lane notes this makes Jesus half man and half God, a chimera of sorts, "a sort of *tertium quid* [or third thing] of the type that the early fathers so rightly fought to exclude." The idea is one expressed by the Apollinarians, who referred to the Christ as neither man nor God, but some sort of a mixture of the two, constituting a "third thing", a heresy dismissed in the fourth century.

When we draw the connection between the Virgin Birth and the Incarnation, we are not saying the Virgin Birth contributed in any way to the Divinity of Christ, for that too is a theological error. Again, Anthony Lane describes the problem and its solution.

Why Mary Matters

Clearly the Incarnation of the Son of God requires a special intervention of God and this can be seen in the operation of the Holy Spirit described by Luke. But it is hard to see how Mary's virginity, the absence of a human father, can contribute to Jesus' deity. It has only been thought to do so because of confusion between the doctrines of the virgin birth and the Incarnation.

It is essential clearly to grasp the distinction between the Incarnation and the virgin birth. The virgin birth concerns the origins of the humanity of Christ. It states that Jesus, as man, had no human father. It does not state that God was his human father. The virgin birth is not like the stories of pagan gods mating with beautiful women. The miracle of the virgin birth is that of birth without a father, not of the mating of God and Mary. The doctrine of the Incarnation, on the other hand, concerns the deity of Christ. It states that this man Jesus was in fact God himself, the Logos, the Son of God come in the flesh. Jesus was divine not because he had no human father but because he is God become man. He is the Son of God (in the Trinitarian sense) not because of his human parentage (or lack of) but because he is the eternal Son of the Father, 'begotten from the Father before all ages'. To summarise the distinction, the Incarnation means that Jesus is the Son of God become flesh, the virgin birth means that he had no human father. It is not hard to see how the two have come to be confused. The one states that God is his Father, the other that Joseph was not. It has been fatally easy to put these two together and to conclude that God was his father instead of Joseph, because Joseph was not. But this is a serious confusion. God is his Father at the level of his eternal existence as God, not at the biological level. It was at the latter level that Joseph failed to be his father. When it is stated that Jesus did not need a human father because God was his Father the two levels are being confused. Such thinking, if pursued consistently, will lead to a grossly perverted form of either the virgin birth or the Incarnation or both.[59]

So while the Virgin Birth was necessary so that God might become man — might constitute a new beginning — this does not mean that because Joseph was not the father of Jesus, that God was His father. This is incorrect. The Christ has no father after His humanity, but has God for His Father after His divinity. The Virgin Birth was necessary so that the full humanity of Jesus could be united with the full divinity of the Son of God.

6: Mariology and Christology

A proper and catholic[60] Mariology is inextricably bound to Christology, and is therefore a necessary component of the true faith. St. Ignatius of Antioch, disciple of the apostle John, calls the virginity of Mary a mystery hidden from the prince of this world, a mystery wrought in silence by God: "Now the virginity of Mary was hidden from the prince of this world, as was also her offspring, and the death of the Lord; three mysteries of renown, which were wrought in silence by God."[61] Now as we know, the term mystery is also the source of the term sacrament; sacrament and mystery have the same scriptural meaning. Protestants, including Lutherans, jettisoned much of the spiritual heritage bequeathed them from the church catholic — specifically that church whose bishop resides in Rome.[62] Of course they would not consider this as an abandonment, but rather a recovery of a primitive Christianity uncorrupted by nearly fifteen centuries of hierarchal and heretical development within the Roman Catholic church. However, the loss of one of St Ignatius of Antioch's "three mysteries of renown" — the virginity of Mary, her offspring, and the death of the Lord — raises the question of whether Protestantism has recovered primitive Christianity, or rather whether in jettisoning Roman Catholicism they also jettisoned something essential to Christianity.[63]

Peter Gillquist writes:

The highly charged emotional atmosphere which surrounds this subject serves to blunt our objectivity in facing up to Mary. Many of us were brought up to question or reject honor paid to Mary in Christian worship and art. Therefore, we often have our minds made up in advance. We have allowed our preconceptions to color our understanding even of the Scripture passages concerning her. We have not let the facts speak for themselves.[64]

34

To be fair, whether one sees the veneration of the Virgin Mary in Sacred Scripture depends in part upon one's theological background and interpretive framework. Scot McKnight, the Karl A. Olsson Professor in Religious Studies at North Park University and author of the book "The Real Mary", states: "[T]he story about the real Mary has never been told. The Mary of the Bible has been hijacked by theological controversies whereby she has become a Rorschach inkblot in which theologians find whatever they *wish* to find."[65] So far, so good. However, McKnight then attempts to find a version of Mary palatable to Evangelicals, ignoring the witness of history and the church, and creates version of Mary befitting his thesis. McKnight's great mistake is his dismissal of what historic Christianity believed, taught, proclaimed, and for which some have even died, regarding the theology surrounding Christ and the Virgin Mary.

To be fair to those from a "Scripture Alone" background, we must admit that the overt scriptural evidence for the veneration of Mary seems rather sparse. Orthodox theologian Vladimir Lossky notes: "If we desired to consider biblical evidence apart from the Church's devotion to the Mother of God, we should be obliged to limit ourselves to the few New Testament passages relating to Mary and the one Old Testament passage cited in the New Testament with reference to her (the prophecy of the Virgin-Birth of the Messiah in Isaiah)."[66] Therefore, the starting place for an understanding of the veneration of Mary must begin with a proper understanding of Christology, and of its dogmatic development as a defense against Christological heresy. Vladimir Lossky notes that even here, the evidence for a Mariological connection is sparse.

If we were to limit ourselves to the dogmatic data, in the strict sense of the word, and were dealing only with dogmas affirmed by the Councils, we should find nothing

35

except the name Theotokos, whereby the Church has solemnly confirmed the divine maternity of the Holy Virgin. The dogmatic subject of the Theotokos, as the name was affirmed against the Nestorians, is Christological before it is anything else; that which is thereby defended against the gainsayers of the divine maternity is the hypostatic unity of the Son of God, when he had become the Son of Man. It is Christology which is directly envisaged here; it is indirectly that at the same time there is a dogmatic confirmation of the Church's devotion to her who bore God according to the flesh. It is said that all those who rise up against the appellation Theotokos, all who refuse to admit that Mary has this quality given to her, are not truly Christians, for they oppose the true doctrine of the Incarnation of the word. This should demonstrate the close connection between dogma and devotion, which are inseparable in the Church.[67]

John Breck notes: "The mystery of the Holy Virgin Mary belongs, as much as any other in Christian experience, to the *disciplina arcani*: the secret, inner life of the Church."[68] Thus we cannot truly understand the place of the Holy Virgin Mary in the economy of salvation apart from the church — for, as Breck notes: "[T]he person of Mary and her place within God's work of salvation is in the broadest sense ecclesial, and not merely scriptural."[69] While the biblical evidence for Mariology exists, the interpretation of the evidence is informed by the church's dogma and devotion (which, as we have shown, is Christological in its orientation).

Still, the question deserves an answer: If the veneration of Mary is truly part of Christianity, why is it not more widely and clearly proclaimed in Sacred Scripture? Hilda Graef provides a potential answer.

The paganism of the Byzantine world round the shores of the Mediterranean was no longer the comparatively sober affair of the Greco-Roman Olympus, of Jupiter and Juno, of Minerva and Mars. It had become a syncretistic religion with very disturbing elements of ecstatic frenzy and sexual promiscuity, and one of its most prominent figures was the Mother Goddess, worshipped under many names, as the Magna Mater, the Phrygian Kybele, the Palestinian Ashtaroth, the Egyptian Isis and the Diana of the Ephesians whose devotees so violently opposed St. Paul (Acts 19). ...When Christianity began to spread, not only among the Jewish communities of the Roman Empire but, under the leadership of St. Paul, also among the pagan population, its teachers had to make it clear that there was only one God, incarnate in Jesus Christ, who could tolerate no rivals, whether male or female, and who was both the creator and the redeemer of the world. A strong [public] emphasis on his virgin mother would have led to unfortunate comparisons and, possibly, identifications.[70]

And so we see why the veneration of the Virgin Mary might be part of the "*disciplina arcani*: the secret, inner life of the Church". Alexander Hislop, in his book *The Two Babyons*, presumes that the veneration of Mary to be evidence of the early apostasy of the church;[71] I propose an alternate point of view — the early church knew that the open veneration of the Blessed Virgin would invite ill-informed comparisons to the mystery religions of the Mediterranean region, and so kept her veiled from view, hidden in plain sight. The evidence for this view is provided by the use the Gnostics (and others) made of the Blessed Virgin.

The earliest Gnostic heresy was Docetism, which taught that Jesus had only appeared to be a man, but did not take on a real human body. The first mention of Mary by a father of the Church appears in the works of Ignatius of Antioch, and is a defense of the full humanity of Christ by means of His birth of the Virgin Mary. In Chapter VII or his

Epistle to the Ephesians, titled "Beware of False Teachers", Ignatius provides the following formulation of the Christ, being both true God and true man.

For some are in the habit of carrying about the name [of Jesus Christ] in wicked guile, while yet they practise things unworthy of God, whom ye must flee as ye would wild beasts. For they are ravening dogs, who bite secretly, against whom ye must be on your guard, inasmuch as they are men who can scarcely be cured. There is one Physician who is possessed both of flesh and spirit; both made and not made; God existing in flesh; true life in death; both of Mary and of God; first passible and then impassible, even Jesus Christ our Lord.[72]

From there we begin to see references to the Virgin Mary pop up in early Gnostic writings. The gnostic Gospel of Philip contains the following passage:

Some said, "Mary conceived by the Holy Spirit." They are in error. They do not know what they are saying. When did a woman ever conceive by a woman? Mary is the virgin whom no power defiled. She is a great anathema to the Hebrews, who are the apostles and the apostolic men. This virgin whom no power defiled [...] the powers defile themselves. And the Lord would not have said "My Father who is in Heaven" (Mt 16:17), unless he had had another father, but he would have said simply "My father".[73]

To sum up: Mary did not conceived by the Holy Spirit, for the Holy Spirit is female, a mother figure. As in "Father, Son, and mother (Holy Spirit)". Jesus therefore had an earthly father as counterpart to His heavenly Father. Although Mary was inseminated by man, she remained a virgin. Such blasphemy!

These Gnostic writings provide us with evidence of what the Church was trying to avoid — the syncretic identification of the Mother Goddess with the Virgin Mary. Hilda Graef mentions two works — the *Ascension of Isaiah* and *Odes to Solomon* — both of which describe the birth of Jesus as something other than a true birth. In fact, these are the earliest literary sources (if perhaps not the theological sources) for the doctrine that Mary maintained her virginity *in partu*, in the birth, and that this was something other than an ordinary vaginal delivery.[74]

I note in passing the relative impossibility of keeping secrets. The *"disciplina arcani*: the secret, inner life of the Church" was bound to slip out. Witness for example the description of Christianity by Pliny the Younger in his letter to the Emperor Trajan where he seeks council on how to deal with Christians (*Epistulae* X.96).[75] This letter, written early in the second century, provides the earliest literary description of the Eucharist, something that was hidden from the catechumenate, and which the Church forbade discussion of to those outside the Church. Even today we pray (in the pre-Communion prayer of St. John Chrysostom): "Of thy Mystical Supper, O Son of God, accept me today as a communicant; for I will not speak of thy Mystery to thine enemies, neither like Judas will I give thee a kiss; but like the thief will I confess thee: Remember me, O Lord, in thy Kingdom."

Having discussed the existence of the Virgin Mary as part of the secret, inner life of the Church, we must also state that the veneration of the Blessed Virgin is indeed to be found in Sacred Scripture. We will follow the example of Archimandrite[76] Lev Gillett in using only the Gospels and the book of Acts for this; the more symbolic witness of the Old Testament and the book of Revelation cannot be understood without a proper evaluation of the more straightforward evidence.[77] Lev Gillett writes:

The Gospel itself ascribes to Mary a privileged place among the creatures. The angel Gabriel said to her: 'Hail, thou that are highly favoured, the Lord is with thee' (Luke i:28). The place occupied by Mary in the divine scheme of our salvation is not only privileged, but unique. Therefore, Elisabeth said to Mary: 'Blessed art thou among women, and blessed is the fruit of thy womb' (Luke i. 42). The Gospel observes that Elisabeth, when she saluted Mary in this manner, was 'filled with the Holy Ghost' (Luke i. 41). Every 'evangelical' (in the Protestant sense) Christian will acknowledge as true and inspired these words of the angel Gabriel and Elisabeth. The same words form the greatest part of the text of the Latin Ave Maria, which many 'evangelical' Christians mistrust, and the whole text of the corresponding Byzantine prayer. Could 'evangelicals' object to our addressing the glorified Virgin Mary in the same words with which she, on earth, was greeted by an angel and by a woman filled with the Holy Ghost? Could they object to our repeating such words, as recorded in the Gospel? If they did, would they still be 'evangelical'?[78]

A standard argument against the veneration of Mary is that Jesus himself did not honor her. The contention is that when a woman tried to honor Mary for having given birth, Jesus instead rejected her. This line of reasoning is faulty, as Lev Gillet explains.

Jesus himself explained in what is the blessing of God which rests on Mary. When a certain woman out of the multitude lifted up her voice and said to our Lord: 'Blessed is the womb that bare thee, and the paps which thou hast sucked', he answered: 'Yea rather, blessed are they that hear the word of God, and keep it' (Luke xi. 27-38). These words are part of the lesson from the Gospel which the Orthodox Church reads at the liturgy on every feast of the Virgin; this shows that the Orthodox Church considers them as the most perfect expression of her own mind concerning Mary's holiness. The words of Jesus must certainly not be interpreted as a disavowal of the praising of his mother by the woman or as an underestimation of Mary's excellence; but they emphasize the real point and show where lies the merit of Mary.[79]

St. Nikolai Velimirovich, in his Prayer number XXII, explores this idea. "O my Majestic Lord! You dance on Your Mother's lap, quickened by the All-Holy Spirit ... You fill the whole soul of Your Mother, all Her virgin breast; and there is nothing in Your Mother's soul except You. You are Her radiance and Her voice, truly Her eye and Her song."[80] Herein we see the connection between the witness of the Sacred Scriptures and that of the inner life of the Church. The meaning of Jesus' words regarding His mother are unclear, and could be interpreted any number of ways. Historically, Christianity has interpreted these words of Christ as expressing the true measure of Mary's greatness, and the reason why she is to be specially honored today. This is in line with the Lukan account of how "Mary kept all these things, and pondered them in her heart" (Luke 2:19; see also 2:51).

By way of contrast to the "*disciplina arcani*: the secret, inner life of the Church", the Protestant notion of *sola scriptura* is informed by and maintained in the context of antipathy towards Rome. Therefore Protestants must inevitably reject the witness of the church fathers, church tradition, and the whole liturgical life of the church — without which it seemingly becomes increasingly difficult (although not impossible) to find scriptural evidence of support for Marian doctrine, and therefore increasingly easy to explain it away. Alexander Schmemann sums up Protestant thought regarding the veneration of Mary in this way: "*To worship God and Christ is understandable. But hasn't Mary been given too much attention and hasn't her icon overshadowed the icon of her Son in popular piety?*

Hasn't this praise and devotion been exaggerated beyond all reasonable proportion?"[81]

As an example of Protestant thought, recall the description of my former belief that Mary was just an incubator for the Christ. In the second century, Irenaeus argued against this concept in his polemic against the various Gnostic heresies.

Those, therefore, who allege that He took nothing from the Virgin do greatly err, [since,] in order that they may cast away the inheritance of the flesh, they also reject the analogy [between Him and Adam]. For if the one [who sprang] from the earth had indeed formation and substance from both the hand and workmanship of God, but the other not from the hand and workmanship of God, then He who was made after the image and likeness of the former did not, in that case, preserve the analogy of man. ...Superfluous, too, in that case is His descent into Mary; **for why did He come down into her if He were to take nothing of her?** *Still further, if He had taken nothing of Mary, He would never have availed Himself of those kinds of food which are derived from the earth, by which that body which has been taken from the earth is nourished; nor would He have hungered, fasting those forty days, like Moses and Elias, unless His body was craving after its own proper nourishment; nor, again, would John His disciple have said, when writing of Him, "But Jesus, being wearied with the journey, was sitting [to rest];" nor would David have proclaimed of Him beforehand, "They have added to the grief of my wounds;" nor would He have wept over Lazarus, nor have sweated great drops of blood; nor have declared, "My soul is exceeding sorrowful;" nor, when His side was pierced, would there have come forth blood and water. For all these are tokens of the flesh which had been derived from the earth, which He had recapitulated in Himself, bearing salvation to His own handiwork.*[82] *[emphasis added]*

Mariology and Christology

The mystery of the Incarnation has been constantly under attack since the times of the apostles. The Gnostics believed that the material world was evil, and therefore was not created by God; since God is transcendent and the world evil, God could not have taken a human body. The heretic Marcion believed that the God of the Old Testament and the God of the New Testament were different; that Christ was God manifest, not God incarnate; that Christ had a putative body, not a fleshly one, meaning that he only appeared to be flesh and blood. Adoptionism was the idea that Christ was simply a man upon who the Spirit of God had descended; this is also known as psilanthropism.[83] The Ebionites believed that Jesus was the Messiah, but denied the virgin birth and the divinity of Christ. The Docetists believed that Christ's manhood and passion were "unreal, phantasmal."[84] The Arians believed the Son of God was a created being and not God from eternity. The Apollinarians believed the Son had a human body and soul, but a divine mind. The Nestorians believed that the Virgin Mary was the Mother of Christ (Christotokos) and not the Mother of God (Theotokos). The Monophysites believed that Christ was not only a single person, but had a single nature.[85]

The veneration of the Virgin Mary protects the humanity of the Christ or, as is specifically the case with the Nestorians (and others), the divinity of Christ. Our secular era sees Jesus as a human being, but denies the divinity of Christ. It is curious that modern Protestants proclaim both the divinity and the humanity of Christ, while in effect denying the means by which our Lord became human. Here is the issue: if God did not become man by partaking of Mary's flesh, then the Incarnation was in no sense a recapitulation of the creation accounts, and the analogy between Jesus and Adam (and between Mary and Eve, which we will discuss later), breaks down. If the divine Son of God took nothing from Mary at the Incarnation, then Jesus wasn't really and truly a man in every way like us, yet

43

without sin. If our God is not a human being with a human body, nature, and will, then our sin cannot be forgiven and our nature is not and cannot be healed, for as Gregory of Nazianzus writes: "[T]hat which He has not assumed He has not healed."[86]

Dumitru Staniloae expands upon this idea

When explained through the climactic power of the Spirit, supernatural acts concerning the person of Christ, such as his supernatural birth and resurrection, do not nullify the nature he took from us with its own contribution; instead, they lead our human nature to the summit of its own realization, for our nature has the spirit as its highest component, and our spirit seeks, in a natural way, to expand its inherent potential in the divine Spirit. Christ's human nature thus remains within an eternal existence. Consequently, supernatural acts which touch his human nature, first and foremost among which is the resurrection, are to be understood rather as acts which restore the nature of man and that of the world in general. The incarnation of Christ represents, at one and the same time, both the descent of God to full communion with humanity and the highest assent of the latter.[87]

Vladimir Lossky notes the intermingling of scripture, dogma, and tradition in the life of the Christian.

We face the impossibility of separating dogma from life and scripture from tradition. Christological dogma obliges us to recognize the divine maternity of the Virgin. Scriptural evidence teaches us that the glory of the Mother of God does not reside merely in her corporal maternity, in the fact of her having carried and fed the Incarnate Word. Then Church tradition, the holy memory of those who 'hear the Word of God, and keep it', gives to the Church the assurance with which she exalts the Mother of god, ascribing to her an unlimited glory.[88]

Mariology and Christology

Protestants operate from within their own tradition, as do all other forms of Christianity. Each particular tradition provides its own coloration to the analysis and interpretation of scripture. For example, it is assumed that a Protestant would only accept what is written in Sacred Scripture, and would deny that which is not written.[89] Yet when it comes to the Virgin Mary, this principle is turned on its head, and the argument is often against Sacred Scripture in favor of Protestant tradition.[90]

One of the more interesting and pronounced theological distinctions maintained by Protestants over and against other Christians is Protestantism's treatment of the Virgin Mary, the Mother of God. Of this, Roland A. Sebolt comments: "The common position of Protestantism and recent Lutheranism has been to ignore Mary altogether."[91] Another wag jocularly asked: "Isn't it strange that Christ was such a good Protestant when his mother was a Roman Catholic?"[92] Kenneth R. Samples, writing in the Christian Research Journal, poses the following question: "What separates Roman Catholics from evangelical Protestants"; he then discusses Mariology as one of several areas of clear doctrinal distinctions.

It might rightly be said that evangelicals have a tendency to ignore Jesus' mother Mary. Catholics, on the other hand, greatly exalt her. Such dogmas as the Immaculate Conception and bodily Assumption, coupled with such titles as "Queen of Heaven," "Queen of all Saints," and the "Immaculate Spouse of the Holy Spirit," make Mary in the minds of Catholics the most exalted of all God's creatures.

While Catholics propose Mary as a point of unity with other Christians, most evangelicals see Mariology as a formidable barrier between themselves and Catholics. Even evangelicals who are for the most part sympathetic to Catholicism generally view this element of Catholic belief as grossly unbiblical. One evangelical commission on evaluating

Catholic Mariology stated: "We as evangelical Christians are deeply offended by Rome's Marian dogmas because they cast a shadow upon the sufficiency of the intercession of Jesus Christ, lack all support from Scripture and detract from the worship which Christ alone deserves." Although the documents of Vatican II inform us that Mary's exalted role "neither take away from nor add anything to the dignity and efficacy of Christ the one Mediator," most evangelicals believe Catholic Mariology actually undermines the foundation of orthodox Catholic Christology.[93]

This blind spot regarding the honor due to Mary has important implications for theology. Mary is at the center of the Incarnation story in the Gospels; she is the nexus between Israel and the Church, between the Old and New Testaments; and as the flesh through which God became man, the Virgin Mary is — if not the nexus between the human and the divine — is at the very least the means by which that nexus came into the world. Thus the inattention paid to Mary cannot help but affect the doctrine of the Incarnation.

7: The Trinity and the Incarnation

The theologian Emil Brunner notes one of the great antimonies in scripture: that the God who is immovable, ineffable and without change, nevertheless *comes*.[94,95] Like it or not, accept it or not, but our Lord came *to* Mary first, before He came *through* or *by means of* Mary.[96] As a result, Mary serves to connect the orders of creation, the gospel, and the eschaton.[97] Sally Cunneen writes: "The image of Mary as mother holding the child on her lap is probably the most palpable expression of Christian theology's insistence on God's incarnation in our world; it also serves as a compact symbolic description of humanity itself."[98] Our God is a human being, and became a human being by building for himself a body of the flesh of Mary, just God built a body for Eve of flesh and bone taken from Adam.

Maximus the Confessor writes the following in his "Commentary on the Our Father" regarding the Trinitarian action at work in the Incarnation:

In becoming incarnate, the Word of God teaches us the mystical knowledge of God because he shows us in himself the Father and the Holy Spirit. For the full Father and the Full Holy Spirit are essentially and completely in the full Son, even the incarnate Son, without being themselves incarnate. Rather, the Father gives approval and the Spirit cooperates in the incarnation with the Son who effected it, since the Word remained in possession of his own mind and life, contained in essence by no other than the Father and the Spirit, while hypostatically realizing out of live for man the union with the flesh.[99]

This Trinitarian action is visible at the Annunciation, where the Archangel Gabriel said to the Blessed Virgin: "The Holy Ghost shall come upon thee, and the power of the Highest shall overshadow thee: therefore also that holy thing which shall be born of thee shall be called the Son of God" (Lu 1:35). Thus it was that the Triune God was first revealed to and by means of Mary. In another place it is said of Mary that she "kept all these things, and pondered them in her heart" (Lu 2:19). The Trinitarian revelation and action of God at the Annunciation suggests that Mary indeed played a part in the Incarnation, contrary to what some Protestants would prefer to believe.

George Gabriel sums this up for us when he states: "Orthodox belief in Mary, as the fathers teach us, can exist only in the context of Christology and the Incarnation, that is, in the context of who and what Jesus Christ is and of the meaning of the Incarnation in history and in the eternal will of God before the ages."[100] With all this in mind, any diminution of the role Mary plays in Sacred Scripture has unfortunate implications for — and perhaps results from — an alternative understanding of creation & the fall of man, of the Incarnation, of the church (ecclesiology), and of eschatology.

8: The Abandonment of Marian Theology

In his book *The Ancestral Sin*, John Romanides presents what is, for western theology, the alternative view of salvation history.

[T]he juridically framed problem of guilt inherited from Adam and the consequent punishment of mankind because of an offense against divine justice do not even exist for the Greek Fathers simply because they teach that God is not the cause of death. Man's withdrawal from God unto his own death, like for freedom of human will, is outside of God's jurisdiction. And it is outside of His jurisdiction by His own will. The fact that God desires the salvation of all does not mean that all are saved. God saves only through love and freedom.[101]

The turning away of the Reformation from any sort of Marian theology was no accident; the heirs of the Reformation did it deliberately. The original Reformers themselves retained a great deal of Marian devotion. Bernard Leeming quotes Lutheran Professor K. E. Skydsgaard: "Luther and the Reformers retained a positive view of the Virgin Mary and an understanding of the fact that Mary truly has her place in God's plan of salvation." Her person, Skydsgaard notes, ought not to be considered "as that of an unimportant individual, but must be placed within the context of the great biblical, theological, and historical account of salvation."[102]

Likewise, Leeming quotes J. Gresham Machan's book *The Virgin Birth of Christ:* 'We are, indeed, as far as anybody from accepting the Roman Catholic picture of the Blessed Virgin. But we also think that Protestants, in their reaction against that picture, have sometimes failed to do justice to the mother of our Lord."[103]

John Calvin argued for the perpetual virginity of Mary,[104] as did the Swiss reformer Ulrich Zwingli.[105] Martin Luther, perhaps the most conservative of the reformers,[106] was especially insistent upon retaining Mary's place in the theological life of the church. Beth Kreitzer points out that Luther adhered to Christological orthodoxy and its attendant Marian doctrines based on "[t]he authority of many [ecumenical] councils and church fathers, particularly Augustine."[107] Yet the disciples of Calvin, Zwingli, and Luther, along with the corpus of the Protestant Reformation, have removed Mary as one of the loci of theology and of the church.

Despite the evident love and affection the Reformers felt for the Virgin Mary, their theological heirs lost no time in pressing forward with theological innovations the Reformers themselves were unwilling to make. For example, Beth Kreitzer goes to great lengths to demonstrate how the 16th century Lutheran pastors reoriented the role of Mary to one they considered proper for women, that of living out a woman's vocation within the house and home.[108]

Mary also regularly serves as a special model for females. ...The image of Mary most popular among Lutheran preachers seems to be of the pious and chaste girl, happy to serve her relatives, but otherwise gladly remaining and working at home. Mary did not leave her family to join a convent, but instead shows all girls how they should be happy in their domestic and familial vocations. The domesticating ideology often found in these sermons gains particular weight when it is declared that Mary, the blessed Mother of God, acted in just these recommended ways.[109]

The reimagining of Mary's role in our salvation story continues to this day. Stephen J. Shoemaker writes of "certain lingering prejudices" which affects the thinking of most scholastics doing research in the area of early Christian studies.

> *There is a palpable tendency in much scholarship to minimize any evidence of Marian devotion in the ancient church, exemplified, for instance, in Hans von Campenhausen's study "The Virgin Birth in the Theology of the Ancient Church", whose stated purpose is [to] demonstrate that Mary was not an important figure in earliest Christianity. Nor is this tendency merely an isolated vestige from the past: the lingering impact of nineteenth-century Protestantism on early Christian studies continues to be seen particularly with regard to Mary.*[110]

As I will attempt to demonstrate, the children of the Reformation have remade the biblical Mary into an image of their own design and, by doing so, have diminished or ignored Mary's place in Scripture, in the Incarnation, in ecclesiology, and in eschatology. They have also, along with the Roman Catholics, played up Eve's part in the fall[111] as a means of making Mary a role model for women, while making Mary a special case, and therefore separate from women. The diminution of the role Mary plays in salvation history, along with an exaggeration of the role Eve played in the fall of man, has important implications for the way Protestants view women, the way they treat their wives and daughters, and the way they view the church — which is, after all, the spotless and virgin bride of Christ.

Part III: Cosmology and Anthropology

9: Christian Cosmology, Christian Anthropology

The standard approach to Mariology involves the use of apologetics. This is a valuable approach, but for most Protestants this approach is insufficient. The veneration of the Virgin Mary is not based simply on an assemblage of facts, but involves facts developed and interpreted from within a particular framework. Apart from an understanding of that framework, the facts are open to alternate interpretations. Thus, the honest critic of Marian theology must at least make an attempt to understand not only what the alternative viewpoint is, but the *why* of it. The summary dismissal of Marian doctrine as idolatry is intellectually dishonest if one does not at least understand the reasons behind the alternate viewpoint. If Protestants do not understand the framework from within which Marian doctrine exists, they will never be able to come to terms with it. It is one thing to understand a thing and reject it; it is quite another to decide to ignore the arguments of those you disagree with before hearing them out.

Father John Anthony McGuckin, of the Romanian Orthodox Church, writes:

> *Avoiding apologetics, time is better spend directly studying the Orthodox understanding of the Blessed Virgin as a guide to an authentic understanding of the Gospel, in so far as she herself is understood to be the perfect image of a disciple; herself perfected and redeemed by her divine Son, and rendered luminous among, and above, all saints and angels by the perfect harmonization of her life with that of the Lord. The Blessed Virgin Mary figures as a dogmatic element supporting several aspects of the Christian faith, therefore, but she herself is a figure who belongs to what some Orthodox theologians have called the 'inner tradition' of Christianity. This signifies a mystery of intimacy; things that*

are known to the elect and the illuminated, but not necessarily understood by those further out in the 'wings' of Christian mystical experience.[112]

For this reason we shall pause our apologetic for the Virgin Mary, and develop the framework within which the Virgin Mary takes her rightful place. To do this, we begin with a discussion of the Incarnation — for the mystery of the church, along with veneration of the Virgin Mary, is inseparably bound to the mystery of the Incarnation. From the Incarnation, from God becoming one with humanity, that we know the nature, worth, and meaning of our human existence. And we can have knowledge of the nature and character of God through the person of the Christ, the incarnate Son of God. The person of Christ points us towards the Father; the Holy Spirit points us to the Son. The Incarnation of the Son of God by the Holy Ghost of the Virgin Mary provides us not only with an example of the love of God, but also of the importance of humanity in the plan of God.

Nicolas Cabasilas, in what Paul Evdokimov refers to as "a neat synthesis of Patristic thought",[113] writes:

The Incarnation of the Word was the work not only of the Father, Whose good pleasure it was, and of His Power, Who overshadowed, and of His Spirit, Who descended, but also of the will and faith of the Virgin. For, just as, without those Three, it would have been impossible for this decision to be implemented, so also, if the All-Pure One had not offered her will and faith, this design could not possibly have been brought to fruition.[114]

While most Protestants would likely disagree with the concept that the Virgin Mary was somehow intimately connected to the Incarnation, may I suggest some early scriptural evidence? Examine the protoevangelium, the first announcement of the gospel message: "I will put enmity between thee and the woman, and between thy seed and her seed; it shall bruise thy head, and thou shalt bruise his heel" (Ge 3:15). In this passage God says he will put enmity between Satan and the woman. Not Satan and the man, but specifically the woman and the seed of the woman. Moreover, while Satan will bruise the heel of the woman's seed, the seed of the woman will crush Satan's head. Thus the woman (who can only be the Virgin Mary)[115] is intimately connected with the Incarnation of Him who is of the seed of a woman, and therefore with the crushing of sin, death, and the devil. She is not the *cause* of Satan's downfall, but she is intimately involved.

The fullest definition of the meaning of the Incarnation — and the Virgin Mary's involvement — developed gradually and in response to heresy. We should expect this, for Christian dogma was first formally explicated in response to Christological heresies, meaning heresies regarding the divinity and humanity of Christ. Evdokimov notes:

From the beginning, discussion centred on the Incarnation as the means of salvation: Cur Deus Homo? — Why God-Man? It is the question of life or death, a theology of Salvation at its most dramatic and historical. The mystery is above all Christological.[116]

To move forward in our discussion, we must first discuss theological cosmology, as many theological errors and heresies are based upon a faulty division of the cosmos into the material and spiritual. This false cosmology begins by thinking of the material realm as lower (meaning lesser in worth), and the spiritual realm as higher. This has a number of unfortunate consequences. First, since the created order is lower, physical and material things are devalued over and against the spiritual realm, making the material world an object of disdain, something to be used up and discarded. Second, if the physical realm is of little value, this raises questions as to why (and if) God actually became a man. Third, it is but a short step from thinking of the material realm as lower than the spiritual realm, to thinking of the material world as something to be despised, and perhaps actually evil. This is the mindset of pagan philosophy, out of which so many Christological heresies sprang. The problem was that this faulty cosmology, applied as an interpretive lens to Sacred Scripture, resulted in a distaste for God becoming man; therefore Christ must have only appeared to be a man, or the Son of God was not fully God. Either position protected the nature of God from being sullied through intimate contact with matter.

This faulty cosmology, this division of the cosmos into spiritual and material, is very much how the West tends to view the world. But the creation accounts tell us a much different story. There, in the first chapters of Genesis, we see the cosmos divided into the created and the uncreated. Both the spiritual realm of the angels and material realm of the perceptible universe are part of the created order.[117]

Jesus Ben Sirach, the author of the Wisdom of Sirach (aka. Ecclesiasticus), describes the judgment with which our Lord created all things, and the manner in which they form a unified whole. In other words, the created order is not divided into material and immaterial, physical and spiritual, and all is blessed by God.

My son, hearken unto me, and learn knowledge, and mark my words with thy heart. I will show forth doctrine in weight, and declare his knowledge exactly. The works of the Lord are done in judgment from the beginning: and from the time he made them he disposed the parts thereof. He garnished his works for ever, and in his hand are the chief of them unto all generations: they neither labor, nor are weary, nor cease from their works. None of them hindereth another,

57

and they shall never disobey his word. After this the Lord looked upon the earth, and filled it with his blessings. With all manner of living things hath he covered the face thereof; and they shall return into it again. (Sir 16:24-30)

As Pseudo-Dionysius, writing regarding "The Celestial Hierarchy", writes: "One truth must be affirmed above all else. It is that the transcendent Deity has out of goodness established the existence of everything and brought it into being."[118] Thus the spiritual and material realms are alike in being created; and humanity, being created in the image and likeness of God, bridges the gap between the spiritual and material realm. Thus God could become man without sullying himself, without lowering himself from the spiritual realm to the world of matter. The lowering was the uncreated and only begotten Son of God assuming unto Himself the nature of created things, thereby uniting himself to both the spiritual and material realm. Therefore matter is not simply the prison of the soul, neither is death a release from the material existence; rather, death is the tragic sundering of spirit, soul, and body, which together constitute the tripartite existence of man.

It is curious that most Protestants spend very little time contemplating the mystery of the Incarnation, especially as the mystery of the Incarnation has been and remains the source of so many theological problems. David B. Currie writes: "Evangelicals are uncomfortable with the implications of the Incarnation. Whenever we are uncomfortable with something, we tend to neglect or ignore it. That is the reaction of many Evangelicals. They accept the Incarnation, believe in it firmly as an orthodox dogma, but do not delve into its implications."[119] This was certainly true of me, and seems to have been true of those around me. We understood that Jesus was God, and that God had become man. But we never dwelt on the idea that God loves our fleshly bodies, or that it took a physical act for God to counter sin, death, and the devil. We never considered how through the creation of a unique hypostasis — the God-man — that the Son of God assumed and healed our humanity. We never connected the description of the recreation and renewal of humanity with the Incarnation, instead leaving that to the eschaton, the age to come.

Because God chose to take on flesh, to become one with one of His creatures and a part of His creation, we are forced to reevaluate what it means to be human. We know "God is a Spirit: and they that worship him must worship him in spirit and in truth" (John 4:24) But God also became and remains a human being, a creature of flesh and bone; of meat and viscera; of skin and hair and teeth. God took on the "feeling of our infirmities" (Heb 4:15), and was subject to the consequences of the fall, even unto death. As the apostle writes: "The sting of death is sin" (1 Cor 15:56). Death has no sting for one without sin, and therefore death could not hold the God-man: "Death is swallowed up in victory" (1 Cor 15:54).

Fr. John Anthony McGuckin, Nielsen Professor of Early Christian and Byzantine Church History at Union Theological Seminary, discusses the relation and importance of the creation accounts to an understanding of the Incarnation, and of our own identity as beings created in the image and likeness of God.

In order to understand this ascent to the knowledge of the True God, the Father of Our Lord Jesus, it is necessary to be moved in the path of the economy by which the gift of the knowledge of God was given to the world. In its most precise form this path is a triadic economy of grace. It begins with the universal Spirit of the Father, manifested and hovering over the chaos of the world order in the act of governance of all created being, which is the order which the Divine Logos brings to material being. The book of Genesis suggests this poetically in its opening stanza: 'In the beginning God created the heavens and the earth. The earth was without form and void, and darkness was upon the face of the deep; and the Spirit of God was moving over the face of the waters. And God said, Let there be light; and there was light.' Orthodoxy understands the spoken word of God to be the Logos. So it appears from the opening words of the Scripture that the power of God's creative will, in the root of all material being, is manifested from the Father's will through the action of the Word in the power of the formative Spirit. This was (in the sense of a broad analogy), like a universal 'incarnation' (or more properly 'enspiration') of the presence of God among his creations. It was initiated by the Will of the Father, set into action by the Word of the Logos, who enlightens all things with his Father's light, and empowered and diffused among creation by the energy of the Divine Spirit. Such is how the pattern of the knowledge of God always works. Always in this order and with this energy of direction.[120]

Since God thought the flesh of humanity was worth saving, and thought highly enough of humanity and the material realm to have taken unto himself createdness — to have chosen to become and still remain a human being — then perhaps we need to spend some time thinking not only about what it means for the uncreated to take on createdness, but what it means for the uncreated to have chosen humanity out of all His creation. Only then can then understand the meaning and purpose of the Incarnation; only then will we be guided into a fuller understanding of the faith, an understanding which serves as a protection against heresy.

10: A Communitarian Anthropology

Alexander Schmemann notes that the term heresy comes from the Greek αἵρεσις (airesis), meaning the action of taking a choice. By extension, a heresy is a choice for something lesser or something other; therefore a heresy is a reduction or deformation of the faith.[121] When Christianity is deformed, when it loses something vital, the Church counters by creating dogma to preserve the "faith which was once delivered to the saints" (Jude 1:3).

When examining a particular dogmatic formula such as Mariology, it is helpful to study the particular deformation of doctrine causing its development. As John Meyendorff writes: "the question 'Who is Christ?" must precede our understanding of the Pauline concept of life 'in Christ'. More to the point, "Christology is of necessity soteriological", meaning that it has to do with salvation.[122] So then, unless we understand both divinity and humanity, and the manner in which both existed in the person of Christ, we will not understand the meaning of our salvation as Christ in us, "the hope of glory" (Col 1:27).

Alexander Schmemann points out that Mariology, in particular, was developed by church councils (in the context of Christology) to combat an anthropological problem in theology.[123] We must therefore examine our Christian anthropology to determine if Mariology is itself the deformation, or if the deformation is the abandonment of Mariological doctrine. While this might seem like a long and pointless digression, a faulty anthropology will affect the way we view the Virgin Mary, leading to the sense that she is of no consequence in and to the Gospel story. If we have a faulty Mariology, we have a faulty anthropology; and if a faulty anthropology, we have a deficient Christology.

Cosmology and Anthropology

We begin our own anthropological quest with Gustaf Aulén's description of the theological consequences of Augustine's anthropology.

Theology has attempted to find in the birth of Christ without the will of man an explanation of his "sinlessness," or at least of his "freedom from original sin." It is perfectly evident that this "explanation" explains nothing. If one wants to gain an explanation this way, one must be consistent and remove "inherited sin" also from Mary. The Roman doctrine of the immaculate conception of Mary is at least consistent. It must be added, however, that this rationalistic explanation has a semblance of legitimacy only as long as one, disregarding the fact that "God is Spirit" (John 4:24), conceives "the Son's unity of substance with the Father" in a physical sense; but that it loses even this semblance of legitimacy as soon as it becomes evident that the unity of substance, about with faith never ceases to speak, does not consist in some special physiological nature, which would jeopardize Christ's true humanity, but in nothing less than this: that we possess "the heart and will of the Father in Christ." Under such circumstances Christian faith must reject these rationalistic explanations of theology.[124]

Gustaf Aulén makes the point that if we have a certain understanding of the nature of man, in this case the doctrine of original sin (often attributed to St. Augustine), it affects our view of the Incarnation and the two natures in Christ. Having devised the rationalistic doctrine of original sin, we must then devise a rationalistic explanation of how Jesus managed to be born *without* original sin. At some level the focus becomes on the special physiology of Jesus, which is somehow separate and apart from ours, in which case Christ is not entirely human.[125] This has been a consistent theme of various Christian heresies.

A Communitarian Anthropology

If Jesus was free from original sin because he took this special physiology from Mary, then she must also have had a physiology separate from ours, which is the position of the Roman Catholic church (the Immaculate Conception). The rejection of this Romish theological innovation by Protestants has led by a seemingly natural extension into a reaction against the place of the Blessed Virgin in theology. In this way we see that one's anthropology affects one's theology. We need to ensure that our anthropology was developed as a consequence of our theology, and not the other way around.

I never connected anthropology with theology until I noticed the term in Joseph Ratzinger's (now Benedict XVI) book "Eschatology".[126] When he used the term anthropology, it startled me. It seemed out of place, for what connection did a theologian in his ivory tower have with James Harrison among the Pygmies, or Margaret Mead among the Samoans? Yet, as it turns out, the theologian, the philosopher, and the anthropologist are all seeking an answer to the riddle of humanity, the human condition, and the meaning of life. We find the riddle of humanity expressed very early in the Hebrew Scriptures. "What is man?" asks Job (Job 7:17; 15:14). The psalmist echoes the question, and the writer of Hebrews reminds us of the psalmist's question (Ps 8:4; 144:3; Heb 2:6). The exploration of and answer to this question comes in three parts: 1) What was man in the state of original righteousness; 2) What has man become after the fall; and 3) What will be the state of man at the end?

11: Cosmology and the Christianization of Anthropology

As we have seen, modern anthropology is ill suited to provide answers to its ultimate question — what is man, and how shall he think of himself? Likewise, the answers provided to these questions by Greek philosophy result only in disturbance, dissolution, and loss. To find the answers to the ultimate questions, we need religion. To be more precise, a fulfilling definition of our humanity and the meaning thereof is only provided within Christianity. If we accept this proposition as true, then it follows that a faulty definition and a false understanding of humanity — of Christian Anthropology — has profound consequences. Just as Mariology is linked to Christology, and Christology to the Incarnation, so too is the Incarnation linked to Cosmology. From the linkage between the Incarnation and Cosmology is derived the essence of what it means to be human: created in the image and likeness of God, yet subject to the ravages of sin and death.

For our purposes, it is not necessary to discuss the *how* and *when* of creation. A preoccupation with these questions will be irrelevant for our purposes, and may well prevent us from examining the question at hand — the *who* and *why* of creation. I might also argue that the focus on the literal meaning of the creation accounts turns us away from the *who* and *why* of creation, which is the primary interpretation of the creation accounts. The creation accounts are a sacred history, a prophetic history. As such, the creation accounts transcend time and space; they discuss matters that delve into the mystery of godliness (1 Tim. 3:16). If we read the creation accounts in a purely literalist fashion, as a dry and purely historical rendition of events, we can miss out on the deep prophetic implications contained in the accounts. We may miss the connections between the creation of the cosmos, the creation of humanity, and the Incarnation — connections that form the very warp and woof of these accounts.

The connections between cosmology, anthropology, and the Incarnation are well-documented in historic Christianity, as evidenced in part by St. Athanasius in his most famous work, *On the Incarnation.*

You may be wondering why we are discussing the origin of men when we set out to talk about the Word's becoming Man. The former subject is relevant to the latter for this reason: it was our sorry case that caused the Word to come down, our transgression that called out His love for us, so that He made hast to help us and to appear among us. It is we who were the cause of His taking human form, and for our salvation that in His great love He was both born and manifested in a human body. For God had made man thus (that is, as an embodied spirit), and had willed that he should remain in incorruption. But men, having turned from the contemplation of God to evil of their own devising, had come inevitably under the law of death. Instead of remaining in the state in which God had created them, they were in process of becoming corrupted entirely, and death had them completely under its dominion.[127]

Athanasius makes the point that God had willed that we remain in incorruption, but that we chose to turn away from God and embrace evil.

This, then, was the plight of men. God had not only made them out of nothing, but had also graciously bestowed on them His own life by the grade of the Word. Then, turning from eternal things to things corruptible, by counsel of the devil, they had become the cause of their own corruption in death; for, as I said before, though they were by nature subject to corruption, the grace of their union with the Word made them capable of escaping from the natural law, provided that they retained the beauty of innocence with which they were created. That is to say, the presence of the Word with them shielded them even from natural corruption, as also Wisdom says: "God created man for incorruption and as an image of His own eternity; but by envy of the devil death entered into the world."[Wisdom ii:23][128]

The question at hand boils down to this: are our actions after the fall still free, being derived from our creation in the image and likeness of God? Alternatively, are our actions after the fall governed by the loss of the image of God and the resultant loss of free will, forcing us into subservience to the Sovereignty of God? For the purposes of our discussion, how we think about the Virgin Mary depends on whether her response to the Annunciation was based on her actual free will, or whether it had been predetermined from all eternity; whether her free choice was actual, or was divine compulsion masquerading as human freedom.

Regarding this, Fr. John Romanides writes:

The basic premise of the entire life and thought of the ancient Church is the biblical teaching of the creation of the world from nothing by a perfectly positive and completely free act of God. ...The ancient Christian teaching on the fall is inseparably bound to biblical cosmology. The key to understanding this cosmology and the relationship between God and the world is the dogma of creation ex nihilo [out of nothing]. This dogma constitutes the whole premise of the church's teaching on freedom.[129]

The creation of the cosmos was not necessary, but was an entirely free act of God. Humanity, being created in the image and likeness of God, thereby partakes of this freedom, a freedom which is an essential part of what it means to be human. There are those who say that we are not free agents; that one of the effects of the fall is the loss of our free will. However, we never see this in scripture. In the account of the fall of man, and the subsequent curse, there is no inkling of a loss of free will. What God describes is a life of hard work, pain, and death — all the result of sin. In the Wisdom of Sirach, we see God presenting man with a choice, allowing man to choose of his own free will.

He himself made man from the beginning, and left him in the hand of his counsel; if thou wilt, to keep the commandments, and to perform acceptable faithfulness. He hath set fire and water before thee: stretch forth thy hand unto whether thou wilt. Before man is life and death; and whether him liketh shall be given him. (Sir 15:14-17)

Sirach describes the result of sin — death —as a covenant, thereby connecting the covenant of the law with the covenant of death.

All flesh waxeth old as a garment: for the covenant from the beginning is, Thou shalt die the death. As of the green leaves on a thick tree, some fall, and some grow; so is the generation of flesh and blood, one cometh to an end, and another is born. Every work rotteth and consumeth away, and the worker thereof shall go withal. (Sir 14:17-19)

After the fall, we were no longer in constant communion with God, so we became subject to the covenant of death. But the existence of sin and death does not require a belief in the loss of the image of God, nor a completely negative view of the human condition. Yet Evangelicals seem bound to this negative view of humanity. In her book *God's Many-Splendored Image*, the Orthodox nun and university professor Dr. Nonna Verna Harrison describes how a false understanding of Christian Anthropology, of what she calls a "Theological Anthropology", has become part of our Christian and secular culture.

Cosmology and Anthropology

The difficulty is that folks today frequently see a Christian understanding of human identity as part of the problem. This is because an oversimplified negative version of humanity is taken for granted in popular culture, and churches often reflect this negative vision without even thinking about it ...Let's say there is a big financial scandal. ...Commentators in the newspapers and on television explain that the fraud occurred because people are greedy, and greed is human nature. Without thinking, folks routinely identify "human nature as the cause of weakness, error, and ethical lapses and as the source of all the world's troubles. ...When those troubled by questions about who they are step into a church, where they can reasonably expect to find healing, the same negative message is often repeated. For example, the preacher may talk about the financial scandal from the pulpit and conclude that since greed is human nature, we are all greedy and need to ask God for forgiveness. We have to condemn ourselves and turn to God. ...Such a message cannot heal the pain of depersonalization and the lost sense of human dignity; it only makes the person seeking Christ's healing word feel misunderstood and even more hurt.[130]

The problem is not only cultural, but theological. Lutheran theologian Peter Brunner writes:

The focal point of God's plan of salvation is the incarnation of the eternal Son of God in Jesus of Nazareth, His cross, and His resurrection. God's redemptive activity in Jesus is the light in which we behold the totality of these acts of God in the mirror of His Word, from creation on through to the consummation. Therefore the creation of man, his fall, his preservation by God, his pathway in paganism and in Israel become perceptible to us only "in Jesus Christ." ...[O]nly he who is acquainted with the center of this entire course, the birth, work, suffering, death, and resurrection of Jesus Christ, will know that sector of the way in God's plan of salvation that tends toward this center and the sector that radiates from it.[131,132]

Peter Brunner's description of the Incarnation is a wonder of concision and precision, yet somehow lacking. Peter Brunner is dealing with the Incarnation as an abstraction. When dealing with the Incarnation as a concrete reality, one must come to terms with the Mother of our Lord and the place she played in the Incarnation. To quote the Nicene Creed, our Lord "was incarnate of the Holy Spirit and the Virgin Mary, and became man." Abstracting the Incarnation of the Son of God from His mother is in some sense a denial of His humanity. If you think that too strong, perhaps we could agree that separating the Mother from her Son in this manner is shortsighted — the result of a failure to think through the implications of the Incarnation and a failure to comprehend the reasons for the Virgin's inclusion in the Gospel story.

Many Christians, including many who are considered to be theologians, have never really thought through the implications of the Incarnation and Chalcedonian Christology. This is especially true when it comes to the definition of what it means for God to be personal, for the personal God to assume humanity into His person, and for human beings to be likewise persons in the image and likeness of God. For many Christians, the focus on the person of Christ is limited to the divine economy — to His work in this world. Missed in this assessment of Christ is the inner life of the trinity as three divine persons (ὑπόστασις, or hypostases) sharing the one divine nature (ousía — the substance or essence), in perfect communion with each other. By extension, then, the nature of humanity as the image of the inner life of the trinity is missed. Salvation then becomes a matter of what we are saved *from*, not what we are saved *for* — which is to become partakers of the divine likeness and to live in communion with God. To put it another way, western theology separates salvation from sanctification and teleology[133], treating each atomistically rather than holistically.

12: The Meaning of God's Image and Likeness

St. John of Kronstadt writes:

What a wonderful creation is man! Look! that which was created from earth contains the breath of God — personal, independent, free — the image of God Himself. How much wisdom and beauty there are in the construction of man's bodily tabernacle, how much wisdom and love — in a word, how much likeness to God is shown in the life itself of the man who has dominion over the earth; as it is said: "Let us make man in our image, after our likeness: and let them have dominion . . . over all the earth."[134]

In the account of the creation of man, God said: "Let us make man in our image, after our likeness" (Ge 1:26). Some treat this as though it is a simple case of parallelism, as though image and likeness are synonymous. Marc Cortez, for example, writes:

"Image" and "lines are largely or entirely synonymous. Many patristic and medieval exegetes argued that there was an important theological distinction intended by the use of 'selem' and 'demut' in Genesis 1:27-28. Contemporary exegetes, however, agree that these two terms are largely synonymous and that we should not read any strong distinction into their use in this text.[135]

In a footnote, Marc Cortez describes the view of Irenaeus as to the distinction between image and likeness, but totally fails to take into account the wealth of patristic literature. He cites the fact that contemporary exegetes reject the distinction between the two terms, and accepts that at face value without providing any information that would allow the reader to distinguish the rationale between each view, let alone to determine for him or herself which perspective is likely to be correct.

For the church fathers, the image and likeness are two separate things. For some, the image and likeness represents the difference between the essence and the person. In this view, humanity is a unity of essence, expressed through a diversity of persons. The image correlates to a single human nature, originally made to be in perfect communion with God; and the likeness would correlate to the multiplicity of persons, sharing that single nature without confusion of persons. In other words, God created humanity after the similitude of the trinity: unity in diversity, and diversity of unity.[136] Others make another distinction; the image correlates to the inner human being, to that which, being created in the image of God, constitutes the essential difference between humanity and the rest of creation; the likeness correlates to the free choice of man to accept or reject God, and thereby the capacity for sanctification, for growth into the likeness of God. The genius of Orthodoxy is that we need not choose between one or the other explanation; both explanations are true in their own sphere, and both complement each other.

What I find interesting is that while Marc Cortez rejects the view that image and likeness are describing two different things, he nevertheless ends up describing the view of the fathers when he describes what amounts to their definition of God's likeness.

The image of God is teleological. Finally, most thinkers affirm that the image is not an entirely static concept; instead, they view it as developing toward something it has a teleological dimension. Thus, as we have seen, Paul portrays the image as something that is being "transformed" (2 Cor. 3.18) and "renewed" (Col. 3.10) in human persons as they are drawn ever closer to the person of Christ. For many theologians, this teleological element is a result of sin. That is, humans were fully in the image of God at creation, but that image was lost or marred after the Fall and stands in need of restoration. For other theologians, particularly those in the Eastern Orthodox tradition, the teleological dynamic of the image has been there from the beginning. Adam and Eve themselves were created with the intention that they would grow toward the image, who is Christ. Humans were thus "predestined to become conformed to the likeness of his son" (Rom. 8.29) from creation. Either way, theologians largely agree that the image of God in humans is a work in progress. It is moving toward its Christological goal, its telos.[137]

In his two Homilies entitled *On the Human Condition,* St. Basil the Great discusses the meaning of being created in God's image.

"Let us make the human being according to our image." It speaks of the inner human being. "Let us make the human being." But you will ask, "Why does it not speak to us of the rational part?" It says that the human being is according to the image of God, but the rational part is the human being. Listen to the apostle say, "Although our outer human being is perishing, the inner is renewed day by day" [2 Cor 4.16].

How?

I recognize two human beings, one the sense-perceptible, and one hidden under the sense-perceptible, invisible, the inner human. Therefore we have an inner human being, and we are somehow double, and it is truly said that we are that which is within. For I am what concerns the inner human being, the outer things are not me but mine. For I am not the hand, but I am the rational part of the soul. And the hand is a limb of the human being. Therefore the body is an instrument of the human being, an instrument of the soul, and the human being is principally the soul in itself.[138]

Cosmology and Anthropology

According to St. Basil, the image of God is hidden under the sense-perceptible portion of humanity. We are more than what is merely sense-perceptible. We have the ability to stand outside ourselves, to monitor and evaluate our actions and reactions as they are happening. This suggests that humanity has an inner reality, something very real, yet not accessible by means of the senses.

While not using these same terms, St. Gregory Palamas describes the ability of the mind (by which he means something more than mere intellect), to supersede merely sensory perceptions.

Although the mind can come down to the level of human reasoning, and by it to a life full of complexities, since its energies are available for all, yet it indubitably has another, superior mode of operation, which it is capable of putting into action by itself. For it is able to remain on its own, either when separated from the body and the things pertaining to the body, or when, although still bound to it, it is enabled, by means of diligence, and assisted by divine grace, to leave behind this varied, complex and lowly way of living.[139]

Somehow most Christians know this to be true. We are not solely our bodies, but our bodies are part of us. Thus someone born with some physical deformity or cognitive abnormality does not cease to be human, nor is someone with profound gifts something more than human. All are human because they partake of and share in the humanity common to us all. This is the Christian argument against the horrors of the ancient world which are rapidly becoming normative in modernity: abortion, infanticide, eugenics, and the death or abandonment to death of the elderly and infirm. These deaths affect us all, diminish us all, for we all partake of the common humanity.

Having discussed the image, St. Basil the Great addresses himself to the likeness of God, which in a sense the spiritual side of humanity or (to use St. Basil's term), the hidden, inner man.

> *"And God made the human being. According to the image of God he made him" [Gen 1.27]. So then, did you not say that the proposition was incomplete? "Let us make the human being according to our image and likeness." The plan had two parts, "according to the image" and "according to the likeness." ...Or perhaps it is saying the same thing. "Let us make the human according to our image and likeness." Yet to say "according to the image" is not to say "according to the likeness." Whichever we choose, we would be rejecting what has been written. For if it says the same, it is perverse to say the same things twice.*[140]

Lars Thunberg, in his study on the thought of Maximus the Confessor, describes the likeness of God as our potential — or our freedom to choose and our ability to change and grow — and the image of God as what we may become in Christ. The idea is that man was not created in a state of moral perfection, and was neither mortal nor immortal by nature. Humanity was created with the ability to grow in Grace, to take on more and more of the characteristics of the divine image.

> *The incarnation of the Logos, according to Maximus, is not caused or motivated only by the fall and by sin, but by man's position vis-à-vis God, by what we have called the divine-human reciprocity. Maximus shows very clearly that the Incarnation would have taken place even without the fall. With this understanding Maximus places himself in line with a tradition in the ancient Church that may be traced back at least to Irenaeus of Lyon (died c. 190). According to this tradition man is not created perfect, so his original state is never one of human perfection. He is called to mature and to develop his likeness to God to the point of perfection of his nature as image of God. Likeness is thus the realization*

(tropological[141] in Maximus, as we have seen) of all that is given as possibility because of man's nature as image of God.[142]

The Protestant Argument

Protestants generally would not accept that image and likeness are different things. Lutheran professor Dr. Eugene F. Klug expresses the Protestant view most forcefully in his article entitled "The Doctrine of Man".

Some have tried to distinguish sharply between image (zelem) and likeness (demuth), as though the first referred to man's bodily and rational faculties, and the second to his spiritual likeness with God. There is no solid linguistic evidence supporting such a division; scripture uses the terms interchangeably (cf. Gen. 1 :26,27; 5: 1 ; 1 Cor. 15:49; Col. 3: 10). Both mean the same thing, referring especially to the fact that man desired what God desired.[143]

If linguistic evidence were the only evidence for differentiating between the image and likeness, we would have to agree with Dr. Klug. However, the distinction between image and likeness is theological, not linguistic, and therefore rests upon different foundations. Theologically, Dr. Klug is forced to believe that the image and likeness of God are the same thing because of his view of the fall of man and its effects upon human nature. Note first what he states as the content of the image: "man desired what God desired." This neglects the import of the second creation account, where woman was created of the same essential stuff as Adam, and therefore like unto him. Theologically, the two accounts are related; we are made in God's likeness, just as Eve was fashioned in Adam's likeness. Eve was like Adam, in that she was built of the same flesh; it had nothing to do with her desire for what Adam desired — for, as we know, her desire was for her husband (Ge 3:16).

The Meaning of God's Image and Likeness

If your Christian Anthropology begins with the fall and works backwards to the creation accounts (as well as forward to the Incarnation and redemption accounts), you are forced to believe that image and likeness are the same thing. If you derive your Christian Anthropology from the creation accounts and move forward from there, the theological result is much different. Dr. Klug expresses this when he writes: "This image, or likeness with God, was lost by the fall; man by nature was now ignorant of God, hostile to Him and His will, disdainful and incapable of things spiritually sound (1 Cor. 2: 14)."[144] It is important to note that the concept of the fall as the loss of the divine image does not come from any clear statement of Sacred Scripture, but is rather derived and read into scripture in a manner that does not accord with the standard Protestant hermeneutic (let Scripture interpret Scripture), and is accepted solely on the basis of conformance to Protestant tradition.

The Creation Accounts

St. Gregory of Nazianzus, in Oration 38, draws a distinction between the mind, between the natures that are intellectual, and the creaturely world of the senses. "[A]kin to Deity are those natures which are intellectual, and only to be comprehended by mind; but all of which sense can take cognisance are utterly alien to It."[145] Gregory emphasizes the distinction and distance between the spiritual and the material world, and then describes the manner in which God created man of spirit and flesh, thereby enabling man to bridge the gap between the spiritual and the temporal.

Mind, then, and sense, thus distinguished from each other, had remained within their own boundaries, and bore in themselves the magnificence of the Creator-Word, silent praisers and thrilling heralds of His mighty work. Not yet was there any mingling of both, nor any mixtures of these opposites, tokens of a greater Wisdom and Generosity in the creation of natures; nor as yet were the whole riches of Goodness made known. Now the Creator-Word, determining to exhibit this, and to produce a single living being out of both — the visible and the invisible creations, I mean — fashions Man; and taking a body from already existing matter, and placing in it a Breath taken from Himself which the Word knew to be an intelligent soul and the Image of God, as a sort of second world. He placed him, great in littleness on the earth; a new Angel, a mingled worshipper, fully initiated into the visible creation, but only partially into the intellectual; King of all upon earth, but subject to the King above; earthly and heavenly; temporal and yet immortal; visible and yet intellectual; half-way between greatness and lowliness; in one person combining spirit and flesh.[146]

Notice that St. Gregory of Nazianzus draws a distinction between the immortality of God, and the temporality of humanity. Man was not created immortal by nature, but with the potential to be immortal by grace — by participation in and communion with God, who alone is immortal by nature. Scripture attests to this in numerous places. Jesus himself says: "I am the resurrection and the life" (John 11:25). And again: "He who eats of My flesh and drinks of My blood has eternal life, and I shall raise him up on the last day" (John 6:54). And yet again: "For as the Father raises the dead and gives life, likewise the Son also gives life to whom He wishes" (John 5:21). From these citations we know that Jesus is God, the source of life, and that life eternal is a gift which He gives freely to whomsoever He wishes.[147]

We are so familiar with the Genesis accounts of creation that we get caught up in the details of the stories, and therefore miss the overall significance of these accounts. These are not primarily historical narratives describing a sequence of events; instead, we find the importance of these creation accounts in their theological and anthropological details. In the second creation story the first man is not immediately named. Of him it is said "the LORD God formed man *of* the dust of the ground, and breathed into his nostrils the breath of life; and man became a living soul" (Ge 2:7). This singular and solitary man does not have, at first mention, a name; and having no name, this solitary man thus encompasses all of humanity in his singular person. In his synthesis of the teaching of Pope John Paul II, Fr. J. Brian Bransfield notes that the biblical description of the solitary man is an ontological description, a description of the human as an individual, not a person.[148] God takes notice of humanity as individuals, and comments that this is "not good." This man is temporal rather than eternal, yet not at this point subject to death. Being made in the image of God, man is created with the freedom to choose his destiny; and being made in the likeness of God, man has the capacity to become partakers of the divine likeness (2 Peter 1:4).

God does not create a companion for the man out of nothing, but builds the woman from flesh and bone taken from this first man.[149] This man is no longer in solitude; this humanity is no longer an individual. Instead, this humanity has become a multiplicity of persons bearing a single nature — the image and likeness of God. The body of Eve, being built from the flesh and bone of Adam, partakes of the same nature, the same image and likeness of God. This image and likeness is then passed from Eve to all of humanity.

At the Incarnation, in a similar manner, God builds for Himself a body of flesh taken from the Virgin Mary, thus ensuring that the nature of the Son of God would join to Himself a human nature in the one person of Christ. What we are by nature, so too is Christ — so that as Christ is by nature, so we too may become by grace (2 Pet 1:4).[150]

Therefore, all of humanity — being created in the image of God and freed from the law of sin and death (Rom 8:2) — has been set free and thereby granted the potential to grow into the participation in the divine likeness.

13: The Ecumenical Councils

St. Maximus the Confessor sums up the witness of the ecumenical councils regarding Christian anthropology and the Incarnation in this manner:

In the mystery of the divine incarnation the distinction between the two natures, divine and human, in Christ does not imply that He is divided into two persons. On the one hand, a fourth person is not added to the Trinity, which would be the case if the incarnate Christ was divided into two persons; while on the other hand, since nothing can be coessential or cognate with the Divinity, there must be a distinction between the divine and human natures in Him. In other words, in the incarnation the two natures have united to form a single person, not a single nature. Thus not only does the hypostatic union formed by the coming together of the two natures constitute a perfect unity, but also the different elements which come together in the indivisible union retain their natural character, free from all change and confusion.[151]

The redemption of our bodies — and of the entire creation — began with the Incarnation, by which the entirety of humanity is inseparably connected with the divine by redeeming us from sin, death, and the devil. The Council of Chalcedon (A.D. 451) expressed the mystery of the Incarnation this way:

Following the holy Fathers we teach with one voice that the Son [of God] and our Lord Jesus Christ is to be confessed as one and the same [Person], that he is perfect in Godhead and perfect in manhood, very God and very man, of a reasonable soul and [human] body consisting, consubstantial with the Father as touching his Godhead, and consubstantial with us as touching his manhood; made in all things like unto us, sin only excepted; begotten of his Father before the worlds according to his Godhead; but in these last days for us men and for our salvation born [into the world] of the Virgin Mary, the Mother of God according to his manhood. This one and the same Jesus Christ, the only-begotten Son [of God] must be confessed to be in two natures, unconfusedly, immutably, indivisibly, inseparably [united], and that without the distinction of natures being taken away by such union, but rather the peculiar property of each nature being preserved and being united in one Person and subsistence, not separated or divided into two persons, but one and the same Son and only-begotten, God the Word, our Lord Jesus Christ, as the Prophets of old time have spoken concerning him, and as the Lord Jesus Christ hath taught us, and as the Creed of the Fathers hath delivered to us.[152]

Chalcedon made the following points: 1) The Son of God and Jesus (who is the Christ) are one and the same Person; 2) Christ is perfect God and perfect man; 3) Christ has both soul and body; 4) Christ's divinity is of the same essence as the Father, and Christ's humanity is of the same essence as ours (except without sin); 5) the Son of God was begotten of the Father before all worlds, but in His humanity was born into this world of the Virgin Mary, for which reason we rightly venerate her as the Mother of God; 6) Christ has both a human and divine nature, which are unconfusedly, immutably, indivisibly, & inseparably united, with the two natures in Christ being preserved and united in the one person of Christ.

The Council of Chalcedon declared the Son of God and the Son of Mary to be the same person, containing both a divine and a human nature. This was not enough for the Monophysites, who felt the decree of Chalcedon divided the Christ's unity of Person and work, and was a denial of His sacrifice.[153] An attempt was made to find some theological language that would bridge the divide between the two sides by saying that the Christ had both a divine and human nature, but only a single action and will.[154] This error was corrected by the Sixth Ecumenical Council (680-681), which stated the following:

> We likewise declare that in him are two natural wills and two natural operations indivisibly, inconvertibly, inseparably, inconfusedly, according to the teaching of the holy Fathers. And these two natural wills are not contrary the one to the other (God forbid!) as the impious heretics assert, but his human will follows and that not as resisting and reluctant, but rather as subject to his divine and omnipotent will. For it was right that the flesh should be moved but subject to the divine will, according to the most wise Athanasius. For as his flesh is called and is the flesh of God the Word, so also the natural will of his flesh is called and is the proper will of God the Word, as he himself says: "I came down from heaven, not that I might do mine own will but the will of the Father which sent me!" where he calls his own will the will of his flesh, inasmuch as his flesh was also his own. For as his most holy and immaculate animated flesh was not destroyed because it was deified but continued in its own state and nature (ὅρῳ τε καὶ λόγῳ), so also his human will, although deified, was not suppressed, but was rather preserved according to the saying of Gregory Theologus: "His will [i.e., the Saviour's] is not contrary to God but altogether deified."[155]

And so we see the Incarnation as encompassing the entirety of our humanity; our flesh, our spirit, our nature, and our will. As Gregory of Nazianzus explains it, this is necessary for our salvation.

> For that which He has not assumed He has not healed; but that which is united to His Godhead is also saved. If only half Adam fell, then that which Christ assumes and saves may be half also; but if the whole of his nature

fell, it must be united to the whole nature of Him that was begotten, and so be saved as a whole. Let them not, then, begrudge us our complete salvation, or clothe the Saviour only with bones and nerves and the portraiture of humanity.[156]

The Son of God, begotten of his Father before all worlds (Nicene Creed), did not think it robbed Him of his divinity to be joined with humanity (Php 2:5-11), to be inseparably united with a human body, a human nature, and a human will. While we sometimes despise these bodies of flesh, nevertheless our Lord became one of us — skin and bones, meat and viscera. The implications of the Incarnation can never be fully grasped by our finite minds. Nevertheless, it is clear that while the pagans and even some Christians long to be released from this fleshly prison, our Lord felt otherwise. Even after His resurrection, He appeared to His disciples in a body of flesh and bones (Lu 24:39). Not only this, but to demonstrate His permanent victory over death, his resurrected body still retains the marks of His crucifixion (Jo 20:29).

The Nicene Creed attributes the Incarnation to both the Holy Spirit and the Virgin Mary. The connection between the Holy Spirit's mothering of creation and the Holy Virgin's mothering of the Son of God are drawn out by Paul Evdokimov, who writes:

In its Christological section, the Creed adds an important specification: "Incarnate of the Holy Spirit and the Virgin Mary." Here, the Holy Spirit conveys the presence of the Father who alone begets; but, at the same time, this presence allows us to say that the Son is born of the Holy Spirit. Likewise, at the time of the Epiphany, the Holy Spirit, in the form of a dove, descends upon the Son at the precise moment when the fatherhood of the Father is revealed: "This is my Son, the Beloved" (Mt 3:17). Here, the dove is certainly the Holy Spirit, the breath of the eternal birth-giving. He is the image, the expression, of hypostatic motherhood.[157]

The correspondence between the Holy Spirit and the Holy Virgin is made even clearer as Evdokimov writes: "The biblical story of creation already presents the Holy Spirit in His function of "hovering over" ("incubating") the abyss from which the world will emerge (Ge 1:2) — the Church and the Body of Christ as potentialities. The Holy Spirit descends on the Virgin, and this is the Nativity of Christ."[158] Moreover, there is a correspondence between the eternal fatherhood of God the Father, from whom the Son was begotten according to His godhead, and the motherhood of the Holy Virgin, from whom the Son was begotten according to his manhood.

For us men and for our salvation, our Lord built for Himself a body of the flesh of the Virgin Mary, by whom he was born according to the flesh as fully man, yet fully God. The flesh taken from the Virgin Mary became the realized and fulfilled tabernacle of God (Joh 1:14), of which the tabernacle of Moses was merely the type and shadow (Heb 8:5; 10:1). This was a complete humanity: a human nature uncorrupted by sin, and a deified human will voluntarily subjected to the divine will. It was this deified humanity, along with the divinity of the Son, which suffered death on the cross, so as to destroy death and hell, thereby breaking the curse we placed on ourselves by choosing the works of the devil over the works of God.

By virtue of His resurrection and ascension to the right hand of the Father, our Lord is able to present His own broken body and shed blood as food for the life of the world. The incarnate Lord declares:

Verily, verily, I say unto you, Except ye eat the flesh of the Son of man, and drink his blood, ye have no life in you. Whoso eateth my flesh, and drinketh my blood, hath eternal life; and I will raise him up at the last day. For my flesh is meat indeed, and my blood is drink indeed. He that eateth my flesh, and drinketh my blood, dwelleth in me, and I in him. As the living Father hath sent me, and I live by the Father: so he that eateth me, even he shall live by me. This is that bread which came down from heaven: not as your fathers did eat manna, and are dead: he that eateth of this bread shall live for ever (John 6:53-58).

As humanity partakes of this world's food for the maintenance of the body, so too humanity must partake of the broken flesh and shed blood of Jesus for the maintenance of the whole of humanity. Man is, indeed, what he eats.

14: Heresy and Christian Anthropology

Oskar Skarsaune, in his book *In the Shadow of the Temple*, writes that the "challenge from Gnosticism & Marcion" led to one of the earliest and simplest definitions of heresy. "[F]or the early Christians the distinction between orthodoxy and heresy amounted to something very simple and basic: Do you confess faith in the God of the Old Testament as the one and only God, creator of heaven and earth, or do you not?"[159] The Gnostics were dualists, believing that "matter is opposed to spirit as evil [is] to good." The human spirit is a divine spark imprisoned in a material body. Because of this, the God of the Old Testament could not be the creator of heaven and of earth, of spirit and flesh, for this would make God the creator of both good and evil. Thus the world was created by a lesser deity. Moreover, because the flesh was the prison of the soul, of the divine spark, the Gnostics denied bodily resurrection, asserting that at death the spirit ascended towards its final reward. The Gnostics share these points in common with Marcion, for whom the God of the Old Testament was an "inferior deity", and for whom anything connected with matter was suspect. Thus the church responded to the challenge of the Gnostics and of Marcion with what amounts to the first part of the Nicene Creed, along with an assertion of the bodily resurrection.[160]

Although Christianity and Judaism use the same sacred texts to describe the origin of man, they have developed fundamentally different anthropologies — primarily because the Christian tradition can make use of the Christ event. Fr. John Breck writes:

Christian anthropology is firmly grounded in the Old Testament understanding of the origin and destiny of the human person. It makes its greatest departure from Hebrew teaching with its proclamation of Christ's incarnation, resurrection, and ascension. These momentous events provide the conditions for the general resurrection of humankind "at the last day" and for the glorification or deification (theōsis) of those who dwell "in Christ."[161]

The Psalmist expressed the human condition best when he exclaimed: "What is man, that thou art mindful of him" (Ps 8:4)? And again: "LORD, what is man, that thou takest knowledge of him! or the son of man, that thou makest account of him" (Ps 144:3)! These are expressions of both comparison and relationship: of comparison, because man ought to be beneath the notice of such as God; and of relationship, because God deigns to notice us, to have created us, and to have ordered the universe for our benefit. Job expressed much the same when he cried out: "What is man, that thou shouldest magnify him? and that thou shouldest set thine heart upon him" (Job 7:17)? A more telling exclamation was when Job cried out: "What is man, that he should be clean? and he which is born of a woman, that he should be righteous" (Job 15:14)? And finally, in the Wisdom of Sirach:

What is man, and whereto serveth he? what is his good, and what is his evil? The number of a man's days at the most are an hundred years. As a drop of water unto the sea, and a gravelstone in comparison of the sand; so are a thousand years to the days of eternity. Therefore is God patient with them, and poureth forth his mercy upon them. He saw and perceived their end to be evil; therefore he multiplied his compassion. The mercy of man is toward his neighbor; but the mercy of the Lord is upon all flesh: he reproveth, and nurtureth, and teacheth, and bringeth again, as a shepherd his flock. He hath mercy on them that receive discipline, and that diligently seek after his judgments. (Sir 18:8-14)

Here is the crux of the matter; here is our first glimpse into the human problem: how do we account for both the greatness and the depravity of man? how do we account for beauty and destruction? how do we account for joy and sorrow? how do we account for the marvel that is life and the horror that is death? To these questions, the philosophers and anthropologists have no answer. The world's religions offer some comfort and solace, but no answers. All, that is, except for Christianity.

This is therefore the economy of salvation: our Lord had compassion upon us, and shows us great mercy. He takes upon himself our corruption, and gives us back his own body and blood for our food, food given for the life of the world. We are what we eat. Both because of and through the Incarnation, the Virgin Mary plays an important role in this economy of salvation. The Incarnation has far-reaching implications for the development of a distinctly Christian anthropology, which not only counters a purely secular anthropology, but helps us discover ourselves as human beings. In doing so, we will discover our true place in the salvation story; by doing so, we will begin to discover why the Blessed Virgin enjoys such an important place both in popular piety and in theology.

Within the Christian orbit, so to speak, we encounter differences regarding the human question, the nature of humanity, humanity's relationship to the rest of creation, and of humanity' relationship with God. These differences most often they arise as theological misunderstandings, as errors that approach, but generally do not rise to the level of theological heresy. In some specific cases these errors actually cause a departure from the faith. Fr. Georges Florovsky writes of the connection between heresy and anthropology using the example of Apollinarianism. Apollinarius espoused a particular Christological heresy: that Christ had a human body and soul, with the divine Logos taking the place of the human rational mind. Florovsky writes:

Apollinarianism is, in its deepest sense, a false anthropology, it is a false teaching about the God-Man Christ. Apollinarianism is the negation of human reason, the fear of thought — "it is impossible that there be no sin in human thoughts". ["ἀδύνατον δέ ἐστιν ἐν λογισμοῖς ἀνθρωπίνοις ἁμαρτίαν μὴ εἶναι" — Gregory of Nyssa, Contra Apollin. II, 6, 8; I, 2]. And that means that human reason is incurable — ἀθεράπευτον ἐστι [it is incurable] — that is, it must be cut off. The rejection of Apollinarianism meant therefore, at the time, the fundamental justification of reason and thought. Not in the sense, of course, that "natural reason" is sinless and right by itself but in the sense that it is open to transformation, that it can be healed, that it can be renewed. And not only can but also must be healed and renewed.[162]

Florovsky makes the point that the manner in which we view humanity necessarily affects the way we view the Incarnation, of the person and work of Christ, and of the meaning of salvation. Thus there is an anthropological component to theology. If we accept the dualistic view that spirit is good and matter is evil, as in the case of Manichaeism, we must therefore accept that Christ only appeared to be human, and that the human body is the prison of the soul.[163] If this is the case, then Christ redeemed the spirit but not the body; and if Christ did not redeem the body, then death is a release and not a curse. If we accept that Christ was fully human, but assumed divinity at some point; and if we accept the possibility that the divinity left Christ before his actual death; then the entirety of our human life has not been sanctified, death has not been conquered, and we are yet in our sins.

The question "What is man?" is therefore central to theology, to who we are as humanity, to the purpose of God becoming incarnate of the Virgin Mary, to the two natures in Christ, to the meaning of our death (and His), and to our ultimate destiny. We know this because in both creation accounts, man is unique. In the first account, God determines to make humanity "in our image, after our likeness", (Ge 1:26) after which it is said "male and female created he them" (Ge 1:27). Thus both men and women alike share in the image and likeness of God. In the second account, it is said: "the LORD God formed man of the dust of the ground, and breathed into his nostrils the breath of life; and man became a living soul" (Ge 2:7.) Thus we see that man is both a creature of flesh, and a creature of spirit.[164]

The human person is consubstantial, of two essences; the human person is entirely fleshly, and entirely spiritual, and is therefore able to bridge the gulf between the temporal and spiritual worlds. It is therefore incorrect to imply, as some do, that this body is the prison of the soul. Death is a tragedy, for it sunders body and spirit. We cannot say that the dead are in a better place, for they are separated from their bodies. And when Jesus says that Lazarus is sleeping, he was not referring to soul sleep, but referring to his body sleeping in the ground, awaiting the resurrection and the reunion of soul and body.

It is here that we see the divide beginning between east and west, between Orthodox and Roman Catholic anthropology. For the Latins (and for western Christianity in general), theological anthropology is essentially moral, involving a change in the nature of our relationship with God, but not a change in our essence. This must be so on account of the logically derived concept of the absolute simplicity of God, who is the Highest Good. The goal of western theological anthropology is to obtain the Highest Good through "beautifying actions within the workings of the Church Militant in order to overcome the world."[165]

Evdokimov describes the theological anthropology of the Orthodox Church as follows.

Orthodox anthropology is not "moral" but ontological; it is the ontology of deification. It is centered not on overcoming this world, but on "seizing the Kingdom of God" (cf Lu 16:16), on the inner transformation of the world into the Kingdom, on the world's gradual illumination through the divine energies. The Church, then, is viewed as the place where this metamorphosis occurs through worship and the sacraments, and is revealed as being essentially Eucharistic, the manifestation of the divine life in human reality, the epiphany and the icon of the heavenly reality. In this dimension as Ecclasia orans (the praying Church), the Church blesses and sanctifies more than she teaches.[166]

We shall speak more on the subject of humanity's division into male and female, specifically the conjugal and virginal states, in the chapter entitled *Marriage and Virginity*. For now, it is enough to describe the basic parameters of the discussion; that this is not a question of Marriage vs. Virginity as though these two modes of Christian life are in opposition to one another, but rather that Marriage and Virginity describe the restoration of sexuality as an expression of the inner Trinitarian love life, and by extension the relationship between God and man.

15: The Theology of the Body

In her book *Path to Sanity*, Dee Pennock writes:

According to the great spiritual counselors of ancient Christian history, God gave us the Adam and Eve account to show us exactly how our souls now work. The saints who became taught of God tell us that we have the same psychological structure and behavior patterns that Adam and Eve had during and after their fall from Paradise.[167]

This means that Christian anthropology begins in the book of Genesis with the creation stories. This is why John Paul II — in his development of what he terms a theology of the body — points to the creation accounts where we see an individual man, created alone, which God pronounces as "not good".[168] This is significant because up to this point God had pronounced everything He created as "good"; yet a man in solitude is "not good". When God found no help for the man among all that He had created, God then builds a woman from the flesh and bone of the man, a help who is the counterpart to and compliment of the man. God brings the woman to the man and, with man and woman by nature being in full communion, God announces his judgment that the *entire* creation is now "very good".

Art historian Irina Yazykova examines this passage as follows:

The book of Genesis (1:31) tells us that the Creator, not unlike a painter surveying a just-completed canvas, was filled with admiration for his creation: "And God saw everything that he made, and, behold, it was very good. Wanting to share with others a delight in the world that he made, God concluded the creation by creating humans.[169]

Paul Evdokimov further explains the implications of God's pronouncement upon His creation: "Everything that

God created is *very good* (Ge 1:31). Evil does not by any means lie in the very condition of being a creature: its source is alien to being, which was good from the start."[170]

And finally, Pope Paul VI writes:

The transition of God's description of His creative efforts as being "good, to His description of the creation of man as "not good", and finally (after the creation of Eve) to His assessment that all of creation is now "very good" is highly important; the transition suggests humanity (male and female) is the capstone of God's creation, and that the full communion of the persons is the point of creation. The remarkable transition also makes clear that God made man for woman, just as woman is built for man. A man — and by extension, a woman — a man in solitude is not good, but man and woman in "communion of persons" is "very good".[171]

We see that the creation of the material world is "good", but the creation of humanity as male and female in their state of original righteousness makes the entirety of creation "very good". For this reason it is clear that man and woman share humanity in common. One is not lower, or lesser, or weaker than the other, despite what our cultures or false understandings of scripture may say. The apostle writes:

For the man is not of the woman; but the woman of the man. Neither was the man created for the woman; but the woman for the man. ... Nevertheless neither is the man without the woman, neither the woman without the man, in the Lord. For as the woman is of the man, even so is the man also by the woman; but all things of God (I Cor 11:8-9, 11-12).[172]

We are equally glorious, because we share in God's image; we are equally pitiable, because we are equally subject to death. Having been made from the same lump of clay, sharing of the same flesh and bone, we are equally "homo communio". Pope John Paul II notes that the "hono communio" is the essence of what scripture means by the term "help meet" (רזע, ezer) for him (Gen 2:20).[173] This communion of persons has three points of reference: first, in the solitude of both man and woman apart from each other; second, in the distinction of mankind from the other animals; and third, in the way in which this communion of persons defines what it means to be human.[174]

The uniqueness of mankind among God's creations is shown most clearly through the account of the naming of the animals, whereby the dominion of man over the earth and the difference between mankind and the animals is expressed. Thus it is quite important that in the naming of the animals, Adam found no one who could exist beside him as an equal partner, as a help meet for him. (Ge 2:18-20) Despite this fact, animals are not entirely beneath us; we share our createdness and our physicality with them. Animals can certainly provide assistance to us as companions, as beasts of burden, and even protection; yet none of the animals can exist beside us in the full communion of persons.[175] None of the animals share in that which was breathed into us — the "breath of life", by which we can be the priests of creation. As priests of creation, our role is not merely to be served by creation, but to serve creation, and to offer it back up to God.

Having found no partner among the creatures, one was built for Adam from flesh and bone taken from Adam's side. Adam's statement upon seeing the woman is highly significant for our Christian anthropology. The importance of this statement is often missed, as it is incorrectly separated in most of our bibles. The versification breaks the entire statement into two verses, making it seem as though Adam's statement is only about woman being taken from man, with the second statement being Moses' own commentary. Taken in this way, the full impact of the statement regarding "leaving and cleaving" is missed. Moreover, when properly punctuated, Adam's statement regarding Eve is not simply a statement of recognition, but is prophetic. Adam's statement, the second eschatological statement in Sacred Scripture, is as follows: "*This is now bone of my bones, and flesh of my flesh: she shall be called Woman, because she was taken out of Man; therefore shall a man leave his father and his mother, and shall cleave unto his wife: and they shall be one flesh*" (Ge 2:23-24).

The significance of Adam's prophecy is demonstrated by Jesus' repetition of this prophecy regarding "leaving and cleaving" in His answer to the Pharisees regarding divorce (Matt 19:3-12). Jesus response draws a clear connection between the communion of persons and the communion with God in the state of original righteousness; and to the purpose of Christ's redemptive work, which has the effect of drawing mankind into a personal communion with each other through the communion we share in Christ (I Cor 10:15-17). This communion, this personal relationship, is in a sense a return to Eden, a return to the purpose for which we were created: perfect communion with God, and perfect communion with each other.

16: The Communion of Persons and the Gift of Self

Since the communion of persons is a constituent element of both the orders of creation and Christ's redemptive work, we must speak of it in detail. Fr. John Breck describes this as key to the doctrine of the human person.

> *Orthodox anthropology — the doctrine of the human person — begins with the Genesis affirmation that every human being is created "in the image and likeness of God." However the term "image" is to be defined; it implies what theologians today call "being-in-communion." The human person is not an isolated entity but a member of a community. And the primary and primordial community is that of the Church, the Body of the risen and glorified Lord, Jesus Christ.*
>
> *The Ultimate model for the ecclesial community is God Himself; the eternal life-in-communion of Father, Son and Holy Spirit. "Be perfect," Jesus instructs His followers, "as your heavenly Father is perfect." That perfection, as God expresses it, consists above all in self-sacrificing love, offers as a free gift to the other: to the other Persons of the Holy Trinity, and to the created world, particularly to human persons.*[176]

What Pope John Paul II called a theology of the body is a useful means of continuing this discussion. Michael Waldstein, writing in the introduction to John Paul II's *Man and Woman He Created Them*, encapsulates the theology of the body into a simple diagram he terms the Sanjuanist triangle, which is his way of describing the essence of the Theology of the Body. I have used this example at a starting point to describe the tripartite nature of the Theology of the Body.

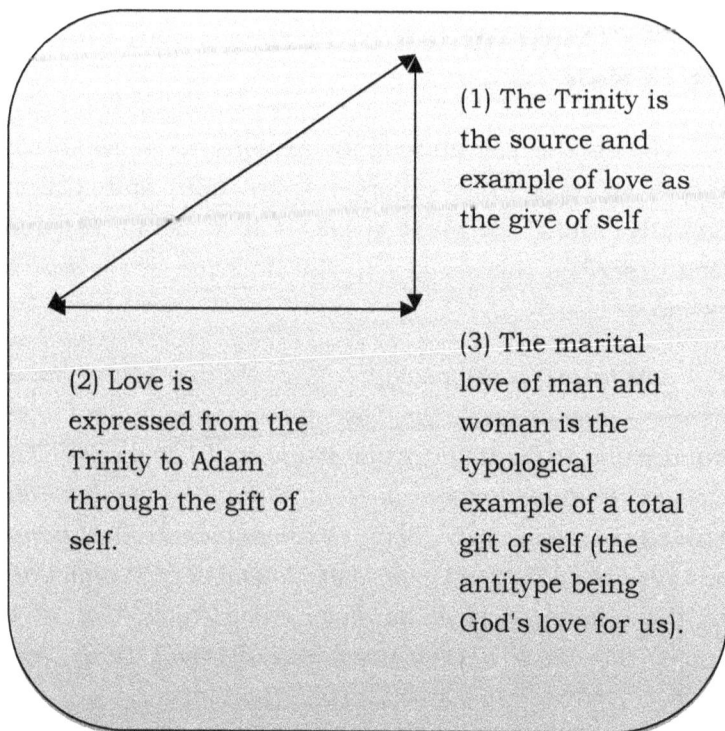

Figure 1: The Tripartite Theology of the Body

The Communion of Persons is a description of the inner Trinitarian life, which is by nature a superabundant love for each other, a gift of self. This superabundant love is expressed through creation of the immaterial and material realms, and through immaterial and material beings. In the creation accounts God gifts Himself to His creation through Adam, and through God's making Eve of Adam's flesh and bone. Now the inner life of the trinity can be expressed in creation through the relationship between husband and wife.

Paul Evdokimov, in his discussion of Andre Rublev's icon of the Trinity, discusses the nature of Trinitarian love as paradigmatic of the relationship between God and His creation. "God is love in himself in his threefold essence, and his love towards the world is only the reflection of his Trinitarian love. The gift of himself...is never a loss, but the

The Communion of Persons and the Gift of Self

expression of the superabundance of love."[177] The love of God is His gift of Himself, which finds its reflection in the gift of self between a husband and wife, and the gift of self between each of them and God.

The relationship expressed in the Tripartite Theology of the body is found in Jesus' High Priestly Prayer, which is the prayer Jesus prayed in the Garden before His betrayal and crucifixion. In this prayer, Jesus expresses the relationship that He has with the Father, and the relationship they share with His disciples. "And this is life eternal, that they might know thee the only true God, and Jesus Christ, whom thou hast sent" (Jo 17:3). This verse is important for many reasons. First, because it defines eternal life not as a heavenly continuation of this earthly existence, but rather that eternal life is relational, as an act of love. This understanding is key to understanding what the Orthodox mean when they use the word deification. Second, this relationship is defined in triangular form; we know the Son who was sent by the Father, through whom we know the Father. Because this prayer was addressed by the Son to the Father, we do not see here a mention of the Holy Spirit; we know from other passages that full manifestation of the Holy Spirit would not occur prior to Jesus' ascension into heaven (Jo 14:25-26).

Now that we are tuned to understand the relational aspects of the High Priestly Prayer, we should turn to the capstone verses of this passage: "Neither pray I for these alone, but for them also which shall believe on me through their word; That they all may be one; as thou, Father, art in me, and I in thee, that they also may be one in us... I in them, and thou in me, that they may be made perfect in one" (Jo 17:20-21, 23). Jesus expresses his desire not only that we may be one, as though disparate elements are being alloyed together; but rather that we may be "made perfect in one".

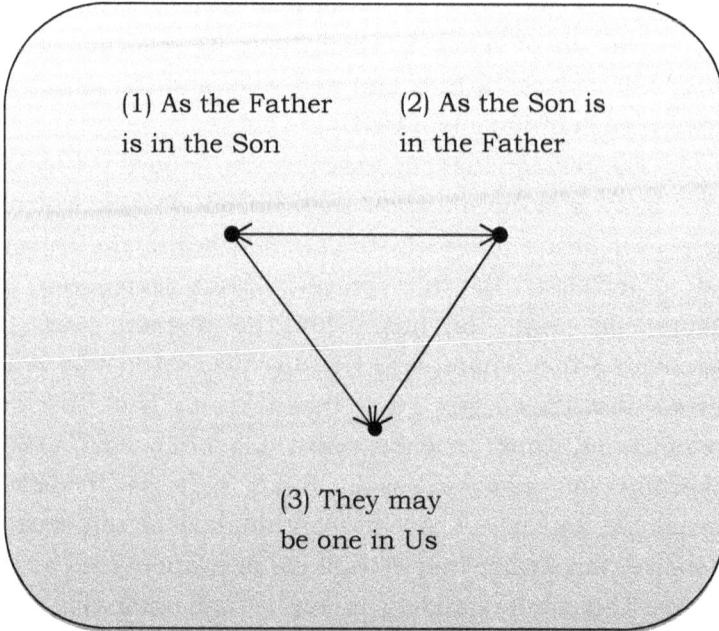

Figure 2: The Communitarian Triangle

Jesus is here expressing the essential unity and unicity (oneness, uniqueness) of human nature from the beginning, a unity which sin has fractured and prevented us from expressing, but which exists nonetheless. This unity is the same as that which exists between the Father and the Son, who are distinct persons sharing a common nature (together with the Holy Spirit). Jesus is praying for a restoration of that humanity which was torn asunder through the primordial departure, which rupture can be healed only through Christ's defeat of sin, death, and the Devil. Christ, in giving of Himself, enables us to give of ourselves in like measure.

The apostle John returns to this them in his first epistle when he writes: "That which we have seen and heard we relate to you, in order that ye also may have communion with us; and our communion also is with the Father and with His son, Jesus Christ." (1 John 1:3, The Orthodox New Testament, Volume 2)

The Communion of Persons and the Gift of Self

This means that people find themselves — which is to say they find the true meaning of their lives — in the gift of self. The gift of oneself is given both to God and to the spouse who is other than ourselves, and yet by nature is and by grace becomes "one flesh". This mutual gift of self, which constitutes the spousal communion of persons, is representative of the communion the Trinity has with itself. This is shown through the descending line of the Sanjuanist Triangle, giving evidence that the marital life and the conjugal act "flows as an image [of] God's own Trinitarian communion".[178]

The gist of Pope John Paul II's statement that "Love is the gift of self" is described by Vladimir Moss in the following manner: "The end of love is union, which of its nature involves a mutual 'exchange of properties', so that what belongs to the one belongs to the other. ...[L]ove presupposes the existence of another person to love."[179] Vladimir Moss explains the Trinitarian aspect of this in this manner.

Now in the beginning the only person of the same nature as himself to whom Adam could exercise his personhood through love was Eve. Therefore if he was to show in himself the image and likeness of God as a multiplicity of Persons united in love, he could do so only in his relationship with Eve. We come to the conclusion, therefore, that the image of God in man was revealed in the beginning not only in Adam and Eve as individuals, but also in Adam and Eve in their relationship with each other, more specifically in their love for each other. Thus the love between man and woman is in the image of the love between the Divine Persons of the Holy Trinity.[180]

This gift of self is best expressed through God's desire to create a helpmate for Adam (Ge 1:20); and by Adam in the garden when he looked upon Eve and declared:

101

"This is now bone of my bones, and flesh of my flesh" (Ge 1:23). As was described earlier, the fall sundered the natural unity of humanity; what was once one a communion of persons has been divided into male and female, even though both male and female remain persons made in the image and likeness of God. However, as Paul Evdokimov notes, "among human beings the religious principle is expressed by women." Evdokimov notes this religious principle is expressed even within the world of matter: "While man extends himself in the world by means of tools, woman does so by her gift of self."[181,182] While it may appear sexist to say so, the natural extension of Evdokimov's thought is that women's primary means of interacting with the created order, the gift of self, indicates women may be inherently more spiritual than men. Certainly this was shown in the account of the fall, where Eve was deceived while Adam sinned willfully.

Dumitru Staniloae describes the gift of self in this fashion:

For love demands that each of those who love one another moves towards the other. Through all things, God gives himself to man, and man to God...This faith expresses the incontestable fact that the world has been made for a purpose and, therefore, that it is the product of a creator who gives meaning and [this world] is guided by that creator towards the fulfillment of its purpose in himself. Moreover, with this goal in view, the creator himself leads our being towards the closest union with himself.[183]

At the Annunciation, we see God announcing his intentions towards humanity. We also see humanity's response by means of a representative person, the Virgin Mary, making her move towards God, being her free gift of self, and God's corresponding move towards the Blessed Virgin, and his gift of self to her, a gift of self that came through her and by means of her to all humanity — and by means of humanity, to all of creation. In Mary's response, we see an illustration of the gift of self by means of her *fiat* (her free choice), as well as a recapitulation of the communion of persons, a matter we will take up again in our discussion of the Virgin Mary in the New Testament.

We see at the Annunciation a reciprocal gift of self when the offer is made to Mary — an offer freely made from one person to another, and freely accepted. Thus our personhood is respected by God. In this exchange God offers Himself to Mary, and Mary offers herself to God. God becomes one with His creation; He who is "the brightness of his glory, and the express image of his person (Heb 1:3) became at the same time His own image; the archetype became one with the type. Staniloae writes: "If the human person is created 'in the image' of the Logos, the model potentially implies Himself in the image. The Logos achieves His image in a subsistent and ultimate way by assuming human nature as an image developed in Him and as an image inseparably united with the model."[184]

17: The Priest of Creation

Even after by one man sin entered into the world, and death by sin, man is still made in the image of God. And, as Fr. John Breck writes, since God is of inestimable value, so too is man. *"The human person, created in the image of God and called to progress toward the divine likeness, is unique and of infinite value."*[185] The exercise of our spiritual perception, our progress toward the divine likeness, is our calling as Christians. We are called to beware, lest we fall away. We are called to grow in grace, to strive against sin, to work out our salvation, to deny ourselves and take up our cross daily. In theological terms, this is the path of sanctification, of theosis, of divinization, of salvation.

Salvation is not an event, but a journey. We cannot say "I am saved," in the same manner in which we can say "I am baptized"; we cannot say "I am saved," but we can say "I was saved, I am being saved, and I will be saved." The apostle likened salvation to running in a race, a race that would be finished only at the time of his death. In his first epistle to the Corinthians, the apostle speaks of salvation (the Christian life) as being in training for the great race. Not only that, but the apostle suggests that he has not arrived, but that he keeps himself in subjection so that he might not be a castaway (1 Cor 9:24-27). Paul's implication is that the Christian life is much like the period of athletic training leading to the games. The writer of the epistle to the Hebrews takes up a similar athletic metaphor, indicating that the Christian life is an endurance race, one for which we put off the sin that weighs us down so that we might run with patience the race set before us, keeping always before us the example of our Lord, and of the prize set before us — which is our Lord himself (Heb 12:1, 2). The point in both metaphors is there is no salvation event that suffices once for all, but that the Christian life is more like a long period of athletic training, or like a marathon, with salvation as the ultimate goal.

The reason all this is so important is that man is unique among God's creations. St. John of Kronstadt writes: "I myself am a miracle of God's goodness, wisdom and omnipotence. I myself — on a small scale — am a whole world; my soul is the representative of the invisible world; my body — of the invisible one."[186] The angelic hosts are spiritual, non-corporeal beings. The universe and all that is in it is physical & corporeal. Of all of God's creations, only humanity is comprised of both body and spirit; only humanity has both a rational and a spiritual consciousness.

St. Gregory Palamas describes the value of humanity as both the recapitulation and culmination of His creative work.

Man, the greater world contained in a lesser, is the combination of all things, the recapitulation of God's creation, which is why he was produced last of all, just as we put an epilogue at the end of speeches; in fact, you could say that this universe is the composition of the person of the Word Himself. Man, then, brings his mind and senses into unity with the greater wisdom of Him who is able to mingle elements that cannot be mixed, by using his imagination, opinion and thought as intermediaries, as genuine bonds of the extremes.

Man and the world are in communion with each other, but whereas the world is greater than man in magnitude, man transcends it in intelligence. He is stored up like treasure within the world, like a very precious object kept in a large house and worth much more than the building that contains it.[187]

Humanity was created to exist in a communion of persons, as an ecclesial being. The role of humanity is to serve as the priest of creation, to unite the physical world to the spiritual and refer it back to God. Lutheran theologian Gerhard Forde notes the following: "The creature is never meant to stand or operate alone but to be one through whom the creator works. The creature is turned about to take care of creation, to seek the good of the other, not of the self."[188,189]

Metropolitan John of Pergamon expounds on the idea of humanity as the priest of creation in this way:

The priest is the one who freely and, as himself an organic part of it, takes the world in his hands to refer it to God, and who, in return, brings God's blessing to what he refers to God. Through this act, creation is brought into communion with God himself. This is the essence of priesthood, and it is only the human being who can do it, namely, unite the world in his hands in order to refer it to God, so that it can be united with God and thus saved and fulfilled. This is so because, as we said earlier, only the human being is united with creation while being able to transcend it through freedom.

This role of the human being, as the priest of creation, is absolutely necessary for creation itself, because without this reference of creation to God the whole created universe will die. It will die because it is a finite universe, as most scientists accept today. This is theologically a very fundamental belief, since the world was not always there, but came into being at some point and, for this reason, will 'naturally' have an end and come into non-being one day.

Therefore, the only way to protect the world from its finitude which is inherent in its nature, is to bring it into relation with God. This is because God is the only infinite, immortal being, and it is only by relating to him that the world can overcome its natural finitude and its natural mortality.

In other words, when God created the world finite, and therefore subject by nature to death and mortality, he wanted this world to live forever and to be united with him -- that is, to be in communion with him. It is precisely for this reason that God created the human being. This underlines the significance of man as the priest of creation, who would unite the world and relate it to God so that it may live forever.

Now, the human being did not perform this function, and here lies for theology the root of the ecological problem. The human being was tempted to make himself the ultimate point of reference, i.e. God. By replacing God with himself, a finite created being, man condemned the world to finitude, mortality, decay and death. In other words, the human being rejected his role as the priest of creation by making himself God in creation.

This is what we call in theology the 'fall of man.' When this occurred, God did not want the world to die and brought about a way of restoring this lost communion between himself and creation. The incarnation of the Son of God was precisely about this. Christ is the one who came in order to do what Adam did not do: to be the priest of creation. Through his death and resurrection, Christ aimed precisely at this unity and communion of the whole of creation with God, at the reference of creation back to God again. It is for this reason that Christ is called the 'second Adam', or the 'last Adam', and that his work is seen as the 'recapitulation' (anakefalaiosis) of all that exists, i.e. of the entire creation.

Now it is this role, which Christ performed personally through his cross and resurrection, that he assigned to his Church, which is his Body. The Church is there precisely in order to act as the priest of creation who unites the world and refers it back to God, bringing it into communion with him. This takes place in the Church particularly through the sacraments.[190]

Cosmology and Anthropology

The communion of persons between the Blessed Mother and her Holy Child, described for us by means of her being overshadowed or clothed with the glory of God (Lu 1:35; Rev 12:1), is paradigmatic of the blessed communion between Christ and His Virgin Bride. Human nature is a unicity, expressed through a division into human persons. God created we human beings to be in perfect communion with each other and perfect communion with God, so that as priests of His creation, we may bring together the physical and the spiritual creation, thereby uniting this world and referring it back to God.

Adam chose to become his own god, and to refer the world to Himself. Human nature became marred by sin, creating a distinction between the person and the individual governed by egoism and self-will, the individual who defines him/herself over against others. As a result of the fall, human nature has become divided — split into individuals.[191] The unification of humanity in the image and likeness of God becomes possible only through the Incarnation of Christ of the Blessed Virgin, whose paradigmatic example prefigures the perfect communion we will enjoy in heaven as the Virgin Bride of Christ. Mary, as the Mother of God, has become the mother of all believers, which makes her the Mother of the Christian Race. And it is in and through the Church that we partake of the Eucharist. By eating His flesh and drinking His blood, we partake of His life (John 6:53-58). His blood flows through our veins, uniting us as the family of God. It is the church, the family of God, the priesthood of believers, which is given the role of acting as the priest of creation, with the mission of creating order out of chaos by resacrilizing the entire creation so as to offer it back to God.

In his book "The Eucharist", Alexander Schmemann describes the sacramental nature of creation, and of our relation to it. A sacrament (or mystery) is not merely a referent to some past action, but in some mysterious way is a revelation. The sacrament is truly *sui generis*, truly in a class of its own. The sacrament is a more true truth, a more real reality.

> [I]n the Orthodox ecclesial experience and tradition a sacrament is understood primarily as a revelation of the genuine nature of creation, of the world which, however much it has fallen as "this world," will remain God's world, awaiting salvation, redemption, healing and transfiguration in a new earth and a new heaven. In other words, in the Orthodox experience a sacrament is primarily a revelation of the sacramentality of creation itself, for the world was created and given to man for conversion of creaturely life into participation in divine life. If in baptism water can become a "laver of regeneration," if our earthly food — bread and wine — can be transformed into partaking of the body and blood of Christ, if with oil we are granted the anointment of the Holy Spirit, if to put it briefly, everything in the world can be identified, manifested and understood as a gift of God and participation in the new life, it is because all of creation was originally summoned and destined for the fulfillment of the divine economy — "then God will be all in all."
>
> Precisely in this sacramental understanding of the world is the essence and gift of that light of the world that permeates the entire life of the Church, the entire liturgical and spiritual tradition of Orthodoxy. Sin is itself perceived here as a falling away of man, and in him of all creation, from this sacramentality, from the "paradise of delight," and into "this world," which lives no longer according to God, but according to itself and in itself and is therefore corrupt and mortal. And if this is so, then Christ accomplishes the salvation of the world by renewing the world and life itself as sacrament.[192]

Our mission as the church is to expose this sacramental reality to the world, to be the kingdom of God within the world, to clothe ourselves and the world in the glory of God, and to offer the sanctified creation back to God. As we intone in the liturgy: "*Thine own of Thine own we offer unto Thee on behalf of all and for all.*" Of our own volition we assemble ourselves together as the body of Christ. Our choice is but an echo and fulfillment of Mary's own choice, when she answered the angel: "*Behold the handmaid of the Lord; be it unto me according to thy word.*" Mary's choice opened the door to our redemption, and to the redemption of the world. Therefore with the Virgin Mary, we accept our calling; and with the apostle, we "*press toward the mark for the prize of the high calling of God in Christ Jesus*" (Php 3:14). Glory to thee, oh Lord; glory to thee.

18: Clothed with the Glory of God

In light of the discussion regarding the communion of persons, which is a sign[193] and symbol of the communion the trinity has with itself, we can understand what the scriptures mean when they speak of Adam and Even being naked, and not ashamed (Ge 2:25).[194] By nature the man and the woman were in full communion with each other, and full communion with God (Ge 2:8). The fathers of the church believed Adam and Eve were thereby clothed with the glory of God.

The obvious question is whether the idea of the original and prototypical humanity being clothed with the glory of God has any scriptural foundation. In the introduction to Robert Alter's translation of Psalms, he notes the way the language of Psalms presents the idea of light's being a mythological property of deity, of God wearing light as a garment, and of God stretching out the heavens as a garment.

God, as we noted in a verse quoted from Psalm 27[195], is associated with light — in that instance, because light, archetypically, means safety and rescue to those plunged in fearful darkness, but also because radiance is a mythological property of deities and monarchs. Psalm 104 is a magnificent celebration of God as king of the vast panorama of creation. It begins by imagining God in the act of putting on royal raiment: "Grandeur and glory you don" (hod wehadar lavashta). The psalmist then goes on: "Wrapped in light like a cloak, / stretching out the heavens like a tentcloth" (verse 2). What makes the familiar figure of light for the divinity so effective is its fusion with the metaphor of clothing. The poet, having represented God donning regalia, envisages Him wrapping Himself in a garment of pure light (the Hebrew verb used here is actually in the active mode, "wrapping"). Then, associatively continuing the metaphor of fabrics, he has God "stretching out the heavens like a tent-cloth," the bright sky above becoming an extension of the radiance that envelopes God.[196]

The association of God with light is the source for the phrase describing Jesus Christ as "light from light" in the Nicene Creed. Since Sacred Scripture speaks of God being clothed in light, and of spreading out the heavens like a tentcloth, it is only natural to extend that idea to original and prototypical humanity. St. Ephrem the Syrian writes: "God clothed Adam in glory"; and again: "It was because of the glory with which they were clothed that they were not ashamed. It was when this glory was stripped from them after they had transgressed the commandment that they were ashamed because they were naked"[197] In like manner, St John Chrysostom writes: "[W]hile sin and disobedience had not yet come on the scene, they were clad in that glory from above which caused them no shame. But after the breaking of the law, then entered the scene both shame and awareness of their nakedness."[198]

The 17th century mystic Jacom Böhme remarks:

Man should have walked naked upon the earth, for the heavenly [part] penetrated the outward, and was his clothing. He stood in great beauty, glory, joy and delight, in a child-like mind; he should have eaten and drunk in a magical manner; not into the body, as now, but in the mouth there was the separation; for so likewise was the fruit of Paradise.[199]

Such was the state of humanity in Paradise. Yet once Adam had sinned and the glory of God had departed from him, it was immediately clear to him that he no longer belonged in Paradise. St. Ephrem the Syrian, explains this in the seventh verse of his second Hymn on Paradise:

At its boundary I saw
figs, growing in a sheltered place,
from which crowns were made that adorned
the brows of the guilty pair,
while there leaves blushed, as it were,
for him who was stripped naked:
there leaves were required for those two
who had lost their garments;
although they covered Adam,
still they made him blush with shame and repent,
because, in a place of such splendor,
a man who is naked is filled with shame.[200]

There are striking parallels between this hymn and the account of the Philistines capturing the Ark — how the pregnant wife of Phineas, upon hearing this, gave birth. *"And she named the child Ichabod, saying, The glory is departed from Israel"* (I Sam 4:21). It is only after the fall, after the glory has departed, and after full communion of persons has been lost, that the man and the woman objectified each other as individuals rather than persons partaking of the same nature; in their fallen state they saw themselves as naked before each other and before God.[201]

The reader will no doubt be reminded of how the Ark of the covenant was shrouded in the "thick darkness" of the Holy of Holies (I Kings 8:12); and of how in Ezekiel chapters 8-10, the prophet is given a vision of the glory of God, the defilement of the temple, and how the glory of God departed from the temple as a consequence for Israel's sin. In this manner we come to the understanding that the glory with which Adam and Eve were clothed, or overshadowed, is natural to mankind in the state of original righteousness, a state of communion with God. We also understand that the glory of God, with which they were clothed, would quite rightly depart as a consequence of Adam's sin. In this context, we note that after the Babylonian captivity and the rebuilding of the temple, Ezra makes no mention of the glory of God returning, filling the temple, and overshadowing the Ark. Instead, the return of the Shekinah glory came at the Annunciation, when the angel Gabriel informed the blessed virgin that the Holy Ghost would come upon her and the power of the highest would overshadow her. What we see at the annunciation (and in Revelation 12), is the blessed virgin clothed with the glory of God, as was Eve in the garden — which points to the Incarnation as the inauguration of God's plan for reconciliation and recreation, for the reestablishment of that perfect communion between God and man, and between each human person.

19: The Marian Bridge

When we consider the Incarnation, we must be aware of the manner in which the Blessed Virgin Mary serves to bridge the gulf between the God who is pre-existent and transcendent, yet is somehow immanent and involved in the processes of this world. The Word became flesh and dwelt among us (John 1:14) by means of the voluntary obedience of Mary. She is the means through which the transcendence of God becomes immanent; she is "God's way of giving structure to the world of nature and yet avoiding complete identification with that world."[202] The entire plan of God for the reconciliation of the world to Himself rested on the free choice of a single person, on the voluntary obedience of the blessed virgin. Through her free choice to be obedient, He who transcends creation emptied Himself, was incarnate of the Holy Ghost, and was made man, thereby becoming God with us (Phil 2:5-7; Matt 1:23).

This claim is a startling one for most Protestants. A common objection is that God could have chosen anyone. If Mary had refused, then God would simply have moved on to someone else. But let us first examine the scriptural record. "When the fulness of the time was come, God sent forth his Son, made of a woman, made under the law, to redeem them that were under the law" (Gal 4:4-5). The plan of God came down to one specific moment in time — the fullness of time.

Moreover, Micah writes: *But thou, Bethlehem Ephratah, though thou be little among the thousands of Judah, yet out of thee shall he come forth unto me that is to be ruler in Israel; whose goings forth have been from of old, from everlasting (Mic 5:2).*

And Luke writes: *And it came to pass in those days, that there went out a decree from Caesar Augustus, that all the world should be taxed. (And this taxing was first made when Cyrenius was governor of Syria.) And all went to be taxed, every one into his own city. And Joseph also went up from Galilee, out of the city of Nazareth, into Judaea, unto the city of David, which is called Bethlehem; (because he was of the house and lineage of David:) To be taxed with Mary his espoused wife, being great with child. And so it was, that, while they were there, the days were accomplished that she should be delivered (Lu 2:1-6).*

So if not Mary, then God would have had to have chosen some other unwed young woman, a woman betrothed to a man whose family happened to come from Bethlehem — a town so small it nearly escaped the notice of biblical history. How many young girls could there have been who, in the fullness of time, met all these criteria? Now remember the Protestant hermeneutical principle: to accept what is written in Sacred Scripture, but to deny that which is not written. We read that God chose Mary, but we do not read that God was prepared to choose someone else. If the argument is that God was prepared to choose someone else, the argument is not from Sacred Scripture; instead, the argument is from the basis of a Romaphobic bias and a tradition of disregard of and occasional hostility towards Mary.

At the Annunciation, we are given the chance to see the entire trinity at work in and through the Incarnation of the Son by the Holy Spirit in the womb of the Blessed Mother; in the Incarnation we see God as both transcendent and immanent. God the Father overshadows her, and the Son is made incarnate by the Holy Spirit — *of the Virgin Mary.* In Genesis we see woman being built from a man; in the Gospels we see man being built from a woman. The Virgin Mary is the material used to fashion the humanity of the Christ, who is the Son of God — the transcendent made immanent. Mary is therefore the gateway for speaking of God's intimate involvement in this world.

The Marian Bridge

One of the questions raised by people who oppose any form of Mariology is what difference this makes. This is not a simple question to answer because it has to do with the very structure of theology, with the deep connections between the Old and New Testaments, and with our eschatological hope. Jaroslav Pelikan makes the point that without Mary, theology is at a loss when trying to make a connection between the God who is transcendent and the God who is immanent; between the God who is other and the God who is involved in the natural world.[203]

In emphasizing God's involvement with nature too much, the theologian risks losing God altogether and ends up talking about natural processes only; in emphasizing God's transcendence too much, God appears abstract and remote: distant, uninvolved, and uninterested. For Protestant theologians this is a problem that appears most visibly in the debates over the various theories of origins, but appears most importantly in the idea of inspiration.[204] Pelikan describes the solution to this dilemma:

[Mary] represents involvement in the processes of nature; after all, what is more directly involved in them than motherhood, even virginal motherhood? Yet she is the Mother of God. By being born of her, Christ becomes truly man, involved with nature; yet he remains truly God, sovereign over nature.[205]

Christ is the seed of the woman; the Holy Spirit used the flesh of Mary in the conception of our Lord. This was a natural process, aided and enhanced by the Holy Spirit. Through Mary (and the incarnate Son of God) we have a way of talking about a God who is involved in the natural world, is hidden within it, yet still transcendent.

In addition, Mariology is an important branch of theology because it binds the entire redemptive process together — from the Protoevangelium, through the sacrificial system, and into the past, present, and future history of the church. Mariology is able to make connections between the

117

earliest eschatological promises in Genesis and their eschatological fulfillment in John's Revelation. In all this, Mariology is intimately connected with Christology, which is the key to unraveling the mysteries of the Kingdom of Heaven. In a very real sense, a Christology without Mariology is incomplete. Mary is also important as a counterpart to Eve, connecting our theology to the creation accounts — thereby helping us develop a Christian anthropology. Furthermore, Mary serves to connect our theology forward into an eternal life in communion with God.

The problem with focusing too much on Mary, as we see with the Latins, is Mary becomes the exclusive way of talking about the immanence of God. This has important Christological implications; it makes Jesus more remote and transcendent — reachable primarily through the mediation of Mary, and secondarily through the saints. But by failing to deal with the Mariological implications of the Incarnation, Protestants tend to worship Jesus as either the Son of God or the Son of Man, but not both at the same time. The modern worship practice emphasizes the humanity of Christ; we modern Christians sing him love songs and treat him as a friend, as a buddy, as one of us. We have trouble dealing with His transcendence, because apart from the proper appreciation of the Virgin Mary, we lack the theological framework for doing so.

Vigen Guroian sums up for us the importance of the Virgin Mary for our Christian life in this way.

Our relationship to Jesus is not merely bilateral, as many modern Christians assume. Jesus has a mother who he has given to us as our mother also. In like manner, my personal holiness does not belong to me alone. Holiness comes about in relationship to Christ and our Mother Mary. It is shared. Holiness consists in keeping and remembering what God has done in Christ through his mother for all of humankind. Holiness is a personal state of wholeness and spiritual wellness. But it also is an active virtue of service rendered to others, which Mary embraced by declaring herself the handmaid of the Lord. Holiness is ecclesial, entirely related and connected to the other great marks of the church: unity, catholicity, and apostolicity.[206]

Part IV: Mariology in the Life of the Church

20: The Historical Development of Mariology

As a young Protestant, I remember being taught that the Hebrew people did not encourage virginity. The argument was that due to their literalistic interpretation of the command to "be fruitful and multiply", the Hebrews viewed virginity with disdain and childlessness as a curse from God. There is some scriptural evidence for this idea, such as the Nazarite vow which did not preclude the Nazarite from enjoying marital relations (Num 6:1-21); or Jephthah's dreadful vow (Jud 11:30-40). But there is also ample evidence favoring virginity, as well as a life characterized by chastity and asceticism. After all, what is keeping kosher if not an ascetic discipline? (Additional scriptural and historical evidence will be provided in the chapters entitled: "Marriage and Virginity", and "Aeiparthenos, or Ever-Virgin".)

One Protestant objection is that we do not see a well-developed Mariology in Sacred Scripture or in the writings of the earliest church fathers. To answer this objection, we need to examine the concept of catechesis — of instruction in the faith. For a number of reasons, catechesis in the early church was primarily oral.

- First, because there was no New Testament canon in the ante-Nicene church. For nearly thirty years there were no epistles; for nearly forty years there were no gospels; for many years different bishops promulgated different canons, and the canon as we know it today wasn't standardized until the late 4th century.
- Second, there were no books as we know them today, only scrolls; different churches had different collections of scrolls.[207]

- Third, scrolls were hand-copied, and therefore expensive.
- Fourth, literacy was not widespread, especially among the lower classes that formed the bulk of the Christian Church.[208]
- Fifth, because scrolls were hand-copied and errors were frequent, the written word was not considered to be as trustworthy as the oral word passed on from teacher to student.
- And finally, because the Christian Church was an underground movement. As Christianity was technically an illegal religion in the Roman Empire, and also so as not to cast pearls before swine, the mysteries of the faith were kept hidden from non-believers. It is perhaps for these reasons that we do not see well-defined theology on a great many subjects within the writings of the earliest church fathers.

As evidence, let us examine some of the works preserving the church order of the early church. The Didache (a.k.a. the *Teachings of the Apostles*), is a very early work, perhaps written as early as 50 AD (but certainly before 70 AD), which was accepted as scripture by many church fathers and within several jurisdictions, and was not officially excluded from the canon until the 4th century.[209,210] The Didache contains very little doctrine, but is mostly concerned with matters of church order, church practices, and holy living.[211] In the third century, Hippolytus (c. 170-c. 236) wrote his Apostolic Traditions, preserving the church order and practices in use in Alexandria, but containing none of what we today would call doctrine.[212] The Didascalia Apostolorum, probably from the early third century, preserves the early church order and practices in use in Syria, likely close to Antioch. The so-called Constitutions of the Holy Apostles appears to be a second or third century work (with fourth or fifth century interpolations), which preserves the church order and practices of the churches in Asia Minor, and appears to be "a revised and enlarged edition of the Didascalia."[213] This work consists of eight books, most of which are solely concerned with church order and holy living. Only the sixth book, "Against Heresies", contains any doctrine — and apart from a creedal portion in Section III entitled *An Exposition of the Preaching of the Apostles,* most of the work consists of a description of various errors or of the prescriptions of the apostles. What we would term the doctrinal portion of this work is surprisingly brief.[214]

Given this, it is likely that Marian doctrine was considered to be a mystery, preserved orally and passed on to catechumens only after their baptism. It is also possible that Marian doctrine, along with Christology, was not especially well developed in the primitive church; but when heretics such as Arius began to attack the nature of Christ, Christology became increasingly important and well-defined. In this view, Marian doctrine developed as an outgrowth of and in support of Christology. In any case, it seems the primitive church had no need of a written dogmatic tradition, being content with the apostolic witness passed on orally to the catechumens. Sergius Bulgakov notes the relative absence of dogma concerning the Virgin Mary; this is "in accordance with the general spirit of Orthodoxy, for which life is more adequate than formulas."[215]

As some hold that Mariology was a creation of the later Ecumenical Councils, what are they to make of the 2nd century fresco entitled "Virgin and Child with Balaam the Prophet", preserved in the Catacomb of St Priscilla?[216] What are they to make of the early 4th century Fresco of the Adoration of the Magi in the catacomb of Marcellinus and Peter?[217] What are they to make of the 4th century marble sarcophagus with its image of the Adoration of the Magi?[218]

Or of another similar mid-4th century sarcophagus with its image of the Adoration of the Magi, including one of the figures carrying a gold wreath which was a gift "offered only to the emperor"?[219]

Even the earliest witness of the fathers contains the seeds of Mariology. Of course this Mariology never stands alone; in line with Sacred Scripture, Mary is always linked with her son, who was both Son of Man and Son of God. Thus Mary was eventually referred to as the Mother of God, a title derived from that used by Elizabeth in the Visitation account: "Mother of my Lord" (Lu 1:43), with the word "Lord" being a widely used circumlocution (or indirect expression) for the Tetragrammaton, the divine name of God. Thus we see the origins of Marian doctrine began with the witness of Sacred Scripture over against the pagans and heretics.

Ignatius of Antioch (ca. 35 or 50-between 98 and 117) is the earliest patristic source for Mariology. Ignatius is important for a number of reasons. First, along with Polycarp, Ignatius is known to have been a disciple of the apostle John. Second, he was the third bishop of Antioch, which was an important center of Christianity (being the church that commissioned Paul and Barnabas). And third, while on his way to martyrdom in Rome, Ignatius wrote seven epistles which survive to this day. In them, Ignatius defends the birth of Jesus through the Virgin Mary as proof both of Jesus' humanity and His divinity.[220] Justin Martyr (ca. 100 or 110-165) is the first author to describe the parallels between Eve and Mary. This doctrine was developed from two sources: first, the Scripture calls Eve the mother of the living (Ge 3:20), which would make Mary the mother of the living in a truer sense of the term; and second, as a necessary byproduct of the Pauline doctrine of the first Adam/last Adam, which formed the basis for Paul's doctrine of recapitulation. For Justin Martyr, the Eve/Mary parallels are profoundly connected with Christology, with the double generation — the two natures in Christ, even though this was not formally defined until the Council of Nicea.[221] Other patristic sources exist, but these two are enough to demonstrate that Mariology is a product of the primitive church.

21: Mariology and the Church

Mariology is profoundly important in the life of the church. Our views on women determine how we think about Mary, and our views about Mary determine the manner in which the church organizes itself and how if functions. Without a proper view of Mary, Christianity becomes a fraternity of and for men, supported by women. Dr. Albert Outler, a Methodist observer at Vatican II, makes the following statement: "we've got to take seriously the whole idea of the maternal dimension of Christianity. Protestantism has stressed to an almost exclusive degree the paternal and fraternal dimensions of religion."[222] It is fascinating to see the manner in which this works in practice. Both Orthodoxy and Roman Catholicism can be said to have a high view of Mary, and both of them create and maintain a substantive place for women within the life of the church. Within conservative and/or confessional Christian denominations, women are seemingly irrelevant to the fraternal and theological life of the church. Without a high view of Mary, the fraternal element of the church is exclusively patriarchal. It is a curious thing that the two church bodies with the most highly developed Mariology are also the two bodies with the strictest adherence to a male-only priesthood, while the church bodies hostile to Mariology seem to require either the subordination of women or are drifting slowly towards women's ordination. As counter-intuitive as it may sound, a high view of the Virgin Mary appears to give women another outlet for their legitimate aspirations.

The churches of the Reformation, along with most Christian communities, fail to notice or deal with the fact that the primary metaphor of the church — the bride of Christ — as is the word used in the New Testament for the church, *ecclesia*. The implications of neglecting the feminine aspect of theology are profound. As Joseph Cardinal Ratzinger (now Pope Benedict XVI) points out, our current modes of thinking about, existing within, and living out the church are masculine.

In today's intellectual climate, only the masculine principle counts. And that means doing, achieving results, actively planning and producing the world oneself, refusing to wait for anything upon which one would thereby become dependent, relying rather, solely on one's own abilities. It is, I believe, no coincidence, given our Western, masculine mentality, that we have increasingly separated Christ from his Mother, without grasping that Mary's motherhood might have some significance for theology and faith.[223]

Russian lay theologian Paul Evdokimov begins his description of the significance of women for theology as follows.

Structurally, the human being is in the image of God; both man and woman resemble the one who is Father in His essence — but a strange discovery awaits every human being: the fact that a man does not possess the paternal instinct in the same way as a woman possesses the maternal instinct. Though he may be conqueror, adventurer, builder, a man is not paternal in his essence — and this is a great paradox. It means that there is nothing immediate in a man's nature that corresponds directly to the religious category of fatherhood. This also means that among human beings the religious principle is expressed by the woman; that the special sensitivity to the truly spiritual lies in 'anima', not in 'animus'; and that it is the feminine soul that is closest to the sources of creation.[224]

This concept is not unique to Evdokimov, or to theologians. H.L. Mencken, the American journalist and all-around curmudgeon, writes:

The essential traits and qualities of the male, the hallmarks of the unpolluted masculine, are at the same time the hall-marks of the Schafskopf[225]. The caveman is all muscles and mush. Without a woman to rule him and think for him, he is a truly lamentable spectacle: a baby with whiskers, a rabbit with the frame of an aurochs[226], a feeble and preposterous caricature of God.[227]

Among theologians, and within the church, the marks of a false understanding of fatherhood, of what it means to be a man, are clearly evident to those with eyes to see. An example of the masculine principle, falsely understood, is found in the hyper-masculine statements of Mark Driscoll, co-founder and preaching pastor of Mars Hill Church in Seattle, Washington. In answer to a question regarding the greatest challenge young Christians faced in the next ten years, Driscoll made the following comment:

There is a strong drift toward the hard theological left. Some emergent types [want] to recast Jesus as a limp-wrist hippie in a dress with a lot of product in His hair, who drank decaf and made pithy Zen statements about life while shopping for the perfect pair of shoes. In Revelation, Jesus is a pride fighter with a tattoo down His leg, a sword in His hand and the commitment to make someone bleed. That is a guy I can worship. I cannot worship the hippie, diaper, halo Christ because I cannot worship a guy I can beat up.[228]

Contrast this with how the Orthodox Bishop Kallistos Ware writes regarding Christ:

Loving humility is a terrible force: whenever we give up anything or suffer anything, not with a sense of rebellious bitterness, but willingly and out of love, this makes us not weaker but stronger. So it is, above all, in the case of Jesus Christ. "His weakness was of strength", says St. Augustine. The power of God is shown, not so much in his creation of the world or in any of his miracles, but rather in the fact that out of love God has "emptied himself" (Phil. 2:7), has poured himself out in generous self-giving, by his own free choice consenting to suffer and to die. And this self-emptying is a self-fulfillment: kenosis is plerosis.[229] *God is never so strong as when he is most weak.*[230]

To be fair, most Protestants would likely not agree with the tone and content of Mark Driscoll's statement, and would possibly see these extreme statements as evidence of a man insecure with his own masculinity, as a projection of his own insecurities onto his reimagining of the biblical Jesus. Not for Driscoll the lamb led to the slaughter. Not for Driscoll the Jesus who, while surrounded by armed men prepared to put up a fight, meekly submitted to his unjust arrest. Not for Driscoll the Jesus who, after Peter lopped off the ear of Malchus, not only healed Malchus but told Peter to put up his sword. Not for Driscoll is the God unwilling that any should perish, but that all should come to repentance; instead, Driscoll sees Jesus returning to cause death and destruction: a Jesus who brings the pain. Yet although we may view Driscoll as extreme, there is a relationship between the denial of and outright hostility towards Mariology in the Protestant branch of Christianity, and the Protestant denial of the feminine principle within ecclesiology, a denial of which Driscoll serves as an extreme, yet paradigmatic example.

Cardinal Ratzinger describes the import of the masculine principle on the Church, and its antidote, in this manner:

We treat the Church almost like some technological device that we plan and make with enormous cleverness and expenditure of energy. Then we are surprised when we experience the truth of what Saint Louis-Marie Grignon de Montfort once remarked, paraphrasing the words of the prophet Haggai, when he said, "You do much, but nothing comes of it" (Hag 1:6) When making becomes autonomous, the things we cannot make but that are alive and need time to mature can no longer survive. ...When the Church is no longer seen in any but a masculine, structural, purely theoretical way, what is most authentically ecclesial about ecclesia has been ignored — the center upon which the whole of biblical and patristic talk about the Church actually hinges.[231]

Much of what passes for the right ordering of the church — to say nothing of the church growth movement that has made its way across America — is the outworking of the masculine principle: a marketing device that is planned, programmed, enervated, and actualized with the same integrity as an Amway sales pitch. It is all a numbers game: market your church a particular way, have a certain set of programs, perform a certain set of activities a certain number of times, and you will have a positive outcome — by which is meant, of course, growth in numbers, income, staff, and salary. Stephen R. Lloyd-Moffett describes the modern mentality in this way: "In a mechanized and multifaceted modern world, this seemingly simple task [of allowing God to work] has become all the more difficult. We have become a society guided by plans, programs, and proposals. We want change quantified and measured. And we want it right away."[232] The masculine principle makes the right ordering (or *bene esse*) of the church, and the hoped for church growth, a matter of personal cleverness and energy rather than the work of the Holy Spirit — with the most successful practitioners becoming wealthy and influential, thereby perpetuating the masculine principle. Moreover, the metrics of growth are touted as *prima facie* evidence of the movement of the Holy Spirit (as any pastor of a small to moderately-sized church can attest to, when measured by his mega-church brethren.)

Balthasar and Ratzinger contrast the "*masculine, activistic-sociological populous Dei (people of God) approach*" with the feminine nature of the *ecclesia*. Whereas church is often treated or thought of as a building, a set of programs, a fraternal organization, or even an ethnic, familial, and/or cultural group, the church is actually a mystery. "*The Church contains the living mystery of maternity and of the bridal love that makes maternity possible. There can be ecclesial piety, love for the Church, only if this mystery exists.*"[233]

22: Mariology and Catholicity

An important and yet neglected line of reasoning is that those who have rejected Mariology have denied an article of faith for the church catholic, and have therefore no cause to consider themselves to be in the line of orthodoxy. Mariology is quite ancient, with evidence for the veneration of Mary extending to the Primitive church, and seemingly to the apostolic era. One of the earliest icon types is that of the Virgin *Hodegetria*, or "She who shows the way."[234] The icon shows Mary holding the infant in one arm, looking out of the frame directly at us, and with her other arm directing our attention toward the Christ child. This type of icon is said to be modeled after one painted by St. Luke himself.

This is not the place to discuss the Vincentian Canon in great detail; it is enough to say that orthodoxy consists of that faith which has been believed everywhere, always, and by all. The sudden denial of what has long considered a vital part of the faith should give us pause. What right does anyone have to consider themselves orthodox, to claim apostolicity for their church, if they reject a doctrine the fathers and the church have long considered crucial to an understanding of Christ himself?

Moreover, what does it say about who Protestants are as Christians, if their method of scriptural interpretation so differs from the fathers that they, looking at the same passages, come to very different conclusions? What has changed — the techniques of analysis and of scriptural interpretation, or the presuppositions they bring to the text? I would argue that our theological traditions and presuppositions have a dramatic impact upon the conclusions we draw. The problem is that the tools of scriptural interpretation are of no use without a theological blueprint. This is why a Catholic, a Lutheran, a Presbyterian, and a Baptist will look at the same passage of scripture, very likely using the same tools, and come to very different conclusions. It also explains why, on certain issues, a Catholic, a Lutheran, a Presbyterian, and a Baptist will begin the discussion of a doctrine by using very different passages and discuss these passages in very different ways, and why each faith tradition will produce different proof texts in support of their respective positions.

H.L. Mencken, despite his being an atheist, nevertheless notes that Mariology is not the invention of the Mediaeval popes, but is found in the Gospels.

The glad tidings preached by Christ were obviously highly favourable to women. He lifted them to equality before the Lord when their very possession of souls was still doubted by the majority of rival theologians. Moreover, He esteemed them socially and set value upon their sagacity, and one of the most disdained of their sex, a lady formerly in public life[235], was among His regular advisers. Mariolatry is thus by no means the invention of the mediaeval popes, as Protestant theologians would have us believe. On the contrary, it is plainly discernible in the Four Gospels. What the mediaeval popes actually invented (or to be precise, reinvented, for they simply borrowed the elements of it from St. Paul[236]) was the doctrine of women's inferiority, the precise opposite of the thing credited to them. Committed, for sound reasons of discipline, to the celibacy of the clergy, they had to support it by depicting all traffic with women in the light of a hazardous and ignominious business. The result was the deliberate organization and development of the theory of female triviality, lack or responsibility and general looseness of mind. Woman became a sort of devil, but without the admired intelligence of the regular demons. The appearance of women saints, however, offered a constant and embarrassing criticism of this idiotic doctrine. If occasional women were fit to sit upon the right hand of God — and they were often proving it, and forcing the church to acknowledge it — then surely all women would not be as bad as the books made them out. There thus arose the concept of the angelic woman, the natural vestal; we see her at full length in the romances of mediaeval chivalry. What emerged in the end was a sort of double doctrine, first that women were devils and secondly that they were angels. This preposterous dualism has merged, as we have seen, into a compromise dogma in modern times. By that dogma it is held, on the one hand, that women are unintelligent and immoral, and on the other hand, that they are free from all those weaknesses of the flesh which distinguish men.[237]

Mencken identifies the flaws and logical contradictions of the western view of women as being both somehow demonic and angelic. These derive from a false and/or underdeveloped theological anthropology. Secular anthropology supplies no corrective to this view, which pervades western society (even though divorced from its theological roots.) Only a theological anthropology, grounded in the human person as the image and likeness of God, can provide the proper balance and unite the two halves of humanity.

23: Mariology and Prayer to the Saints

Prayer to the saints is one of the areas where most Protestants differ with the Catholic Church. Actually, this is not fully accurate; as it turns out, non-Protestant Christians — whether Roman Catholic, Eastern Rite Catholic, Eastern Orthodox, Oriental Orthodox, and Coptic Christians — all have no problem praying to the saints, of whom the blessed Virgin Mary is the paradigmatic example, being the greatest of all the saints.

Perhaps the most clear argument against prayer to Mary, to the saints, and to angels is found in the Smalcald Articles, part of the Lutheran's Book of Concord. Here Martin Luther draws from and expands upon Philip Melanchthon's arguments from the Augsburg Confession, and from the Apology to the Augsburg Confession.

The invocation of saints is also one of the abuses of Antichrist conflicting with the chief article, and destroys the knowledge of Christ. Neither is it commanded nor counseled, nor has it any example [or testimony] in Scripture, and even though it were a precious thing, as it is not [while, on the contrary, it is a most harmful thing], in Christ we have everything a thousandfold better [and surer, so that we are not in need of calling upon the saints]. And although the angels in heaven pray for us (as Christ Himself also does), as also do the saints on earth, and perhaps also in heaven, yet it does not follow thence that we should invoke and adore the angels and saints, and fast, hold festivals, celebrate Mass in their honor, make offerings, and establish churches, altars, divine worship, and in still other ways serve them, and regard them as helpers in need [as patrons and intercessors], and divide among them all kinds of help, and ascribe to each one a particular form of assistance, as the Papists teach and do. For this is idolatry, and such honor belongs alone to God. For as a Christian and saint upon earth you can pray for me, not only in one, but in many necessities. But for this reason I am not obliged to adore and invoke you, and celebrate festivals, fast, make oblations, hold masses for your honor [and worship], and put my faith in you for my salvation. I can in other ways indeed honor, love, and thank you in Christ. If now such idolatrous honor were withdrawn from angels and departed saints, the remaining honor would be without harm and would quickly be forgotten. For when advantage and assistance, both bodily and spiritual, are no more to be expected, the saints will not be troubled [the worship of the saints will soon vanish], neither in their graves nor in heaven. For without a reward or out of pure love no one will much remember, or esteem, or honor them [bestow on them divine honor].[238]

In the passage, Martin Luther does not argue from scripture. Instead, his argument is that prayer to the saints is against the chief article of faith — Justification, as defined by Lutheran dogma. This is a highly curious stance, as it can be argued that prayer to the saints and to angels is supported in scripture, even in the Protestant's truncated canon.

The Scriptural Witness

The book of Zechariah is important for a number of reasons, but for our purposes we will focus on the importance of Zechariah for its development in the theology of angels. In particular, God communicates to Zechariah through angels, and Zechariah questions them as to the meaning of the visions he has been seeing. In the first chapter of Zechariah receives a series of visions, after which is recorded an extensive conversation with an angel, beginning as follows:

Then said I, O my lord, what are these? And the angel that talked with me said unto me, I will shew thee what these be. ... And the LORD answered the angel that talked with me with good words and comfortable words. So the angel that communed with me said unto me, Cry thou, saying, Thus saith the LORD of hosts; I am jealous for Jerusalem and for Zion with a great jealousy. ... Then lifted I up mine eyes, and saw, and behold four horns. And I said unto the angel that talked with me, What be these? And he answered me, These are the horns which have scattered Judah, Israel, and Jerusalem (Zec 1:9, 13-14, 18-19).

The careful reader will notice that Zechariah inquired of the angel what these things meant; the angel asked the LORD, the LORD replied to the angel, and the angel told Zechariah. For our purposes, this demonstrates that prayer (which may be described as a conversation) may be made to angels. In Zechariah there seems to be little difference between asking an angel for an interpretation, and asking the LORD himself. Moreover, Zechariah treats the answer from the angel as though it came directly from the LORD. This same back and forth between Zechariah and the angel continues throughout the book. This idea is also found in the book of Daniel, where Daniel prays to God for the interpretation of his vision, and then discusses the interpretation with an angel. And of course Mary herself had a conversation with an angel, a non-corporeal, spiritual being, a conversation we know of as the Annunciation, and which will be discussed more fully in Part V: Mariology in Sacred Scripture. Not only did Mary converse with the angel, but treated the angel's words as being those of God Himself.

Another Old Testament passage from 2nd Maccabees clearly indicates that prayer to the saints is not only heard, but answered.

And this was his vision: That Onias, who had been high priest, a virtuous and a good man, reverend in conversation, gentle in condition, well spoken also, and exercised from a child in all points of virtue, holding up his hands prayed for the whole body of the Jews. This done, in like manner there appeared a man with gray hairs, and exceeding glorious, who was of a wonderful and excellent majesty. Then Onias answered, saying, This is a lover of the brethren, who prayeth much for the people, and for the holy city, to wit, Jeremias the prophet of God. Whereupon Jeremias holding forth his right hand gave to Judas a sword of gold, and in giving it spake thus, Take this holy sword, a gift from God, with the which thou shalt wound the adversaries (2 Mac 15:12-15).

You may argue that 2 Maccabees is not in the Protestant canon of Scripture, and you would be correct. It is, however, in the scriptural canon used by every other Christian body (not just the Roman Catholics). Moreover, 2 Maccabees was in Martin Luther's German translation of the Holy Bible, and in the original 1611 King James Bible (although in both it was separated from the books that make up the current canon of the Hebrew Scriptures.) This is not the place to discuss canonical issues, other than to state that there are good and valid arguments to make for its being part of the Christian canon. But what we can say is that it is clear that the Jews of the diaspora 1) believed the saints were alive, 2) believed the saints were able to hear their prayers, and 3) believed the saints were able to respond. Therefore, it is not much of a stretch to understand how the early Christian church, being comprised mainly of Jews, did not have a problem with intercessory prayer to the saints.

A belief in prayer to the Virgin Mary appears to be a quite early development. The John Rylands Papyrus 470 is a fragment dated to around 250 A.D., and containing the following prayer to the Theotokos:

Under your
mercy
we take refuge,
Mother of God! Our
prayers, do not despise
in necessities,
but from the danger
deliver us,
only pure,
only blessed.[239]

Notice, if you will, the dating of this fragment — well before the time of the edict of Milan in 313 A.D.; this papyrus dates to the time of Emperor Decius, under whose reign there was a persecution of Christian laity across the empire. This prayer, dating from a time of great persecution, is still contained in the Greek Orthodox "Book of Hours", where it is one of the concluding prayers of the evening services; also, the Orthodox sing this hymn as the last dismissal hymn of daily Vespers during Great Lent.[240] The prayer is also used in the Roman Catholic Church, where it is known as the *Sub tuum praesidium.*[241]

Shawn Tribe and Henri de Villiers provide us with the following theological analysis of this prayer.

Three fundamental theological truths are admirably synthesized:
1. *The special election of Mary by God ("only blessed").*
2. *The perpetual Virginity of Mary ("only pure").*
3. *The Divine Motherhood ("Mother of God"; "Mother" may be considered as a poor translation of Genitrix).*[242]

We should also add the idea that Mary hears our prayers and, in some sense, answers them. Thus prayer to the Theotokos, along with a belief in her remaining ever-virgin, is an expression of ante-Nicene Christianity, rather than (as some suggest) a syncretic grafting of paganism onto Christianity by a post-Constantine, apostate church.

St. John of Kronstadt waxes lyrical on this topic.

Pray, my brethren, to the Mother of God when the storm of enmity and malice bursts forth in your house. She, Who is all-merciful and all-powerful, can easily pacify the hearts of men. Peace and love proceed from the one God, as from their Source, and Our Lady--in God, as the Mother of Christ the Peace, is zealous, and prays for the peace of the whole world, and above all--of all Christians. She has the all-merciful power of driving away from us at Her sign the sub-celestial spirits of evil — those ever-vigilant and ardent sowers of enmity and malice amongst men, whilst to all who have recourse with faith and love to Her powerful protection, She soon speedily gives both peace and love. Be zealous yourselves also in preserving faith and love in your hearts; for if you do not care for this, then you will be unworthy of the intercession for you--of the Mother of God; be also most fervent and most reverent worshippers[243] of the Mother of the Almighty Lord; for it is truly meet to bless Her--the ever-blessed; the entirely spotless Mother of our God, the highest of all creatures, the Mediatrix for the whole race of mankind. Strive to train yourself in the spirit of humility, for She Herself was more humble than any mortal, and only looks lovingly upon the humble." He hath regarded the low estate of His handmaiden" (said She to Elisabeth), of "God, Her Saviour."[244]

I must admit that this troubled me for some time. Even as I write this, after being chrismated into the Orthodox Church, I am still not entirely comfortable with prayer to the saints. Yet I consider this more a matter of my sloppy prayer habits rather than conviction, for I have become convinced that prayer to the saints is the most natural thing in the world.

Mariology in the Life of the Church

One of the best places to start is with the words of Jesus: "God is not the God of the dead, but of the living" (Mat 22:32). The context of this passage has to do with the Sadducees and their disbelief in the resurrection from the dead. Jesus responded not with a defense of resurrection per se, but instead with the statement that the God of Abraham and Isaac and Jacob was the God of the living. In other words, the mortal bodies of Abraham, Isaac, and Jacob may have died, but they were still very much alive. Jesus made much the same claim in his story of Lazarus and the rich man. This is likely not a parable, because Lazarus is named in the story; therefore he is a real person, despite his having suffered bodily death. Even after death, the rich man recognizes both Abraham and Lazarus, and actually converses with father Abraham (Luke 16:19-31).

St. John of Kronstadt writes:

The saints of God live even after their death. Thus, I often hear in church the Mother of God singing her wonderful, heart-penetrating song which she said in the house of her cousin Elizabeth, after the Annunciation of the Archangel. At times, I hear the song of Moses; the song of Zacharias--the father of the Forerunner; that of Hannah, the mother of the prophet Samuel; that of the three children; and that of Miriam. And how many holy singers of the New Testament delight until now the ear of the whole Church of God! And the Divine service itself--the sacraments, the rites? Whose spirit is there, moving and touching our hearts? That of God and of His saints. Here is a proof for you of the immortality of men's souls. How is it that all these men have died, and yet are governing our lives after their death--they are dead and they still speak, instruct and touch us?[245]

Thus the souls of those asleep in Jesus, while disembodied, are kept conscious and alive, awaiting the resurrection of their bodies (1 Thes 4:13-18). Jesus describes one conversation in particular, a conversation in which the rich man seems aware of the spiritual condition of his brothers. This would seem to allow for the possibility that those asleep in Jesus are aware of us. Moreover, at the Transfiguration, Jesus spoke with Moses and Elijah, both of whom seemed aware of Jesus' upcoming death (Mat 17:1-9).

Peter Gillquist writes:

If Saint Paul instructs us as a holy priesthood to pray "always ...for all the saints" (Ephesians 6:18), is it so outrageous to confess with the Church that holy Mary (along with all the saints who have passed from death to life and continually stand in the presence of Christ) intercedes before her Son on behalf of all men? For Mary is the prototype of what we are all called to be.[246]

It is with all this in mind that we read the roll call of faith in Hebrews chapter 11. Despite the Lutheran confessions arguing against intercessory prayer to the saints, Lutheran theologian Gustaf Aulén notes:

The koinonia of the church is not limited to the church as it exists now in the present. Death does not constitute a boundary. The fellowship of the church includes the witnesses to the faith in all ages. When the Letter to the Hebrews in the eleventh chapter has enumerated a long line of witnesses from the time of the old covenant, it continues in chapter twelve to stress the significance of the fact that "we are surrounded by so great a cloud of witnesses," and especially that we look "to Jesus the pioneer and perfecter of our faith" (Heb. 12:1-2). In these words the author of the letter has disclosed the true perspective of the relationship between the many and the one. Just as the old covenant has its heroes of faith, so the new has "so great a cloud of witnesses."[247]

Mariology in the Life of the Church

Lutheran pastor Berthold Von Schenk writes in "The Presence" regarding the presence of our dear departed, worshiping with us around the altar:

As we seek and find our Risen Lord, we shall find our dear departed. They are with Him, and we find the reality of their continued life through Him. The saints are a part of the Church. We worship with them. They worship the Risen Christ face to face, while we worship the same Risen Christ under the veil of bread and wine at the Altar. At the Communion we are linked with heaven, with the Communion of Saints, with our loved ones. Here at the Altar, focused to a point, we find our communion with the dead; for the Altar is the closest meeting place between us and our Lord. That place must be the place of closest meeting with our dead who are in His keeping; The Altar is the trysting place where we meet our beloved Lord. It therefore, must also be the trysting place where we meet our loved ones, for they are with, the Lord.

How pathetic it is to see 'men and women going out to the cemetery, kneeling at the mound, placing little sprays' of flowers and wiping their tears from their eyes, and knowing nothing else. How hopeless they look! Oh, that we could take them by the hand, away from the grave, out through the cemetery gate, in through the door of the church, and up the nave to the very Altar itself; and there put them in touch, not with the dead body of their loved one, but with the living soul who is with Christ at the Altar!

Oh, God the King of Saints, we praise and magnify Thy holy Name for all Thy servants, who have finished their course in Thy faith and fear, for the Blessed Virgin Mary, for the Holy Patriarchs, Prophets, Apostles, and Martyrs, for all Thy other righteous servants; and we beseech Thee that, encouraged by their example and strengthened by their fellowship, we may attain to everlasting life, through the merits of Thy Son Jesus Christ our Lord. Amen.[248]

144

The saints are living, are aware of us (as seen in the conversations between Moses, Elijah, and the transfigured Christ), fellowship with us, worship with us at the heavenly altar (of which the earthly altar is but a shadow), and are able to speak with Jesus. The author of Hebrews charges us to keep in mind the saints in heaven, the great cloud of witnesses (Heb 12:1) — of whom constant mindfulness in some way helps us avoid sin and keep us on the path towards salvation.

Many Protestant churches are aware of the saint's perpetual involvement in the life of the church, even if they do not fully comprehend it. Why is it that many Protestant churches have graveyards on the church grounds? If you ask some of them, the more theologically sophisticated will say that the departed are still members of the church. Some sacramental Protestants (such as Lutherans) will go so far as to say that every time they celebrate the Lord's Supper, the departed dead are celebrating it with them in heaven.[249] If this is true, then why would we not ask the saints to intercede for us, just as we might ask the pastor or a trusted friend?

Prayer to the Queen of Heaven

In Part VII of this book I discuss some of the various Marian Types, Symbols, and Titles. Of particular importance to this discussion is the title "Queen of Heaven". We hear this term with western ears, and find it offensive. Yet as the Sacred Scriptures are a Semitic book, a product of a Semitic culture, we must develop some degree of Semitic understanding. In the nation of Israel, it was not the wife of the king who was queen, but his mother. If you wanted something from the king, very often you would make your request to the queen, who would intercede with the king on your behalf (1 Kin 2:12-25; 2 Kings 11:1-20). Thus, of all the saints, it is the Blessed Virgin who occupies this special position, which is why she occupies such a special place in our prayers.

It is with this understanding in mind that we can come to an understanding of what St. John of Kronstadt writes:

> *If enemies surround you, and you are in spiritual distress, call immediately upon our Most Holy Lady. She is Queen in order that she may reign, by Her sovereign power, over the powers that oppose us, and may mightily succor us, for we are Her inheritance.*[250]

I confess to an intellectual understanding of this, yet I sometimes find it uncomfortable to pray to the saints. Perhaps I am still culturally Protestant, or perhaps I do not truly believe in life after death. Sometimes, in that dark night of the soul, I have to admit to myself that the second is more likely to be true. Could it be that this is the case for others as well? I would like to believe that I am unique, but experience tells me this is not the case; what is true of me is often true of others as well. Could it be that the problem with prayer to the saints is that we do not truly believe the saints are truly alive — that unbelief is truly the state of our heart? Lord, I believe; help thou my unbelief.

Part V: The Perpetual Virginity of the Virgin Mary

24: Marriage and Virginity

One of the typical problems for Protestants is the idea that Mary remained ever-virgin. This is a scandal to many. It is likely that the objection is to life-long abstinence within marriage, rather than an objection to virginity outside of marriage. And yet, as Fr. John Hainsworth suggests, the question can be inverted: "Why *not* believe in her ever-virginity?"[251] But related to the objection to abstinence within marriage is a general hostility towards virginity when connected to the monastic calling. The implication is that Joseph's marriage of the Virgin Mary not only implied, but necessitated his sexual conquest of the Virgin Mary. And yet, Protestants never really examine the implications of such a conquest, something the Jodie Boychuk addresses quite nicely in her blog.

One of the most powerful arguments in defence of the ever-virginity of Mary is simply to consider what kind of madness it would have been for Joseph, a devout Jew to dare touch a woman who had given birth to God. Joseph knew what had happened to Uzzah when he had touched the ark of the covenant - he died instantly. That only held tablets on which God had written. Mary however, is a living ark, which had held God in the flesh. Joseph would never have viewed her as his conjugal partner because of this. He would have certainly kept her pure and cared for her as a father-figure and guardian.[252]

Marriage and virginity are sometimes thought to be in opposition to each other, such that proponents of the one must, of necessity, be opposed to the other. If you argue for virginity, you must be arguing against marriage. Conversely, the Apostle Paul's preference for virginity over marriage is sometimes interpreted as indicating that that virginity (and therefore the monastic calling) is the higher and more

148

spiritual state. Nothing could be further from the truth: "Marriage is honourable in all, and the bed undefiled" (Heb 13:4). Paul Evdokimov writes:

> On the face of it, monasticism and marriage are utterly opposed. But at a profounder level, where our life is intertwined with the life of the Spirit, we can see that they are intimately related and complementary. The sacrament of marriage internalizes in its own way the monastic state; indeed, it originally included the specifically monastic right of the tonsure. Two aspects of the same mystery are both directed towards the supreme and universal human value of spiritual virginity.[253]

Clark Carlton describes the integrity of the person as the concept that forms the keystone of the arch between marriage on the one hand, and virginity on the other: "[W]e understand virginity not merely as a biological fact, but as a symbol for the integrity of the whole person."[254] This does not mean that virginity is opposed to marriage, or that marriage is a barrier to the integrity of the whole person. Instead, virginity on the one hand, and radical monogamy on the other, are the two halves of the same coin; they are different paths to the same goal.

G.K. Chesterton noted that critics of Christianity often accuse it of contradictory things.

> [C]ertain skeptics wrote that the great crime of Christianity had been its attack on the family; it had dragged women to the loneliness and contemplation of the cloister, away from their homes and their children. But, then, other skeptics (slightly more advanced) said that the great crime of Christianity was forcing the family and marriage upon us; that it doomed women to the drudgery of their homes and children, and forbade them loneliness and contemplation. The charge was actually reversed.

The Perpetual Virginity of the Virgin Mary

...To the skeptic, Christianity appears to assert two contradictory things; either Christianity values marriage too highly, or it denigrates marriage in favor of virginity. To the one, Christianity appears to condemn women to the cloister; to another, it confines them to the kitchen. What is lacking, some might say, is a middle ground, a balance between the two extremes.[255]

Chesterton sees this search for balance as the approach of paganism, whereas the genius of Christianity is in its embrace of both extremes.

Paganism declared that virtue was in a balance; Christianity declared it was in a conflict: the collision of two passions apparently opposite. Of course they were not really inconsistent; but they were such that it was hard to hold simultaneously.[256]

Aristotle held the principle of non-contradiction to be axiomatic. According to Aristotelian logic, a thing cannot be both one thing and another thing at the same time. This is related to the law of the excluded middle — that for any proposition, either the proposition is true or its negation is true. Christianity is an explicit challenge to such philosophy. The central assertion of Christianity, that Christ was both fully God and fully man, is in stark contrast to the wisdom of this world. In like manner, Chesterton demonstrates that the Christian view of marriage and virginity is evidence of its embrace of antimonies. Again, Chesterton writes:

It is true that the historic Church has at once emphasised celibacy and emphasised the family; has at once (if one may put it so) been fiercely for having children and fiercely for not having children. It has kept them side by side like two strong colours, red and white, like the red and white upon the shield of St. George. It has always had a healthy hatred of pink. It hates that combination of two colours which is the feeble expedient of the philosophers. It hates that evolution of black into white which is tantamount to a dirty gray. In fact, the whole theory of the Church on virginity might be symbolized in the statement that white is a colour: not merely the absence of a colour. All that I am urging here can be expressed by saying that Christianity sought in most of these cases to keep two colours coexistent but pure. It is not a mixture like russet or purple; it is rather like a shot silk, for a shot silk is always at right angles, and is in the pattern of the cross.[257]

G. K. Chesterton is saying nothing new here; his view is that of the early church. The Shepherd of Hermas,[258] written around A.D. 160, raises the issue of marriage vs. virginity. The specific issue was whether a person sinned by remarrying after the first spouse died; the answer is that no, it was no sin, but there was greater honor and glory in remaining unmarried thereafter. "If a wife or husband die, and the widower or widow marry, does he or she commit sin?' 'There is no sin in marrying again,' said he; 'but if they remain unmarried, they gain greater honour and glory with the Lord; but if they marry, they do not sin.'"[259]

St. Gregory Palamas, the 14th century monk and Bishop of Thessaloniki, does not despise married life, but along with St. Paul reckons that marriage can be a distraction from and even an impediment to the striving for purity (1 Cor 7:28).

He came...to make us His brethren and coheirs. This, it seems, is the reward granted 'in all its fullness' to those who hasten to the life-giving Vine and establish themselves as branches in it, who labour on behalf of themselves and who cultivate it on behalf of themselves. And what do they do? First, they cut away everything that is superfluous and that, instead of promoting, impedes the bearing of fruit worth of the divine cellars. And what are these things? Wealth, soft living, vain honours, all things that are transitory and fleeting, every sly and abominable passion of soul and body, all the litter gathered while daydreaming, everything heard, seen and spoken that can bring injury to the soul. If you do not cut out these things and prune the heart's offshoots with great assiduity, you will never bear fruit fit for eternal life.

Married people can also strive for this purity, but only with greatest difficulty. For this reason all who from their youth have by God's mercy glimpsed that eternal life with the mind's keen eye, and who have longed for its blessings, avoid getting married, since likewise in the resurrection, as the Lord said, people neither marry nor are given in marriage, but are 'as the angels of god' will even in this present life, like the sons of the resurrection, rightly place themselves above bodily intercourse.[260]

We should note that St. Gregory Palamas wrote this to a nun and fellow monastic. We should careful not to presume a message addressed to a particular person in a particular situation is intended for a wider application, just as a bespoke suit will likely not fit any but the one for whom it was made. What may appear as a gentle condemnation of marriage is actually given to a fellow monastic as an exhortation to stay the course. It is with that in mind that we should address ourselves to the following passage, also from St. Gregory Palamas:

How will the woman, who is tied by natural bonds to a husband, children and all her blood relations, possess that freedom for which she is enjoined to strive? How will she, when she has taken upon herself the care of so many, devote herself, free from care, to the Lord? How will she possess tranquility when entangled with such a multitude?

For this reason she who is really a virgin — who models herself on Him who is virgin, who was born of a

Virgin and who is the Bridegroom of the souls that live in true virginity — will shun not merely carnal wedlock but also worldly companionship, having renounced all kindred, so that like St Peter she can say boldly to Christ, 'We have left all and followed Thee' (Matt. 19:27). If an earthly bride leaves father and mother for the sake of a mortal bridegroom and cleaves to him alone, as Scripture says (cf Gen 2:24)), what is untoward in a woman leaving her parents for the sake of an immortal Bridegroom and bridal chamber? How can she whose 'citizenship is in heaven' (Phil 3:20) have kinship on the earth? How can she who is not an offspring of the flesh but of the Spirit (cf. John 1:13) have a fleshly father or mother or blood relative? How will she who has renounced the carnal life, and so as far as possible has spurned and continues to spurn her own body, entertain any relationship whatever to bodies that are not her own?[261]

There are some interesting things here. First, note that this passage, which is part of "the most substantial of Palamas's ascetic writings", is written not from the perspective of a man, but of a woman. It is also devoid of any hint of female subordination or assumption of female guilt for the fall of man. Woman is seen as coequal with man before the Lord, and as a fellow warrior in the struggle for ascetic mastery.[262] Second, we see in this passage an echo of the Lord's own words: "If any man come to me, and hate not his father, and mother, and wife, and children, and brethren, and sisters, yea, and his own life also, he cannot be my disciple" (Lu 14:26). From this passage we understand that we are to love our Lord more than our relatives, those who share our bloodline. Thus we understand not that we are to be selfish and individualistic, nor that we are to put the family, the clan, and the tribe above our common humanity, but that we so love the kingdom of God that by comparison it is as if we despise our flesh and our fleshly relations. This is what it means to take up your cross daily (Luke 9:23); this is what it means to die daily (1 Cor 15:31); this is what it means to be crucified with Christ, nevertheless yet to live (Gal 2:20).

Metropolitan Hilarion Alfeyev expands upon this train of thought:

The entire philosophy of monasticism is expressed in the following words of Christ: 'If you would be perfect, go, sell what you possess and give to the poor, and you will have treasure in heaven; and come, follow Me'; [Matt.19:21] 'If any man would come after Me, let him deny himself and take up his cross and follow Me. For whoever will save his life will lose it, and whoever loses his life for My sake will find it';[Matt.16:24-25] 'He who loves father and mother more than Me is not worthy of Me'.[Matt.10:37] Monasticism is for those who want to be perfect, to follow Christ and to give their life for Him, to sell everything in order to have heavenly treasure. Like a merchant who goes and sells all his possessions in order to buy a pearl, a monk is ready to deny everything in the world in order to acquire Christ. And the sacrifice is worth making, for the reward is great:

Then Peter said in reply, 'Lo, we have left everything and followed You. What then shall we have?' Jesus said to them, 'Truly, I say to you... Everyone who has left houses or brothers or sisters or father or mother or children or lands, for My name's sake, will receive a hundredfold, and inherit eternal life'.[Matt.19:27-29][263]

Notwithstanding St. Gregory Palamas' previous quote regarding the ascetic life, he is careful not to condemn marriage as an institution, nor even as a sacramental act.

Do not be astonished or distressed by the fact that no criticism is made in Scripture of women who live in wedlock, caring for the things of the world but not for the things of the Lord (cf. 1 Cor 7:34), while at the same time those who have vowed themselves to virginity are forbidden even to approach worldly things and are never allowed to live in comfort. Yet St Paul also warns those who live in wedlock: 'The time is short; so let those who have wives live as though they had none and those involved in worldly affairs as though they were not involved' (1 Cor. 7:29, 31); and this, I think, is harder to accomplish than the keeping of one's virginity. For experience shows that total abstinence is easier than self-control in food and drink. And one might justly and truly say that if someone is not concerned to save himself, we have nothing to say to him, but if he is so concerned, then he should know that a life led in virginity is more easily accomplished and less laborious than married life.[264]

Palamas writes much the same in his later work *A New Testament Decalogue*, written from the Bishop to his flock. What is interesting is how closely Palamas adheres to the themes developed in his writings to the nun Xenia, taking advice written to a specific individual and situation and adapting it to a general audience.

'You shall not be unchaste' (Exod. 20:14), lest instead of being united to Christ you become united to a prostitute (cf 1 Cor. 6:15), severing yourself from the divine body, forfeiting the divine inheritance and throwing yourself into hell. According to the law (cf. Lev. 21:9), a daughter of a priest caught whoring is to be burnt, for she dishonours her father; how much more, then, does the person who defiles the body of Christ deserve endless chastisement. If you are capable of it, embrace the path of virginity, so that you may become wholly god's and may cleave to Him with perfect love, all your life devoting yourself undistractedly to the Lord and to what belongs to Him (CF. 1 Cor 7:32), and in this way anticipating the life to come and living as an angel of God on earth. For the angels are characterized by virginity and if you cleave to virginity you emulate them with your body, in so far as this is possible. Or, rather, prior to them you emulate the

Father who in virginity begot the Son before all ages, and also the virginal Son who in the beginning came forth from the virginal Father by way of generation, and in these latter times was born in the flesh of a virginal Mother; you likewise emulate the Holy spirit who ineffably proceeds from the Father alone, not by way of generation, but by precession. Hence if you practice true chastity in soul and body you emulate God and are joined to Him in imperishable wedlock, embellishing every sensation, word and thought with virginal beauty.

If, however, you do not choose to live in virginity and have not promised God that you will do this, God's law allows you to marry one woman and to live with her alone and to hold her in holiness as your own wife (cf. 1 Thes 4:4), abstaining entirely from other women.[265]

Note here the description of virginity as being something other than mere celibacy; Palamas describes the path of virginity as becoming wholly God's, as cleaving to Him with a perfect and undistracted love. This is a path open to more than just the cloistered monk; more than just the unmarried virgin. Palamas describes virginity as being a characteristic of the heavenly angels, who according to our Lord neither marry, nor are given in marriage. Thus the chastity and virginity is not characterized by the absence of sexual relations, but rather of a life lived as one of the Church, which is the virgin bride of Christ.

St. Cyril of Jerusalem, in his Catechetical Lectures, writes concerning chastity, which he describes as the avoidance of wantonness.

But let us all by God's grace run the race of chastity, young men and maidens, old men and children; not going after wantonness , but praising the name of Christ . Let us not be ignorant of the glory of chastity: for its crown is angelic, and its excellence above man. Let us be chary of our bodies which are to shine as the sun: let us not for short pleasure defile so great, so noble a body: for short and momentary is the sin, but the shame for many years and for ever. Angels walking upon earth are they who practise chastity : the Virgins have their portion with Mary the Virgin. Let all vain ornament be banished, and every hurtful glance, and all wanton gait, and every flowing robe, and perfume enticing to pleasure. But in all for perfume let there be the prayer of sweet odour, and the practice of good works, and the sanctification of our bodies: that the Virgin-born Lord may say even of us, both men who live in chastity and women who wear the crown, I will dwell in them; and walk in them, and I will be their God, and they shall be My people. 128 To whom be the glory for ever and ever. Amen.[266]

Regarding the relationship between the monastic vocation and marriage, the 19th century monk Alexander Bukharev (Aleksandr Matveevich Bukharev, a.k.a. Archimandrite Feodor), is quoted by Elisabeth Behr-Sigel as follows:

Monastic life is called angelic...because monks, like angels, are called to serve all and to work for the salvation of mankind. Their vocation in its essence does not differ from that of other Christians, in particular that of married couples. But the monastic vocation surpasses that of marriage in its emphasis on the universal. Married couples must discern, cherish, and respect the image of God in each other. The monk, in taking the monastic vow of celibacy, prepares himself to 'see through the vision of faith the Lord himself in each person.' In all his relationships, he desires only to gain Christ. Strangers as well as family and friends, honest and dishonest people alike, all are for the untarnished soul the true bridegroom, Jesus Christ. Inspired by the love of Christ...the man of God opens his arms to each one.[267]

The Perpetual Virginity of the Virgin Mary

There are different forms of martyrdom. When our Lord exhorts us to take us our cross daily (Luke 9:23); when the apostle says of himself that "I die daily" (1 Cor 15:31); and when the author of Hebrews discusses resisting sin, even to the shedding of blood (Heb 12:4); we understand that this dying is not always a physical death, nor is it always a physical shedding of blood. Bishop Kallistos (Timothy) Ware quotes a famous seventh century Celtic text to describe the different forms of martyrdom.

Now there are three kinds of martyrdom which are accounted as a Cross to a man, white martyrdom, green martyrdom, and red martyrdom. White martyrdom consists of a man's abandoning everything he loves for God's sake ...Green martyrdom consists in this, that by means of fasting and labour he frees himself from his evil desires, or suffers toil in penance and repentance. Red martyrdom consists in the endurance of a Cross or death for Christ's sake.[268]

The concept of monasticism as a form of martyrdom is quite ancient, and is widespread throughout Christendom. (In fact, much of the Old Testament law created an entire nation that existed as a community characterized by asceticism, which ultimately is what keeping kosher is all about.) Not all are called to the red martyrdom of physical suffering and death; not all of us are called to the white martyrdom of the monastic; yet all of us are called to the green martyrdom of abhorrence of one's passions, and of repentance in sackcloth and ashes (Job 42:6).

Orthodox lay theologian Paul Evdokimov describes the idea that monasticism is a form of martyrdom, and takes Archimandrite Feodor's description of monastic life as angelic a step further.

St. Athanasius's description of St Anthony, the Father of monasticism, as one who achieved perfection without

158

tasting martyrdom, marks an important turning-point in the history of Christianity. The 'baptism of blood' of the martyrs is transformed into an 'eschatological baptism' of asceticism. The true monk attains not simply a state of the soul, but the integrity of 'an angel on the earth', he is 'isangelos' — equal to the angels — with the face of 'crucified love; witnessing to the last things, he already experiences the 'little resurrection'. In the command, 'if you wish to be perfect, sell what you have,' he hears, 'sell what you are.' This is total offering; ethical renunciation leads to ontological renunciation, the giving up of self. Having given away all that you have, and become poor, you offer all that you are, and become rich in God. That is why the old cannons permit suicide in only one case, that of a virgin threatened with violation. The free offering of virginity reveals the inner meaning of martyrdom: 'Thy lamb, O Jesus, crieth aloud unto thee; I long for thee, my Bridegroom, and, seeking for thee, I endure sufferings, I am crucified with thee, and in Baptism I am buried with thee. I suffer for thy sake that I may reign with thee, and I die with thee that I may live with thee.'[269,270]

Our Lord was made, like us, "a little lower than the angels" (Ps 8:5; Heb 2:7, 9). Yet scripture also says that we are to "judge angels" (1 Cor 6:3). Why then would we think it strange that some in this earthly existence taste of the "little resurrection" being but a foretaste of the general resurrection? Should it seem unlikely that some, having tasted of the "little resurrection", should be considered as "equal to the angels?"

Paul Evdokimov provides a perfect summation of Orthodox thought on virginity. "It must be understood that the monastic chastity, the 'angelic state', is never opposed to marriage but is a sign, valuable in itself, of the *Parousia* and the Kingdom. What matters is chastity of the soul, 'purification of the heart', something quite different from merely formal, physical chastity."[271,272] This purity of heart forms the basis for what Fr. Thomas Hopko calls "radical monogamy", a life lived as a response to and reflection of the constancy of God in His relationship towards us.[273]

In this manner we see the Pauline resolution of the antimony of marriage and virginity. It is not that one is more better or more holy than the other, nor that one is the source of evil, but that the married life offers all manner of distractions from the sanctified life. When Paul said that he wished all men were as he was, it was not a slam on marriage, but a recognition that married people will have trouble in the flesh, from which he hoped to spare them. It is a recognition that those who have chosen marriage have chosen the more difficult path to righteousness.

25: Virginity in Church History

Philip Van Ness Myers, in his book "Rome: its rise and fall", states: "It was during the period between the third and the sixth century that there grew up in the Church the institution known as Monasticism."[274] The timing is correct insofar as the rise of monasticism as a distinct, identifiable movement is concerned. However, as Alexander Schmemann notes, there is a close connection between the "monastic ideal" and the "ideal and cosmic sense of the early church". Schmemann traces the origins of monasticism to the "ethical and spiritual maximalism of the pre-Nicene epoch"; as well as the "undoubted connection with the early Christian summons to the 'one things needful'" which is now "regarded as established and proved".[275]

One need only read (in the "Apostolic Tradition of Hippolytus of Rome) the list of professions forbidden by the Church to her members[276] (all connected in one way or another with the official paganism of the state) to be convinced of the truth of K. Heussi's opinion that the life of Christians in the age of persecution was "monastic." "If we can imagine," he writes, "the position of the early Christians and Christian communities within the pagan world, their complete separation from the life of society, from the theatre, the circus, from all religious and imperial holidays, and the narrow confines within which their external life was passed, then we will understand the monastic character of the world of early Christians, living in the world but as if separated from it..."[277]

Lynn H. Nelson points out that, in a sense, monasticism was nothing new.

One must remember that the distinction between the tilled and irrigated fields surrounding the villages of Egypt

161

and Syria was very clear. Beyond the fields was "the desert," rocky and waterless land, with a sparse vegetation of brambles, nettles, and thornbushes, and incapable of supporting human habitation. It was the site of caves and small springs of brackish or salty water, abounding in poisonous snakes, lizards of all sorts, and watched over by vultures. From time immemorial, however, men and women had left their villages to live nearby in these badlands and to seek — with the aid of solitude, exposure to the weather, and in hunger and thirst — a deeper knowledge of the universe and the role of human beings in it, and perhaps to experience a mystic ecstacy[sic] in which they felt themselves united with the universe and its god.

Such people, hermits [a word that comes from eremus, or "desert," and meaning "desert dwellers"], were regarded by the local villagers as holy men. They would take offerings of food to the hermits near their village, and the hermits would give them wise advise[sic]. Some hermits subjected themselves to rather extreme forms of self punishment to drive out cravings for worldly things, and the villagers, admiring such conduct, would sometimes travel long distances to see and offer sustenance.

Associated with this custom was the popular custom of going out into the desert to seek enlightenment, particularly when confronted with some important decision or when dissatisfied with life in general. Moses, Elijah, Jesus, and Muhammad, as well as the entire Israelite people, among many others, retreated into the desert and found their life's mission there.

Many early Christians went into the desert to escape the persecutions of Diocletian's reign, and some were hunted down and martyred there, thus enhancing the idea in the minds of the early Christians that the desert was in some special way the place to seek communion with God.[278]

In his introduction to the *Lives of the Desert Fathers,* the Rev. Benedict Baker provides the following brief description of Jewish and early Christian monasticism.

> *The prophets of the Old Testament, from the call of Abraham, Elijah and onwards, were no strangers to desert life (cf. 1 Kings,19); they were often alone, and either much sought after by authority or else totally unpopular with it. They had one concern only, to discern and proclaim the word of the Lord. Besides the named prophets of the Old Testament there were apparently many others, as the references to the 'sons of the prophets' show (1 Kings,20, 2 Kings,2).*
>
> *Within the Jewish nation at about the time of Christ, there was the Essene community, a group of people living outside society, in the desert, under a strict ascetical rule. The Alexandrian Jewish philosopher Philo (c.20 BCE-c.50 CE) gives an account in his De Vita Contemplativa of them and of the Therapeutae, another Jewish community at Lake Mareotis near Alexandria, who lived in strict seclusion, meeting together only on the Sabbath and high festivals. The Vitae Patrum records that as early as the beginning of the second century a certain Frontonius with seventy brothers left the world and went to live in the desert, 'labouring yoked together in the work of the Lord, meeting the challenges of spiritual trials' (VP,I, Vita Frontonii.i).*[279]

And so monasticism was nothing new. Yet Christianity gave this impulse to retreat from the world a new emphasis, a new focus, a new urgency. Schmemann notes that the church met on the first day of the week, which connected it with ordinary time; yet the church also met on the eighth day of the week, connecting the liturgy with the "New Aeon".[280] The church was within the world, was manifesting a reality apart from the world, and was actualizing that reality for the life of the world. The pre-

The Perpetual Virginity of the Virgin Mary

Constantine church was, therefore, truly a monastic brotherhood.

26: Persecution, Secularization, and Monasticism

Carolinne White, author of *Early Christian Lives,* provides the following threefold description of early Christian monasticism: "If solitude and withdrawal from the world were characteristic of early Christian monasticism, another element considered essential was celibacy, the commitment to a life of chastity."[281] Philip Van Ness Myers, author of *Rome: its Rise and Fall*, writes: "The term 'monasticism,' in its widest application, denotes a life of austere self-denial and of seclusion from the world, with the object of promoting the interests of the soul."[282] Monasticism existed first in its private form, as described by Carolinne White; later its normative form became the coenobitic brotherhood. Some view monasticism as a reform movement within the church, as an attempt to call the church to remembrance of her initial purity of purpose, of her sense of herself as the eschatological Kingdom of God. Even as a reform movement, it is essential to understand that monasticism was not a protest from outside the church, but existed within the church. Monasticism called the church to remember that "one thing needful", and served as an antidote to the secularizing tendency of the post-Constantine era. It is only in this sense in which we can say that monasticism was a product of the post-Constantine era.

Alexander Schmemann writes:

Monasticism arose as an almost unconscious and instinctive reaction against the secularization of the Church — not only in the sense of a reduction of her moral ideal or pathos of sanctity, but also in the sense of her entrance, so to speak, into the "service of the world" — of the Empire, civic society, natural values; into the service of everything that

165

The Perpetual Virginity of the Virgin Mary

(after the downfall of paganism) was waiting to receive from Christianity a religious "sanction" and "sanctification".[283]

But we must also consider that there were other motivations for the development of monasticism, as Carolinne White so beautifully describes:

Why did people at this period opt for such a radical lifestyle? ...As for the period after Constantine's conversion and his edict of toleration in 313 [A.D.] which promised religious freedom, the period when the ascetic life seems to have become increasingly popular, the principal theory for this sudden popularity is that many were driven by a desire to find a new means of proving their dedication to Christ at a time when the persecution had been replaced by tolerance and martyrdom by privilege. Certainly this may have been one motive, but it would be wrong to suppose that after 313 [A.D.] life as a Christian suddenly became a soft option. Christians could still be subject to pagan attacks, particularly under the anti-Christian emperor Julian (361-3), but also to persecution by heretics, particularly the Arians, a very powerful group who even had imperial backing under the emperors Constantius (337-61) and Valens (364-78). Such persecution could take the form of being compelled to do military service, being driven into exile, or falling victim to physical violence. ...Orosius, who wrote his 'History Against the Pagans' in the early fifth century at Augustine's suggestion, mentions the monks as a particular target of the persecutors.[284]

It is clear that the church saw monasticism as a reaction against the secularization of the church and as the return to and continuation of the early ascetic lifestyle of the church. Schmemann writes: "From this standpoint we can begin to understand the de facto agreement made by the Church's hierarchy with monasticism, which in Byzantium led to the actual control of the Church by the monks." This in itself may seem unusual, as monasticism began as both a lay and a private movement. Neither of the founders of organized monasticism — both the private monasticism of St. Anthony and the group or coenobial monasticism of St. Pachomius — were priests. In fact, as Schmemann notes, they considered sacerdotal or priestly orders as "incompatible with the monastic vocation."[285] And yet, unlike the 16th century reformation, monasticism was embraced by the early church. Perhaps this is because monasticism was not a schismatic movement, but behaved as though it were part of the church; as such, it was regarded "as a realization of the ideal bestowed on and in the Church."[286]

Fr. Michael Koblosh writes of his personal experience of this spiritual "band of brothers":

When I was in Russia in 1974, during the Soviet period, standing in the churches among hundreds of fellow Orthodox Christians was a very powerful experience because their very presence in the church was an act of defiance against Soviet persecution. There was certainly a strong sense of unity and bondage — and a powerful force that lifted one up and gave courage — because people could lose their jobs if some communist ideologue boss caught them there. In such a situation, the normal social barriers that tend to keep people apart, collapse, and social relations among believers become direct and immediate and anything but superficial.

In the war against demonic powers, the "army" is not just those around you-although God sends people into your life when you need them-but the whole Tradition as such, past and present. The holy fathers and mothers are truly "army buddies" who, through their lives and writings, care about you and your eternal life, and whose words can keep you from being destroyed. You know that St. Anthony, who was asked what he learned after living as a solitary in a cave for many years ("forty years"), answered: "I learned that my brother is my life." And a variant interpretation of "love your neighbor as yourself" is "love your neighbor because he is yourself."

The content of genuine love is a dying: "He increases, I decrease..." As the beloved is brought into the "center," the "I" has to move to the side. During persecution, being put to death because one is a Christian was (is) precisely a sign of victory and resurrection. It is a partaking in the "life-creating" death of Christ. After the persecutions, death as a way of life remained central — and that [is] what monasticism is all about. Whether the Red Martyrdom of blood, or the White Martyrdom of ascetic self-denial; whether through monastic virginity or marital union-one way or another-you are going to have to "do" Christ's death before resurrection can be accomplished: "Unless a grain of wheat falls into the ground and dies ..." The eschatological Kingdom can be incarnated and can radiate only through those who have "made good" on their baptisms into Christ's death. How you go about doing this is what the Tradition and the community of the Church is all about — because, though the Kingdom is one and the same for all, getting there will be different for each. Each needs a specific, personal Word that is given to no one else. "Seek ... knock ..." Struggle to hear that Word — and sometimes the struggle itself is the Word — though not always.[287]

27: The Virgin Mary as the Prototypical Christian

One of the ways in which the struggle against sin played out among the early church was reflected in the status of the Virgin Mary. To understand this, we must return again to a discussion of the Incarnation of our Lord. Maximus the Confessor, in his "Commentary on the Our Father", writes:

He purified nature from the law of sin in not having permitted pleasure to precede his incarnation on our behalf. Indeed his conception wondrously came about without seed, and his birth took place supernaturally without corruption: with God being begotten of a mother and tightening much more than nature can the bonds of virginity by his birth. He frees the whole of nature from the tyranny of the law which dominated it in those who desire it and who by mortification of the sensuality of the earthly members imitate his freely chosen death. For the mystery of salvation belongs to those who desire it, not to those who are forced to submit to it.[288]

This language may be difficult for modern people to hear, especially the children of the sexual revolution, as it demonstrates a preference for virginity as a sign and symbol of a life wholly given over to the service of God. It may also be difficult for some Protestants to accept, as it creates a space for free will. But only within this context can we see how the Virgin Mary could be honored as the prototypical virgin, the one whose entire life was an example of service to God, and therefore the one in whom is best manifest our Lord. Furthermore, as a byproduct of the Holy Virgin's example, she elevated her entire gender — so much so that women veil themselves when they pray on account of Mary's glory which emanates from them (1 Cor 11:10).[289]

The Perpetual Virginity of the Virgin Mary

The Protestant theologian and church historian Philip Schaff, in his "History of the Christian Church", draws the connection between the Virgin Mary and the state of women within the Christian church, between paganism and the changed nature of Christian family life, a change which included an enthusiasm for celibacy.

The Virgin Mary marks the turning point in the history of the female sex. As the mother of Christ, the second Adam, she corresponds to Eve, and is, in a spiritual sense, the mother of all living.

Henceforth we find woman no longer a slave of man and tool of lust, but the pride and joy of her husband, the fond mother training her children to virtue and godliness, the ornament and treasure of the family, the faithful sister, the zealous servant of the congregation in every work of Christian charity, the sister of mercy, the martyr with superhuman courage, the guardian angel of peace, the example of purity, humility, gentleness, patience, love, and fidelity unto death. Such women were unknown before. The heathen Libanius, the enthusiastic eulogist of old Grecian culture, pronounced an involuntary eulogy on Christianity when he exclaimed, as he looked at the mother of Chrysostom: "What women the Christians have!"

Thus raising the female sex to its true freedom and dignity, Christianity transforms and sanctifies the entire family life. It abolishes polygamy, and makes monogamy the proper form of marriage; it condemns concubinage with all forms of unchastity and impurity. It presents the mutual duties of husband and wife, and of parents and children, in their true light, and exhibits marriage as a copy of the mystical union of Christ with his bride, the church; thus imparting to it a holy character and a heavenly end.

Henceforth the family, though still rooted, as before, in the soil of nature, in the mystery of sexual love, is spiritualized and becomes a nursery of the purest and noblest virtues, a miniature church, where the father, as shepherd, daily leads his household into the pastures of the divine word, and, as priest, offers to the Lord the sacrifice of their common petition, intercession, thanksgiving, and praise.

With the married state, the single also, as an exception to the rule, is consecrated by the gospel to the service of the kingdom of God; as we see in a Paul, a Barnabas, and a John, and in the history of missions and of ascetic piety. The enthusiasm for celibacy, which spread so soon throughout the ancient church, must be regarded as a one-sided, though natural and, upon the whole, beneficial reaction against the rotten condition and misery of family life among the heathen.[290]

It is out of this historical context — this opposition to and conflict with the pagan world system — that the apostle writes his instructions to the church of Corinth concerning virginity and marriage (1 Cor 7). When the apostle writes: "*it is* good for a man not to touch a woman"; and "to the unmarried and widows, It is good for them if they abide even as I", it is within this understanding of virginity as a life of service to the kingdom of God. And when he writes: "*to avoid* fornication, let every man have his own wife, and let every woman have her own husband"; and "if they cannot contain, let them marry: for it is better to marry than to burn", it is with the understanding that both virginity and marriage are alike a gift of God. One person is determined to live a life of chastity outside of marriage, while another person is determined to live of chastity within marriage. The resolution of the antinomy, spoken of by Chesterton, is in the opposition of both to a life of sin in general, and specifically to the opposition of both to the pagan world system.

And thus we see the Virgin Mary, in her virginity, as the prototypical Christian — rather than (as some would have it) an aberration.

28: Virginity for the Sake of the Kingdom of Heaven

In Matthew 19 the Pharisees tempt Jesus by asking him a question concerning the legitimacy of divorce. Jesus turns this question on its head by returning to Genesis 2 and the orders of creation. The Pharisees asked why then did Moses permit divorce, to which Jesus answered that divorce was permitted because of the hardness of their hearts: that a man who puts his wife away for any reason except fornication and marries another woman commits adultery, and anyone who then marries the divorced woman also commits adultery.

The disciples responded that if this were true, it was not good to marry. In their Jewish context the injunction to be fruitful and multiply was taken quite literally; marriage and procreation were duties owed to the community and to God. It is interesting that Jesus does not point to his own example in this area; instead, He gives the unexpected answer.

All men cannot receive this saying, save they to whom it is given. For there are some eunuchs, which were so born from their mother's womb: and there are some eunuchs, which were made eunuchs of men: and there be eunuchs, which have made themselves eunuchs for the kingdom of heaven's sake. He that is able to receive it, let him receive it (Matt 19:11-12).

Jesus teaches that there are those to whom the gift of virginity is given *for the sake of the kingdom of heaven.* The Apostle Paul later expounds on this teaching in I Cor 7, indicating that marriage is good, but virginity is better — but that virginity is only for those who are gifted for it. Neither Jesus nor Paul implies anything negative about marriage, about the material body, or about sexual union.

Virginity for the Sake of the Kingdom of Heaven

St. Ignatius, 3rd Bishop of Antioch (following the apostle Peter and Evodius), wrote the following in his Epistle to the Philadelphians:

Wives, be ye subject to your husbands in the fear of God; and ye virgins, to Christ in purity, not counting marriage an abomination, but desiring that which is better, not for the reproach of wedlock, but for the sake of meditating on the law...Virgins, have Christ alone before your eyes, and His Father in your prayers, being enlightened by the Spirit. May I have pleasure in your purity, as that of Elijah, or as of Joshua the son of Nun, as of Melchizedek, or as of Elisha, as of Jeremiah, or as of John the Baptist, as of the beloved disciple, as of Timothy, as of Titus, as of Evodius, as of Clement, who departed this life in [perfect] chastity, Not, however, that I blame the other blessed [saints] because they entered into the married state, of which I have just spoken. For I pray that, being found worthy of God, I may be found at their feet in the kingdom, as at the feet of Abraham, and Isaac, and Jacob; as of Joseph, and Isaiah, and the rest of the prophets; as of Peter, and Paul, and the rest of the apostles, that were married men. For they entered into these marriages not for the sake of appetite, but out of regard for the propagation of mankind.[291]

Both Jesus and Paul describe virginity "for the kingdom of heaven's sake" as being a special gift, a *charisma*. This gift of virginity is an exceptional vocation, while marriage is the ordinary vocation, the normal course of events in the world.[292,293] As a reaction to the abuses of monasticism, the 16th century Lutheran reformers rejected chastity in monasticism in favor of marriage, which they insisted was the preferred state, because only in marriage could one love and serve the neighbor. In his *Winterpostille* of 1528, Luther himself argues against scripture in favor of his own innovative doctrine.

Marriage is far superior to the celibate religious life, and not only because it is clearly instituted and honored by God. It is an estate of "faith," for those who enter into it should be convinced that they are doing God's work and fulfilling their calling. It is an estate of love, for in it one "must and should" help and serve others.[294]

Luther's clear implication is that the monastic is not helping and serving others — a position which, as we have seen, does not accord with the historic understanding of monasticism. Nor does his implication accord with Luther's own experience, for as a priest-monk he wrote, taught theology, preached, presided at the Eucharist, and heard confessions. In this he helped and served as much as an Augustinian monk as he did as a Lutheran pastor.

29: Virginity in Sacred Scripture

Let us discuss various instances of virginity in the Sacred Scriptures. First among the virgins is the prophetess Miriam, the older sister of Moses, who seems to have never married. Miriam is the Hebrew form of Mary, making the typological connection between the virginal Miriam with the Virgin Mary plain. Moreover, just as Scripture records Mary's Magnificat, so too Scripture records the song of Miriam (Ex 15:20-21), sung after pharaoh's army was swallowed up in the Red Sea. And just as the Virgin Mary is held in high esteem, so too was Miriam, who not only is one of the few women who figures prominently in Scripture, but is one of an even smaller group whose death is recorded in Scripture.

No discussion of virginity would be complete without making mention of Jephthah's daughter who, because of Jephthah's dreadful vow, was offered up to God and remained a virgin her entire life (Jud 11:36-40).[295] This is indeed the first explicit case in Scripture of one who was given over to the Lord, who served God through abstaining from the ordinary pleasures and consolations of this life. In this sense, making oneself a eunuch "for the sake of the kingdom of heaven" is an intentional act, an act that is not only about sexual abstinence. Instead, sexual abstinence is the sign and symbol of a life wholly given over to the service of God.

Elijah the Tishbite is an Old Testament example of one who made himself a virgin "for the sake of the kingdom of heaven". Not only is there no mention of Elijah's wife anywhere in the scriptural record, but Elijah's mode of existence precluded any family ties. During the three and a half year drought recorded in I Kings, Elijah stayed in a cave beyond the Jordan; then with the widow of Zeraphath; then after the encounter with the prophets of Baal he fled for

175

The Perpetual Virginity of the Virgin Mary

forty days to Mt. Sinai. None of this would have been possible if Elijah had a wife. Indeed, although Nazarite vows do not require virginity, Elijah is nonetheless thought to have lived a Nazarite style existence.[296] Thus the prophecy of the coming of Elijah (Mal 4:5) is fulfilled in John the Baptist, who from birth was a Nazarite (Luke 1:13-15); and who, like Elijah, was a virgin.

Elisha is another interesting example. On Mt. Sinai God told Elijah to anoint Elisha to be prophet in his stead. After Elijah spread his mantle on Elisha's shoulders, Elisha left his father's house and followed Elijah. Before Elijah was bodily assumed into heaven, he granted Elisha's request for a double portion of his spirit. Like Elijah, we have no mention or indication in Scripture of Elisha taking a wife; additionally, the Works of Josephus never indicate that either prophet was married.

In the book of Daniel we have the example of four young Hebrew captives pressed into service in the Babylonian court, all of whom were virgins. We have no indication in Scripture that Daniel, Hananiah, Mishael, and Azariah ever married, as confirmed by church history and tradition. Indeed, Scripture tells us the king entrusted the four to "Ashpenaz the master of his eunuchs" (Dan 1:3). The Hebrew word translated as eunuchs in Daniel is used of Potiphar, who was married (Ge 37:36), and therefore had "trouble in the flesh" (I Cor 7:28). While the word in its broadest sense refers to court officials, to those who were dedicated to the king's service, it does appear that by the time of Nebuchadnezzar and in the Babylonian court the king's servants were castrated so they could serve the king without being "troubled in the flesh". Thus Daniel and his companions were likely among those "made eunuchs of men" (Matt 19:12).[297] Still, it is interesting that virginity, even though compulsory in this case, is connected with the service of the king, which further illuminates Jesus' meaning regarding those who make themselves eunuchs

176

"for the sake of the kingdom of heaven". Moreover, it could be argued that through their refusal to eat meat offered to idols, these four young men proved to have been given the gift of chastity, which we understand to pertain to more than simple abstinence from sexual pleasures, but also abstinence from pleasures of the flesh. This special *charism* was made manifest in their lives in a special way, through various signs and wonders, through gifts of prophecy, and through angelic visitations.

We also learn from the Old Testament record that virginity is not a requirement for the Lord's service. The last judge and prophet of God, Samuel, was given to the Lord and declared to be a Nazarite even before his birth (1 Sam 1:11), yet married and had sons (1 Sam 8:1). We also know that virginity was not a prerequisite for being a prophet; Isaiah, who prophesied perhaps 100 years after Elijah, was married (Isa 8:3). In addition we have the example of Anna the prophetess, who had lived with her husband for seven years before his death, and who, after the death of her husband, lived a chaste life of prayer and fasting in the temple for the next 84 years. This Anna was given the *charism* of being a witness to the messiah (Luke 2:36-38).

From the scriptural witness we understand that virginity is a special gift from God, given to some to perform extraordinary service "for the sake of the kingdom of heaven". We also understand that sexual abstinence is only part of this calling, that chastity is the sign and symbol of a life wholly dedicated to the service of God. In this way we can understand difference between the "sons of the prophets" (I Ki 20:35; 2 Ki 2:3,5,7,15; 4:38; 5:22; 6:1) who could be married (2 Ki 4:1), and Elijah. We also understand the service of God does not require virginity per se, and that a life dedicated to the service of God can still encompass ordinary family life. Yet to some is given a special grace, of which virginity is the sign, by which some dedicate themselves wholly and completely to God, "for the sake of the kingdom of heaven".

30: Virginity as an Eschatological Sign

What are we to make of Jesus' referencing to virginity "for the Kingdom of Heaven's Sake"? In what way is virginity related to the Kingdom of Heaven? For the answer we need to reflect upon Jesus response to the Sadducees, recorded in Matthew 22, Mark 12, and Luke 20. Jesus is being tempted with a question concerning a wife with seven husbands, each of whom died. They asked:

Therefore in the resurrection whose wife shall she be of the seven? for they all had her" (Matt 22:28). *"And Jesus said to them: The children of this world marry and are given in marriage: But they that shall be accounted worthy of that world and of the resurrection from the dead shall neither be married nor take wives. Neither can they die any more for they are equal to the angels and are the children of God, being the children of the resurrection* (Luke 20:34-36).

Jesus' answer indicates that marriage is for this world, this age, but that virginity is the ordinary state of the resurrected life. The reason given is that in the resurrection, they are like the angels, and are the children (υιος, huios) of God. It is interesting to note that Jesus does not refer back to the orders of creation, but makes an eschatological and teleological statement. Marriage, even in the state of original righteousness, is a sign and symbol for this world, while virginity is a sign and symbol for the next. Therefore marriage is normative in the temporal manifestation of the Kingdom of Heaven, and virginity is the exception, pointing towards its eschatological manifestation of the Kingdom of Heaven.

Because Protestants have such poorly developed theology in this area, it is necessary to look outside the Protestant orbit to understand the significance of both the married and the virginal state. For this purpose, John Paul

II's seminal work on the theology of the body is exceptionally useful.

Pope John Paul II first points out that virginity "for the Kingdom of Heaven's sake is an expression of finality. Christ's own life is one of continence, of which virginity is the sign. Thus virginity has some meaning for and connection to the Kingdom of Heaven. There is a value attached to virginity which makes if valuable in and for the Kingdom of Heaven. This virginity is not utilitarian, in that virginity is a prerequisite for the Kingdom of Heaven. Nor does Christ indicate that marriage is of no value for the Kingdom of Heaven. To understand Christ's meaning, we must abandon all attempts at finding a utilitarian explanation for either marriage or virginity. Instead, the value of marriage exists as a sign and symbol of the relationship between Christ and the Church. Likewise, virginity, while remaining the exception rather than the rule, still exists as a sign and symbol — which is demonstrated through the initial creation of man alone, and only latter by the creation of woman.[298]

What is rejected is a purely utilitarian meaning of marriage, by which we mean the purely temporal and bodily usage. In the orders of creation, which Jesus used in his dispute with the Pharisees on divorce, man was originally created in solitude, which God said was "not good" (Ge 2:18). God then created Eve from one of Adam's ribs; God made another like unto him, one who was made for him (Ge 2:18, 21-23). What is especially interesting about this is that only after Eve was created do we find a reference to gender, to being male and female. It is not that Adam was not male before, but rather an acknowledgement that we are truly male and female only in relationship with each other. This communion of persons, this gift of self — of which the sexual act is a mere outward expression — is a sign and symbol of the communion of persons within the trinity.

Virginity as an Eschatological Sign

In this communion of persons we understand the ultimate meaning of the two becoming one flesh (Ge 2:24). This is not, as among animals, purely for the purpose of generation.[299] Nor is it purely for companionship. Rather, the communion of persons is ontological, an icon of and participation in the relationship the trinity has with itself. The communion of persons also has an eschatological component, something Jesus alludes to in his dispute with the Sadducees. And finally, the relationship between husband and wife — the two becoming one flesh — is sign and symbol of the mystery, which is the relationship between Christ and His church (Eph 5:25-32), the bride of Christ (Joh 3:29; Rev 21:2), which is His body (I Cor 12:27).

St. John Chrysostom, in his homily "Against Publishing the Errors of the Brethren", speaks in this manner concerning the gift of virginity granted to Mary:

*[H]ear the words of Gabriel which were addressed to her — For when he had come and said to her, "thou shalt conceive in the womb and bear a son, and thou shalt call his name Jesus;" the Virgin was astonished and marvelled, and said, "how will this be to me, since I know not a man." What then said the Angel? "The Holy Ghost shall come upon thee." Seek not the sequence of nature, he says, when that which takes place is above nature; look not round for marriage and throes of child-birth, when the manner of the birth is too grand for marriage. "And how will this be," she says," since I know not a husband." And verily on this account shall this be, since thou knowest no husband. For didst thou know a husband, thou wouldest not have been deemed worthy to serve this ministry. So that, for the reason why thou disbelievest, for this believe. And **thou wouldest not have been deemed worthy to serve this ministry, not because marriage is an evil; but because virginity is superior;** and right it was that the entry of the Master should be more august than ours; for it was royal, and the king enters*

The Perpetual Virginity of the Virgin Mary

through one more august. It was necessary that He should both share us to birth, and be diverse from ours. Wherefore both these things are managed. For the being born from the womb is common in respect to us, but the being born without marriage is a thing greater than on a level with us. And the gestation and conception in the belly belongs to human nature; but that the pregnancy should take place without sexual intercourse is too august for human nature.[300] [Emphasis added]

Virginity is a good gift and calling of God. Since marriage is good but virginity "for the sake of the kingdom of heaven" is better (I Cor 7:38), and since the gifts and calling of God are without repentance (Rom 11:29), it is unreasonable to expect that the one who had been overshadowed by the Father, and in whom Jesus Christ our Lord was incarnate by the Holy Spirit "for the sake of the kingdom of heaven", to have abandoned that holy estate for the lesser estate of marriage. Moreover, as Mary is typologically speaking the new Ark of the new Covenant, and since no one was allowed to touch the Ark of the Covenant on pain of death (II Sam 6:6-7), it is reasonable for Joseph to never have had relations with Mary. Instead, in keeping with both Scripture (and, I might add, the Lutheran understanding of vocation), it is likely that Mary — following the example of (and being the archetype for) Jephthah's daughter (Jud 11:36-40) — gave herself over willingly over to virginity "for the sake of the kingdom of heaven", and that God supernaturally protected her virginity in childbirth.

Virginity "for the sake of the kingdom of Heaven" is not a repudiation of the body, because Jesus in his dispute with the Sadducees looks forward to the resurrection of the body in which we are equal to the angels. This resurrection brings us into a spiritual communion with God, which is the fulfillment of the sign and symbol of temporal marriage. As marriage is the sign and symbol of the communion of persons within the trinity, and also of the relationship between Christ and the church, so virginity "for the sake of the kingdom of heaven" is an eschatological sign, looking forward to its spiritual fulfillment both as the bride and body of Christ. Looked at in this light, the perpetual virginity of Mary is a theological necessity, for as the angels proclaimed (Luke 2:14), the Incarnation and virgin birth is the eschatological sign of the inbreaking of the kingdom of heaven.

31: The Supposed Sons of the Virgin Mary

It is an article of faith that Mary is Mother of the Lord and still a virgin.[301]

Little in theology is more curious and strange than the Protestant renewal of the formerly heretical supposition that Mary had other children after Jesus. This suggestion was maintained by the heretic Helvidius, a position easily disproved by Jerome in his tract entitled *The Perpetual Virginity of the Virgin Mary.*[302] Even within Protestantism, the rejection of the perpetual virginity of the Virgin Mary is a late theological development: of the *Semper Virgo* the early Protestant Reformers had no doubt; the idea that the mother of our Lord had other children of natural generation is, for those who will have eyes to see, clearly contradicted in Scripture.

Some would no doubt argue that the marriage of Joseph and Mary must have included a sexual component, for what is marriage without sex? Yet where is in written that Joseph ever married the Blessed Virgin? In fact, just the opposite: in Luke we see Joseph travelling to Nazareth "with Mary his espoused wife, being great with child" (Luke 2:5). Given the Protestant predilection for Scripture Alone, why must we assume a marriage existed where no marriage is proclaimed? It is not as if the Scriptures are shy about using metaphors for sexual activity; beginning in Genesis chapter 4 we have the account of Adam's knowing Eve, and her conceiving. Something similar is contained in the account of Zacharias and Elizabeth, the cousin of Mary. So why the strange reticence in the case of Joseph and Mary? Could it be that the argument from silence is actually compelling? Is there something more than simply an argument from silence?

However obvious the perpetual virginity of the Mother of God may seem to some of us, it should be acknowledged that the purely scriptural evidence would seem to be weak. Jaroslav Pelikan acknowledges as much. Three of the Gospels — Matthew, Mark, and John, but not Luke — did speak in later chapters about "brethren" of Christ [Matt 12:46; Matt 13:55; Mark 3:31; John 2:12; John 7:3,5], as did the apostle Paul [1 Cor 9:5; Gal 1:19]. The apparently obvious and natural conclusion from this would seem to have been that after miraculous conception of Jesus by the power of the Holy Spirit, Mary and Joseph went on to have other children of their own. Jaroslav Pelikan writes:

But that was not the conclusion that the vast majority of early Christian teachers drew. Instead, they came to call Mary Ever-Virgin, Aeiparthenos, Semper Virgo. To do this in the light of biblical materials about the "brethren" of Jesus, they had to resort to some elaborate biblical arguments. The biblical support for calling Mary Ever-Virgin, however, came not chiefly from the New Testament but from the Song of Songs: "A garden enclosed is my sister, my spouse; a spring shut up, a fountain sealed." ...Thus Jerome, after stringing together a series of texts from the Song of Songs, came to this verse, which he took to be a reference to "the mother of our Lord, who was a mother and a Virgin. Hence it was that no one before or after our Savior was lain in his new tomb, hewn in the solid rock [Jerome, Against Jovionian I:31]" An interesting process of creative biblical interpretation was going on here. For according to the Gospels at the other end of the story of the earthly life of Jesus Christ, the grave of Jesus was "a new sepulcher," belonging to Joseph of Arimathea, where no one had ever been buried before. The Gospels said nothing about the later history of the sepulcher, after the resurrection of Jesus, just as they said nothing about the later history of the womb of Mary. But on the strength of the "hortus conclusus" [enclosed garden] of the Song of Songs, Jerome, who was arguably the greatest biblical scholar in the history of the Western Church, felt justified in concluding both that there would never be another person buried in the sepulcher and that there was never another person born of the Virgin.[303]

The perpetual virginity of Mary protects the doctrine of the Incarnation, the theandric mystery of God becoming man, and of the two natures in Christ. Proclus, Bishop of Constantinople (d. 446 or 447), delivered a Christmas homily against Nestorius, in which he expounded upon the importance of the *Semper Virgo*. "*If the mother had not remained a virgin, then the child born would have been a mere man and the birth no miracle.*" And again: "*Nor was he solely God, without humanity. For he had a body, you Manichee! Had he not clothed himself in me, he would not have saved me. Rather, when he appeared in the Virgin's womb he clothed himself in him who was condemned; there it was that the awesome contract was concluded.*"[304]

Why the Virgin Birth

You may well ask Mary's own question: why should these things be? Why the virgin birth, and why the necessity that she remain a virgin? St. Athanasius, the great defender of Orthodoxy against the Arian heresy (*Athanasius contra mundum*; Athanasius against the world), writes that in taking up residence in the virgin's body, her body became His temple.

For He did not simply will to become embodied, or will merely to appear. For if He willed merely to appear, He was able to effect His divine appearance by some other and higher means as well. But He takes a body of our kind, and not merely so, but from a spotless and stainless virgin, knowing not a man, a body clean and in very truth pure from intercourse of men. For being Himself mighty, and Artificer of everything, He prepares the body in the Virgin as a temple unto Himself, and makes it His very own as an instrument, in it manifested, and in it dwelling.[305]

From the idea of the Virgin Mary being the temple of God comes the understanding of the temple and its furnishings as being the type, of which Mary is the archetype. She is the Ark of the Covenant that is overshadowed by the glory of God; she is the urn containing the manna, the bread of life; she is the table on which reposes the bread of life; she is the inviolate, immaculate, and perpetually unsullied holy of holies. He that is mighty has done to her great things; from henceforth and unto all generations may her name be praised.

St. Maximus the Confessor, in his First Century of Various Texts, writes of the manner in which the miracle of the Incarnation is demonstrated in and by means of another miracle, the protection of Mary's virginity.

Christ our God is born and becomes man by adding to Himself flesh endowed with an intellective soul. He who from non-being brings created things into being is Himself born supranaturally of a Virgin who does not thereby lose her virginity. For just as He Himself became man without changing His nature or altering His power, so He makes her who bore Him a Mother while keeping her a Virgin. In this way He reveals one miracle through another miracle, at the same time concealing the one with the other. This is because in Himself, according to His essence, God always remains a mystery. He expresses His natural hiddenness in such a way that He makes it the more hidden through the revelation. Similarly, in the case of the Virgin who bore Him, He made her a Mother in such a way that by conceiving Him the bonds of her virginity became even more indissoluble.[306]

Perpetual Virginity as Guarantee of the Incarnation

The mystery of Mary's perpetual virginity protects the mystery of the Incarnation; without the first, you cannot be certain of the second. For if Mary had other children after Jesus, born of natural generation, what assurance do we have that Jesus was not born of natural generation as well? The Christian Apologetics Society points out that Islam, atheists, and cultists all deny Mary's perpetual virginity, out of necessity, as its existence would call into question their understanding of the person and work of Jesus.

Why do most of the world's Christians still continue to hold and teach the doctrine of the perpetual virginity of Mary? Because denial of the doctrine pulls the rug out from beneath the doctrine of the divinity of Christ. Islamic apologists, atheists, and cultists see the denial of Mary's perpetual virginity as the gateway to disproving the divinity of Christ. They argue, if Mary had seven children and these six are human, then the seventh is human as well. Therefore, Christianity is a sham as it is built on a lie. God is one and there is no Trinity. Allah Ahkbar![307]

Note well the argument here. If Mary was not a virgin in the conception and in the birth, and if she is not a virgin still, then the virgin birth is merely an interesting story, a pleasant but essentially meaningless bit of piety. Absent the her perpetual virginity, one might even argue that the virgin birth itself was unnecessary, and that our Lord need not have been born of a virgin. He could have been a mere man who was indwelt by the Spirit at his baptism; he could have been God who merely appeared to be a man. But he was not any of those; instead, he was conceived, was born, died, and was resurrected as the God/man — one person in two natures, fully God and fully man, as prophesied by Isaiah: "Therefore the Lord himself shall give you a sign"; and "Behold, a virgin shall be with child, and shall bring forth a son, and they shall call his name Emmanuel, which being interpreted is, God with us" (Isa 7:14; Mt 1:23).

The Modern Protestant and Mary's Virginity

Bernard Leeming notes that despite approving of the necessity of the Virgin birth as a sign, for some reason Protestant theologians are not especially concerned with the perpetual virginity of Mary.

[I]t is strange that Barth, like Skydsgarrd, von Loewenich, Pelikan, J. Gresham Machan, and even Max Thurian, see little significance in the perpetual virginity of our Lady. Yet Pelikan points out that Luther "not only repeated the tradition (of our Lady's perpetual virginity) but vigorously defends it against its detractors".[308] Max Thurian says: "Calvin himself will have it that Mary had no other children, and attacks Helvidius — not, it seems, in order to defend the perpetual virginity of Mary so much as to affirm the plenitude of the gift of God in Jesus Christ.[309]

The prophet Isaiah expressly states that the virgin birth was given as a sign. The perpetual virginity of the Theotokos is a perpetuation and demonstration of that sign. Protestants fail to understand that virginity is not the point, but is merely an outward sign of a life dedicated to God. Thus Protestants fail to realize that the virginity is a sign of the Incarnation, and that protecting Mary's virginity after Jesus's birth is necessary for the preservation of the sign. The notion that Mary had other children after Jesus detracts from the signal event of the Incarnation, and creates doubt as to the truth of its existence. Moreover, the perpetual virginity of Mary has typological significance, such that the Virgin Mary, as the archetype, is proleptically[310] present in and gives meaning to the typological event. John Breck writes:

The Perpetual Virginity of the Virgin Mary

As a final example of typological interpretation, that to some degree summarizes the witness of the liturgical texts of both Nativity and Theophany, we can note the following passage. This is the "Dogmaticon" or celebration of the Virgin's role in redemptive history.

In the Red Sea of old
A type of the Virgin Bride was prefigured.
There Moses divided the waters;
Here Gabriel assisted in the miracle.
There Israel crossed the sea without getting wet;
Here the Virgin gave birth to Christ without seed.
After Israel's passage, the sea remained impassable;
After Emmanuel's birth, the Virgin remained a virgin.
O ever-existing God who appeared as man,
O Lord, have mercy on us?[311]

By way of contrast, Merrill F. Unger — Protestant theologian and professor of Old Testament Studies at Dallas Theological Seminary — provides the following summation of contemporary Protestant thought in *Unger's Bible Dictionary:*

Was Mary the mother of any other children than Jesus? *is a question that has caused almost endless controversy. Of course, the advocates of her perpetual virginity assert that she was not. From the accounts in Matt. 13:55; Mark 6:3, it would seem more than likely that she had a number of children. This presumption is increased by the fact that the persons named as the "brethren" of Jesus are mentioned in connection and in company with his sisters and mother. Indeed, the denial of the natural interpretation of these passages owes its origin, in all probability, to the tradition of perpetual virginity, the offspring of the false notion of the superior sanctity of celibacy.*[312]

Dr. David Scaer, writing in Logia, implies that the notion of Mary's perpetual virginity, which clearly predates the council of Nicea, was nevertheless not part of the apostolic deposit of faith, but a rather late development (very much like support for virginity). Curiously, he never states this outright, but simply creates that impression in the reader.

The 'semper virgo' means that after giving birth to Jesus, his mother refrained from sexual relations with Joseph. Not only was Jesus conceived 'ex Maria virgine', but she remained so for the rest of her life. The highly fanciful second-century Protoevangelium of James, which combines and expands the Matthew and Luke birth narratives, is the first known document to offer the idea. It gained momentum with the Roman Empire's recognition of Christianity as a legal religion. Martyrdom as a certain way to heaven was replaced by asceticism, which included celibacy, and Mary was held up as an example to be followed. Virginity became the new martyrdom.[313]

After creating doubt in the reader's mind as to the historicity of the doctrine of Mary's perpetual virginity, Dr. Scaer declares the issue to be *theolegoumenon*, a theological opinion suggested as a possibility, but not decisive. Not doctrine, in other words.

While the appearance of the 'semper virgo' hypothesis can be explained and traced historically, several factors may explain the current interest. It may come from a romanticism that desires to revive the faith of a pristine church[314] in which this was a settled view. Reasons for recent interest in the 'semper virgo' are theological; it is what is called a theolegoumenon. This means that although the biblical support is not foolproof, there are theological reasons for it. In this case it is subliminal conviction, perhaps unrecognized by the mostly married, Lutheran proponents, that celibacy reaches a higher level of sanctity than the married life. Paul can be counted on for support for remaining single rather than living the married life, not because he saw a higher virtue in celibacy, but because it allowed him more time to care for the churches.

The theolegoumenon argument, the one taken from theology, can be taken in another direction, if the starting point is the homo factus est [and became man].[315] Jesus did not become a human being in a morally neutral sense, but he was burdened with sin and lived in a sinful environment. He did not live in what our Evangelical friends would call "a Christian family," as if after Eden such a family ever existed. His own family thought he had lost his senses (Mk 3:21). Part of his humiliation is that they rejected him. But Jesus said to them, "A prophet is not without honor except in his own country and in his own house" (Mt 13:57).

The 'semper virgo' cannot in any sense be regarded as a doctrine or even a pious opinion, especially if the opposing view is seen as unequal or lacking in piety. Proponents of one or the other view cannot be seen as more pious than others, but it may be that the piety of one person may account for current interest in the 'semper virgo' hypothesis.[316]

Dr. Scaer's argument here is curious. He defines *theolegoumenon,* or theological opinion, as being things for which the biblical support is not foolproof, but for which there is nonetheless a theological rationale. This is a rather curious definition, for it places nearly everything that is not explicit in scripture in the realm of *theolegoumenon.* For the record, I simply state that many of the core doctrines of Christianity are not explicit. For example: the Holy Trinity is nowhere explicit in Sacred Scripture, although it is everywhere implicit. Likewise the deity of Christ is nowhere explicit, at least not in terms that modern man would accept — "I and the Father are one" may have been for the ancient Jew the functional equivalent of declaring oneself to be God, but it doesn't have the same ring to the modern ear. If we accept Dr. Scaer's definition of *theolegoumenon*, than most theological heresies could be redefined as theological opinions, and most of the doctrine's we hold today would be simply our way of expressing our piety.

It is also curious that Dr. Scaer chooses to begin his argument against the doctrine of Mary's perpetual virginity with the humanity of Jesus. The perpetual virginity of Mary does not protect the humanity of Christ, but rather protects His divinity. Mary did not stay a virgin because she gave birth to a man, but because she bore God. There is a curious symmetry here between the Protestant's development of the Doctrine of Man from the fall, and Scaer's denial of Mary's perpetual virginity from the humanity of Christ.

Merrill F. Unger's description of an "endless controversy" over Mary's perpetual virginity is a rather new development in the history of Christian doctrine. The earliest extant accounts regarding Mary evince no such controversy; apart from the heretics, Mary's perpetual virginity did not become a controversial matter until well into the Protestant reformation. This was not even a matter of controversy amongst the earliest Protestant reformers; the three most important reformers — Martin Luther, Ulrich Zwingli, and John Calvin — all believed in and had no difficulty with the orthodoxy of existing Marion doctrine, to include Mary's perpetual virginity. This is not to say that they did not have problem with certain elements of popular piety, elements which later became enshrined in Roman Catholic dogma. Instead, this means that those elements of Marian doctrine which had been held for the previous 1,500 years were also held by the founders of the Protestant Reformation.

There are Catholic scholars who have a view more in line with Protestants than with the historic Christian church. Sally Cunneen, writing about the Mary of the New Testament, makes the following claim:

The Perpetual Virginity of the Virgin Mary

Although Catholic teaching has consistently held otherwise, Catholic New Testament scholar [Fr.] John Meier finds no reason not to believe that Jesus had sisters and brothers. Nothing in Scripture supports the idea that Mary remained physically intact while giving birth, or that she had no sexual relations with her husband after Jesus was born, though both of these claims become important in later Marian theology and devotion.[317]

What is curious about the statement above is that Cunneen, a Catholic, states there is no evidence for the perpetual virginity of Mary. Even more curious is that she does this without acknowledging, presenting, discussing, and finally dismissing the evidence presented by her own Church; she simply treats it as if it does not exist. Moreover, she does not care to think about the theological implications of her view. She simply states there is nothing to see here, and then moves on.

Clans, Tribes, and the Supposed Sons of Mary

While we moderns are fond of categorizing everything to the nth degree, things were a lot looser in the ancient world. We westerners primarily think in terms of our immediate family, and perhaps our extended family, but do not think of family in terms of clans and tribes. Yet clans and tribes are important to many people in the world today, just as they were important to the Jews in the Old Testament and in the time of Christ. In the Hebrew tongue, there is no word for cousin; the same word is used for brother as well as for cousin, since it was easier than using a circumlocution (like son of my uncle). The bible was written in an idiomatic, Hebraized Greek — making the use of "brother" a Hebraism. Although Greek has a word for cousin, the bible doesn't use it, seemingly because the Hebrew culture didn't deem the distinction to be important.[318]

The Supposed Sons of the Virgin Mary

It should be noted that this is not merely a Semitic idea, but a similar concept can be found within Europe. Edith Durham, writing in her book "High Albania", makes the following observation regarding the Albanian concept of familial relations.

The men and women descending from a common male ancestor, though very remote, regard one another as brother and sister, and marriage between them is forbidden as incestuous. Though the relationship be such that the Catholic Church permits marriage, it is regarded with such genuine horror that I have heard of but one instance where it was attempted or desired, when against tribe law. Even a native priest told me that a marriage between cousins separated by twelve generations was to him a horrible idea, though the Church permitted it, "for really they are brothers and sisters."[319]

Dr. David Scaer dismisses this argument. Beginning with a discussion of the author of the book of James, he writes:

In the strictest sense this James was not a half-brother, because Jesus had no human father. "Uterine brother" best expresses their relationship. Five boys, including Jesus and James, all had the same mother. James is named along with the other brothers, Joseph, Simon, and Jude, and the unnamed sisters (Mt 13:55-56) and they are found in the company of Mary, who is identified as Jesus' mother (Mk 6:3). At the wedding of Cana, Jesus' mother and his brothers are present, but his brothers are not named (Joh 2:12). The salutation of the last of the catholic epistles, "Jude, a servant of Jesus Christ and brother of James," corresponds with Matthew and Mark, and indicates that James and Jude were brothers and hence Jesus' brothers. On top of this, James is explicitly called the brother of the Lord (Gal 1:19) and takes precedence over Peter and John as a pillar of the church (Gal 2:9). Like Peter, he also merited a separate appearance of the resurrected Jesus (1 Cor 15:5, 7).

Proponents of the 'semper virgo' hypothesis cite the cross scene in which Jesus commits his mother to the care of the beloved disciple (Jn 19:26-27), assuming that she has no one else to provide for her, but this can hardly be the case. After Jesus' ascension she appears in the assembly of believers with his brothers (Acts 1:14). Even if these were Joseph's sons by a previous marriage, her step-children, or Jesus' cousins, her nephews, she was not abandoned. All four evangelists, assuming that Acts was written by Luke, speak of Mary and place her with Jesus' brothers, and one Gospel also places her with his sisters. She is also that Mary who stands at a distance from the cross and is identified as "the mother of James and Joseph" (Mt 27:56).

Denying that Mary had other children requires an explanation for how those who were called Jesus' brothers and sisters were related to him. No one questions that in some sense they were family members. Eastern Orthodoxy generally saw them as cousins, as members of Jesus' extended family. In Roman Catholicism they were seen as Joseph's children from a previous marriage. Proponents of the 'semper virgo' hypothesis offer four scenarios, all complex, to explain Jesus' relationship to those who are called his brothers and sisters, but they are not agreed on which one is right. Least satisfactory is the hypothesis that they were first cousins, simply because in the same Gospels, 'adelphos', the Greek word for brother, is used of the relationship of Peter to Andrew and James to John, who were real brothers.[320]

At first glance, this seems a damning argument. What an assortment of scriptural citations, all supporting the idea that Mary had other children besides Jesus. Scaer gives the alternate points of view short shrift, and is generally dismissive of them.

The Supposed Sons of the Virgin Mary

Firstly, Dr. Scaer dismisses the account in John's gospel of Jesus committing his Mother to the care of the apostle John, and commiting the apostle John to his Mother. That this account is only found the theological gospel is highly significant, indicating that this was not merely a matter of Jesus arranging for the temporal care of His mother, but rather that this was a matter of some theological import.[321]

Secondly, Dr. Scaer he has been rather selective in his choice of texts. The plain fact is that the word used for to describe Jesus brothers is used in a wide variety of ways in the New Testament. Vine's Expository Dictionary of Old and New Testament Words provides the following list of ways in which the word *adelphos* is used:[322]

1. Male children of the same parents (Matt 1:2)
2. Male descendants of the same parents (Acts 7:23)
3. Male children of the same mother (Gal 1:19)
4. People of the same nationality (Acts 3:17, 22)
5. Any man, a neighbor (Lu 10:29)
6. Persons united by a common interest (Mt 5:47)
7. Persons united by a common calling (Rev 22:9)
8. Mankind (Mt 25:40)
9. The disciples (Mt 28:10)
10. Believers (Mt 23:8) [323,324]

The term Brethren is rather common in scripture, and is used in a wide variety of ways. It is clear that while it can mean brother in the technical sense, as in male children of the same mother or the same parents, it can and usually does have a broader meaning. In fact, this broader usage is widespread amongst Protestants. There are many different Protestant denominations named "Brethren", and in many Protestant churches, people use the terms 'brother' and 'sister' as terms of address, as a way of highlighting that we are all brothers and sisters in Christ.[325]

The Perpetual Virginity of the Virgin Mary

Saint John (Maximovitch) of Shanghai & San Francisco writes:

It is likewise incorrect to think that the brothers and sisters of Christ were the children of His Most Holy Mother. The names of "brother" and "sister" have several distinct meanings. Signifying a certain kinship between people or their spiritual closeness, these words are used sometimes in a broader, and sometimes in a narrower sense. In any case, people are called brothers or sisters if they have a common father and mother, or only a common father or mother; or even if they have different fathers and mothers, if their parents later (having become widowed) have entered into marriage (stepbrothers); or if their parents are bound by close degrees of kinship.

In the Gospel it can nowhere be seen that those who are called there the brothers of Jesus were or were considered the children of His Mother. On the contrary, it was known that James and others were the sons of Joseph, the Betrothed of Mary, who was a widower with children from his first wife. (St. Epiphanius of Cyprus, Panarion, 78.) Likewise, the sister of His Mother, Mary the wife of Cleopas, who stood with Her at the Cross of the Lord (John 19:25), also had children, who in view of such close kinship with full right could also be called brothers of the Lord. That the so-called brothers and sisters of the Lord were not the children of His Mother is clearly evident from the fact that the Lord entrusted His Mother before His death to His beloved disciple John. Why should He do this if She had other children besides Him? They themselves would have taken care of Her. The sons of Joseph, the supposed father of Jesus, did not consider themselves obliged to take care of one they regarded as their stepmother, or at least did not have for Her such love as blood children have for parents, and such as the adopted John had for Her.

The Supposed Sons of the Virgin Mary

Thus, a careful study of Sacred Scripture reveals with complete clarity the insubstantiality of the objections against the Ever-Virginity of Mary and puts to shame those who teach differently.[326]

The argument that Dr. Scaer so blithely dismisses — that Jesus entrusted his mother to the apostle John because Mary had no other children — is a much more telling argument than he is willing to admit. But it is not the only argument, for the scripture tells us that the so-called brothers of Jesus were in fact the children of another Mary, the wife of Clopas. Let us now examine the evidence.

The Scriptures and the Supposed Brothers of Jesus

Since we are primarily talking to biblical literalists, to those who claim the literal sense of is the only sense (as my father used to say), let us examine the scripture in its plain and literal sense. I will demonstrate how the literal interpretation of Sacred Scriptures proves that Jesus did not have brothers and sisters.

Dr. Scaer and others would "proof text" their hostility to the perpetual virginity of Mary with the following passage: "Is not this the carpenter's son? is not his mother called Mary? and his brethren, James, and Joses, and Simon, and Judas? And his sisters, are they not all with us" (Matt 13:55-56)?" The use of the terms brother and sister in this context are a Hebraism, which is easily proven when we let Scripture interpret Scripture. Of the four "brothers", let us discuss James, because the same arguments apply to the rest of Jesus' supposed siblings.

Examine and compare the following gospel descriptions of the women standing beneath the cross: "among whom were Mary Magdalene, and Mary the mother of James and Joseph, and the mother of the sons of Zebedee" (Matt. 27:56); "There were also women looking on from afar, among whom were Mary Magdalene, and Mary

199

the mother of James the younger and of Joses, and Salome" (Mark 15:40). "But standing by the cross of Jesus were his mother, and his mother's sister, Mary the wife of Clopas, and Mary Magdalene" (John 19:25).

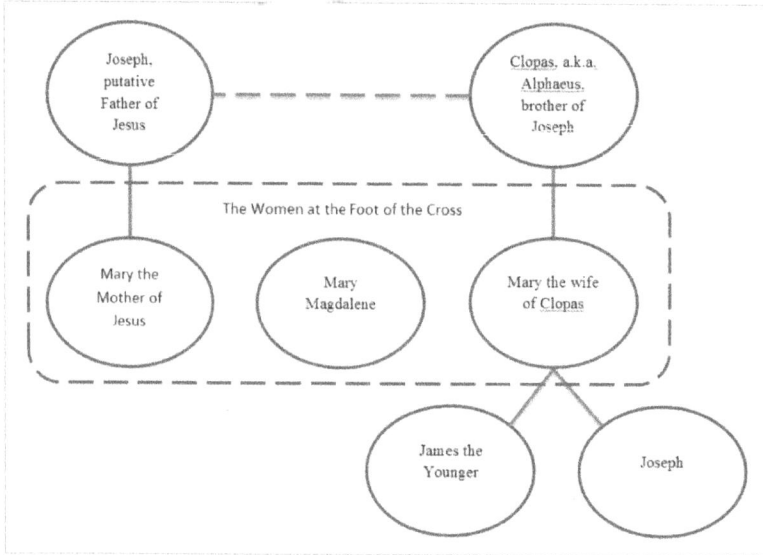

Figure 3: Mary, the Wife of Clopas

A comparison of these parallel accounts clearly shows the mother of James and Joseph must be the wife of Clopas. When Matthew describes James as the son of Alphaeus, he is using Aramaic (Mt 10:3; cf Mk 2:14; 3:18; Lu 6:15; Ac 1:13). The same name can be rendered in Greek as Clopas; therefore, it is likely that James the Younger is the son of Mary and Clopas. As recorded by the church historian Eusebius, Hegesippus explains that Clopas was the brother of Joseph, the putative father of Jesus, which would make James the Younger the nephew of Joseph and the cousin of Jesus — or a brother, in Semitic parlance.

A note in Eusebius (NPNF2-01) makes a similar point regarding Symeon.

The Supposed Sons of the Virgin Mary

This Symeon is to be distinguished from the apostle Simon, the Canaanite, and also from Simon, the brother of our Lord (mentioned in Matt. Xiii. 55 and Mark vi. 3). It is noticeable that Hegesippus nowhere calls him the "brother of the Lord," though he does give James that title in Bk. II. chap. 23. Clopas is mentioned in John xix. 25, as the husband of Mary, who is without doubt identical with Mary the mother of James (the little) and of Joses; mentioned in Matt. Xxvii. 56, Mark xv. 40, &c. If Hegesippus' account be accepted as trustworthy (and there is no reason for doubting it), **Symeon was the son of Clopas** *and Mary, and therefore brother of James the Little and Joses. If, then, Alphæus and Clopas be the same, as many claim, James the Little is to be identified with James the son of Alphæus, the apostle, and hence the latter was the brother of Symeon. This identification, however, is entirely arbitrary, and linguistically difficult, and we shall do better therefore to keep the men separate, as Renan does.*[327] *[Emphasis added]*

Hegesippus specifically declares Symeon to not be the son of Joseph, but the son of Clopas.

And after James the Just had suffered martyrdom, as the Lord had also on the same account, **Symeon, the son of the Lord's uncle, Clopas**, *was appointed the next bishop. All proposed him as second bishop because he was a cousin of the Lord.*[328] *[Emphasis added]*

There are other indirect scriptural evidences of Jesus being not only the first-born son of the Virgin Mary, but her only child.

1. The pericope of Jesus in the temple when he was twelve years old implies he had no brothers and sisters, as no mention was made of them (Luke 2:41–51).
2. The people of Nazareth called Jesus *the* son of Mary, not *a* son of Mary (Mark 6:3).

201

The Perpetual Virginity of the Virgin Mary

3. While the gospels speak of the brethren of our Lord, these brethren are never referred to as sons of Mary, as was Jesus. Jesus brethren are seen as giving him advice (John 7:3-4), or seeking to restrain him (Mark 3:21). In Eastern cultures, younger brethren do not advise their elders, as it is disrespectful. The behavior described in the Gospels is a clear implication that Jesus' brethren were older, thereby eliminating them as biological siblings of our Lord, since Jesus was Mary's "first-born" son (Luke 2:7).

4. When Jesus was dying on the cross, he directed the apostle John to take care of his mother (John 19:26–27). If Jesus had other biological brothers, the care of Mary would have been entrusted to them. It is difficult to imagine a situation in which Jesus would have disregarded family ties in favor of John, and in which Jesus' biological siblings would not have stepped up and taken on the responsibility.

An interesting theological argument for Jesus being an only child can be made from John's gospel.

*And the **Word** was made flesh, and dwelt among us, (and we beheld his glory, the glory as of **the only begotten of the Father**,) full of grace and truth. John bare witness of him, and cried, saying, This was he of whom I spake, He that cometh after me is preferred before me: for he was before me. And of his fulness have all we received, and grace for grace. For the law was given by Moses, but grace and truth came by Jesus Christ. No man hath seen God at any time; **the only begotten Son**, which is in the bosom of the Father, he hath declared him (John 1:14-18). [emphasis added]*

In this passage Jesus Christ is called the Word, the only begotten of the Father, and the only begotten Son. His humanity and divinity are both on display in the one passage; He is the only begotten of the Father according to

His divinity, and the only begotten Son according to his humanity. This is demonstrated by the twofold reference to the Word being the only begotten; the first time, as the only begotten of the Father, and the second being (possibly) a veiled reference to Jesus being the only begotten Son of Mary. The symmetry of this argument fits well with what we know from Old Testament references to Mary, such as the reference to the sealed gate. Another more subtle argument is that John is the only gospel writer to not include a birth narrative. The gospel of John is the theological gospel, and therefore John included a theological rather than a historical accounting of Jesus' birth. By this is meant a reference to Jesus being the only begotten both of God the Father, and of the Virgin Mary.

Against Mary's Perpetual Virginity

The usual and most trifling arguments against Mary's perpetual virginity consist in a willful misinterpretation of Scripture. In Matthew 1:25, it is said that Joseph did not know Mary "until" she gave birth to her "first-born" son. Two things are derived from this one verse: that "until" implies that Joseph "knew" Mary *after* the birth of Jesus, and that "first-born" implies additional children.

For example, Dr. David Scaer concludes his article against Mary's perpetual virginity with the following quote from Dale C. Allison:

"When Joseph woke from sleep, he did as the angel of the Lord commanded him; he took his wife, but knew her not until [ἕως] she had borne a son; and he called his name Jesus." Allison says that the word "... need not entail the resumption of sexual relations, ...the First Evangelist nonetheless would surely not have chosen such an expression if he thought Mary 'ever virgin.'"[329]

This is a very strange way to end a scholarly article, as it presupposes the conclusion and fails to deal with the variety word usages and alternative explanations. This argument over the meaning of 'until' is not new; it was an early argument of the heretic Helvidius, and it is a flawed argument. Consider that "until" means only that a condition existed up to a certain point, but not that the condition must have changed after that point. For example: "Michal the daughter of Saul had no children till the day of her death" (2 Sam. 6:23). Does "till" imply she had children after death? The account of the burial of Moses by God concludes with the statement that no one knew where his grave was "until this present day" (Deut. 34:6). Obviously this does not imply that his grave was or would be discovered at a later date. In fact, the word "until" often implies and is therefore a circumlocution for eternity.

Saint John (Maximovitch) of Shanghai & San Francisco writes:

"After the birth of Jesus," said the false teacher Helvidius in the 4th century, and likewise many others before and after him, "Mary entered into conjugal life with Joseph and had from him children, who are called in the Gospels the brothers and sisters of Christ." But the word "until" does not signify that Mary remained a virgin only until a certain time. The word "until" and words similar to it often signify eternity. In the Sacred Scripture it is said of Christ: In His days shall shine forth righteousness and an abundance of peace, until the moon be taken away (Ps. 71:7), but this does not mean that when there shall no longer be a moon at the end of the world, God's righteousness shall no longer be; precisely then, rather, will it triumph. And what does it mean when it says: For He must reign, until He hath put all enemies under His feet? (I Cor. 15:25). Is the Lord then to reign only for the time until His enemies shall be under His feet?! And David, in the fourth Psalm of the Ascents says: As the eyes of the handmaid look unto the hands of her mistress, so do our eyes look unto the Lord our God, until He take pity on us (Ps. 122:2). Thus, the Prophet will have his eyes toward the Lord until he obtains mercy, but having obtained it he will direct them to the earth? (Blessed Jerome, "On the Ever-Virginity of Blessed Mary.") The Saviour in the Gospel says to the Apostles (Matt. 28:20): Lo, I am with you always, even unto the end of the world. Thus, after the end of the world the Lord will step away from His disciples, and then, when they shall judge the twelve tribes of Israel upon twelve thrones, they will not have the promised communion with the Lord?[330]

Clearly, the Scriptures cannot be used to argue against the perpetual virginity of Mary by arguing she bore additional children, and that these children were the biological brothers and sisters of Jesus. The literal interpretation of Scripture appears to assign the parentage of James and Joses to Clopas and the other Mary — likely being the sister of the Virgin Mary.[331] The literal interpretation of Scripture is that Simon and Judas were also the sons of Clopas, and therefore cousins to our Lord. Salome, the only named sister of James, Joses, Simon, and Judas, was likewise the daughter of Clopas and cousin of our Lord.

The arguments over the meaning of the word 'until' are puerile at best. Moreover, arguing against the perpetual virginity results — al la Helvidius — in virginity being "ranked below matrimony".[332] The apostle says that marriage is good, but virginity is better (1 Cor 7:38); those who vociferously maintain that the Blessed Virgin bore children of natural generation find themselves arguing for their position over and against Scripture.

Part VI: The Virgin Mary in the New Testament

32: Scripture Alone and the Virgin Mary

Protestants hold to the idea of Sola Scriptura, which means "by scripture alone." This concept is a problem, as it has many different meanings. Fr. Andrew Stephen Damick writes: "At the beginning of the Reformation, it did not mean a total abandonment of all church tradition, but simply attempted to elevate Scripture to the highest and most central point of Christian life."[333] The Lutheran Reformation taught the primacy of Scripture over other sources of authority (which they held to be derivative of scripture, and therefore dependent upon it). The use of the phrase "Sola Scriptura" to describe the Lutheran position of the primacy of scripture was unfortunate, as its adoption by other reformers came without the particular Lutheran understanding. In the Reformed tradition, as described by Fr. Damick, the Sacred Scriptures are not the primary authority, but the only authority.

Under the Swiss Reformer Hudlrych Zwingli, sola scriptura came to mean much more than before, going so far as to claim that the Bible is the single, exclusive source of all Christian doctrine and practice (which led Zwingli to abolish every Christian ritual he couldn't find in the Bible). This view is the position of most Protestant denominations today, who have largely abandoned the notion of tradition entirely. Some differ on whether what is not mentioned in Scripture is forbidden or to be left to local custom to decide. Either way, all idea of authoritative tradition is rejected.[334]

With all this in mind, we will first examine the scriptural record regarding Mary, as these are the only references which will be universally accepted by Protestants. To begin with, we must somehow deal with the fact that there are few explicit scriptural references to the Virgin

Mary. Anglican theologian L. S. Thornton acknowledges the problem.

> *If we attend only to surface impressions the amount of space given to our Lady in scripture is not large. Apart from the infancy narratives there are only two or three incidents in the gospels in which she appears. She is also mentioned near the beginning of the Acts in the incident which precedes the Day of Pentecost; and that is all. There is, or course, the strange picture of the Woman with Child in Revelation xii; but that is a symbolical vision, of which the precise meaning is open to dispute.[335]*

Orthodox theologian Vladimir Lossky also discusses the difficulties inherent in a *nuda scriptura* (naked scripture) approach.

> *It is very hard, if not impossible, for an Orthodox theologian who has to speak about the Mother of God to limit himself to one of the three groups of materials to be employed, and to be concerned with either scriptural, or dogmatic, or devotional data. The three are indissolubly linked together in the life of the Church, where devotion, scripture, and dogma are present simultaneously in theological thought.[336]*

Although the Orthodox see the written Scripture as being part of Tradition, and in fact growing out of it, it is not necessary to accept this point of view to accept tradition and pious devotion as sources of theological understanding. One could take the approach of the Lutheran theologian Robert Preus, who described a three-fold tier of authority: scripture, confessions, and other good Christian literature.[337] The Protestant preference for explicit scriptural evidence is a problem if only explicit scriptural evidence is accepted. For example, there is little explicit evidence for the Holy Trinity in the bible; the existence of the triune God is implicit within and inferred from Sacred Scripture, and was defined by church councils over and against various heresies such as Adoptionism, Sabellianism, and Arianism, which each appealed to Sacred Scripture to prove their position.[338] I submit that if the witnesses to the truth of the triune God are accepted, then the same witnesses may and should be used to establish the veracity of Mariology. Thornton discusses the relationship between "revealed truth and ecclesiastical orthodoxy" as expressed in certain Marian teachings: first, the "Eva-Ave" doctrine whereby "the disobedience of Eve is reversed in the response of Mary"' and second, "the liturgical use of certain scriptural passages concerning Holy Wisdom upon festivals of our Lady".[339]

This current work will not delve deeply into the vast devotional or liturgical literature in both the eastern and western church concerning the Virgin Mary; the subject is too deep and too broad for this endeavor. But it is enough to suggest that there exists a great wealth of dogma and piety contained in both liturgical traditions which would occasion further investigation. Such an investigation should not be undertaken lightly, or without serious thought. If you cannot accept the little that has & will be expressed in this work, you will be in no position to understand the liturgical tradition.

33: The Virgin Mary and the New Testament

Contrary to what many say, the New Testament actually contains a great deal of information about or concerned with the Virgin Mary, especially if one is willing to acknowledge the typological significance of the Old Testament as a witness to the Blessed Virgin. Father John Anthony McGuckin writes:

The New Testament shows, evidently enough, that Mary was one of the leading figures of the Good News. If she does not feature strongly in the writings of the apostle Paul, the deficiency is more than made up by the manner in which the evangelists Luke, Matthew, and John paint her icon in profoundly deep theological colours. In the New Testament texts of the Annunciation, the Nativity, the wedding feast of Cana, the Crucifixion, and the account of Pentecost, we find major streams of evangelical tradition that set out the counterpoint of music which the Holy Virgin plays in response to the invitation of her son. The pattern of her own discipleship is recounted there as a model and archetype of the 'true disciple'. It is amazing to consider that some thinkers have regarded her as a peripheral figure, compared, for example, to Peter of the other apostles, when so much focus is given to her within the New Testament texts themselves, that she clearly emerges as prima omnium [first of all] among the disciples.[340]

The scriptures give us no information about the family or life of the Virgin Mary, before or after her marriage to Joseph. Joseph is himself a cipher; apart from his occupation, his hometown, and his conversation with the angel, the scriptures record almost nothing about him (which is significant in itself). But the scriptures are theological, not biographical; they exist to satisfy our spiritual needs, not our intellectual curiosity. Think for a moment about the gospels — except for His three-year ministry, we have very little information about Jesus; and even during his ministry, we have very few details about Jesus' daily life. In the Epistles, we have even less. Yet is with the epistles that we will begin.

34: The Witness of Paul and the Gospel of Luke

Professor Tim Perry, in his book "Mary for Evangelicals," begins what he calls the "Pre-Pauline Witness", which are fragments of ancient creedal formulas found in Romans and Philippians. Perry first discusses the *Carmen Christi*, or the Hymn of Christ, found in Philippians 2:5-11. Perry's point, which is relevant to us, is that the *Carmen Christi* is a witness to the Incarnation; of Christ's pre-existence in the form of God, yet who emptied himself and became a man. Perry acknowledges that the Incarnation of the Son of God is "undeveloped," yet nonetheless present.[341]

Next Perry discusses what may well be a more interesting passage, if only because it is so rarely noticed or commented upon, as it is part of the introduction to the Book of Romans.

Concerning his [God's] Son Jesus Christ our Lord, which was made of the seed of David according to the flesh; And declared to be the Son of God with power, according to the spirit of holiness, by the resurrection from the dead (Romans 1:3-4).

This passage contains a number of items of importance. First, we notice that the phrase "his Son" means that Jesus Christ our Lord was the Son of God, which tells us some important things. William Smith, author of "A Dictionary of Greek and Roman Antiquities," tells us that during the Roman Era, the power of a Father was expressed by the term *Patria Potestas*, which is defined as the power of a Father "over the persons of his children, grandchildren, and other descendants."[342]

The Virgin Mary in the New Testament

"The term patria potestas strictly expresses the power of the father, as such, which arises from the paternal relation; but the term also imports the rights of the child as a filius familias or filia familias. Of these rights the most important was the capacity of being the suus heros [an heir] of the father.[343]

So basically, everything that belonged to the son, belonged to the father, and the son had the right of inheritance. This relationship is perfectly expressed in Jesus' High Priestly Prayer in John 17. Speaking of His disciples, Jesus prays: "Thine they were, and thou gavest them me."(v. 6) Jesus expresses the monarchy of the Father when he prays: "All things whatsoever though has given me are of thee," (v. 7) and again; "For I have given unto them the words which thou gavest me; and they have received them, and have known surely that I came out from there" (v. 8) But there is something more here; the passage is an expression not only of Roman law, but of a Semitic understanding of familial relationships; a son of his father was the expression of his father, was everything the father was, and a reflection of his father.

Both the idea of God the Father as having *pater potestas* and the idea of the kinship of a son to his father are in view when Jesus stated: "I and my Father are one." For this, the Jews tried to stone him: "because that thou, being a man, makest thyself God" (John 10:30, 33). Jesus was not merely saying God was the progenitor of his line, but by proclaiming an essential unity between God and himself, was identifying himself as God. Moreover, this is promulgation of what eventually was understood as the doctrine of the Trinity; Jesus was basically saying: "I and my Father, we are both one." This was considered blasphemous in part because, as every pious Jew knew and prayed each day, God is One: "Hear, O Israel: The LORD our God is one LORD" (Deut 6:4).

The Witness of Paul and the Gospel of Luke

Another item of importance is the phrase: "made of the seed of David according to the flesh" (Rom 1:3). Tim Perry writes:

Romans 1:3 presents Jesus as descended from David's seed. Although the Greek verb can mean "to be born," it more often denotes "to come into being," a minor grammatical point with significant theological implications. If the former reading is correct, the verse simply describes Jesus' human descent; if the latter reading is followed, it alludes to the preexistence of the divine Son. ...Whether a human birth or an incarnation is meant, the context stresses Jesus' humanity. Hence, "according to the flesh" (Rom 1:3) does not carry the moral tone that Paul often employs (E.g., Rom 8:4-9; Gal 3:2-3; 5:16-19).[344]

Regarding the mention of Jesus Christ our Lord being of the seed of David, Perry writes that this a reference to Jesus being of the lineage of David, and also a reference to the preexistence of Jesus. What Perry does not mention is the veiled reference to the *protoevangelium* — to Jesus being of the seed of the woman (Ge 3:15), which intimately ties the Virgin Mary with the Gospel.

There is a curious reference in the apostle's first epistle to the Corinthians that, when properly understood, draws the connection between Even and Mary, between the creation of Eve from Adam, and the Incarnation of the Son of God from Mary. Paul writes: "For as the woman is of the man, even so is the man also by the woman; but all things of God (I Cor 11:12)." Just as Eve is of Adam, so also is Jesus of the Virgin Mary.

It has long been the position of the Christian church that Mariology does not stand on its own, but is a component of Christology. As such, Mariology protects the doctrine of the Incarnation, that God became man. The Virgin Birth, the holiness of Mary, the perpetual virginity of

Mary — all these are in service to the Incarnation of the Son of God.[345] What we do know of Mary from Sacred Scripture is mainly from Luke's gospel: the Annunciation, the Visitation, the Presentation, and Jesus' visit to the temple at twelve years of age. John's Gospel is the sole source for the wedding at Cana. Only four instances of Mary speaking are recorded in the Gospels: the Annunciation, the Magnificat, Mary's words to the twelve-year-old Jesus when she found him in the temple, and the Wedding at Cana. In each instance, the situation and her response are theologically significant.[346] In Luke's Gospel, Mary is the central figure in his first two chapters, with all of the action revolving around her. All this is summed up in the second to the last verse of chapter 2: that Mary *"kept all these sayings in her heart"*. Once the ministry of Jesus begins, Mary fades into the background, which should be every believer's response to Jesus. Mary lives out the saying of John the Baptist: "He must increase, but I must decrease" (Jo 3:30). Luke also records Mary's presence in the "apostolic college (Acts 1:14)", where she is the only person named, and whose presence "embodies universal joy...in the icons of Pentecost".[347]

Luke's focus on Mary makes his gospel especially important for Mariology. The early church fathers were of the opinion that that Paul influenced the theological structure and narrative of the Luke's Gospel. This in no way diminishes the importance of Luke as a historian — it simply indicates that Paul was not only an important source of Luke's gospel, but likely influenced its theological structure and content.[348] Irenaeus, writing in the 2nd century, states the following: "Luke also, the companion of Paul, recorded in a book the Gospel preached by him."[349] Eusebius quotes Origen's description of Luke's Gospel in this way: *"And the third by Luke, the Gospel commended by Paul, and composed for Gentile converts"*.[350][351] Eusebius, in

The Witness of Paul and the Gospel of Luke

describing the spread of the Gospel throughout the world, offers the following:

> *But Luke, who was of Antiochian parentage and a physician by profession, and who was especially intimate with Paul and well acquainted with the rest of the apostles, has left us, in two inspired books, proofs of that spiritual healing art which he learned from them. One of these books is the Gospel, which he testifies that he wrote as those who were from the beginning eye witnesses and ministers of the word delivered unto him, all of whom, as he says, he followed accurately from the first. The other book is the Acts of the Apostles which he composed not from the accounts of others, but from what he had seen himself. And they say that Paul meant to refer to Luke's Gospel wherever, as if speaking of some gospel of his own, he used the words, "according to my Gospel."[352,353]*

The early Christian idea that Paul was the authority and theological source for the Gospel of Luke is quite interesting, for Luke gives us more detail regarding Mary than any other Gospel writer. Furthermore, Luke is seemingly more liturgical than the other synoptic gospels; the Lutheran Divine Service (for example) contains quite a lot of material from the Gospel of Luke.[354] In addition, Luke 1:28-35 and Luke 1: 42-48 are the source material for the first half of the prayer the Latins call the Hail Mary: "*Hail Mary, full of grace. Our Lord is with thee. Blessed art thou among women, and blessed is the fruit of thy womb, Jesus*". Moreover, Luke records Mary's words in the Magnificat to the effect that "*from henceforth all generations shall call me blessed.*"[355] This is in marked contrast to the modern view that Paul was anti-woman, for alone of the Gospel writers Luke records the primary information that resulted in the veneration of the Blessed Virgin Mary by the ancient church.

35: The Witness of the Apostle John

The gospel of John the Evangelist is quite interesting, for he never mentions Mary by name. She is explicitly referenced only twice (Jn 2:1-12; Jn 19:25-27), each time only as the mother of Jesus. Each time, however, her presence is theologically significant. At the Wedding in Cana, Mary is not only present at, but the proximate cause of the first miracle attributed to Jesus — the turning of water into wine. Mary is also present at the crucifixion, where John provides the only record of Jesus saying to John "Behold your mother", and to Mary, "Behold your son."

Mary's lack of visibility in John's gospel proves no great difficulty, for as Paul Evdokimov writes, the "pneumatological character" of John's gospel "derives from the intimacy, the very mysterious correspondence, between John the Evangelist and the Virgin."[356] As Origen notes, this correspondence relates to the identification of each believer with Christ, and Mary's identification as the Mother of the Christian Race.

We might dare say, then, that the Gospels are the firstfruits of all Scriptures, but that the firstfruits of the Gospels is that according to John, whose meaning no one can understand who has not leaned on Jesus' breast nor received Mary from Jesus to be his mother also. But he who would be another John must also become such as John, to be shown to be Jesus, so to speak. For if Mary had no son except Jesus, in accordance with those who hold a sound opinion of her, and Jesus says to his mother, "Behold your son," and not, "Behold, this man also is your son," he has said equally, "Behold, this is Jesus whom you bore." For indeed everyone who has been perfected "no longer lives, but Christ lives in him," [Gal 2:20] and since "Christ lives" in him, it is said of him to Mary, "Behold your son," the Christ.[357]

We will speak more of this in the chapter entitled "Mother of the Christian Race". Suffice it to say that this passage is important for many reasons. It is used as one piece of evidence for Mary's perpetual virginity; it is used to demonstrate that Mary had no other children besides Jesus; it is used typologically to show the close relationship between Mary and the Church.

36: The Implicit Witness regarding Mary

Orthodox author and theologian George S. Gabriel reminds us, as most Protestants would agree, that many of the Mariological doctrines are not explicit in scripture. "It was many years after the death of the mother of Jesus that the New Testament was completed, yet it is silent about her ever-virginity, the final years of her life, and her dormition and burial itself."[358] Gabriel quotes St. Theodore the Studite regarding various doctrines not explicitly contained in Sacred Scripture.

There are a great many things that are not written in the Scriptures with the same words but are proclaimed in the fathers and are of equal force as the Scriptures. Indeed, the Son's being of the same essence (μοούσιος) with the Father, for example, is not found in the divinely inspired Scriptures; it was made clear later by the fathers, and likewise that the Holy Spirit is God, and that the Kyriatokos[359] is Theotokos. There are other things also, and it takes a long time to enumerate them. If they were not professed, however, our true worship would be disavowed."[360]

Despite the acknowledged difficulties, we dare not say that the Sacred Scriptures are silent on Mariological doctrine. Peter Gillquist, writing of his journey from being a Protestant pastor to an Orthodox priest, acknowledges the difficulties Protestants have. When discussing the New Testament witness of Mary, Gillquist asks: "What is it, then, that the New Testament teaches concerning the Virgin Mary? We can find at least four crucial answers."[361] The framework presented by Peter Gillquist is as follows:

Mary is the Greatest Woman Who Ever Lived.

Here, Gillquist cites both the Archangel Gabriel and Elizabeth: "Blessed are you among women." (Luke 1:28, 42)

The Implicit Witness regarding Mary

Gillquist points out that Mary in particular found favor with God. "Hail, thou that art highly favoured, the Lord is with thee: blessed art thou among women. ...Fear not, Mary: for thou hast found favour with God." (Luke 1:28, 30).

Mary is our Model for the Christian Life.

Gillquist notes that we are all to "receive Christ" (John 1:12), and that Mary was the first human being who actually did so. "Behold the handmaid of the Lord; be it unto me according to thy word." (Luke 1:38) Beth Kreitzer notes that for some Mary is seen not as *the* model believer, "but as a fruitful model *for* believers, whose real importance lies in her role in bringing Christ into the world." Kreitzer that states that as a model *for* believers, Mary recedes into the "background of the 'christological moment' taking place in this gospel."[362] This was somewhat of a stumbling block for me, because my religious upbringing taught me not to give credence to a woman in spiritual matters. The idea that I should model my Christian life after a woman, even the Virgin Mary, was a difficult pill to swallow.

Mary is our model of obedience.

This should be no problem for Protestants. I have heard numerous sermons where Mary's primary virtue was obedience. While this is applied to all Christians, Beth Kreitzer points out the primary interpretation is often that Mary serves as a model for women, especially as a representation of "faith, humility, and good conduct." However, Kreitzer notes that Mary's humility is often represented not as a cover for her actual status, but as an ontological state, a state of being.[363] Sally Cunneen quotes Marina Warner as saying Mary's acceptance of her low estate as a woman is "used to denigrate both humanity and women." Cunneen points to the prevalence of certain "misogynist and puritanical interpretations of Mary."[364]

The Virgin Mary in the New Testament

Peter Gillquist notes that the angel Gabriel answered Mary's question as to how she could bear a child, since she was a virgin; the angel then waited for her response, which was one of obedience. Mary's advice to the servants at the wedding of Cana is applicable to us as well: "Whatsoever he saith unto you, do it."[365] (John 2:5) Thus Mary's obedience, her humility, was not an inherently female characteristic, but an example for us all of Christian participation with the will of God.

Mary is our model of purity and holiness.

Peter Gillquist writes:

We who are called holy brethren (Hebrews 3:1) are commanded to be holy as God is holy (1 Peter 1:15, 16). We are to present our bodies as a living sacrifice (Romans 12:1). Is it so unthinkable that she whose holy body was the recipient of God Incarnate should be called "most holy" by the Church? If we as the Church as called to be without "spot or wrinkle or any such thing, but ...holy and without blemish" (Ephesians 5:27), does it not follow that she who is the birth-giver of the Lord of that Church should be of that same holy character?"[366]

The point Gillquist is making needs further explanation, as the connection with Mary is less than clear. The problem for us is that sometimes we don't really think through the implications of the Incarnation. What would it mean to be in actual physical contact with God, to have the Lord of all growing in side you? There are scriptural precedents.

In the book of Isaiah, the prophet has a vision of a heavenly liturgy, in which the holiness of God comes in contact with Isaiah, purging his sin.

The Implicit Witness regarding Mary

In the year that king Uzziah died I saw also the Lord sitting upon a throne, high and lifted up, and his train filled the temple. Above it stood the seraphims: each one had six wings; with twain he covered his face, and with twain he covered his feet, and with twain he did fly. And one cried unto another, and said, Holy, holy, holy, is the LORD of hosts: the whole earth is full of his glory. And the posts of the door moved at the voice of him that cried, and the house was filled with smoke. Then said I, Woe is me! for I am undone; because I am a man of unclean lips, and I dwell in the midst of a people of unclean lips: for mine eyes have seen the King, the LORD of hosts. Then flew one of the seraphims unto me, having a live coal in his hand, which he had taken with the tongs from off the altar: And he laid it upon my mouth, and said, Lo, this hath touched thy lips; and thine iniquity is taken away, and thy sin purged.(Isa 6: 1-7)

Lutheran professor and theologian John Kleinig, in the introduction to his commentary on Leviticus, discusses the contagious quality of God's holiness, how it is transmitted from God to man.

The Lord alone is inherently and permanently holy. His holiness is his godliness, his nature, and his power as God. It is inseparable from him and his presence. Holiness is derived only from him; it is available only by way of contact with him. People and things borrowed their holiness from their association with him at Mount Sinai and at the sanctuary. He sanctified the tabernacle and its precincts so that they became God's "sanctuary" (שׁקמ). He has called the Israelites to be holy (Ex 19:6) and had sanctified them with the blood of the covenant at Mount Sinai (Ex 24:8). He had, in fact, redeemed them from Egypt so that he could be their God and sanctify them (Lev 11:45; 22:32-33). His presence with them, his glory, made and kept them holy (Ex 29:43, 44). Yet holiness was something that they never possessed for themselves, but kept on receiving from God. It was an acquired state of being, a contingent condition, an extrinsic power, something that was lost as soon as contact with him was lost.[367]

Given the above, does it not seem likely that if a coal from the heavenly altar could purify Isaiah, that coming into direct physical contact with God would have the same affect? If seeing our Lord at the end of days can will work a change in us, what sort of change was wrought in Mary? Would not that change have a transformative and lasting effect? Germanos of Constantinople, in his *Oration on the Consecration of the Venerable Church of Our Supremely Holy Lady, the Theotokos, and on the Holy Swaddling Clothes of our Lord Jesus Christ*, provides a remarkable metaphor which may help. He writes: "A vessel which has been in contact with myrrh even for a short time knows how to preserve its sweet smell for a long time after it has been emptied."[368] How much more so would a person retain the scent of holiness? For this reason, because contact with God changes a person, we venerate Mary as our model of purity and holiness.

Mary is our model of royalty and intercession.

When discussing the Virgin Mary in the Old Testament, we took note that Psalm 44[45]:10-18 and the Song of Solomon appear to bear some reference to Mary as Queen. This seeming exaltation of the Virgin Mary is a problem for most Protestants, yet it is unclear exactly why this is. Perhaps it is because, absent the larger theological and cultural framework, it appears that calling Mary the Queen of Heaven means she is the wife of a member of the Triune God. Or perhaps it is thought this gives Mary too much honor.

Peter Gillquist writes:

The Implicit Witness regarding Mary

If the sacred Scriptures declare that we are all kings (Revelation 1:6), is it so strange that the Church refers to Mary as Queen? If the Holy Bible promises that you and I shall judge angels (1 Corinthians 6:3), is it so odd that the Church should sing that Mary is "more honorable than the cherubim and more glorious beyond compare than the seraphim"?

We will discuss this in greater detail in Part VIII, "Marian Types, Symbols, and Titles", but for now let me close by saying that in Semitic cultures, the title of Queen was given to the mother of the King.

Mary is the Mother of God.

In church history, the Nestorians called Mary the *Christotokos*, the Mother of Christ, but not the *Theotokos*, the Mother of God. The third ecumenical council condemned this as a Christological heresy, as a denial that the Christ was both God and man, with a divine and a human nature, consubstantial in the one person of Christ. The title *Theotokos* was applied to Mary not merely as an honorific, but as an essential component of Christology. Again, we will discuss this in greater detail in Part VIII, "Marian Types, Symbols, and Titles".

The Nestorian heresy continues to bedevil the Church, in ways that are both fascinating and pernicious. The Nestorians were banished from the empire, but did not disappear. The Reformed theologian Robert Letham describes the influence of the Nestorians on the prophet Mohammed.

During his early travels, Muhammad probably encountered merchants with a smattering of knowledge of Nestorian Christianity. It is likely that Theotokos — or its entailments — may have cropped up on some occasion, probably in garbled fashion, and contributed to Muhammad's

225

belief that Christians worshipped a trinity consisting of Allah, Jesus his Son, and the Virgin Mary, Jesus' mother.[369]

Now to be fair, Nestorius never taught anything remotely like this, and neither do the Nestorian Christians who exist today. Yet the radical monotheism of Islam and its hostility to the doctrine of the trinity, are a theological reaction to the outgrowth of a faulty Christology, and something Christianity struggles with to this day.

We Are to Honor Mary and Call Her Blessed.

If you accept the scriptural evidence that Mary is the greatest woman who ever lived, our model for the Christian life, and the Mother of God, it should be no great leap to honor Mary and call her blessed. Moreover, as Peter Gillquist notes, the Bible tells us to do just this. First, as we will discuss shortly, the Angel Gabriel called Mary "highly favored". Next, Elisabeth greets Mary by saying: "Blessed art thou among women, and blessed is the fruit of thy womb. And whence is this to me, that the mother of my Lord should come to me?" (Luke 1:42-43). Finally in the Magnificat, "Mary prophesied "henceforth all generations will call me blessed" (Luke 1:48). This is why Christians throughout history have venerated the Virgin Mary: in honoring the Mother of God, they honor Him who was born of her for us, and for our salvation.

37: Protestants on the Annunciation

The Anglican L. S. Thornton notes that in "St Luke's account of the Annunciation...the Church saw the reversal of Eve's seduction by the serpent."[370] And as the reversal of the seduction of Eve is in a sense the essence of salvation, the importance of the Lukan account of the annunciation is crucial to a proper appreciation of the Virgin Mary's place within Christology. To demonstrate modern Protestant thinking on the annunciation, we will begin by discussing three Protestant commentators on this passage.

The Concordia Heritage Series includes William F. Arndt's *Bible Commentary on the Gospel according to St. Luke.* While this volume is a commendable work, the information on the Annunciation and the Magnificat is limited — so much so, in fact, that Arndt is clearly providing an apologetic for the Protestant tradition. Of Mary, Dr. Arndt says: *"The meaning of it [Gabriel's description of Mary as 'highly favored'] is that God looked upon Mary with satisfaction and was intending to bestow blessings upon her. It implied that Mary was a true child of God, a humble believer in the Lord's promises."*[371] Arndt shows a remarkable lack of insight into the Lukan account of the Annunciation, and displays a telling lack of academic rigor in this area.

R. C. H. Lenski, in his *Interpretation of Luke's Gospel,* contains some important exegetical information on the Annunciation, the Visitation, and the Magnificat, and in doing so lays the ground work for a proper hermeneutic of the subject.[372] However, both Lenski and Arndt miss the connection between Mary and Eve; both fail to reference the Protoevangelium, the so-called "First Gospel" found in Genesis 3:15; both neglect any discussion of Jesus being the seed of a woman, when the ancients held that women were the fertile soil into which men planted their seed; and both fail to discuss the implications of Mary's voluntary obedience, without which the Incarnation would not have occurred. Truly it can be said that both Dr. Lenski and Dr. Arndt capture the essence of the Protestant tradition, but miss much of what the early church believed concerning Mary.

Dr. Arthur Just, Professor of Exegetical Theology at Concordia Theological Seminary, might be said to have a higher view of Mary. In the first volume of his commentary on the Gospel of St. Luke, Dr. Just spends a great deal of time on the Annunciation and Magnificat. Where Dr. Arndt discerns no structure in the Magnificat,[373] Dr. Just discerns a shape in the pericope for the birth of both Jesus and John the Baptist,[374] as well as a parallel structure in the Annunciation[375] and Magnificat[376] narratives. Moreover, Dr. Just points out that the annunciation is drenched with eschatological portent: *"The entire OT hope is about to be realized. ...Mary stands as one through whom the fulfillment is accomplished."*[377] This eschatological portent is one reason why Mary is so important to the plan of God. In his later book on the Divine Service, Dr. Just makes mention of Mary as being the new Israel, the new temple, *"perhaps the ark of the covenant"*, and Mary's womb being the vessel that housed the holiness of God.[378] This suggests that Mary was the fulfillment of that which was, in the temple, only the shadow of the heavenly realities (Heb 8:5). But despite Dr. Just's somewhat higher view of Mary, there remain depths of Marian doctrine that remain unexplored.

38: The Annunciation: the Courtship of the Virgin

A sense of the unexplored depths of Marian doctrine may be found in the homilies of the Syrian poet and theologian Jacob of Serug (b 451 – d. 29 November 521). In his Homily Concerning the Blessed Virgin, Mother of God, Mary, he writes:

Our Lord descending to earth beheld all women;
>*he chose one for himself who among them all was pleasing.*
He searched her and found humility and holiness in her,
>*and limpid impulses and a soul desirous of divinity.*
And a pure heart and every reckoning of perfection,
>*because of this he chose her, the pure and most fair one.*
He descended from his place and dwelt within the glorious one among women,
>*because for her there was not a companion comparable to her in the world. ...*
She who was full of the beauty of holiness looked to the Lord;
>*he sought to dwell solemnly in her pure womb.*
Then He sent a Watcher from the heavenly legions,
>*that he might bring the good tidings to the blessed one, most fair.*
Gabriel, the great chief of the hosts, descended;
>*he went down to her as he had been sent from God.*
Because she alone was worthy of the great mystery
>*which was rich in divine revelations.*
With prayers and in limpidity and in simplicity,
>*Mary received that spiritual revelation.*[379]

How may we account for the difference between the extravagant praise of the Virgin Mary by Jacob of Serug, and the more restrained accounts by modern Protestant theologians? The simmering hostility of Protestants toward Catholicism certainly has something to do with it, as does the Protestant reaction against the 1854 declaration by Pope Pius IX of Mary's Immaculate Conception. The problem is that the anti-Catholic bias ends up affected the Protestant interpretation of the Lukan account of the Annunciation, an account that is much richer than Protestant commentators are willing to admit.

Jodie Boychuk writes: "There is no Christianity apart from the Incarnation of God and Mary played a vital role in it, not only by carrying God in her womb, but also by giving Him flesh and bones of her flesh and bones."[380] This simple quote exemplifies the nature of the debate over the role of the Virgin Mary within the greater Christian communion, more so than most citations from the more learned and celebrated theologians. This is the central issue; without Mary, there was no Christ. Without Christ, there was no death and resurrection. Without Christ's death and resurrection, we are still in our sins. Therefore we can say that without the Virgin Mary, we are still in our sins. (This is perhaps why the Latins call Mary the Redemptrix).

In his address to the Members of the Fellowship of St Alban and St Sergius, Catholic theologian L. S. Thornton introduces us the scriptural and theological riches of the Annunciation account.

[T]here are in this brief story several clear echoes of the Old Testament and at least one definite quotation. For example, the angelic greeting to Mary is verbally identical with a like salutation of Gideon before a memorable restoration of Israel (Judges vi. 12). 'The Lord is with thee' might also recall 'Emmanuel, God with us' from the prophecy of Isaiah; and if so we can understand the Virgin being 'troubled at the saying'. There follow appropriately several phrases from the messianic oracle: 'Unto us a child is born', which comes a little later in Isaiah (ix. 7 following vii. 14): 'He

shall reign...for ever' upon 'the throne of his father David'. This restoration of Israel was to be the final one.[381]

Mary was troubled at the angel's greeting and (unlike Eve) questioned the angel further. The answer of the Angel Gabriel is highly significant.

The Holy Ghost shall come upon thee, and the power of the Most High shall overshadow thee: Wherefore also that which is to be born shall be called holy, the Son of God (Luke i. 35).

L. S. Thornton notes that this verse is "central" to the Lukan narrative, and contains "two distinct echoes from the book of Exodus."

In the second clause of the quotation the word rendered 'overshadow' is significant. Its literary associations suggest the cloud of the divine presence which rested upon the tabernacle. This appears from Exodus xl. 35, where the cloud 'abode' upon the tent of meeting. From 'shakan' ('abode') is formed 'shekinah', a word coined to represent the divine presence over the ark in the Holy of Holies. In the Greek bible, moreover, 'shakan' is rendered by a word of similar sound meaning 'overshadowed'. It is this word (episkiazein) which St Luke employs in the phrase: 'the power of the highest shall overshadow thee'. That the word is here used designedly by the evangelist is evident from the story of our Lord's Transfiguration, where all three gospels have it. There St Peter's talk of three tents or tabernacles is answered by the divine voice from the overshadowing cloud indicating the true tabernacle in the flesh of 'Jesus only'. So here, in the earlier scene at Nazareth, the origination of that same tabernacle of flesh is announced in the angelic words. The tabernacle of the divine indwelling is the flesh of Mary which Jesus took. Once more scripture shows by its language that we cannot separate our Lady from her Son.[382]

The Virgin Mary in the New Testament

Thornton goes on to point out a more subtle echo of the tabernacle and the sacrificial system found in the angelic explanation.

When the firstborn of Egypt were slain, Israel, God's own firstborn son (Ex iv. 22), went free. In grateful acknowledgement of this fact it is laid down that all the firstborn males of Israel and of their live-stock shall be set apart of 'sanctified to the Lord'. To that expression Westcott and Hort refer us, in their edition of the Greek Testament, when they come to St Luke's phrase: 'that which is to be born shall be called holy', in the crucial verse which we are considering. This interpretation fits the context well. For the tabernacle was not simply and solely the abode of the divine presence, the place where God meets man. As such, it was also the centre of the cultus, the place in which sacrifice was offered. If Mary is here the sanctuary, Jesus her promised Son is already the victim.[383]

Metropolitan Hilarion Alfeyev, writing about God in the Old Testament, reminds us that the Glory of God was usually a localized phenomenon, tied to specific places and objects.

The glory of God frequently seems to be localized in a concrete place or connected with this or that other holy object: the cloud of the glory of God fills the tabernacle of the covenant (cf. Ex 40.34-35); it even appears on the golden cover of the mercy-seat (cf. Lev 16-13). The glory of God and the mercy-seat are closely related; losing the mercy-seat means the loss of the glory of God (cf. I Sam 4.21-22). The cover of the mercy-seat, or more accurately, the space above it, was the place of the particular presence of the glory of God: "There I will meet you ... from above the mercy-seat" (ex 25.22). Subsequently in targumim literature, the presence of God above the mercy-seat would be known by the term Shekhina, meaning "the presence of God."[384]

The Annunciation: the Courtship of the Virgin

In the New Testament the glory of God is revealed to a person or persons, as in the Transfiguration of Our Lord, but only in the Annunciation account is it said to overshadow a material object. What L.S. Thorton calls "the centre of the cultus" of the Old Testament may be thought of as the localization of God's Shekinah glory in the person of the Virgin Mary. An email exchange with Fr. John Cox noted: "the glory of God is manifest to a person *through* a person."[385]

As we can see, the Annunciation text is rich in scriptural allusions and contains deep theological insight. It is high time Protestants stopped letting their antipathy towards Catholicism affect their interpretation of the text, and begin by simply using their hermeneutic of letting Scripture interpret Scripture. The narratives concerning the Virgin Mary are not there just because they are a good story, or to put us in a sentimental mood, but because they are theologically significant. There is a reason God chose her; there is a reason Mary was allowed to make her own choice; there is a reason why all generations call her blessed. If we pretend that Mary is simply an example of womanly virtue, or an example of obedience for us to follow, for then we read onto her our own cultural biases and theological preconceptions and do violence to Sacred Scripture. We must pay attention to what the God of our fathers is saying through His Word, and in the life of the Mother of God.

St. John Damascene (676-787), in his book *Exposition of the Orthodox Faith*, provides the following summary of the Annunciation.

So then, after the assent of the holy Virgin, the Holy Spirit descended on her, according to the word of the Lord which the angel spoke, purifying her, and granting her power to receive the divinity of the Word, and likewise power to bring forth. And then was she overshadowed by the enhypostatic Wisdom and Power of the most high God, the Son of God Who is of like essence with the Father as of Divine seed, and from her holy and most pure blood He formed flesh animated with the spirit of reason and thought, the first-fruits of our compound nature: not by procreation but by creation through the Holy Spirit: not developing the fashion of the body by gradual additions but perfecting it at once, He Himself, the very Word of God, standing to the flesh in the relation of subsistence. For the divine Word was not made one with flesh that had an independent pre-existence, but taking up His abode in the womb of the holy Virgin, He unreservedly in His own subsistence took upon Himself through the pure blood of the eternal Virgin a body of flesh animated with the spirit of reason and thought, thus assuming to Himself the first-fruits of man's compound nature, Himself, the Word, having become a subsistence in the flesh. So that He is at once flesh, and at the same time flesh of God the Word, and likewise flesh animated, possessing both reason and thought. Wherefore we speak not of man as having become God, but of God as having become Man. For being by nature perfect God, He naturally became likewise perfect Man: and did not change His nature nor make the dispensation an empty show, but became, without confusion or change or division, one in subsistence with the flesh, which was conceived of the holy Virgin, and animated with reason and thought, and had found existence in Him, while He did not change the nature of His divinity into the essence of flesh, nor the essence of flesh into the nature of His divinity, and did not make one compound nature out of His divine nature and the human nature He had assumed.[386]

St. Hilary of Poitiers (c. 300 – c. 368), in his book *De Trinitate*, or *On the Trinity*, writes concerning similar things. But he also notes that "fastidious minds" may be offended by the mingling of the divine with our animal nature. Yet it this vision of the Son of God as a wailing infant that moves Hilary to wonder at the condescension of God.

> *But lest perchance fastidious minds be exercised by cradle and wailing, birth and conception, we must render to God the glory which each of these contains, that we may approach His self-abasement with souls duly filled with His claim to reign, and not forget His majesty in His condescension. Let us note, therefore, who were attendant on His conception. An Angel speaks to Zacharias; fertility is given to the barren; the priest comes forth dumb from the place of incense; John bursts forth into speech while yet confined within his mother's womb; an Angel blesses Mary and promises that she, a virgin, shall be the mother of the Son of God. Conscious of her virginity, she is distressed at this hard thing; the Angel explains to her the mighty working of God, saying, The Holy Ghost shall come from above into thee, and the power of the Most High shall overshadow thee. The Holy Ghost, descending from above, hallowed the Virgin's womb, and breathing therein (for The Spirit bloweth where it listeth), mingled Himself with the fleshly nature of man, and annexed by force and might that foreign domain. And, lest through weakness of the human structure failure should ensue, the power of the Most High overshadowed the Virgin, strengthening her feebleness in semblance of a cloud cast round her, that the shadow, which was the might of God, might fortify her bodily frame to receive the procreative power of the Spirit. Such is the glory of the conception.*[387]

The Annunciation is no slight thing, but a matter of great importance. The Annunciation is the beginning of salvation history, of divinity which created and transcended time and space, being enclosed within space at a particular point in time. This is an expression not only of the power of God, but of God's humility. The creator became one of His own creatures; the ineffable and incomprehensible God took flesh of the Virgin Mary — not by force or compulsion, but by her free choice. In this manner the Blessed Virgin became the Mother of God, becoming part of the salvation history of the world. Jesus was the man of sorrows, and acquainted with grief (Isa 53:3). In like manner, the sword pierced her heart also (Lu 2:35).

39: Hail, Full of Grace

Protestants take an immediate dislike to the use of the phrase "Hail, full of grace". It is not the translation itself, which is certainly no better or worse than any other. Instead, this phrase is associated in the Protestant mind with the idea of Mary as Mediatrix, a concept most Protestants abhor. "Hail, full of grace" is also associated with the Rosary, a bit of Marian piety which some Protestants take to be "vain repetitions" (Mt 6:7). This is too bad, because this mindset is the cause of much disregard for the theological richness contained the account of the Annunciation. Indeed, we are meant to be taken aback by the statement of the angel Gabriel, no matter how it is translated — just as the Virgin was. Who is this young woman to have attracted the notice of God? What exactly does Gabriel's statement mean? How do we explain it, or do we merely explain it away? Our treatment of this passage depends as much on our theological traditions as it does on the text itself.

A proper translation of Gabriel's greeting requires more than a passing familiarization with the original language.[388] Of the form of the greeting, the Lutheran commentator Lenski notes that the use of the word "Hail" (*chairo*, χαιρε) is in itself unremarkable. *"[Chaire], the present imperative, is the common form of greeting in the Greek. No person now greets another, either on arriving or on leaving, by saying, 'Hail!' yet this translation persists. Perhaps the translation, 'Greetings!' will do as well as any; in the Aramaic it must have been the common wish: 'Peace to you!'"*.[389] However, what Lenski fails to appreciate is that the word does not stand alone, but is part of a peculiar phrase in Greek: *chairo, kecharitomene* (χαῖρε, κεχαριτωμένη). Moreover, Lenski fails to place this phrase in its scriptural context.

The Virgin Mary in the New Testament

The manner in which the angel addresses Mary offers a challenge to the translator, for the word *kecharitomene* is particularly difficult to translate.[390] The word *kecharitomene*, by which Gabriel addresses Mary, is variously translated as "highly favoured", "favored by the Lord", "favoured one", or "full of grace". Even the casual observer must realize these different ways of translating the word in question have different meanings, and therefore it seems that none of these translations is entirely satisfactory.

The Lutheran scholar Jaroslav Pelikan, in his book 1996 book *Mary Through the Centuries*,[391] gives us the following information:

"Hail Mary, full of grace: the Lord is with thee," was, according to the Vulgate, the salutation of the angel Gabriel to Mary. In reaction against that translation, and against the meaning with which it had been freighted when "full of grace" was taken to mean that Mary had not only been the object and the recipient of divine grace, but, possessing that grace in its fullness, also had the right to act as its dispenser, the Authorized Version of the Bible translated the salutation to read: "Hail, thou that are highly favored." The Greek passive participle being rendered by these conflicting translations was kecharitōmenē, whose root, the noun charis and its cognates, meant "favor" in general and, particularly in the New Testament and other early Christian literature, referred to "grace," seen as the favor and unearned generosity of God. In the immediate context of the account of the annunciation, it does seem to have been referring first of all to the primary initiative of God in selecting Mary as the one who was to become the mother of Jesus and thus in designating her as his Chosen one.[392]

Fr. Stefano M. Manelli writes: "The Greek verb charitaô in the active sense means 'to enrich with grace'; in the passive sense, it means 'to be enriched with grace'; in the sense of the perfect passive participle, it means 'to be enriched with grace in a firm and stable way'".[393] Lutheran author R. C. H. Lenski similarly comments: "[kecharitomene]...has the strongest connotation of the present: 'having been favored and as a result still being in this blessed condition.' The root in the verb is [charis], grace, the unmerited favor bestowed by God. The passive voice makes God the agent."[394] Thus the angel Gabriel at a minimum greeted Mary as one who is highly favored of God, one who is compassed with favor, one who is honored with blessings — and in a firm and stable way remaining in this blessed condition. So then, we can be entirely comfortable in saying that Mary was in a state of grace.

The form of address is itself interesting. When looking at the individual words, the greeting seems wholly unremarkable. The greeting made by Gabriel to Mary is similar to the "Hail, Caesar" used in the formal greeting and acclamation of the Roman emperor. In the New Testament, this form of address is used only of our Lord and of Mary. In Matt 26:49, Judas betrays Jesus and addresses him with "Hail, master". In Matt 27:29, Mark 15:18, and John 19:3, the soldiers mock Jesus by saying: "Hail, King of the Jews". And finally, in the Lukan birth narrative, Gabriel's address to Mary: "Hail, full of grace".

The careful reader will have noted that Gabriel did not address Mary by name (as in the "Hail Mary"). In each of the passages mentioned above, the word "Hail" is followed by the title, making this the formal form of address. (The soldiers and Judas may have meant to mock or betray, but nonetheless their words were both a title and an accurate statement.) All this suggests the phrase "thou that art highly favoured" is in fact a title. In turn, this suggests the Douay-Rheims Bible is more correct when it translates the greeting as "Hail, full of grace." A greeting connected with a title is much more formal, indicating something of the status of the greeter vis-à-vis the person being greeted. This being the case, the idea that Gabriel spoke with Mary in such a respectful way indicates her elevated status, her importance place in the economy of God. It is this understanding which is maintained in the Orthodox liturgy, which says of Mary: *"More honorable than the Cherubim, and more glorious beyond compare than the Seraphim: without defilement you gave birth to God the Word: true Theotokos, we magnify you."*[395]

Despite the indication of Mary's status, nothing in this passage suggests the possibility that Gabriel is saying Mary is the seal of divine graces and a bestower of grace. It is not possible to build an entire dogmatic system from this single statement. If this is the sole scriptural evidence (as it appears to be), proper analysis leads us to reject the proposition that Mary is the bestower of grace, for the angel Gabriel once again speaks to Mary, saying: *"Fear not, Mary: for thou hast found favour with God"* (Luke 1:30).

We have been graced in His beloved son, while Mary has either been found either to *be* worthy or has been *made* worthy to be graced with His beloved Son. Yet we are still left with the fact that Mary is addressed by the title "Full of Grace", and with all that implies regarding her character and place in the plan of God. Moreover, we cannot ignore the way the angel Gabriel seems to venerate Mary by using such a formal form of address. If the Blessed Virgin Mary is venerated by Gabriel, dare we do any less?[396]

40: Rejoice, Daughter of Zion

We still have not fully exhausted the context of Gabriel's greeting. Cardinal Ratzinger (Benedict XVI) provides the following literal translation: "Rejoice, full of grace. The Lord is with you." While this construction is similar to the "formulaic greeting current in the Greek-speaking world", it takes on greater import when placed in its scriptural context. Ratzinger compares Gabriel's greeting with Old Testament statements about the "daughter of Zion" which have the same construction in the Septuagint: Zeph 3:14; Joel 2:21; Zech 9:9; and Lam 4:21. Of these passages, Ratzinger draws our attention in particular to Zephaniah, as representative of them all.[397] The import of the passage only becomes clear when we examine it in its context.

Sing, O daughter of Zion; shout, O Israel; be glad and rejoice with all the heart, O daughter of Jerusalem. The LORD hath taken away thy judgments, he hath cast out thine enemy: the king of Israel, even the LORD, is in the midst of thee: thou shalt not see evil any more. In that day it shall be said to Jerusalem, Fear thou not: and to Zion, Let not thine hands be slack. The LORD thy God in the midst of thee is mighty; he will save, he will rejoice over thee with joy; he will rest in his love, he will joy over thee with singing. I will gather them that are sorrowful for the solemn assembly, who are of thee, to whom the reproach of it was a burden. Behold, at that time I will undo all that afflict thee: and I will save her that halteth, and gather her that was driven out; and I will get them praise and fame in every land where they have been put to shame. At that time will I bring you again, even in the time that I gather you: for I will make you a name and a praise among all people of the earth, when I turn back your captivity before your eyes, saith the LORD (Zeph 3:14-20).

The Virgin Mary in the New Testament

This passage opens with the three parallel refrains: "Sing, O daughter of Zion; shout, O Israel; be glad and rejoice with all the heart, O daughter of Jerusalem", which is remarkably similar in construction to Gabriel's greeting: "Hail, *thou that art* highly favoured". The LORD has taken away the judgments of the daughter of Jerusalem; He has cast out the enemy. Because the LORD is in the midst of her, she shall no longer see evil. The LORD is in the midst of her, rejoicing over her, loving her, singing her praises. This passage is clearly messianic; is it any wonder that the angel Gabriel greets this daughter of Jerusalem with rejoicing?

This greeting marks the beginning the Gospel in the strict sense; its first word is 'joy', the new joy that comes from God and breaks through the world's ancient and interminable sadness. Mary is not merely greeted in some vague or indifferent way; that God greets her and, in her, greets expectant Israel and all of humanity is an invitation to rejoice from the innermost depth of our being. ...In order to grasp the sense of this announcement, we must return once more to the Old Testament texts upon which it is based, in particular to Zephaniah. These texts invariably contain a double promise to the personification of Israel, daughter Zion: God will come to save, and he will come to dwell in her. The angel's dialogue with Mary reprises this promise and in so doing makes it concrete in two ways. What in the prophecy is said to daughter Zion is now directed to Mary: She is identified with daughter Zion, she is daughter Zion in person. In a parallel manner, Jesus, whom Mary is permitted to bear, is identified with Yahweh, the living God. He is the Savior — this is the meaning of the name Jesus, which thus becomes clear from the heart of the promise.[398]

Ratzinger draws a connection between Mary and the daughter of Zion spoken of in the Old Testament. She is the personification of Israel; she is Israel in a person. This is a startling claim, one requiring further exploration. The Old Testament uses the phrase "daughter of Zion" twenty six times, and "daughter of Jerusalem" seven times. It is clear that these are parallelisms, that these phrases are simply different ways of referring to the same thing. For example, the Zephaniah passage quoted above uses three parallels: "Sing, O daughter of Zion; shout, O Israel; be glad and rejoice with all the heart, O daughter of Jerusalem." In this passage, the daughter of Zion is equivalent to daughter of Jerusalem, and both of these are identified with Israel. Israel is spoken of as a woman in a variety of contexts: in Jeremiah 3:14 she is the wife of the LORD; in Jeremiah 3:20 she is an adulterous wife; and in Jeremiah 4:30 Israel is a despoiled woman, deserted by her lovers. Yet these examples of feminine imagery do not tell the whole story.

Isaiah speaks of "The virgin, the daughter of Zion" (Isa 37:22). This reference is contained in the account of the siege of Jerusalem by Sennacherib, the Assyrian king. Yet Isaiah begins with a somewhat different view of this daughter of Zion:

Ah sinful nation, a people laden with iniquity, a seed of evildoers, children that are corrupters: they have forsaken the LORD, they have provoked the Holy One of Israel unto anger, they are gone away backward. Why should ye be stricken any more? ye will revolt more and more: the whole head is sick, and the whole heart faint. From the sole of the foot even unto the head there is no soundness in it; but wounds, and bruises, and putrifying sores: they have not been closed, neither bound up, neither mollified with ointment. Your country is desolate, your cities are burned with fire: your land, strangers devour it in your presence, and it is desolate, as overthrown by strangers. And the daughter of Zion is left as a cottage in a vineyard, as a lodge in a garden of cucumbers, as a besieged city (Isa 1:4-8).

The Virgin Mary in the New Testament

Isaiah resolves the contradiction between the despoiled and the virginal daughter of Zion with the promise of a redeemer, who would redeem her without money, loose the bands of her captivity, and the daughter of Zion would not only return to her former beauty, but be preserved from uncleanness.

> *Awake, awake; put on thy strength, O Zion; put on thy beautiful garments, O Jerusalem, the holy city: for henceforth there shall no more come into thee the uncircumcised and the unclean. Shake thyself from the dust; arise, and sit down, O Jerusalem: loose thyself from the bands of thy neck, O captive daughter of Zion. For thus saith the LORD, Ye have sold yourselves for nought; and ye shall be redeemed without money (Isa 52:1-3).*

Psalm 44(45) uses the image of the daughter in relation to the King. This is one of the so-called "messianic psalms", although there is some debate about its interpretation. The notes in the Scofield Reference Bible describe this psalm as looking forward to Christ's "second advent in glory".[399] Charles Haddon Spurgeon, in his work *The Treasury of David*, describes three views of this Psalm:

> *Some here see Solomon and Pharaoh's daughter only — they are shortsighted; others see both Solomon and Christ — they are cross-eyed; well-focussed [sic] spiritual eyes see here Jesus only, or if Solomon be present at all, it must be like those hazy shadows of passers-by which cross the face of the camera, and therefore are dimly traceable upon a photographic landscape. "The King," the God whose throne is for ever and ever, is no mere mortal and his everlasting dominion is not bounded by Lebanon and Egypt's river. This is no wedding son of earthly nuptials, but an Epithalamium[400] for the Heavenly Bridegroom and his elect spouse.[401]*

Rejoice, Daughter of Zion

This is one area, however, where Charles Haddon Spurgeon, the "Prince of Preachers", is incorrect. When we place Psalm 44(45) in context with all the other "daughter of Zion" references in the Old Testament, and compare the imagery with that of the New Testament (especially the Magnificat), it is clear that while the Psalm may have been written on the occasion of David's marriage to a foreign princess from Tyre (v. 13), this princess is a type for which the antitype is the Virgin Mary. Note the image of the "virgins her companions that follow her", an image that prefigures the parable if the five wise and the five foolish virgins. Note as well the idea of the bride of David being remembered and praised to all generations, which is explicitly referenced in Mary's Magnificat.

Hearken, O daughter, and consider, and incline thine ear; forget also thine own people, and thy father's house; So shall the king greatly desire thy beauty: for he is thy Lord; and worship thou him. And the daughter of Tyre shall be there with a gift; even the rich among the people shall intreat thy favour. The king's daughter is all glorious within: her clothing is of wrought gold. She shall be brought unto the king in raiment of needlework: the virgins her companions that follow her shall be brought unto thee. With gladness and rejoicing shall they be brought: they shall enter into the king's palace. Instead of thy fathers shall be thy children, whom thou mayest make princes in all the earth. I will make thy name to be remembered in all generations: therefore shall the people praise thee for ever and ever (Psa 44(45): 10-17).

Jeremiah uses a great deal of spousal imagery to lay out God's case against his people. However, Jeremiah sees Israel, the daughter of Zion, as being connected with the redemptive plan of God. Jeremiah will sometimes see Israel as both despoiled and virginal in the same passage. In Lamentations, the prophet speaks of the "virgin daughter of

245

Zion", then begins to describe her breach which is seemingly too great to be healed, a breach which causes her enemies to hiss and gnash their teeth. It may seem difficult to reconcile the image of the virgin with the image of a despoiled Jerusalem; however, this presents no difficulty as long as we remember symbols are polysemic, that they can have multiple uses and meanings, based on the characteristics of the signifier.

In Jeremiah, after a verse in which we see Israel as a despoiled wife deserted of her lovers, the prophet hears "a voice as of a woman in travail, and the anguish as of her that bringeth forth her first child, the voice of the daughter of Zion, that bewaileth herself, that spreadeth her hands, saying, Woe is me now! for my soul is wearied because of murderers" (Jer 4:31). This remarkable verse is not only applicable to Jeremiah's time; the apostle John takes up this imagery and gives it a greater significance: "And there appeared a great wonder in heaven; a woman clothed with the sun, and the moon under her feet, and upon her head a crown of twelve stars: And she being with child cried, travailing in birth, and pained to be delivered" (Rev 12:1-2). The woman of Revelations 12 is the Virgin Mary, who "brought forth a man child, who was to rule all nations with a rod of iron: and her child was caught up unto God, and to his throne" (Rev 12:5). Thus the daughter of Zion stands in for the Virgin Mary. Mary is Israel in person and as a person; she is the concretization of Israel.[402] Just as the prophets did not separate the two advents of Christ, so also they did not separate the virgin daughter of Zion from image of the despoiled wife, leaving that job to us.

41: How shall these things be?

After Gabriel tells Mary she will conceive in her womb and bring forth a son, Mary asks a curious question. "How shall this be, seeing I know not a man?" Given that most people lived in one room houses and lived near their animals, we cannot expect that Mary would be ignorant of the facts of life. Moreover, Mary was betrothed to a man named Joseph, and in the ordinary course of events we might well expect that at some point in the future she would become pregnant. To an ordinary woman, the unexpected part of the announcement would have been the announcement that she was to bear the Messiah. Why then this curious question? Compare Mary's reaction to that of Zacharias who, after being told by Gabriel that Elizabeth would bear a son in her old age, apparently went right home and had sex with his wife. Yet Mary's question seems to assume that she is now and will remain a virgin; she appears to be asking how she will bear a child of natural generation seeing not only that she is now a virgin, but that she will continue to be a virgin in the future.[403]

Dr. Norman Geisler comes from a non-denominational background (which in his case basically means a Baptist without denominational affiliation). Of Luke 1:28, Geisler writes:

> It is by no means necessary to take the phrase "full of grace" as a proper name. Even contemporary Catholic versions of the Bible do not translate it as a proper name (for example, the New American Bible). It could refer simply to Mary's state of being as a recipient of God's favor.
>
> Even if it were a proper name and referred to Mary's essential character, it is not necessary to take it extensively all the way back to her birth. The only way one could conclude this is by factors beyond the biblical text itself.

Even if it were taken extensively to Mary's beginning, it does not of necessity mean an immaculate conception. It could simply refer to God's grace being upon her life from conception. But that was true of others, including Jeremiah (Jeremiah 1) and John the Baptist (Luke 1), who were not immaculately conceived. Elliott Miller and Kenneth Samples note in The Cult of the Virgin, the Greek term for "full of grace" is charito. But "charito is used of believers in Ephesians 1:6.[404]

Geisler raises the issue of the Vulgate as the source of the phrase "full of grace", and cites it as an "inaccurate" and "misleading rendering". It should be noted that one modern Catholic Bible, the NAB, renders the term as "favored one." Geisler also dismisses the idea that "full of grace" is a name or title. And, having dismissed the idea that "full of grace" is either a title or a circumlocution for Mary's name (on specious grounds, I might add), Geisler then thinks he has grounds to dismiss any derivative theological understandings. What is interesting is that Geisler compares Luke 1:28 and Eph 1:6 and tries to make it appear the words mean the same thing, somehow neglecting to mention the words are in different grammatical cases.

Another interesting thing is that Geisler, in denying the Roman Catholic doctrine of the Immaculate Conception, inadvertently stumbles upon the Eastern Orthodox understanding of Mary's being "full of grace". He writes: "Even if it were taken extensively to Mary's beginning, it does not of necessity mean an immaculate conception. It could simply refer to God's grace being upon her life from conception."[405] When Geisler makes the case that there were others who also received God's Grace upon conception, he only makes the Eastern Orthodox position stronger.

Let me make one thing clear: I do not consider Geisler to be disingenuous, or even a poor scholar, but rather a product of a theological tradition which will not

How shall these things be?

allow him to accept Mary as being anything other than an ordinary peasant girl given an extraordinary task, and who, once that task was over, went back to her ordinary and unremarkable life.

42: The Free Choice of Mary

And the angel said unto her, Fear not, Mary: for thou hast found favour with God. And, behold, thou shalt conceive in thy womb, and bring forth a son, and shall call his name JESUS. He shall be great, and shall be called the Son of the Highest: and the Lord God shall give unto him the throne of his father David: And he shall reign over the house of Jacob for ever; and of his kingdom there shall be no end. Then said Mary unto the angel, How shall this be, seeing I know not a man? And the angel answered and said unto her, The Holy Ghost shall come upon thee, and the power of the Highest shall overshadow thee: therefore also that holy thing which shall be born of thee shall be called the Son of God. And, behold, thy cousin Elisabeth, she hath also conceived a son in her old age: and this is the sixth month with her, who was called barren. For with God nothing shall be impossible. And Mary said, Behold the handmaid of the Lord; be it unto me according to thy word. And the angel departed from her (Luke 1:30-38).

In Part I we developed a Christian Anthropology, in which the communion of persons plays a major part. To recap, humanity was originally created in the image of God, with the potential to grow into the likeness or similitude of God, to become partakers of the divine nature (2 Pe 1:4). This potentiality involved communion with one another and with God, as represented by the Sanjuanist triangle (see Figure 1). In Mary, we see a recapitulation of this communion. God sends his messenger to her, in the garden as it were. Mary hears and accepts the message, at which time God overshadows her and Son is incarnate of her by the Holy Spirit. This was not something done to her; no, it was her active and free choice, her fiat, through and by which Mary was and remains an active participant in the

Incarnation. Any other interpretation does violence to the text.

Rabbi Menachem Mendel Morgensztern of Kotzk, (1787 - 1859) more commonly referred to as the Kotzker Rebbe, is quoted as saying: "God is only where you let Him in."[406] There are different variants of this saying; Fr. Andrew Stephen Damick puts it like this. "The Kotzker Rebbe once asked his students, 'Where is God?' They replied, 'Does not the bible tell us the whole world is full of his glory?' He responded, 'That may be fine for the heavenly angels, but the answer for men is different. God is present wherever human beings allow God to enter.'"[407] While it may seem odd to quote a Hassidic Jew on this matter, it would appear that the Kotzer Rebbe's statement, in whichever formulation you wish, is clearly in line with the Revelation of St. John: "Behold, I stand at the door, and knock: if any man hear my voice, and open the door, I will come in to him, and will sup with him, and he with me." (Rev 3:20) Thus the Christ who is all, and in all, nevertheless does not presume upon his divinity, but in His humility stands outside knocking, patiently waiting for each of us to invite Him in.

So then, what is faith — or more precisely, what is the role of faith? Is faith purely a divine gift imparted to persons apart from their own will or consent? Or is faith purely a human act? Did Mary make a free choice, or was her choice already made for her? Fr. Touma (Bitar), in an essay entitled "There's Doubt, and then there's Doubt", described the resolution between the initiative of God and our response in this way.

Faith, as it occurs to us today, has a human aspect, there is no doubt about this. But it also has a divine aspect. The human aspect is related to receiving on the one hand and on the other hand it is related to response. Initiative in faith belongs to God. We are unable to attain it on our own. Only in Him are we able to attain it. In this way, the initiative towards Mary belonged to the angel Gabriel, "Peace be upon you... the Lord is with you. Blessed are you among women" (Luke 1:28). Mary was, at the beginning, in a state of receiving. Then, after dialogue with the angel, she had her response: "Here I am, the handmaiden of the Lord. May it be to me as you say" (Luke 1.38). It is clear that the Lord God did not impose His will. He leaves the way open for us to respond or to not respond. He does not alter what we are inclined towards or what we desire. Naturally, He knows what is to come in advance. He does not act except at precisely the right time, when we are ready to accept what He offers us and thus are ready to accept His demand and fulfill His will. "My word does not return to Me empty," says the Lord!

This presupposes that if we are to accept what is of God, that our internal state must be prepared for it. "Blessed is the man who has resolved in his heart to go up, in the Valley of Baka, to the place that he intends. There the judge will permit him blessings" (Psalm 83:5-6 LXX).[408]

Paul Evdokimov writes: "It is precisely when our freedom is embedded in the work of God (*opus Dei*) that it never ceases to be true freedom. The Virgin's fiat ("Let it be to me according to your word") is not the result of a mere submission of her will; her will expresses the supreme freedom of her spirit."[409] Evdokimov expands on the significance of the Virgin's fiat in this manner.

As long as our freedom is exercised within the opus Dei [the work of God] it will never cease to be true freedom. The Virgin's 'fiat' was an expression not of mere submission but of a truly free personality. This was the act that all her previous life — in the temple, according to tradition — had been leading up to; she had been watched over by the Spirit, and protected also by her own intense recollectedness — so clearly depicted in the icons of the Annunciation, where she appears not surprised and astonished by the unexpected, but awestruck at the mystery of this long-awaited moment; the angel bringing the tidings and the Virgin listening to him together form a perfect harmony. Here is the history of the world in a nutshell, theology in a single word; the fate of the world, even of God, waits in suspense for nothing but what will be released by her fiat — the childbearing of God; and in this we see that she is utterly consecrated, holy and pure. Even God does not invent the truth, but has it eternally in mind until, 'he spoke, and it was done'. The freedom of humanity made in the image of God is to reproduce that very springing up of the truth which pre-exists humanity.[410]

It is this freedom of the Virgin's spirit — paradigmatic of our own freedom — that presents a monumental problem for many Protestants, especially those with a Lutheran, Reformed, or Calvinistic background.[411] If Mary's choice was truly free, then we, too have a choice; and if we have the ability to choose God and God does not impose His will on us, then much of Protestant theology becomes suspect.

We cannot avoid a certain parallelism in God's choice for man, and in man's choice for God (although we can attempt to explain it away.) We should expect to see that parallelism, based solely on the creation of man as the bearer of God's own image, and as the only created being into which God Himself breathed the breath of life. The creation itself was a creative act of God's own free will. The freedom of will and the creative impulse is an essential part of God's divine revelation. The original image of God remains an essential and integral part of humanity — not merely a substance, or one of many components making up humanity; rather, as Evdokimov writes, "the *whole* human being has been created, sculpted 'in the image".[412] It is because of and by means of this image that we are able to lament out human condition and call out to God for relief. Blessed Augustine famously wrote: "[M]an wants to praise you; man, but a particle of Your creation. You awaken us to delight in Your praise, for You made us for Yourself, and our hearts are restless until they rest in You."[413] Augustine speaks here of God's desire for us, and our corresponding desire for Him. This desire was not eradicated by the Fall, but remains active, compelling man to attempt to fill the void. As Blaise Pascal is famously (and apocryphally) quoted as saying: "There is a God shaped vacuum in the heart of every man which cannot be filled by any created thing, but only by God, the Creator, made known through Jesus."[414]

It is therefore not enough to speak only of Mary's fiat, but also of God's fiat on our behalf. Paul Evdokimov notes that although God desires us, and chooses us, he will not force himself upon us, for that would destroy the communion of essence between God and mankind.

The mere salvation of the world is easily within reach of the omnipotence of God; what is beyond it is the world's affirmation of its salvation through its own free response. God can take upon Himself every iniquity, even unto death. But He cannot pronounce the fiat for man, or answer for him. By contrast, there is an affinity between the Holy One and the saints who say "Amen" — a communion of essence, which allows the Word to come to "his own home..., his own people" (Jn 1:11). To the fiat of the Creator corresponds the fiat of the creature: "Behold, I am the handmaid of the Lord" (Lu 1:38).[415]

Paul Evdokimov goes on to note that the Gospels contain three parallel fiats.

The Virgin's ministry as a woman begins at the moment of the Annunciation, but archetypically it is rooted in the Cross. The close parallelism of the three fiats in the Gospel asserts itself in the full breadth of its meaning. The night of Gethsemane resounds with the fiat of Christ: "Let

*your will, not mine, be done" (Mt 26:39). The fiat of the Virgin
already contains the sorrowing Mother standing next to the
cross, the Stabat Mater Dolorosa. The tragic struggle of faith
in John the Baptist leads him to undergo the trial by fire, and
the words of Christ replying to the disciples of St John (Mt
11:2-6; Lu 7:18-23) confirm his fiat, fulfilled and sealed by
his martyrdom. In these three archetypes, the crucified faith
prefigures the life-bearing Cross. The confirmation of the fiat
is not a mere announcement, but a shining victory over its
potential negation, won in the heart itself, and taking its
place in the act of the crucified Bridegroom and of those who
have been "wounded by the divine Bridegroom."[416]*

The free choice of Mary as given in the gospels finds
a parallel in the free choice of Christ to accept the death on
the Cross, and the free choice of John the Baptist to believe
in Christ and accept martyrdom on His behalf. The Virgin
Mary, by her free choice, gave of herself to her son, who is
the Son. Through Mary, the Father gave his only begotten
Son by means of the Spirit to Mary, and through Mary to
us. Through her participation in this divine communion —
by means of her voluntary obedience to the proclamation —
He who was begotten of the Father from eternity was joined
to a human nature in the womb of the Blessed Virgin.
Through the free and voluntary cooperation of the Virgin
Mary, the Son of God became bone of our bone, flesh of our
flesh.[417]

There is much difference of opinion regarding the
import of Mary's choice. The Calvinist, for whom everything
is predestined through the sovereignty of God, see's Mary's
words as foreordained, representing the illusion of choice.
This brings up a host of troubling issues involving God
forcing Himself upon a young woman. This God is no better
than the pagan Gods, who took by trickery or force any
woman who tickled their fancy. The Lutherans, who speak
of the bound will (unable to respond in spiritual matters

until God gifts them with His grace), might not have this problem. For non-Protestants, the Annunciation, and especially Mary's voluntary response, is "normative of God's dealing with men in the work of salvation."[418] Bernard Leeming cites the Baptist theologian Dr. Neville Clarke who, in an attempt to defend the Baptist's view of believer's baptism, ends up making the case for Mary's fiat, her free choice.

Though we confess the miracle of Bethlehem to be sheer act of divine grace, the humanity of the Lord to have concrete subsistence only in and as a result of the hypostatic union, yet we must never forget that the incarnation itself is preceded and made possible by the obedience of the Virgin Mary — 'Behold the handmaid of the Lord; let it be to me according to your word' (Luke 1:38) — and followed and perfected by the filial human response of the one who 'although he was a Son, he learned obedience through what he suffered' (Heb. 5:8).

Against any excessive Lutheran insistence that justification is a pure act of God, independent of human acceptance, the Papist stand is a counterpoise. Dr. Clark, a little later, says: "Christus pro nobis [Christ for us] must become Christus in nobis [Christ in us], if redemption is to be realized. ...Incorporation into the Totus Christus [the whole Christ], which baptism embodies, is rooted in the substitutionary work of the God-man and shares its character of divine act, but the differentia of the human response must never be denied. If the response itself be opus dei [the work of God], yet the incorporation must wait upon that Amen being spoken."[419]

Bernard Leeming notes: "The response itself is the work of God and from beginning to end our Lady's holiness was God's work in her; and yet her *Fiat* is required."[420] And

The Free Choice of Mary

to demonstrate that Mary is normative for the Christian life, Paul Evdokimov writes the following:

> In the experience of the great spiritual masters, the Eucharist finds its image in the nuptial union. By pronouncing my fiat, I identify with the beloved being. The divine will becomes mine, and wells up from my own will; 'The life I live is not my life, but the life which Christ lives in me' (Gal 2:20).[421]

Paul Evdokimov provides with a greater understanding of the importance of Mary's fiat. True unity with God requires the freedom of the will. The bound will acquiesces reluctantly; the free will obeys with joyful abandon.

> Freedom proclaims, "Let your will be done." It is because we can say equally well, "Your Will shall not be done," that we are able to say, "Amen." The two freedoms harmonize. According to St Paul, "With Him, it was, and is always, Yes" (2 Cor 2:20) — which admirably explains the text of Mt 18:19, "if two of you agree" (symphônêsôsin, literally "agree in sound, in voice") [there am I in the midst of them]. We can only be truly united in the will of God, in the transcendence of every limitation, in the upwelling of the entirely new reality of the Body of which prayer is a direct expression, and which is completely unconnected to any imperative demand. Such a "Yes" must be born in secret, at the wellspring of our being; and this is why the one who utters it for everyone is a Virgin, the Mother of all the living.
> We now understand why God does not give orders, but issues appeals, and invitations. "Hear, O Israel!" (De 6:4). Tyrannical decrees are met with mute resistance; the invitation from the Master of the Banquet calls forth the joyful acceptance of "him who has ears." The chosen one is the one who accepts the invitation, and grasps the gift he receives. "They shall come with shouts of joy to Zion's height, shining

257

*with happiness at the bounty of the Lord, the corn, the new
wine. They shall become like a watered garden" (Jer 31:12).
"He gave them bread from heaven" (Ps 77:25). God has
placed His freedom, His image as creator, in "earthen
vessels" (2 Cor 4:7); and He comes to look at Himself.*[422]

In his magisterial book "Orthodoxy", Paul Evdokimov
provides a summary of the importance of Mary's fiat, her
free choice. "Under scrutiny of the light from Tabor
searching into every geographical place we must all accept
the ultimate freedom: to follow the Virgin in her *fiat* at the
Incarnation, by uttering on behalf of history the
eschatological *fiat* to the Parousia [second coming of
Christ]."[423] In this short summation, Evdokimov ties Mary's
free choice to our salvation, our sanctification, and our
Lord's return in glory. Mary's acceptance of the angelic
message was emblematic of her worthiness, of her
blessedness, of her holiness.

Mary lived the paradigmatic example of the Christian
life. She perfectly exemplifies the statement of John the
Baptist: "He must increase, but I must decrease" (John
3:30). Alone of all Jesus disciples, she is said to have "kept
all these things, and pondered them in her heart" (Lu 2:19).
She clearly did not always understand her son Jesus, but
she alone of all His disciples was present at the Incarnation,
at His birth, at the beginning of His ministry, at His death,
was witness to His resurrection and ascension, and was
present at the day of Pentecost. She alone kept these
things, pondered these things, and was therefore in all
likelihood the only person in a position to be the source for
the opening chapters of Luke's gospel. In addition, because
Mary was given a choice, we know that we too are given a
choice. Like a good captain we can let the let the *Ruach
Elohim* (Spirit or Breath of God) fill the sails of our ship and
drive us forward, or we can ignore the wind and drift
aimlessly. Our veneration of the Virgin Mary is not the

veneration of a demigod. Instead, as the captains of our own ship (so to speak), we use the paradigmatic example of the Blessed Virgin as the chart to guide us home.

43: The Visitation

The connection between the Annunciation and the Visitation is made plan by Fr. John Anthony McGuckin. "Her prophetic utterance of the simple word *chaire* (rejoice) makes the younger prophet, John, leap for joy in his mother's womb, startles into life by the return of the power of the Living Spirit to Israel, as witnessed in her repetition of the angelic evangelization."[424] The Angel's first words to Mary, and Mary's first words to Elizabeth, were the same: Rejoice. But why rejoice? Elizabeth's response makes this clear, for the Mother of her Lord had come. In other words, Mary was announcing the return of the Messiah.

Nothing in the biblical record indicates Mary was of noble birth or high social standing. Mary was from Nazareth in Galilee; Galilee was thought to be a backwards place, and people from Nazareth were not well thought of (John 1:46; 7:52). Mary seems to have internalized this, for in the Magnificat she describes her humble origins (Luke 1:48). On the other hand, Mary's cousin Elizabeth was honored by being the wife of a Priest. In addition, Elizabeth is described as being 'well stricken in years' (Luke 1:7), and old age was respected (Le 19:32; Pr 20:29). Thus it is startling to hear Elizabeth salute Mary, saying: "*Blessed art thou among women, and blessed is the fruit of thy womb. And whence is this to me, that the mother of my Lord should come to me*" (Lu 1:42-43)? This is a complete role reversal; Elizabeth is repeating the words of the angel Gabriel, and is worshipping her incarnate Lord through her veneration of Mary.

It is fascinating to note that Elizabeth appears to be quoting, or at least paraphrasing, the words of King Uzziah and the high priest Joakim to Judith: "*Blessed are you, O daughter, by the Most High God above all women on earth; and blessed by the Lord God, who created heaven and earth and who has guided you to cut off the head of the leader of our enemies*" (Judith 13:18); "*You are the glory of Jerusalem, you are the great boast of Israel, you are the great honor of our people*" (Judith 15:10).[425]

Elizabeth's husband, Zacharias had been serving his rotation as priest for morning and evening sacrifice. The first duty of a priest was to keep himself ritually pure so as not to profane the Holy Name (Lev 22:1-16).[426] Yet Zacharias took Mary into his own home for three months (Luke 1:56). If Mary had been an adulteress, Zacharias was running the risk of becoming ritually impure by coming into contact with her, thus risking death through the profanation of the Holy Name. But previously, Zacharias had his own encounter with the angel Gabriel and it altered his perceptions (Luke 1:19). He, like Mary, was obedient to the will of God, no matter the cost.

44: The Magnificat

Luke records Elizabeth's threefold blessing of Mary: "Blessed art thou among women"; "Blessed is the fruit of thy womb"; and "Blessed is she that believed, for there shall be a performance of those things which were told her from the Lord". Mary responds to this threefold blessing with the best known canticle in Scripture, the Magnificat.

The question is not whether these are inspired scripture, but whether Mary was inspired when she spoke these words. If she was, then we must heed her words. But what if Mary was not inspired by the Holy Spirit when she spoke these words? Perhaps Luke is simply recording her words, telling us that this is what she said, and we are not supposed to attach any doctrinal significance to her words.

The Rev. Curtis A. Jahn, editor at Northwestern Publishing House, describes the Protestant dilemma for us.

Before looking at the song itself, we need to address another question regarding Luke's brief introductory words, "And Mary said": Was Mary inspired when she composed and spoke her song? Is every word of Mary's song to be understood as God's Word in the sense of divine doctrine? Or are these words only Mary's words, which Luke recorded? ...

Think how crucial such a question is for properly understanding the book of Job. Much of the inspired text of Job consists of the speeches of Job's three so-called friends. Because of biblical inspiration, we do not doubt that the text accurately presents what Eliphaz, Bildad, and Zophar actually said to Job. But they did not speak by divine inspiration, even though their words are recorded in the Bible. In fact, the text clearly says so in Job 42:7: "After the LORD had said these things to Job, he said to Eliphaz the Temanite, 'I am angry with you and your two friends, because you have not spoken of me what is right, as my servant Job has.'"[427]

262

This is a issue that only those who hold to Sola Scriptura (Scripture Alone) have. One can hold to an inspired, infallible, and verbally inerrant Scripture, and yet dismiss much of what is contained within Scripture as not doctrinally relevant. The argument made by Curtis Jahn is that because the Scriptures do not state Mary's words were inspired, we may *not* assume Mary was speaking prophetically — which means the Magnificat was not inspired. However, since everything she said she would have been able to deduce from what the angel Gabriel told her, and since the Magnificat is a restating of scripture, she was restating divine truths.[428,429]

Why does this matter? If Mary was quoting divine scripture, why should we care whether or not Mary was led by the Holy Spirit to proclaim her canticle? Although Curtis Jahn does not say so, it boils down to the status of women in the church. If what Mary said was not inspired, we can dismiss everything she says and focus on the references she uses. But if what Mary said was inspired, then perhaps we need to actually listen to women, and perhaps we must be more nuanced in our treatment of women in the church.[430]

N. Clayton Croy and Alice E. Connor, writing in the Journal for the Study of the New Testament, come to a radically different conclusion. In their article, they claim that Luke is presenting Mary as a prophet. The connection is made between the Annunciation to the Virgin Mary, and other annunciations (Ishmael, Isaac and Samson, as well as John the Baptist), and the commissioning stories (Isaac, Moses, Gideon and Samson).[431] By comparing these two, the claim is maid that the Annunciation fits the commissioning model more than the annunciation model. Therefore, while the primary focus of the Annunciation is to announce the Incarnation and Virgin Birth of Christ, the secondary focus of Luke's story is to present Mary as "the bearer of prophetic revelation."[432]

The Virgin Mary in the New Testament

Croy and Conner also point out certain "lexical clues" in the Lukan narrative. The designation of Mary as the Lord's slave is a prophetic designation.[433] Then there are the clues contained in Gabriel's response to Mary's question as to how all this would happen. The response, Croy and Conner note, is a balanced parallel, a form of Semitic poetry.

The Holy Spirit	will come upon you, and
the Power of the Most High	will overshadow you.

The verb 'to come upon' is used in Acts for the Holy Spirit's empowerment of the disciples for service (Acts 1:8; cf. Isa 32:15). The word for 'overshadow" is used elsewhere in the Synoptic Gospels in reference to the Transfiguration. Thus, as Croy and Conner note, we see a "transcendent, empowering presence descending upon Mary from above."[434] Croy and Conner cite other considerations as well, including the connection between prophecy and virginity in the Greco-Roman world, the prophetic content of the Magnificat, and the fact that the fathers of the early Church called Mary a prophet.[435]

So once again, what does this matter? There are several Old and New Testament Prophetesses, such as Miriam (Mic 6:4), Deborah (Jud 4:4), Huldah (2 Kings 22:14), the wife of Isaiah (Isa 8:3), Noadiah (Neh 6:14), Anna (Luk 2:36), and the four daughters of Philip the Evangelist (Acts 21:8-9). If women are on record in scripture as prophesying in both the Old and New Covenants, then there is no reason to presume that Mary could not also be a prophetess, unless you are already predisposed against the Virgin Mary.

The structure of the Magnificat is hidden by the way it is broken up into verses, which distorts the meaning by placing verse divisions between parallel clauses. Dr. Art Just points out that the Magnificat is broken up into two strophes: the first strophe constituting Mary's Hymn of Praise, and the second strophe describing God's Mighty Acts of Salvation for Israel.[436] We will concentrate on the first strophe, which is divided into two statements by Mary, divided over four verses.

Strophe 1: Mary's Hymn of Praise
Statement 1

1:46b-47   *"My soul doth magnify the Lord,*
            And my spirit hath rejoiced in God my Saviour.

1:48   *For he hath regarded the low estate of his*
            handmaiden:

Statement 2

            For, behold, from henceforth all generations
            shall call me blessed.

1:49   *For he that is mighty hath done to me great*
            things;
            and holy is his name.[437]

Mary here proclaims her humble origins, such that she considers it remarkable that God had taken notice of her. She continued to live in poverty her entire life; upon Jesus' death the Apostle John took her unto his own home (John 19:26-27), whereas if she were of even moderate means she would no doubt have had little trouble finding a kinsman redeemer (Lev 25:25; Ruth 3:12-13). Yet despite her humble origins, and what appears to have been a humble end, it is nonetheless true that all generations have called her blessed. However, we should note that the word for blessed used in this passage is not the word we might expect. Instead of εὐλογέω (eulogeō), from which we get our word for eulogize, we see the word μακαρίξω (makarizō), which means happy. This highlights Mary's voluntary and enthusiastic acceptance of the role she was asked to play in the plan of God. Moreover, by saying that God had done to her great things, she excludes all possibility that she had been violated by God, or that what had been done to her somehow dishonored her. She specifically rejects the disdain that Scripture indicates was sometimes heaped upon her;[438] she feels no shame, only joy.

After Elizabeth's threefold blessing, Mary responds with the Magnificat. Regarding Mary's response to Elizabeth's greeting, St. Peter of Damascus quotes St. John of Damascus as follows:

'Heaven was amazed, and the earth's ends were astounded, that God should appear in bodily form to men and that your womb, O Mother of God, became capable of containing the heavens; because of this the orders of angels and of men magnify you.' And again: 'All who heard shuddered at the ineffable condescension of God: how the Most High of His own will descended even to the body, born man from a virgin womb. Because of this we the faithful magnify the pure Mother of our God.'[439]

45: Blessed art thou among women

God is truly transcendent, truly other, truly beyond anything we can imagine, much less comprehend (Eph 3:20). Yet God is gracious and merciful, slow to anger, and of great kindness, changing his mind concerning the evil we so richly deserve (Joe 2:13). The God who is transcendent and wholly other cannot be approached by man; yet the God who is imminent and intimately involved with his creation has humbled himself and taken on the form of a servant. The transcendence and immanence of God are two truths that cannot be balance or reconciled on our own. Instead, we see the entire trinity involved in the Incarnation: the Father sends the Holy Spirit who overshadows her, and the Son of God is incarnate of the Virgin Mary. Thus the Virgin Mary is the initial point of reference in our attempt to deal with the transcendence and immanence of God. Through the Virgin Mary we understand how God can be wholly outside his creation, yet wholly and intimately involved with it, participating in life from its earliest beginnings through to a cursed death. The Incarnation, and the meaning of the Incarnation, depends wholly upon the voluntary acceptance and submission of the Virgin Mary to the path laid out for her.

Hail Mary, full of grace, blessed art thou among women, and blessed is the fruit of thy womb, Jesus.

Part VII: The Virgin Mary in the Old Testament

46: The Typology of the Blessed Virgin

While growing up, I heard little if any scriptural teaching regarding the Virgin Mary in the Old Testament. Among Protestants little to no emphasis is placed upon her prophetic pre-announcement, her predestination, and the Old Testament figures and symbols used to describe her and her role in the economy of salvation. Since Protestants teach little concerning these things, they end up arguing about peripheral Marian issues; and having disposed of a peripheral issue or two, they act as though they have dispensed with the core of Marian teaching.[440] However, the traditional Marian questions remain unexplored, unexamined, and unanswered.

The reason for this is, in part, a faulty and incomplete application of the Christological approach to the Old Testament in favor of an excessively literalist interpretation;[441] in other words, they have adopted a Judaic approach to the scriptures.[442] The Jews in Jesus day, as also Jews today, tended to interpret the Hebrew Scriptures in a very literalistic fashion. However, if the literal interpretation was problematic, as in the conflict between the messiah as both suffering servant and triumphant ruler of all, they interpreted the scriptures symbolically. Tracy R. Rich, who operates the Judaism 101 website, describes it this way.

Jews had a rather clearly-formed idea of the messiah and a messianic age long before Jesus came along. That clearly-formed idea involved the restoration of the Davidic monarchy and a just and peaceful society throughout the world, as foretold by the prophets during the age of the Babylonian Exile. The Jews of the Roman Empire desperately longed for that beautiful ideal as they suffered under Roman tyranny.[443]

The Typology of the Blessed Virgin

By contrast, Christians interpret the Hebrew Scriptures, what we call the Old Testament, in light of the Christ event, by which we mean that we see in the Old Testament a variety of prefigurations, images, types, symbols, and figures of Christ. Many of the arguments used by Protestants against what Paul Ladouceur calls "*Old Testament Prefigurations and Images of the Theotokos*", and what Fr. Stefano Manelli calls "*Figures and Symbols*", would be similar in kind to those used by Jews who argue against the Christological interpretation of the Old Testament.

Vladimir Lossky points out that the Christological interpretation of the Old Testament is the key to understanding the New, but is not the only key.

The Old Testament is not only a series of prefigurations of Christ, which become decipherable after the Good News has come. Before it is that it is the history of the preparations of the human race for the coming of Christ, a story in which human freedom is constantly put to the trial by God. ...All the sacred history and tradition of the Jews is the tale of the slow and laborious journey of fallen humanity towards the 'fulness of time', when the angel was to be sent to announce to the chosen Virgin the coming Incarnation of God and to hear from her lips the human act of consent to that which the divine plan of salvation accomplishes.[444]

Since Mary is explicitly connected to Christology, we are permitted to interpret the Old Testament in light of the Incarnation — to read the Theotokos into the Old Testament as well. If the forerunner is prefigured, would it not be reasonable for the Mother of God to be prefigured as well?

The most explicit reference to this Christian hermeneutic is found in Jesus statement to the disciples on the Emmaus road: "O fools, and slow of heart to believe all that the prophets have spoken: Ought not Christ to have suffered these things, and to enter into his glory? And

271

beginning at Moses and all the prophets, he expounded unto them in all the scriptures the things concerning himself" (Lu 24:25-27). Fr. Stephen Freeman, in a blog post titled "In Accordance with the Scriptures", provides a number of references to this hermeneutical method. Where 1 Cor 15:3-4 uses the phrase "according to the scriptures", Freeman says: "this is a hermeneutical statement, a claim about how the Scriptures are to be interpreted."[445] This passage from Luke is an explicit reference to the Hebrew Scriptures, as the New Testament books had not yet been written, nor had the corpus of the New Testament been determined. Jesus himself made this claim in a number of places, both explicit and implicit. "You search the scriptures, because you think that in them you have eternal life; and it is they that bear witness to me" (John 5:39). Fr. Stephen notes that a reference to this hermeneutic is made by Jesus reference to His rising on the third day. "The resurrection 'on the third day' is no where referenced other than in the oblique imagery of the prophet Jonah's deliverance from the belly of the whale. But it would appear that this is precisely the reference Christ had in mind ('the sign of the prophet Jonah' in Matthew 12:40)."[446] This hermeneutic is not developed from an isolated passage, but was espoused by Christ Himself, and was also the hermeneutic of the apostles. In light of the explicit references by our Lord and the apostles, we are able to look beyond the purely literal to the symbolic references to find Christ and his mother which are found throughout in the Old Testament.

At this point we will deal with the primary Old Testament references to the Blessed Virgin in the Old Testament. Part VIII deals with a greater number of Marian types, symbols, and titles, which are generally of little use until the Primary Marian references are examined and accepted.

Primary Old Testament Marian References

- The Virgin Birth   Isa 7:14
- The Protoevangelium   Ge 3:14-15
- The Woman in Travail Micah 5:1-4a
- The Sealed Gate   Eze 44:1-2
- Queen & Daughter   Ps 44[45]:10-18

NOTE: This list is derived from section headings in Manelli, *All Generations Shall Call Me Blessed;* the Sealed Gate was added because of its importance for the conception of Mary's perpetual virginity.[447]

47: The Virginal Conception and Birth

We have already discussed the meaning of virginity, particularly in the chapter entitled "Marriage and Virginity". In this chapter we focus not on virginity per se, but on the importance of virginity to the Incarnation of our Lord.

Isaiah prophesied long ago: "Therefore the Lord himself shall give you a sign; Behold, a virgin shall conceive, and bear a son, and shall call his name Immanuel" (Isa 7:14). This is a profoundly important passage, repeated by the angel Gabriel to Joseph in Matt 1:23. Therefore we have testimony from one of God's messengers (*angelos* = messenger) that the sign given in Isaiah was both Christological and Mariological. In the Isaiah passage we learn not only that the virgin was to conceive, but that the virgin was to bear a son; Mary was to remain virginal not only in the conception, but in childbirth. The curse given to Eve and her progeny (Ge 3:16) was to be reversed in the case of Mary, who is the antitype of Eve. Thus Eve contained in her womb all sinners, and is the mother of all sinners. By contrast, Mary contained within her womb Immanuel, God with us, and so became the Mother of the Christian Race, of all who believe.

A common Jewish argument against this passage is that the word used in Isaiah is not the specific Hebrew word for virgin, *betûllāh*, but is instead the more generic term for a young woman, *almah*. The Septuagint, the translation of the ancient Hebrew Scriptures into the Greek language, uses the specific Greek word for virgin, *parthenos*. The Septuagint translation is quoted in Matthew 1:22-23, thereby drawing the connection between Isaiah's prophecy and its fulfillment in and by the Virgin Mary.

There are a number of arguments which support the translation of the Septuagint. First, the Hebrew word in Isa 7:14 contains the definite article, making the word in

The Virginal Conception and Birth

question *ha'almah*. The implication is that the prophet had someone definite in mind. Second, in Hebrew culture an unmarried woman was presumed to be chaste; which means, to follow the logic, a young unmarried woman would be assumed to be virginal. In every other instance used in scripture, the assumption is that the word denotes a woman "sexually and chronologically mature", and still a virgin.[448] Thus, even if we assume the Medieval Masoretic text is accurate, it is conceivable that the Septuagint is correct. And third, we must be aware that the Septuagint is the more ancient of the extant texts; we must admit the possibility that the extant Medieval Hebrew texts have been corrupted. Thus we may presume the Septuagint translation to be correct, meaning we must assume the Holy Spirit, speaking through Matthew the apostle, knew of what He spoke.[449]

St. Ambrose (b. 337, d. 397), commenting on Isaiah 7:14, makes the following point: "This is the virgin who conceived, this the virgin who brought forth a Son. For thus it is written, Behold a Virgin shall conceive and bear a Son; declaring not only that she should conceive as a virgin, but also that she bring forth as a virgin".[450] In the Old Testament God to said to Israel: "All that openeth the womb is mine" (Ex 34:19). The implication is that in childbirth the womb is opened, and of course no one with an opened womb could be a virgin. Yet Mary was virgin in the conceiving, and virgin in the bearing. The Blessed Augustine (b. 354, d. 430) states: "A virgin conceived, a virgin bore, and after the birth was a virgin still."[451] St. Leo the Great (b. ~400, d. 460) makes the same case: "[B]y a new nativity [Christ] was begotten, conceived by a Virgin, born of a Virgin, without paternal desire, without injury to the mother's chastity....The origin is different but the nature like: not by intercourse with man but by the power of God was it brought about: for a Virgin conceived, a Virgin bare and a Virgin she remained".[452] Luther (b. 1483, d. 1546)

275

echoes Augustine: "Christ, we believe, came forth from a womb left perfectly intact";[453] and: "Christ did not impair the virginity of His mother's body."[454]

The Blessed Augustine expresses the typological significance of this event: "That same power brought forth the body of the infant from the inviolate virginal womb of the mother, as afterward the Body of Man penetrated closed doors."[455] Note that Augustine describes the resurrected Christ passing through locked doors as the type, of which the birth of Jesus without impairing His mother's virginity is the antitype. We are drawn as well to Ezekiel's Sealed Gate (Eze 44:1-3), which we will discuss at length in the chapter titled "The Sealed Gate."

When we say in the Creed "born of the Virgin Mary", we are confessing Mary to have remained a virgin in the conception and after the birth of Jesus. We are not confessing that Jesus was born of her who *was* a virgin, but of her who is a virgin still. This is because, as George Gabriel tells us, her maternity and virginity were not merely a physical state, but an ontological condition. John of Damascus (b. 676 – d. 749) explains this for us in his first homily on the Dormition of the Theotokos, where he says: "She found an abyss of grace who kept undefiled her double virginity, her virginal soul no less spotless than her body; hence her perfect virginity."[456]

Some of the fathers go so far as to say that the curse of Ge 3:16 did not apply in the birth of Jesus, that Mary's womb was not opened, that she gave birth without pain, without blood, without becoming ritually unclean. As an example of this patristic teaching, in his second homily on the Dormition of the Theotokos John of Damascus says: "How can death claim as its prey this truly blessed one, who listened to God's word in humility, and was filled with the Spirit, conceiving the Father's gift through the archangel, bearing without concupiscence or the co-operation of man the Person of the Divine Word, who fills all things, bringing

Him forth, without the pains of childbirth, being wholly united to God?"[457] How this painless parturition happened we do not know, yet we cannot ignore Augustine's comparison of the resurrection appearance of our Lord to the disciples as they were hiding in a locked room, and we must at least admit the possibility, however unlikely it might seem.

The earlier mention of the "sign of the prophet Jonah" points out another aspect of the Virgin birth, which is as an illustration of the new birth. After Jesus mentioned the new birth, Nicodemus asked incredulously: "How can a man be born when he is old? can he enter the second time into his mother's womb, and be born" (Jn 3:4)? Ambrose of Milan had this question in mind when using both the new birth and the Incarnation when commenting upon the truthfulness and validity of the sacraments.

> So, then, having obtained everything, let us know that we are born again, but let us not say, How are we born again? Have we entered a second time into our mother's womb and been born again? I do not recognize here the course of nature. But here there is no order of nature, where is the excellence of grace. And again, it is not always the course of nature which brings about conception, for we confess that Christ the Lord was conceived of a Virgin, and reject the order of nature. For Mary conceived not of man, but was with child of the Holy Spirit, as Matthew says: "She was found with child of the Holy Spirit." If, then, the Holy Spirit coming down upon the Virgin wrought the conception, and effected the work of generation, surely we must not doubt but that, coming down upon the Font, or upon those who receive Baptism, He effects the reality of the new birth.[458]

We must recall what the prophet Isaiah said: "Therefore the Lord himself shall give you a sign; Behold, a virgin shall conceive, and bear a son, and shall call his name Immanuel" (Isa 7:14). Note that Isaiah prophesied not only the Virgin birth, but also that this birth was to be a sign which, according the distinction between the sign and the thing signified, indicates the sign was itself not an essential element of the thing signified. Bernard Leeming notes that among Protestants, it was Karl Barth who noted that the Virgin birth was not a necessity for the Christ to be the Son of God, but was necessary for the birth to be a sign that Christ was the Son of God.

The Virgin Birth of Christ was declared by the older non-Catholic defenders of orthodoxy to be "a central necessity" for any true doctrine of the Incarnation, and made the touch-stone of orthodoxy. This was correct. But some exaggerated and seemed to say: "Unless Christ was born without a human father, he would not be, and could not be, the Son of God"; and "unless Christ were conceived by the operation of the Holy Ghost alone, he would have inherited original sin and so not have been sinless". Both these statements are incorrect and have given rise to much confusion. They turn the suitability of the Virgin Birth into an absolute necessity. Christ is not the true Son of the eternal Father because of his human but because of his divine generation; and, even though he had, like our Lady, a human father, he could still have been entirely free from original sin. Barth deserves credit for perceiving this and for stating it clearly; in both cases he derives the true doctrine from Catholic sources. He quotes Suarez to show that Christ could have been God even were he born of a human father, and rightly lays the emphasis upon Christ's eternal Sonship; he appeals to the Catholic doctrine of the immaculate conception of our Lady to conclude that Christ could have been sinless even though born of normal conception. The Virgin Birth is a sign, as Isaias says.[459]

The Virginal Conception and Birth

We have already noted Karl Barth's distinction between the sign and the thing signified; that there is both a connection and a difference. Barth then asks if the connection between the sign and the thing signified is arbitrary; and also, in this context, whether a person can truly accept the Incarnation (the thing signified) without accepting the sign (the virgin birth).

Are the signs of which the biblical witness to revelation speaks arbitrarily selected and given? Is the outward part, in which according to this witness the inward part of revelation is brought to ear and eye, merely an accidental expression of the inward? From what standpoint will we really want to establish this point, if we are clear that revelation is something else than the manifestation of an idea? But if we cannot establish it, how can we really want to achieve this abstraction, holding to the thing signified but not to the sign unless we freely choose to do so? When we do this, is it not the case that openly or tacitly we have in mind something quite different? This is the question we have to put to ourselves even in regard to the Virgin birth. Ultimately, the only question that we can ask here, but we very definitely have to ask it, is this: When two theologians with apparently the same conviction confess the mystery of Christmas, do they mean the same thing by that mystery, if one acknowledges and confesses the Virgin birth to be the sign of the mystery while the other denies it as a mere externality or is ready to leave it an open question? Does the second man really acknowledge and confess that in His revelation to us and in our reconciliation to Him, to our measureless astonishment and in measureless hiddenness the initiative is wholly with God? Or does he not by his denial or declared indifference towards the sign of the Virgin birth at the same time betray the fact that with regard to the thing signified by this sign he means something quite different? May it not be the case that the only one who hears the witness of the thing is the one who keeps to the sign by which the witness has actually signified it?[460]

It is noteworthy that Barth draws this distinction, as he was arguing against the attempt to accept scriptural doctrine without accepting the miraculous signs along the way. Barth makes the case that a particular event is marvelous does not make it a miracle. What constitutes the miracle is the connection between the sign and the thing signified, and the necessity of the one for the other.

[J]ust because like all biblical miracles the ex virgine [of the virgin] is essentially a sign, in our interpretation of it we ought not to be content merely to make clear its discontinuity, its "supernaturalness." Miraculous and marvellous are two different things. Merely by establishing the marvellous as such, indispensable though that is, we still remain in the sphere in which there are marvels according to heathen religion and cosmology too, marvels with a strong resemblance to the biblical marvel, even to the natus ex virgine [born of a virgin] itself. The way in which the natus ex virgine appears in the New Testament and the say in which it has been expounded in the Early Church give us no right to abide by that finding and to regard the marvellous as the original motive of the dogma. With full recognition of its formal importance we can as little abide by this finding as by the ex Maria [of Mary] which has an equal claim on our notice and emphasis. By the ex virgine the essential point is plainly expressed that by the Word being made flesh, by God's Son assuming "human nature," this human nature undergoes a very definite limitation. Grace is imparted to it. But this cannot happen without its coming under judgment as well.[461]

Barth draws upon the Covenant Theology[462] of the Reformed communion when he implies the sign of the virgin birth was a matter of both grace and judgment: of Grace, because our Lord was incarnate and became man; of judgment, because human nature possess no capacity to choose the divine or, perhaps, no ability to strive against sin, making humanity guilty of the death of God.[463]

In the ex virgine there is contained a judgment upon man. When Mary as a virgin becomes the mother of the Lord and so, as it were, the entrance gate of divine revelation into the world of man, it is declared that in any other way, i.e., by the natural way in which a human wife becomes a mother, there can be no motherhood of the Lord and so no such entrance gate of revelation into our world. In other words, human nature possesses no capacity for becoming the human nature of Jesus Christ, the place of divine revelation. It cannot be the work-mate of God. If it actually becomes so, it is not because of any attributes which it possessed already and in itself, but because of what is done to it by the divine Word, and so not because of what is done to it by the divine Word, and so not because of what it has to do or give, but because of what it has to suffer and receive — and at the hand of God. The virginity of Mary in the birth of the Lord is the denial, not of man in the presence of God, but of any power, attribute or capacity in him for God. If he has this power — and Mary clearly has it — it means strictly and exclusively that he acquires it, that it is laid upon him. In this power of his for God he can as little understand himself as Mary in the story of the Annunciation could understand herself as the future mother of the Messiah. Only with her Ecce ancilla Domini [Behold the Handmaid of the Lord] can he understand himself as what, in a way inconceivable to himself, he has actually become in the sight of God and by His agency.[464]

The meaning of this judgment, this negation, is not the difference between God as Creator and man as a creature. Man as a creature — if we try for a moment to speak of man in this abstract way — might have the capacity for God and even be able to understand himself in this capacity. In Paradise there would have been no need of the sign of the virgin to indicate that man was God's fellow-worker. But the man who revelation reaches, and who is reconciled to God in revelation and by it, is not man in Paradise. He has not ceased to be God's creature. But according to Barth, Man has lost his pure creatureliness, and with it the capacity for God, because as a creature and in the totality of his creatureliness he became disobedient to his Creator. To the root of his being Man lives in this disobedience. It is with this disobedient creature that God has to do in His revelation. It is Man's nature, Man's flesh, that the Word assumes in being made flesh. According to Barth's understanding, this human nature, the only one we know and the only one there actually is, has of itself no capacity for being adopted by God's Word into unity with Himself, i.e., into personal unity with god. Upon this human nature a mystery must be wrought in order that this may be made possible. And this mystery must consist in its receiving the capacity for God which it does not possess. This mystery is signified by the Virgin Birth.[465]

Barth is guilty here of coming at the scriptures with *a priori* understandings, something we are all guilty of. In his case, it is his Swiss Reformed theological heritage which insists that the human nature was totally corrupted in the fall, leaving nothing left that could respond to God, much less be fellow-workers with God. It should also be noted that Barth is arguing against the judgment of the church fathers, who saw the Incarnation as being part of God's plan even apart from the fall. The idea that the Incarnation is *prima facie* evidence of the guilt of Original Sin is common to many Protestant communions, and derivative of Roman Catholic theology.

The Orthodox theological understandings of the Incarnation are much different. Although it is not dogma, there are some fathers who teach that the Son of God would have become incarnate even if Adam had not sinned, for the scriptures discussing the Church as the body of Christ and the bride of Christ have little or nothing to do with the death of Christ. The Incarnation itself, then, is not a judgment. George Gabriel notes: "[T]he father say that the Virgin was chosen from among women even before women existed and that the Virgin's free consent to become the vessel of the Incarnate "mystery hidden from before the ages" was in God's foreknowledge."[466]

We have already dealt with the Protestant idea of man's total corruption in the fall, which included the idea that as a consequence man lost free will. Because of the importance of Karl Barth for recent theology, as well as the power of his rhetoric, it is important that we repeat ourselves lest the reader fall into despair. The exercise of our spiritual perception is our calling as human beings and especially as Christians.

As Christians, we are called to beware, lest we fall away. We are called to grow in grace, to strive against sin, to work out our salvation, to deny ourselves and take up our cross daily. This is the path of sanctification, of divinization, of theosis. "Ye therefore, beloved, ... beware lest ye also, being led away with the error of the wicked, fall from your own stedfastness. But grow in grace, and in the knowledge of our Lord and Saviour Jesus Christ" (2 Pet 3:17-18). "Ye have not yet resisted unto blood, striving against sin" (Heb 12:4). "Wherefore, my beloved, ...work out your own salvation with fear and trembling. For it is God which worketh in you both to will and to do of his good pleasure" (Phil 2:12-13). "If any man will come after me, let him deny himself, and take up his cross daily, and follow me" (Luke 9:23). "Whereby are given unto us exceeding great and precious promises: that by these ye might be partakers of the divine nature, having escaped the corruption that is in the world through lust" (2 Pe 1:4). It is not that we have the power to make ourselves holy — far from it. But we do have the choice to turn to God, after which God gifts us with power from on high. If we turn away, we lose that connection; if we return, the connection is restored. This is the meaning of the entire Deuteronomic history of the Old Testament, which is a continual illustration and manifestation of this principle.

48: The Protoevangelium

The first Old Testament reference to the Virgin Mary is found in the first book of Moses, commonly called Genesis. The account of the curse placed upon Satan is also known as the Protoevangelium, or 'First Gospel'.

And the LORD God said unto the serpent, Because thou hast done this, thou art cursed above all cattle, and above every beast of the field; upon thy belly shalt thou go, and dust shalt thou eat all the days of thy life: And I will put enmity between thee and the woman, and between thy seed and her seed; it shall bruise thy head, and thou shalt bruise his heel (Ge 3:14-15).

The curse places enmity between Satan and the woman, and the seed of the woman; Satan will injure the heel of her seed, but the seed of the woman will crush the serpent's head. So who exactly is this woman? This is one place where the meaning of scripture is particularly unclear apart from the Christ event. If we took this passage in isolation from the rest of scripture, we might well assume the woman being talked about is Eve. And yet we must deal with this curious reference to the seed of the woman. In the ancient world it was thought that men carried seed (or sperm) which took root in the fertile soil of a woman's womb. Therefore to speak of the seed of a woman is highly unusual, and must be a reference to the virgin birth. But then who is her seed? It can be none other than the Christ, the Son of Mary, who alone defeated the devil. Therefore, if the seed of the woman is Christ, the woman herself can be none other than the Virgin Mary. And therefore, given that Mary is herself a descendant of Eve, the woman is in a sense both Mary and Eve, for it was Mary's obedience that undid the damage done by Eve's disobedience.

The Virgin Mary in the Old Testament

St. Justin Martyr, in his Dialogue with Trypho [the Jew], writes of the fulfillment of the serpent's curse by Christ, who was born of the Blessed Virgin, the second Eve.

He became man by the Virgin, in order that the disobedience which proceeded from the serpent might receive its destruction in the same manner in which it derived its origin. For Eve, who was a virgin and undefiled, having conceived the word of the serpent, brought forth disobedience and death. But the Virgin Mary received faith and joy, when the angel Gabriel announced the good tidings to her that the Spirit of the Lord would come upon her, and the power of the Highest would overshadow her: wherefore also the Holy Thing begotten of her is the Son of God; and she replied, 'Be it unto me according to thy word.' "And by her has He been born, to whom we have proved so many Scriptures refer, and by whom God destroys both the serpent and those angels and men who are like him; but works deliverance from death to those who repent of their wickedness and believe upon Him.[467]

St. John of Kronstadt seconds Justin Martyr with this, his explanation of the way the protoevangelium was fulfilled by Christ.

Though the enemy and devil seduced Eve, and Adam fell with her, yet the Lord not only granted them a Redeemer in the fruit of the seed of the woman Who trampled down death by death, but also granted us all in the woman, the Ever-Virgin Mary Mother of God, who crushes the head of the serpent in herself and in all the human race, a constant mediatress[468] *with her Son and our God, and an invincible and persistent intercessor even for the most desperate sinners. That is why the Mother of God is called the "Plague of Demons," for it is not possible for a devil to destroy a man so long as man himself has recourse to the help of the Mother of God.*[469]

49: The Woman in Travail

The Old Testament prophet Micah connects the woman in travail (or in the throes of childbirth), with the coming of the Messiah.

But thou, Bethlehem Ephratah, though thou be little among the thousands of Judah, yet out of thee shall he come forth unto me that is to be ruler in Israel; whose goings forth have been from of old, from everlasting. Therefore will he give them up, until the time that she which travaileth hath brought forth: then the remnant of his brethren shall return unto the children of Israel (Mic 5:2-3).

This passage is clearly a reference to the birth of the messiah, and therefore the woman in travail is the one from whom the Messiah is born. But is this a reference to the nation of Israel, or to a specific person? John's apocalypse takes the concept of the woman in travail and expands upon it, making it clear that this woman is none other than the Virgin Mary.

And there appeared a great wonder in heaven; a woman clothed with the sun, and the moon under her feet, and upon her head a crown of twelve stars: And she being with child cried, travailing in birth, and pained to be delivered. And there appeared another wonder in heaven; and behold a great red dragon, having seven heads and ten horns, and seven crowns upon his heads. And his tail drew the third part of the stars of heaven, and did cast them to the earth: and the dragon stood before the woman which was ready to be delivered, for to devour her child as soon as it was born. And she brought forth a man child, who was to rule all nations with a rod of iron: and her child was caught up unto God, and to his throne (Rev 12:1-5).

The Virgin Mary in the Old Testament

Both the Gospel of Matthew (Mat 2:3-6) and the Gospel of John (John 7:41-42) mention Micah's prophecy in connection with the Messiah. The Matthean reference comes directly after the birth narrative, making the Marian reference plain.

What is especially noteworthy in Micah's prophecy is that the coming forth from the woman in travail is featured as prominently as the One who came forth. This mention is not in spite of He who came forth, but because of it, indicating the close connection of the woman in travail with He who came forth.

Fr. Stefano Manelli points out that the Micah passage states the goings forth of the one who is to be ruler of Israel have been from of old, from everlasting, but that he would come forth from Judah, from Bethlehem Ephratah, from the woman in travail. Thus Micah foretold both that the Messiah would be from eternity, indicating the divine origin; and from the woman in travail, indicating the human origin.[470] The connection between the woman in travail with the Isa 7:14 prophecy of the virgin who shall conceive and bring forth a son is quite clear, ensuring that Micah would be understood by his intended audience. Moreover, the connection between mother and son is a clear parallel to the Protoevangelium in Ge 3:15, where the battle between the serpent and the son of the woman is first described.

The battle between the serpent and the son we see played out in the Revelation of St. John, where the dragon waited to devour the son of the woman in travail. Despite the seeming helplessness of the woman and her child, the son was nevertheless caught up to God, and to His throne. We are meant to draw the connection here both to Christ's resurrection and defeat of death, and to His ascension to heaven. It is curious that while John's gospel contains little mention of the Virgin Mary, John's apocalypse shows her connected with the fulfillment of the Protoevangelium, with Christ's resurrection and ascension. We also see the woman in travail, yet also clothed with the sun, which is in itself a remarkable image, being connected as it is with her being overshadowed by the power of the Highest (Lu 1:35), with the Shekinah glory of God. It is important to note that the woman is clothed with the Sun prior to her being in travail, which is an indication that the angelic greeting may well and truly be translated "Full of grace."

50: The Sealed Gate

Ezekiel's prophecy concerning the sealed gate fits naturally into a discussion of the Virgin Mary. The passage is clearly prophetic in nature, but what is often missed is its typological significance. The image of the sealed gate, being a type of the Virgin Mary, connects and completes our picture of the Virgin Mary in the Old Testament. If Isa 7:14 was the only indication of the virginal conception and birth, or Mary's remaining virgin after the birth, we could dismiss it as an isolated verse, and our interpretation of that verse as theological opinion (Theolegoumenon) and perhaps a false doctrine. However, when connected to the prophecy of the sealed gate, it is clear that the one passage interprets the other.

To understand Ezekiel's prophecy, it helps to understand the symbology of the temple within ancient Judaism. Orthodox theologian Vigen Guroian writes, in his book *The Melody of Faith:*

> *Ancient Israel not only envisioned Creation as God's temple, but also built its houses of worship as microcosms of the universe. The Hebrew temple incorporated symbols of all the elements and forces of the cosmos. The temple on Mount Zion in Jerusalem "holds down the forces of chaos and sustains the first action of creation," says Douglas Knight. "Zion is the foundation, cornerstone, and navel" of the world. The sacrifice and the smoke of incense symbolize God's presence. God meets humanity in the temple, as heaven and earth are there united.[471]*

With the understanding that temple is a microcosm of the universe, holding down the forces of chaos and sustaining the creation, let us now examine the passage from Ezekiel.

Then he brought me back the way of the gate of the outward sanctuary which looketh toward the east; and it was shut. Then said the LORD unto me; This gate shall be shut, it shall not be opened, and no man shall enter in by it; because the LORD, the God of Israel, hath entered in by it, therefore it shall be shut. It is for the prince; the prince, he shall sit in it to eat bread before the LORD; he shall enter by the way of the porch of that gate, and shall go out by the way of the same (Ezek 44:1-3).

One of the more interesting prophecies in scripture is that of the sealed gate, as it is used in a variety of ways to mean different things. By itself it is not terribly significant; it is only when placed within a theological context that its meaning becomes clear. This is, therefore, one of the clearest examples of how one's own theological traditions affects the way one reads the scriptures. To a Dispensationalist, this passage is part of a description of a literal temple that is to be built at some future time in the millennial kingdom, and provides a purely literal description of events which will take place when Christ rules for a thousand years from the throne of David.[472]

It is interesting, however, to see that this idea is not the consistent witness of the fathers. St. Jerome, writing in A.D. 417 "Against the Pelagians", draws the following connection: "*The heretics refused to acknowledge the mystery, which was prefigured by the Eastern door of the Temple (Ezek. xliv. 2), which closed again when once the High Priest had gone through it.*" To this Philip Schaff adds the following footnote: "*There was an early and widespread belief, afterwards confirmed by a decree of the Council of Ephesus, that the birth of Christ was by miracle, not by a true and proper parturition.*"[473] St. Jerome expanded this argument against the heretic Helvidius in the treatise called "The Perpetual Virginity of the Virgin Mary".[474]

The Virgin Mary in the Old Testament

St. Theodotus of Ancyra (d. 446) compares Christ's coming forth from the womb with His coming forth from the tomb. In doing so, he describes Mary's womb as remaining closed, just as the tomb was closed, and connects both closings to the prophecy of the sealed gate. Seen in this light, the miraculous birth would serve not only as a sign in and of itself, but also as a type of Christ's resurrection.

> The Savior, after three days, came forth from the tomb, not limiting himself to opening his own tomb, but opening the tombs of many saints as well. ...When he rose from the tomb, he opened tombs; when he was born from a womb, he did not open the womb. ...When he is born, he leaves the Virgin's womb closed.
>
> Let us tell, then, the reason why the tombs were opened, while the virginal womb was not opened. The reason is that his Resurrection became the causal principle of all resurrections, while the extraordinary manner of his birth was reserved to him alone.[475]

David J. Halperin, Professor of Religious Studies at the University of North Carolina (which is, interestingly enough, the same university where Bart Ehrman teaches), wrote a provocative book entitled "Seeking Ezekiel", the thesis of which is that Ezekiel had a vindictive loathing of sexuality, a loathing which turned eroticism into revenge fantasies. Yet even Halperin takes time off from his curious thesis to make the following observation.

> In 44:3, we meet a "prince" who sits within the sealed gate of the Temple, there being passively nourished ("he shall sit in it, to eat bread before Yahweh"). Given the female Temple symbolism that we have established for Ezekiel, we can hardly doubt the essential truth of the traditional Christian interpretation that took this passage to be a prophecy of the Virgin Mary. The space within the sealed gate is the womb; the "prince" is the fetus within it.[476]

The Sealed Gate

It is interesting that Protestants typically do not see what liberal scholar David Halperin does — that Ezekiel 44:1-3 is a reference to the virgin birth of Christ, and the perpetual virginity of the Blessed Virgin. In his commentary on Ezekiel, the Anglican priest and reformer John Wesley wrote of the shut gate that this means that it was not normally opened, and that none of the common people could enter thereby.[477] Presbyterian pastor Matthew Henry, in his Complete Commentary on the Bible, Volume IV, states that the gate was kept shut "*both to perpetuate the remembrance of the solemn entrance of the glory of the Lord into the house (which it would remain a traditional evidence of the truth of) and also to possess the minds of people with a reverence for the Divine Majesty, and with very awful thoughts of his transcendent glory.*"[478]

It is true that there are problems with the description of the temple in Ezekiel 40:1 – 46:24. The description is not of the first temple, nor the second temple, nor the second temple after the extensive remodeling by King Herod. Interpreting this temple allegorically is problematic, because so much of the description is left unexplained. Interpreting the temple as a spiritual description of the church also presents problems due to the multiplicity and specificity of the details. Despite this, it cannot be denied that the description of this temple as a spiritual description of the church has been the common interpretation of the fathers. The dispensationalist J. Dwight Pentecost quotes Arno Gaebelein, "The Prophet Ezekiel", where he states the spiritual interpretation is "the most accepted", after which Gaebelein proceeds to argue against it (demonstrating the Protestant predilection for private interpretation).[479]

The gospels of Luke and John both record the post-resurrection appearance of Christ to the eleven, with others also present. Luke records simply that as they were speaking, "Jesus himself stood in the midst of them" (Lu

293

24:36). It is significant that John, the most explicitly theological of the gospel writers, made the point that the doors were shut (John 20:19). In this way we are led to reflect upon the connection of the shut doors with the sealed gate of the prophet Ezekiel. The sealed doors are connected with the perpetual virginity of Mary, and also to the painless parturition; the appearance of Jesus through the shut doors indicates the manner in which Jesus was born while leaving his Mother's virginity intact.

And so we are back to this: one's own theological traditions have a profound effect upon the way one reads the scriptures. One cannot long abide with cognitive dissonance; one finally has to deal with it, and the most effective method of eliminating cognitive dissonance is to dismiss alternate points of view — to dismiss alternative ways of interpreting the text. For whatever reason, it is clear that the Protestant tradition no longer accepts the view of the fathers and Protestant reformers that the sealed gate is a reference to the perpetual virginity of Mary, and thereby misses the rich typological significance of Exekiel's prophecy.

Part VIII: Marian Types, Symbols, and Titles

51: **Symbols and Scriptural Interpretation**

Having examined the more prominent Marian passages, it is time to discuss the various Marian types, symbols, and titles. Before we can do this, however, we need to discuss the nature of types, symbols, and titles. A passage of scripture ought to be understood in the manner the author intended. When the author uses a figure of speech; uses a person or event by way of comparison or contrast with another such person or event; or uses symbolic language; the literal sense of the passage is captured only symbolically, only in the figurative sense. When Galatians 2:9 refers to Peter, James, and John as pillars, this is figurative language; the nature of the pillars are symbolically applied to the character and position of Peter, James, and John. The author of Sacred Scriptures employs various figurative means — types, symbols, and titles — to express theological truths.

In theology, a type (or figure) is a form of foreshadowing, with the type serving as a figure of the fulfillment, or antitype. Typology is the means used to resolve the seeming incongruities between the Old and New Testaments. We have the witness of Christ himself, who "beginning at Moses and all the prophets, he expounded unto them in all the scriptures the things concerning himself" (Luke 24:27). This exposition clearly contained a number of Christological types, as Jesus often used types as a means of demonstrating the continuity between the Old Testament and himself. For example, Jesus drew a typological comparison between the bronze serpent lifted up by Moses with the manner in which the Son of Man, being lifted up, would draw all men to himself (John 3:14; 12:32). Jesus spoke of the prophet Jonas, drawing a comparison between how Jonah spend three days and nights in the whale's belly, to how He would Himself spend three days and nights in the earth. In these passages, the Old Testament type prefigures the New Testament antitype, or fulfillment.

Types and Symbols

Types, also known as archetypes, prefigure their antitype. By comparison, a symbol is an abstraction of a concrete reality. The reality of the object or objects is abstracted through stripping away unnecessary complexities and mapping similar pieces of data onto a single piece of abstract data, thereby revealing a core truth that can be used to make sense of the world. The symbol typifies or represents certain qualities, and the symbol is then associated with a concrete object, fact, or thought.

For example, the prophet Isaiah writes of a "foundation a stone, a tried stone, a precious corner stone, a sure foundation" (Isa 28:16). The apostle Peter picks up and expands upon on the idea of the messiah as a corner stone. Peter speaks of Jesus as the "living stone", with the church as a "spiritual house" made up of "lively stones". He then quotes Isaiah, making it clear that Jesus is the "chief corner stone" of this lively house (1 Pe 2:4-6). Peter uses symbolism to distance the idea of the church, along with its Jesus as its head, from the concrete details of any specific building; he also connects the church with Old Testament symbology.

An important thing to remember, however, is the process of abstraction, of simplification, works the other way as well. Take Peter's symbol of the church as a spiritual house made up of lively stones, with Jesus as the chief corner stone. The apostle Paul also uses a spiritual house as a symbol, but adds the additional detail of the apostles and prophets forming the foundation. Thus the symbol is capable of expanding, of taking on greater concrete detail, while still remaining emblematic of a theological reality.

Peter and Paul both use the image of the spiritual house, but map that image onto reality in different ways.

Symbols and Their Multiple Meanings

Symbols are polysemic, meaning they can have multiple thematically consistent meanings. Some Protestants reject the idea of symbols having multiple related meanings. For many of them, the interpretation of a symbol remains consistent throughout Sacred Scripture. Oil always refers to the Holy Spirit, and birds always refer to evil. An interesting example of this is with the symbolic meaning of leaven (yeast), which for many Protestants always represents sin. Thus when Jesus refers to the Kingdom of Heaven as like leaven hidden in three measures of meal till the whole was leavened, the assumption is that the Church will always contain a measure of sin, and therefore the Church will become more and more corrupt. It would never occur to them that the growth of leaven might be related to the growth of the mustard seed, and that both relate to the growth of the Church from insignificant beginnings. Thus some Protestants can never accept the idea of the Church as an authority, because their hermeneutic requires the Church to be sinful and corrupt.

Yet it is clear that the interpretations of symbols shift within Sacred Scripture. Take the image of the corner stone. The qualities of the corner stone are mapped onto the person of Jesus Christ. The primary characteristic of corner stone is that it determines the placement of the building on the site; the corner stone is put in place first, and the rest of the structure is related in some way to that corner stone. In this way Peter and Paul make clear that Christ is the origin of the church, and that everything belonging to the church is connected to and related to Christ. Paul then speaks of the apostles and prophets as forming the foundation of the building, of laying out its basic shape and dimensions. Peter focuses instead on the idea of the church as being built up of living stones, of the structure as growing, adapting, changing, even while maintaining its basic orientation around the person and work of Christ. Both use the same image in different ways; they draw from the image meanings which are related to each other through the common characteristics of the corner stone in relation to Christ and the church. Interpreting Sacred Scripture in this manner is no flight of fancy; these interpretations are not allegories in the modern sense, where Sacred Scripture is twisted to say something other than the author intended to say. We do not add to the words of Scripture, nor do we take anything away: instead we allow the author of Sacred Scripture to say exactly what He wishes.

We must be careful when discussing the titles given to the Virgin Mary. The issue here is that the titles must be examined in their entirety, not categorized and examined one by one. In addition, the titles must always have some relation to Christology, to the Incarnation, and to the Eschaton. George Gabriel writes:

> Her names are integral and seamless in the theology of who and what Jesus Christ is and in the "mystery that was hidden form the ages" and "hidden in God." For this reason, Latin Mariology is alien to Orthodoxy and rejected by it as a distinct theology with Mary at its center in the place of Christ. On the other hand, a Christian cannot claim to confess the true Jesus without also confessing His mother as the true Theotokos. And it is here that Protestantism and Nestorianism converge. The fathers say, "If one does not accept holy Mary as Theotokos, he is separated from God."[480]

It is unfortunate that in trying to demonstrate the integrity and seamlessness of the types, symbols, and titles of the Virgin Mary, we must explain them individually. It should be understood that this is only for the sake of convenience and clarity.

Specific Marian Prefigurations

- Ladder (Jacob's)   Ge 28:10-17
- Bush (Burning)   Ex 3:1-8
- Dew/Rain on the Fleece/Sheepskin: Jud 6:37-40
- Ladder (Jacob's)   Ge 28:10-17
- Queen, Princess, Daughter of the King, Daughter of God, Sovereign Spouse, Fiancée: Ps 44:10-18; Song passim
- Mountain (Shaded, Sacred, Spiritual, Holy, Divine, Fertile, Uncut, Inviolate, of the Lord's House)   Ex 19:16-20ff; Dan 2:34; Hab 3:3; Is 2:2
- Rod (from the Stem of Jesse, of David)   Is 11:1-10
- Door/Gate (of the Lord, of the King, Heavenly, Luminous, Impassable Eze 43:27-44:4

Other Marian Prefigurations

- Ark (of the Covenant, Holy)   Ex 25:10-16; 37.1-9; Ps 131:8
- Ark (Noah's)   Ge 6:13-22
- Breeze (Light)   1 Kg 19:12
- Chariot (Divine, Spiritual)   2 Kg 2:11-13
- Cloud (Luminous, Storm)   Ex 19:9; 16-18
- Couch (Solomon's)   Song 3:7-8
- Furnace (Spiritual)   Dan 3:19-30
- Great Fish (Sea Monster)   Jon 2
- Manna Ex 16:4-36
- Mountains   Mt:24-16; Mk 13:14; Lu 21:21
- Paradise (Spiritual, of Delights, Magnificent)   Ge 2:8ff
- Rod, Staff, Branch, Scepter (of Aaron)   Num 17:16-26
- Scepter (of Righteousness)   Ps 44:7
- Spring: Fountain (Born of the Rock; of Life; Sealed)   Ex 17:1-7; Song 4:12
- Tables (of the Law)   Ex 20
- Throne (of Fire; Spiritual)   Eze 1:4ff; Ex 19:18
- Tree (of Life)   Ge 2:9
- Zion   numerous

The Temple: its Vessels and Furnishings

- Temple (Spiritual, Living, Sanctified, of the Glory)   1 Kg 6ff
- Sanctuary   Ex 25:8
- Tabernacle (Immaculate)   Ex 26; 35; 36; 40; also Num (passim)
- Holy of Holies   1 Kg 6:16-21
- Table (of Shewbread, Holy)   Ex 25:23-30; 35:13
- Urn, jar (of the Manna) Ex 16:32-33
- Chalice, Jar, Cup (Sacred, Precious, Virgin)   Num 7, passim
- Veil of the Temple   Ex 26:31-37; 2 Ch 3:14
- Incense, Perfume   Ex 30:34-38; Lev 2: 5: 24 passim
- Candle stand, Lamp (Golden, Spiritual) Ex 25:31; 35:14; 1 Kg 7:49
- Censer (Golden) Ex 30:1, 35:15; 40:5; 1 Kg 7:48
- Offering, Sacrifice, Gift Ex 12; 13; 20 passim

52: The Burning Bush

John's Gospel tells us the Word is eternal, the Word is God, and the Word became flesh. For this reason we speak of Christ as "the incarnate Word." In Greek philosophy the Word (or *logos*), was the "divine reason" that coordinated the universe. The apostle John uses the Greek term *logos*, but imbues it with additional meaning. Jesus, as the Word, is the divine expression of God. Jesus, being God, is "of one substance with the Father, by whom all things were made."

What is the actual divine utterance that John refers to as the Word? The Word, the divine expression of God, is the same word spoken to Moses at the burning bush when God declared himself to be the great I AM, the self-existent one, complete and entire in Himself. The same God who veiled His glory in a burning bush later encased His glory in a body of flesh and blood "for us men, and for our salvation."

But what more can we say of the burning bush (Ex 3:1-5)? The author of the book of Hebrews says: "Our God is a consuming fire" (Heb 12:29; De 4:24; 9:3). Yet the bush was not consumed. Martin Luther writes of the naked God, the God in His absolute majesty, the *Deus absolutes*. The naked human cannot stand before the naked God, for no man can see God and live (Ex 33:20). God must hide himself to reveal himself, lest His fallen creation be consumed. And yet, there is that bush, the bush that burned and was not consumed; the burning bush which made the very ground before it holy; the burning bush before which Moses loosed his shoe and bowed the knee. Why was not the bush consumed?

We may well ask the same of Mary. How was it that Mary contained within her womb the all-consuming fire of God? Why was not Mary destroyed? How is it that she, alone of all creation, bore Him who is eternally begotten of the Father, Light from Light, true God from true God; how is it that she bore him who is begotten, not made, of one substance with the Father? Our God formed for himself a body of the Virgin Mary, just as God formed Eve of a rib taken from Adam's side, except in this case our Lord took up residence within that very body. The Virgin Mary lamented her low estate: our Lord enfleshed Himself from this low estate, and it was to this low estate that our Lord was born. As the apostle says, our Lord "made himself of no reputation, and took upon him the form of a servant, and was made in the likeness of men" (Php 2:7).

Meditating upon the burning bush, upon God appearing as tongues of fire in the bush, and upon why the majesty of God did not consume His creation, we come to the inescapable conclusion that God supernaturally protected the bush. The presence of God appearing as tongues of fire in the bush made the bush holy, and made the very dust of the earth holy. The fire from the altar had touched His creation; God's contagious holiness cleansed the stain of sin, and made sacred that which was once common. This is why, for example, we bow before the altar; the altar is a sacred space. And this is why Moses had to loose his shoes from off his feet, why Moses was forced to reverence the bush: the burning bush, the all-consuming fire that nevertheless did not consume.

In like manner Mary was supernaturally protected. The angel Gabriel declared her to be full of grace. Grace is not simply unmerited favor — that definition is incomplete, and more akin to the definition of mercy. No, Grace is a state, a state bestowed as a gift by God. As the apostle says, the blessing of the forgiveness of sins is the gift of faith, by grace (Eph 2:8-9; Rom 4:7, 16). Of this grace, Luther writes: "Grace will not be halved nor quartered, but receives us wholly and completely into favor."[481] Having been justified by faith, we have peace with God through our Lord

303

Jesus Christ, and have access by faith into this grace wherein we stand (Rom 5:1,2). And this is why we venerate Mary, she who was made holy, she who was the sacred stuff of whom our Lord was formed; and she who was the sacred space within which our Lord resided.[482]

Just how exactly was Mary protected from the presence of Almighty God, the all-consuming fire? She was in a state of Grace. Her merits, such as they are (for she is in need of a savior, as we all are) are the reflection of the merits of Christ, just as the moon's light is but the reflection of the sun. And yet, Mary is blessed among women, and all generations have recognized her blessedness. While even Moses could not see the face of God, Mary carried the Son of God in her womb. Therefore, before Mary we loose our shoes from off our feet; for her body was the fertile soil into which our Lord was planted, and the ground before "the bush that burns yet is not consumed" is holy ground.

But how can these things be, seeing Mary is but a women, one of the teeming masses of fallen humanity? But therein lies the problem. Mary is not just *a* woman, she is *the* woman (Ge 3:15; Rev 12:1). She is the *Theotokos*, the Mother of God. She is also the archetype of the church, the virgin bride of Christ; the virgin bride who is sanctified and cleansed with the washing of water by the word; glorious, without spot or wrinkle or any such thing; holy and without blemish. As such, when we venerate Mary we venerate the Mother of God, the bush that burns yet is not consumed; and we give honor to the Christ who justifies, who sanctifies and cleanses with water and the word, who defeated Sn, Death, and the Devil: the Christ who glorifies, who makes us holy in Him.

The burning bush has reference to the holiness of God, contained within ordinary creation, and by which that creation is transformed. That which was common, is common no longer. And in this way we finally come to a discussion of the perpetual virginity of Mary. Andrew Louth writes:

The burning bush of Exodus 3 was taken by the Fathers to be a prefiguring of the perpetual virginity of the Mother of God: the bush burned and was not consumed, just as Mary conceived the Son of God and yet remained a virgin, intact after childbirth. Both of these were seen to speak of the presence of the divine which transfigures but does not harm the creature.[483]

Earlier we discussed the typology of the Sealed Gate as a foreshadowing of the perpetual virginity of Mary. The typology here is, by itself, obscure. Yet when referenced against Mary as the antitype, and against the typology of the sealed gate, the image becomes more clear. Mary was overshadowed by the glory of God; the Son was incarnate by the Holy Spirit of the flesh of the Virgin Mary. Mary could say of Jesus that He was bone of her bone, and flesh of her flesh. Think of it; the Lord of all took up residence within her and, by doing so, made her holy.

You and I can but look forward to the end of days when our Lord shall appear, and we shall be transformed. AS the apostle writes: "For now we see through a glass, darkly; but then face to face: now I know in part; but then shall I know even as also I am known" (1 Cor 13:12). Similarly, John writes: "Beloved, now are we the sons of God, and it doth not yet appear what we shall be: but we know that, when he shall appear, we shall be like him; for we shall see him as he is." We await His appearance; we await the sight of His face. Yet nothing we see or experience will be anything like what Mary experienced; while we are sons of God, God is Mary's own son. While the coal from the altar may touch our lips, the fire from the altar lived within Mary. Mary herself became and remains a sacred person. If is for this reason that we have no problem with the veneration of Mary, just as we have no problem venerating an altar, a sanctuary, or a church.

53: Wisdom Hath Built Her House

In the book of Proverbs, Wisdom has long been understood to be a personification of Christ. St. Ignatius of Antioch writes: "If any one says there is one God, and also confesses Christ Jesus, but thinks the Lord to be a mere man, and not the only-begotten God, and Wisdom, and the Word of God, and deems Him to consist merely of a soul and body, such an one is a serpent, that preaches deceit and error for the destruction of men."[484] We see that Wisdom is a representation of God in various ways. Proverbs 8 is a hymn of praise to Wisdom, and attributes to Wisdom attributes and actions belonging to God alone. "By me kings reign, and princes decree justice. By me princes rule, and nobles, even all the judges of the earth" (Pr 8:15-16). Isaiah adds to this that God also brings princes to nothing: "It is he...That bringeth the princes to nothing; he maketh the judges of the earth as vanity. Yea, they shall not be planted; yea, they shall not be sown: yea, their stock shall not take root in the earth: and he shall also blow upon them, and they shall wither, and the whirlwind shall take them away as stubble" (Isa 22a; 23-24). The apostle likewise writes: "Let every soul be subject unto the higher powers. For there is no power but of God: the powers that be are ordained of God" (Rom 13:1).

Just as we see God as Wisdom involved in the setting up rulers as his civil ministers on earth, we also see Wisdom existing before creation, and involved in creation.

The LORD possessed me in the beginning of his way, before his works of old.

I was set up from everlasting, from the beginning, or ever the earth was.

When there were no depths, I was brought forth; when there were no fountains abounding with water.

Before the mountains were settled, before the hills was I brought forth:

While as yet he had not made the earth, nor the fields, nor the highest part of the dust of the world.

When he prepared the heavens, I was there: when he set a compass upon the face of the depth:

When he established the clouds above: when he strengthened the fountains of the deep:

When he gave to the sea his decree, that the waters should not pass his commandment: when he appointed the foundations of the earth:

Then I was by him, as one brought up with him: and I was daily his delight, rejoicing always before him (Pr 8:23-30).

I would be remiss if I did not point out that the chapter divisions are not part of the original text. Thus chapter 9 flows naturally from chapter 8. From the account of Wisdom's preexistence and involvement in creation comes an exhortation from Wisdom to hearken and keep her ways (Pr 8:32ff; cf Jn 14:15, 21; 15:10). Then we come upon a most interesting passage. "Wisdom hath builded her house, she hath hewn out her seven pillars" (Pr 9:1). I have always been fascinated by the seven pillars of wisdom,[485] but had neglected to contemplate the house which Wisdom built. Of course the tabernacle was, in a sense, a house for God. "[L]et them make me a sanctuary; that I may dwell among them" (Ex 25:8). But when David desired to build a house for God, the response of God through His prophet Nathan is interesting:

Shalt thou build me an house for me to dwell in? Whereas I have not dwelt in any house since the time that I brought up the children of Israel out of Egypt, even to this day, but have walked in a tent and in a tabernacle. In all the places wherein I have walked with all the children of Israel spake I a word with any of the tribes of Israel, whom I commanded to feed my people Israel, saying, Why build ye not me an house of cedar (2 Sam 7:5-7)?

God announces to David that He (God) will build for him (David) a house (v. 11). House in this context could be taken in the sense of children, of progeny, of a kingly dynasty. However, God's promise that the kingdom of David's descendent will last forever clearly takes this promise out of the temporal and into the spiritual realm;[486] this is clearly messianic. The house that God promises is a spiritual house for David. Yet God in His consideration of our weakness allows David's Son to build him an earthly house (v. 12-13), in which the glory of God dwelt, shrouded in thick darkness (1 Ki 8:12-13). This is the same thick darkness in which Moses met with God on Mt. Sinai (Ex 20:21; De 4:11; 5:22).

The prophecy of God, spoken through Nathan to David, is similar in tone to God's answer to Job's complaint. The tone is incredulous: "Shalt *thou* build *me* an house for me to dwell in?" To put it another way, God is saying "Who are you to build Me a house? Since when do you provide for Me? And just when were our roles reversed?" Instead, what we see in Proverbs is that God builds for himself a house. Nonna Harrison provides the following description:

The New Testament often identifies holy people as the temple instead of a holy place and the holy things with which it is furnished. Our Lord Jesus Christ refers to the body he has assumed as the temple, stating that if it is destroyed he will raise it again after three days (Jn 2:19-22). Peter and Paul refer to the church community as the temple and each of the faithful as one of its living stones (1 Cor 3:16; Eph 2:20-22; 1 Pe 2:4-5). Paul also speaks of each Christian as a temple of the Holy Spirit (1 Cor 6:19). All this reveals the inherent personalism of Christianity. Once God has assumed a human body and soul, the primary locus of holiness is in human beings, both individually and communally. The Kingdom of God is a communion of persons: the Father, Son, and Holy Spirit and all those who are joined to them by Grace — the Mother of God, the angels, the saints, and all redeemed humanity.[487]

Insofar as the apostles use temple imagery to refer to individual Christians, we are forced to understand that it is entirely scriptural to use temple imagery to refer to the Virgin Mary, especially as the annunciation narrative uses tabernacle/temple imagery when it speaks of Mary being overshadowed: a term that specifically refers to the Shekinah glory of God which dwelt in thick darkness in the holy of holies, just as Christ dwelt in thick darkness within Mary's virgin womb. Thus it is entirely appropriate to think of Wisdom building her house as being a reference first of the Virgin Mary, and secondly of the Church. Both houses are supported by seven pillars, which is a reference to the Holy Spirit (Re 3:1), and the seven graces: wisdom, understanding, counsel, might, knowledge, godliness, and the fear of God. We gaze in wonder at the Virgin Mary, who alone of all created beings was overshadowed by the Holy Spirit, and who alone of all created beings is supported by the seven pillars of wisdom.

54: Mary as the New Ark

At the announcement of the angel Gabriel, Mary asked how this could be, seeing she had not been with a man. Gabriel replied: "The Holy Ghost shall come upon thee, and the power of the Highest shall overshadow thee" (Luke 1:35). The word translated as overshadow is episkiazo (επισκιαζω) and is used in three places: here in Luke, in the accounts of the transfiguration (Matt 17:5; Mark 9:7; Luke 9:34), and the description of how people would lay their sick in the streets in hope that the shadow of Peter might overshadow them (Acts 5:15). The idea of overshadowing also contains the idea of the hiddenness of God, shrouded in the "thick darkness" of the Holy of Holies (I Kings 8:12), which certainly would have been the referent for the Jews.[488] But the association with the transfiguration also brings with it the idea of enveloping a person with the glory of God. In this way we come to the description of the Virgin Mary in Revelations 12 as being "clothed with the sun" (Rev 12:1), clearly a reference to the manner in which the Holy Spirit came upon her, and the power of the Highest overshadowed her.

We must remember that the verse and chapter divisions are not inspired. The Mariological passage spoken of at the end of the previous section begins at Revelations 11:19, where we see the temple of God opened in heaven, in which was seen the Ark of the Covenant. Of course we understand Jesus to be the new temple,[489] and thus this reference to the temple of God is a reference to Christ. The passage then leads naturally into the description of the woman with child, who we understand to be the Virgin Mary. This close connection with the temple (who is Jesus) makes it clear that the Virgin Mary is the new Ark.[490] Yet, as Dr. Eugenia Constantinou notes, there are other interpretations.

It should be noted at this point that this is not the consistent witness of antiquity. Andrew of Caesarea, author of one of the most ancient commentaries on John's Apocalypse, indicates the ark constitutes the good things prepared for the saints.

By the opening of heaven and the vision of the ark is meant the revelation of the good things prepared for the saints, just as all are concealed in Christ, in whom all the fullness of divinity dwelt bodily, according to the Apostle. At that time they will be revealed, when the awesome sounds of lightening and thunder, the punishments of Gehenna, will come upon the lawless and impious, like hail raining upon them in the transposition of the present things during the earthquake.[491]

Lutheran professor Rev. Dr. Louis Brighton, in his commentary on the Revelation, quotes from the commentary of Oecumenius the heretic[492] to the effect that "the ark represents 'the good things in the coming age that have now been hidden from men.'" This is simply evidence that the understanding of the Ark as a type of Mary grew over time. Dr. Brighton actually expounds upon the representative evidence, but misses its significance.

The ark which first stood in the tabernacle later resided in the Holy of Holies in Solomon's temple (1 Ki 8:6). When Nebuchadnezzar destroyed Jerusalem and the temple, probably the ark was also destroyed (2 Ki 25:9). However, there is a legend (2 Macc 2:1-8) that tells how Jeremiah rescued the ark and the incense altar. He hid them in a cave on Mt. Nebo, from where Moses saw the Promised Land (Deut 34:1). Jeremiah supposedly blocked up the cave's entrance and then made the prophecy that the ark would not be brought to light again until the Lord God would regather his people.[493]

Mary as the New Ark

The original Ark of the Covenant, if you recall, was the only artifact found in the Holy of Holies (Ex 40:3), which remained perpetually shrouded (overshadowed, Luke 1:35) in thick darkness (1 Kings 8:12). The Ark itself contained Aaron's rod, a pot of manna, and the stone tablets upon which the law was inscribed (Heb 9:1-5). This is typologically significant: the manna is fulfilled in Jesus as the bread of life (John 6:35); Aaron's rod that budded is fulfilled by He who is the rod out of the stem of Jesse (Isa 11:1); and the law is fulfilled in Jesus (Matt 5:17), whose own body and blood is the new covenant (I Cor 11:23-26). In fact, the New Testament argues that the entire sacrificial system is a pattern, an example, a type of heavenly realities (Heb 8:5; 10:1). Therefore we can say that the Ark of the Covenant is nothing less than a type and a prefiguring of the Virgin Mary, who is the fulfillment of the Old Testament type.

There are some other interesting Old Testament parallels between the Ark of the Covenant and the Virgin Mary. The Visitation in Luke 1 corresponds well with the story of the Ark in 2 Samuel 6.[494]

1. The same basic journey to a small town in Judah occurred with both the Ark and the Virgin Mary; in fact, even the phraseology is similar between 2 Sam 6:2 and Luke 1:39.

2. The arrival of both the Ark and the Virgin Mary were greeted with shouts of joy (2 Sam 6:15; Luke 1:42). In fact, the word used for Elizabeth's shout is anaphoneo (αναφωνεω) used only here in Luke 1:42. Its literal meaning is to "cry aloud, to proclaim or to intone", and is related to the liturgical ceremonies involving the Ark.[495]

3. In 2 Sam 6:9, David is afraid, saying: "How shall the ark of the LORD come to me?" Likewise, Elizabeth says: "And whence *is* this to me, that the mother of my Lord should come to me" (Luke 1:43)?

313

4. The Ark abode for three months in the home of Obededom the Gittite (2 Sam 6:11), just as the Virgin Mary abode with Zacharias and Elizabeth for three months (Luke 1:56).

5. Moreover, just as the household of Obededom was blessed by the presence of the Ark, so Elizabeth indicates that she will be blessed by the presence of Mary (Luke 1:45, which could mean both Mary and Elizabeth).

6. Upon the return of the Ark, David danced for joy (2 Sam 6:12-16); when the Virgin Mary approached Elizabeth, the baby in Elizabeth's womb leapt for joy (Luke 1:41-44).

7. One of the more interesting restrictions concerning the Ark is that no one could touch it on pain of death (2 Sam 6:6-7). The church catholic has long been witness to the perpetual virginity of Mary, something certainly appropriate to her position as the new Ark. Moreover, this is closely related to the Mosaic law concerning divorce and remarriage; for a woman who left her husband for another man could not remarry her first husband, for she is defiled, and it would be an abomination (De 24:1-4). Therefore, according to a strict reading of the Jewish law as applied to Joseph's situation, he could not have had sexual relations with Mary, for she belonged to the Holy Spirit.

After the angel Gabriel describes the nature of the child she will be carrying and the miraculous manner of her conception, he says: "With God nothing shall be impossible" (Luke 1:37). Mary responds in perfect obedience: "Behold the handmaid of the Lord; be it unto me according to thy word" (Luke 1:38).[496] This is a remarkable statement on her part. The angel Gabriel had pronounced her blessed among women, yet Mary knew that as the recipient of this blessing she was being condemned to a life of shame. She was betrothed, not married: a betrothal is sometimes described as a marriage without privileges.[497] Everyone would assume she had been unfaithful (especially her espoused husband, until the angelic visitation), and that Jesus was the illegitimate child of an adulterous relationship. Mary could have refused the honor of giving birth to the Messiah, but for the joy that was set before her she despised the shame, became obedient, and was made the Mother of God, the new Ark.

St. Andrew of Crete spoke on behalf of the typological significance of the Ark in his Homily: "On the Nativity of Our Supremely Holy Lady, the Theotokos, with proof that she descends from the seed of David", which begins with extravagant praise of St. Anne, mother of Mary.

Let us also offer praise in harmony with these [words] to the one who was once called sterile, but who has now become mother of the virginal bridal chamber! Let us say to her, along with Scripture, let us say, how blessed is the house of David from which you have come forth! And also the belly in which God fashioned an ark of holiness which conceived him without seed! Thus you are blessed and thrice-blessed, who conceived in your womb a most divinely sanctified infant, whose most honored name was Mary, from whom Christ emerged as the flower of life and to whom belonged the esteemed pregnancy and the transcendent childbirth.[498]

The Monk John, Presbyter of Euboea, expresses much the same in his "Homily on the Conception of the Holy Theotokos":

Behold, a new ark is being constructed by the Creator, which is countless thousand times stronger than the one in the time of Noah and in that of Moses! For the latter was a receiver of law, whereas this one is a receiver of God.

Behold, a boat sails the sea and seeks expendable fruit from a cargo. Joachim and Anna were seeking fruit in human form, and behold, they received the unseeded oyster that bore the heavenly and highly prized pearl, Christ our God![499]

And finally, we finish with St. Andrew of Crete, "Oration on the Annunciation of the Supremely Holy Lady, Our Theotokos", in an excerpt from his *chairetismoí* :

Hail, the new ark of glory in which the Spirit of God came down and rested. Ark, in which he who was holy in nature miraculously constructed for himself the sanctuary of new-found glory in the virginal workshop of nature, for the sake of his Incarnation; for he did not change in any way, being immutable, but instead he added that which he was not since he was a lover of humankind.[500]

55: Theotókos, the Mother of God

Among Protestants, there is a reticence, if not outright hostility, toward calling the Virgin Mary the Mother of God. For reasons which may not seem entirely clear to them, the title smacks of heresy. At least that was my impression when I first heard it used; the title had never been used in the churches I attended, nor was it used devotionally in my home. The title and its theological implications were never discussed, and so we were left with no basis for understanding the title and its use in the church.

We never discussed the scriptural foundation of the title Theotokos, nor its history, nor its importance in the creeds of the church. In part this was because church history, for us, began in 1517; prior to this was the Catholic era, which we rejected. Part of this was because we were non-creedal, relying upon "Scripture Alone". And so we were blind to the theological implications of calling Mary the Theotokos.

Father John Andrew McGuckin, in discussing this issue, hearkens back to the era when Nestorius, the Bishop of Constantinople, rejected the title of Mother of God, preferring instead his own appellation: Mother of Christ. He was opposed by Cyril of Alexandria, and this theological quarrel ultimately provoked the First Council of Ephesus, also known as Third Ecumenical Council. Fr. McGuckin writes:

Cyril projected the title Theotokos for the Virgin as the summary and chief bulwark of Orthodox Christology. Mary's status as the Mother of God proclaims prophetically to the church that her Son is no less than the Divine Word, and that he who is eternal in the Father's own being has now come among humanity as a true child of the Jewish Virgin of Nazareth. Again that which is to be seen is more than can be seen by mere eyes. It is the eyes of faith alone that can see the Jewish maiden as truly Theotokos; just as it the illumined heart alone that can see her Son as the Living Word of God. When the church confesses her (a word that rightly means to join in prayerful praise to celebrate the wonders of God) it confesses, therefore, the essence of the mystery of redemption in Christ. The praise and confession of Mary is, to that extent, entirely a celebration of the fundamental kerygma of our salvation: that God himself came in our midst as Emmanuel, to rescue us.[501]

Let us now discuss the scriptural foundation of the Marian title, Theotokos. In Luke's Gospel, Elizabeth exclaims: "And whence is this to me, that the mother of my Lord should come to me?" (Luke 1: 43). The word here translated as Lord is the Greek word *kurios (κυριος)*, which is the Greek word used to translate Adonai, which is itself a circumlocution used in place of the name of God. By extension, Elizabeth was calling Mary the "Mother of God". Jaroslav Pelikan expresses this most forcefully when he writes:

If this verbal exchange between Mary and her "cousin [syngenis]" Elizabeth were to be interpreted as having taken place in Aramaic or even to have employed some Hebrew, the title attributed by Elizabeth to Mary, "the mother of my Lord, which was 'hē meter tou kyriou mou' in Greek, could conceivably be taken as a reference to Jesus Christ as Adōnai, "my Lord," the term used as a substitute for the ineffable divine name, JHWH. That was, at any rate, how from early times Christian interpreters had seen the standard New Testament "Christological title of majesty" kyrios, whether or not the Gospels or the apostle Paul had intended any such identification. And because, in the central affirmation of the faith of Israel, the Shema, "Here, O Israel: the Lord our God is one Lord," repeated by Christ in the

Gospels, there already was the identification between "the Lord" and "our God" as one, the assemble bishops at the Council of Ephesus in 431 did not find it difficult to move from Elizabeth's formula of Mary as "the mother of my Lord" to Cyril's formula of Mary as Theotokos.[502]

56: Protestants and the Mother of God

Bernard Leeming discusses the oddity of Protestant's being uncomfortable with the dogmatic formulation of Mary as Theotokos, the Mother of God.

Barth points out that Luther, Zwingli and Lutheran and Reformed Orthodoxy constantly and deliberately used and defended the term theotokos, "as a legitimate expression of Christological truth: and as a test of the proper understanding of the Incarnation of the Word of God. Many Protestants follow Barth in this and several, like Skydsgaard and Pelikan, recognize the inevitable theological and devotional connection between our Saviour's true Godhead and our Lady's motherhood of God; but many Protestants have strange inhibitions about using the expression "Mother of God", even when they admit its legitimacy. Skydsgaard says: "Luther constantly calls Mary the mother of God in his sermons, a term in and of itself strange and shocking, containing the whole secret of the incarnation: true God and true man."[503]

Bernard Leeming continues to address the issue, noting that Protestants who profess an orthodox understanding of the divine Sonship of Christ, nevertheless are uncomfortable with the title "Mother of God".

Some Protestants who are perfectly sound on the divine Sonship of Christ, and who, like Cullmann, maintain that Christ is named "God" not only in St. John but also in St. Paul, would still, like Calvin, hesitate or refuse to use the title "Mother of God". Professor Torrance frequently cites Chalcedon on Christology, and yet he does not, to my knowledge, ever use the title "Virgin Mary:Mother of God". This may be due to fear lest the title favour a Docetic or Apollinarian view of the Incarnation; or may be from an unreasonable fear lest the use of the title may encourage to Romanist views of Mariology. It is not necessarily due to denial or doubt of Christ's divinity.[504]

Dr. Louis Brighton, in his commentary on the book of Revelation, makes the mistake described by Bernard Leeming. When commenting upon the passage from Revelations 12:1-8, Dr. Brighton admits the passage is about Mary, and that apart from Christ, "no human figure in the entire Bible is so clothed and glorified as this woman."[505] However, in the same context he refers to her as "Mary, the mother of the Christ Child,"[506] something remarkably similar to the Nestorian title: "Mother of Christ." The only other reference to Mary in Brighton's commentary comes in a quotation from the ancient commentary of Oecumenius, in which Mary is called the "θεοτόκος, the 'mother of God'."[507]

I no longer remember why I used to be uncomfortable with the Marian title "Mother of God", and I can find no good theological reason for Protestants to be uncomfortable with it either. The only reason that comes to mind is that it sounds too Catholic, which reason is simply insufficient.

57: The History of the Term Theotókos

The appellation of Theotókos, or Mother of God, was applied very early to the Virgin Mary as a confession of orthodoxy. Peter, Bishop of Alexandria (b. 260-d. 300-311), connects our Lord and the Virgin Mary using the same terms we use today: "...*our Lord and God, Jesus Christ, being in the end of the world born according to the flesh of our holy and glorious lady, Mother of God, and Ever-Virgin.*"[508] In the *Passion of St. Peter, Bishop of Alexandria*, the author writes how after Peter's martyrdom and the collection of his relics: "*they came to the church of the most blessed mother of God, and Ever-Virgin Mary, which, as we began to say, he had constructed in the western quarter, in a suburb, for a cemetery of the martyrs.*"[509] This episode makes it clear that even at this early date, churches were being built in honor of the Ever-Virgin Mary.

Likewise Alexander, Bishop of Alexandria (b. 273– d. 326) writes:

After this we know of the resurrection of the dead, the first-fruits of which was our Lord Jesus Christ, who in very deed, and not in appearance merely, carried a body, of Mary Mother of God, who in the end of the world came to the human race to put away sin, was crucified and died, and yet did He not thus perceive any detriment to His divinity, being raised from the dead, taken up into heaven, seated at the right hand of majesty.[510]

St. Gregory of Nazianzus (c. 330 – 389-390) warns us: "if one does not acknowledge Mary as Theotokos, he is estranged from God."[511]

It is clear, therefore, that the title of Mother of God was used of Mary from antiquity and applied with great seriousness, yet had not yet taken on its full dogmatic force. Nestorius, Archbishop of Constantinople from 428-431 A.D., used his position to object to the term Mother of God, arguing that Mother of Christ was more accurate. The followers of Nestorius, known as Nestorians, held that no one could bring forth that which was anterior in time, and that therefore Mary was the mother of Christ, but not of God. St. John of Cassian, writing against Nestorius, says the following: "*We will now prove by Divine testimonies that Christ is God, and that Mary is the Mother of God.*"[512] This highlights the Christological significance of the Nestorian controversy, for if Mary is not the Mother of God, then Christ is not God; and if Christ is not God, then we are still in our sins. At the third Ecumenical Council, held in Ephesus in 431 to discuss the Nestorian controversy, the title of Theotókos was dogmatically applied to the Virgin Mary to resolve the Christological controversy.[513] The Third Ecumenical Council confirmed by subscription The Letter of Cyril to John of Antioch (which is sometimes styled the "Ephesine Creed"); the relevant extract is quoted below.

We confess, therefore, our Lord Jesus Christ, the Only Begotten Son of God, perfect God, and perfect Man of a reasonable soul and flesh consisting; begotten before the ages of the Father according to his Divinity, and in the last days, for us and for our salvation, of Mary the Virgin according to his humanity, of the same substance with his Father according to his Divinity, and of the same substance with us according to his humanity; for there became a union of two natures. Wherefore we confess one Christ, one Son, one Lord. According to this understanding of this unmixed union, we confess the holy Virgin to be Mother of God; because God the Word was incarnate and became Man, and from this conception he united the temple taken from her with himself.[514]

Marian Types, Symbols, and Titles

The Epistle of Cyril [of Alexandria (c. 376-444)] to Nestorius, quoted in the Acts of the Third Ecumenical Council, states the following:

This expression, however, "the Word was made flesh," can mean nothing else but that he partook of flesh and blood like to us; he made our body his own, and came forth man from a woman, not casting off his existence as God, or his generation of God the Father, but even in taking to himself flesh remaining what he was. This the declaration of the correct faith proclaims everywhere. This was the sentiment of the holy Fathers; therefore they ventured to call the holy Virgin, the Mother of God, not as if the nature of the Word or his divinity had its beginning from the holy Virgin, but because of her was born that holy body with a rational soul, to which the Word being personally united is said to be born according to the flesh.[515]

St. Cyril of Alexandria, in the *Anathematisms* attached to the Acts of the Third Ecumenical Council, writes: "If anyone will not confess that the Emmanuel is very God, and that therefore the Holy Virgin is the Mother of God (Θεοτόκος), inasmuch as in the flesh she bore the Word of God made flesh [as it is written, "The Word was made flesh"] let him be anathema."

The editor's comments on the *Anathematisms*, entitled *Excursus on the Word* Θεοτόκος, writes at length regarding the connection between the Incarnation and the necessity of the dogmatic use of the term Theotokos.

A similar attempt to reduce to a logomachy [dispute over words] the difference between the Catholic faith and Nestorianism has been made by some writers of undoubted learning among Protestants, notably by Fuchs and Schröckh. But as in the case of the homousios so, too, in the case of the theotocos the word expresses a great, necessary, and fundamental doctrine of the Catholic faith. It is not a matter of

324

words, but of things, and the mind most unskilled in theology cannot fail to grasp the enormous difference there is between affirming, as does Nestorianism, that a God indwelt a man with a human personality of his own distinct from the personality of the indwelling god; and that God assumed to himself human nature, that is a human body and a human soul, but without human personality. ... It is no part of my duty to defend the truth of either the Catholic or Nestorian proposition — each has found many adherents in most ages since it was first started, and probably what is virtually Nestorianism is to-day far more widely held among persons deemed to be orthodox than is commonly supposed. Be this as it may, Nestorianism is clearly subversive of the whole Catholic Doctrine of the Incarnation, and therefore the importance of the word Θεοτόκος cannot be exaggerated.[516] [The alternative spelling of Theotokos is in the original]

Regarding the nature of the term Theotokos, Georges Florovsky writes:

The word does not occur in Scripture, just as the term ὁμοούσιος [homoousios; same in substance] does not occur. But surely, neither at Nicaea nor at Ephesus was the Church innovating or imposing a new article of faith. An "unscriptural" word was chosen and used, precisely to voice and to safeguard the traditional belief and common conviction of ages. It is true, of course, that the Third Ecumenical Council was concerned primarily with the Christological dogma and did not formulate any special Mariological doctrine. But precisely for that very reason it was truly remarkable that a Mariological term would have been selected and put forward as the ultimate test of Christological orthodoxy, to be used, as it were, as a doctrinal Shibboleth in the Christological discussion. It was really a key-word to the whole of Christology.[517]

On that note, we shall let Fr. John Andrew McGuckin have the last word.

The Virgin Mary stands not only as a Christological bulwark, epitomizing the ultimate 'scandal of our faith' that if she is called the Theotokos, her Son must be confessed as divine (God of God, Light of Light, true God or true God, as the Creed has it). But in many ways she is a 'Bronze Gate' in a contemporary world abounding in reductionist and faithless exegesis. She who treasured all these stories and tales of wonder about her Son in her heart, as the evangelist tells us, is still one who refused to allow the sacred kerygma of the Gospel to be watered down and made palatable to the tastes and conceptions of those who are far from being deeply rooted in the strange and paradoxical ways of a God who, with the world's salvation in the balance, chose a simple and innocent heart which was ready to say to him: 'Let it be done in me, as I am your servant.' The choice of an unmarried first-century Jewish woman from a rural backwater was a contradiction of the 'wisdom of this world', and still is. It is perhaps, why theological reflection on the Theotokos (so prevalent and powerful in the early church) has fallen into relative silence today. Nevertheless, those disciples who know that God does not see as humans see, but looks into the quality of the heart and faith of human beings, know that the divine election follows ways that often seem surprising, incredible, or plain bizarre to the rational gaze.[518]

The Theotokos and the Creeds

John Meyendorff, in his exposition on the dogmatic formula of Chalcedon,[519] makes the connection between the Christ and the Mother of God clear. "The Latin formulas included in the definition ("each nature preserving its own way of being," "in two natures") ...are balanced by the remarkable insistence on the personal unity of Christ. The word Θεοτόκος [Theotokos], implying the *communication*

326

idiomatum [communication of idioms or attributes], is also used."[520] Thus the title of Theotokos is an oblique reference to and defense of the consubstantial union of the divine and human natures in the person of Christ.

"The name *Theotokos* is an inevitable sequel to the name *Theanthropos,* the God-Man. Both stand and fall together."[521] In this way the title *Theotokos,* or Mother of God, represents a theological appreciation of the two natures in Christ, which the church confesses in the Chalcedonian formula and is preserved in the Athanasian Creed of the western church: "*our Lord Jesus Christ, the Son of God, is at once God and man: he is God, begotten before the ages of the substance of the Father, and he is man, born in the world of the substance of his mother, perfect God and perfect man, with reasonable soul and human flesh.*" The name *Theotokos* is not a celebration of Mary, but rather a confession of the Christ as both God and man, conceived of the Holy Spirit of the flesh of the Virgin Mary. For this reason St. John of Damascus(b. 676 – d. 749), commenting upon the title of Theotokos in his *Exposition of the Orthodox Faith*, writes: "The name of the Mother of God contains all the history of the divine economy in this world."[522,523]

It should be remembered as well that the Christian church had initially reacted against the Gnostics, who held to a dualistic view of soul and body, such that the material world was by nature bad, and therefore beneath the dignity of God.

James Kiefer sums up the distinction between the Gnostics and the Christian church using the Apostles Creed.

A CREED generally emphasizes the beliefs opposing those errors that the compilers of the creed think most dangerous at the time. The Creed of the Council of Trent, which was drawn up by the Roman Catholics in the 1500's, emphasized those beliefs that Roman Catholics and

327

Protestants were arguing about most furiously at the time. The Nicene Creed, drawn up in the fourth century, is emphatic in affirming the Deity of Christ, since it is directed against the Arians, who denied that Christ was fully God. The Apostles' Creed, drawn up in the first or second century, emphasizes the true Humanity, including the material body, of Jesus, since that is the point that the heretics of the time (Gnostics, Marcionites, and later Manicheans) denied. (See 1 John 4:1-3)

Thus the Apostles' Creed is as follows:

* I believe in God the Father Almighty,

* Maker of Heaven and Earth,

The Gnostics held that the physical universe is evil and that God did not make it.

* And in Jesus Christ, His only Son, Our Lord,

* Who was conceived by the Holy Ghost,

* Born of the Virgin Mary,

The Gnostics were agreed that the orthodox Christians were wrong in supposing that God had taken human nature or a human body. Some of them distinguished between Christ, whom they acknowledged to be in some sense divine, and the man Jesus, who was at most an instrument through whom the Christ spoke. They held that the man Jesus did not become the bearer or instrument of the Christ until the Spirit descended upon him at his baptism, and that the Spirit left him before the crucifixion, so that the Spirit had only a brief and tenuous association with matter and humanity. Others affirmed that there was never a man Jesus at all, but only the appearance of a man, through which appearance wise teachings were given to the first disciples. Against this the orthodox Christians affirmed that Jesus was conceived through the action of the Holy Spirit (thus denying the Gnostic position that the Spirit had nothing to do with Jesus until his Baptism), that he was born (which meant that he had a real physical body, and not just an appearance) of a virgin (which implied that he had been special from the first moment of his life, and not just from the baptism on.[524]

For these reasons, as Florovsky writes, the Mariological doubts held by the churches of the Reformation are signs of a confused and an incomplete Christology.

The Christological doctrine can never be accurately and adequately stated unless a very definite teaching about the Mother of Christ has been included. In fact, all the Mariological doubts and errors of modern times depend in the last resort precisely upon an utter Christological confusion. They reveal a hopeless "conflict in Christology." There is no room for the Mother of God in a "reduced Christology." Protestant theologians simply have nothing to say about her. Yet to ignore the Mother means to misinterpret the Son. On the other hand, the person of the Blessed Virgin can be properly understood and rightly described only in a Christological setting and context. Mariology ...belongs to the very body of doctrine. The Mystery of the Incarnation includes the Mother of the Incarnate.[525]

The Theotokos and Chalcedonian Christology

Should someone doubt that Mary, the Mother of God, is an integral part of Christology, we should remember the formula put forth by the Fourth Ecumenical Council — known as the Council of Chalcedon (A.D. 451) — a formula which is definitive for Christology:

Following the holy Fathers we teach with one voice that the Son [of God] and our Lord Jesus Christ is to be confessed as one and the same [Person], that he is perfect in Godhead and perfect in manhood, very God and very man, of a reasonable soul and [human] body consisting, consubstantial with the Father as touching his Godhead, and consubstantial with us as touching his manhood; made in all

329

things like unto us, sin only excepted; begotten of his Father before the worlds according to his Godhead; but in these last days for us men and for our salvation born [into the world] of the Virgin Mary, the Mother of God according to his manhood. This one and the same Jesus Christ, the only-begotten Son [of God] must be confessed to be in two natures, unconfusedly, immutably, indivisibly, inseparably [united], and that without the distinction of natures being taken away by such union, but rather the peculiar property of each nature being preserved and being united in one Person and subsistence, not separated or divided into two persons, but one and the same Son and only-begotten, God the Word, our Lord Jesus Christ, as the Prophets of old time have spoken concerning him, and as the Lord Jesus Christ hath taught us, and as the Creed of the Fathers hath delivered to us.[526]

Martin Chemnitz, the great second-generation Lutheran theologian (known as the second Martin),[527] in his book *The Two Natures in Christ,* confirms the Chalcedonian formula. *"Therefore God, whom we call the Lord, the Son of God, and the Logos by the conception of His own flesh and by His nativity, can be said because of the hypostatic union to have been conceived and born of the Virgin Mary, who is therefore correctly called the mother of the Lord and the God-bearer (Θεοτόκος)."*[528]

Chemnitz describes at length why the Christological title *Theotokos* is necessary.

[T]he Son of God from eternity subsisted in the divine nature before assuming the human nature. For the flesh of Christ was not first formed and animated separately in the womb of Mary in such a way that afterwards the person of the Logos was united with this preformed and animated flesh. For this would mean that the human nature of Christ at some time would have had its own proper and peculiar subsistence before and outside the hypostatic union with the

Logos. Nor would Mary have been the God-bearer (θεοτόχος). Of necessity it would follow that there are two persons in the incarnate Christ. But the angel expressly said that by this conception in and of Mary there should be born the Son of God (Luke 1:35). And He whom Mary conceived is called Immanuel (Matt. 1:23). Therefore, this individual unit of human nature, which by the operation of the Spirit in the conception was separated from the person of the Virgin Mary, at no time and at no moment of time existed or subsisted of and in itself before or outside the hypostatic union with the Logos.[529]

As Martin Chemnitz writes, in line with the common consensus of the Orthodox Fathers, calling Mary the *Theotokos*, the God-bearer, the Mother of God, is a confession of the Incarnation, of the divine and human natures united in the one person of Christ.

In the end, the Protestant failure to use the title "Mother of God" seems to result more from Catholiphobia than doctrinal disagreement. Yet it also cannot be denied that as the title was used to safeguard the two natures in Christ, the failure to use this title reopens the door to Gnosticism and Nestorianism.

58: Aeiparthenos, or Ever-Virgin

It is an article of faith that Mary is Mother of the Lord and still a virgin.[530]
Martin Luther

Helvidius has shown himself too ignorant, in saying that Mary had several sons, because mention is made in some passages of the brothers of Christ.[531]
John Calvin
(Calvin said "brothers" in this context meant cousins or relatives.)

I esteem immensely the Mother of God, the ever chaste, immaculate Virgin Mary.[532]
Ulrich Zwingli, early Swiss reformer.

Belief in the Virgin Birth of Christ is not enough. Islam also teaches His virgin birth, as well as His coming again. For the Muslim, the Virgin Birth is a sign of the role of Jesus as a prophet, but not His being God in the flesh. Muslims will also argue that if Mary has seven children, and six of them were born of the flesh, the seventh was as well.[533] This understanding is the natural manifestation of the radical monotheism of Islam. With this in mind, we begin to understand the manner in which Mary's being ever-virgin protects the God-manhood of the Christ.

Among the orthodox church fathers, the earliest written evidence of the belief in the Virgin Mary's remaining ever virgin comes from a fragmentary work attributed to "Peter of Alexandria (d.311), a predecessor of Athanasius," although Hilda Graef mentions some doubt the authenticity of the document.[534] By contrast, the introductory notice to the works of Peter of Alexandria in the Ante-Nicene Fathers, volume 6, make no mention of any doubtful provenance concerning the fragmentary works. Peter writes: "Jesus Christ ... born according to the flesh from our holy, glorious Lady, Mother of God and Ever-Virgin, Mary."[535]

To discuss the title of Aeiparthenos, or Ever-Virgin, we must return once again to well-trodden ground, if only to remind ourselves of the meaning and its eschatological importance of virginity. Virginity is characterized by sexual abstinence; however, that is just its outward form. Virginity is the external form of chastity, which encompasses the entirety of the person. It is not purely a denial of self, although that is certainly a part of it; in its fullness, it is the means toward and an embrace of the eschatological end. This chastity for the sake of the Kingdom of God is prefigured and exemplified through the Blessed Virgin. George Gabriel writes:

> Incomparably greater than the virginity of all other virgins, her virginity is the only total virginity, for she was perfectly and completely virgin and ever-virgin in a triple manner, "being every-virgin in mind, and in soul, and in body." [John of Damascus, Homily on the Birth of the Theotokos, ch. 5] Her ever-virginity, therefore, was a living affirmation of the "life of the age to come." It was not the bloody battle for virginity waged by those who struggle inside the bounds of nature not yet overcome. Her ever-virginity was the perfect image, even in this life, of the future age and the fulfillment of the Lord's words: "In the resurrection they neither marry, nor are given in marriage." [Mt. 22:30] For the bounds of nature as we presently know them shall be forever overcome at the general resurrection.[536]

Georges Florovsky, writing of the Ever-Virgin Mother of God, makes the following claim: "The whole dogmatic teaching about our Lady can be condensed into these two names of hers: the *Mother of God* and the *Ever-Virgin*, — Θεοτόκος [Theotokos] and ἀειπαρθένος [Aeiparthenos]. Both names have the formal authority of the Church Universal, an ecumenical authority indeed."[537] As we previously discussed, the appellation of Theotokos was subscribed to by the Third Ecumenical Council not to glorify Mary, but to protect Christology. In like manner, the Greek appellation of Aeiparthenos, or Ever-Virgin, was formally applied to the Virgin Mary at the fifth Ecumenical Council, held in Constantinople in 553.[538] Fr. John Anthony McGuckin writes:

> The council of Constantinople II stressed the doctrine of Nicaea more firmly in 553, to afford her the title Aeiparthenos, meaning "Ever Virgin". It is axiomatic to Orthodox belief that the Blessed Virgin was not merely virginal before the conception of Christ, but remained so for all her earthly and heavenly witness afterwards (for as it is with the greatest of the saints and angels, Orthodoxy understands her to be active and powerful in the guidance and help of the earthly church even to the present.). For this reason Orthodoxy understands the New Testament references to the brothers and sisters of Jesus to signify his immediate family in the wider kin-group, but not the biological children of Mary, as if conceived after him (and this is something which is certainly in accordance with biblical idiom, and not in contradiction of it).[539]

Some argue against virginity in general, and of Mary in particular, on the basis of the importance of marriage and child-bearing as part of the covenantal relationship between God and Israel. However, as Fr. John Hainsworth notes, there is scriptural and historical evidence suggesting a more nuanced approach to virginity among the Hebrews.

> To argue against Mary's perpetual virginity is to suggest something else that is greatly implausible, not to say unthinkable: that neither Mary nor her protector, Joseph, would have deemed it inappropriate to have sexual relations

after the birth of God in the flesh. Leaving aside for a moment the complete uniqueness of the Incarnation of the Second Person of the Trinity, recall that it was the practice for devout Jews in the ancient world to refrain from sexual activity following any great manifestation of the Holy Spirit.

An early first-century popular rabbinical tradition (first recorded by Philo, 20 BC-AD 50) notes that Moses "separated himself" from his wife Zipporah when he returned from his encounter with God in the burning bush. Another rabbinical tradition, concerning the choosing of the elders of Israel in Numbers 7, relates that after God had worked among them, one man exclaimed, "Woe to the wives of these men!"[540]

To the ancient Hebrews, as related by rabbinical tradition, it was clear that after bringing their gifts to the tabernacle, whereupon the LORD GOD spoke to Moses from between the cherubim, the elders of Israel were expected to subsequently refrain from sexual relations. There were various other reasons to refrain from sexual relations — for sexual fasting, if you will. For example, a man was not to enjoy conjugal relations with his wife during her monthly cycle, and for seven days afterwards (Lev 15:19-28). Fr. Hainsworth explains that sexual abstinence was not a rejection of the flesh, but instead a matter of consecration to God — which is the sense in which we are to understand the character of Joseph and Mary's marriage.

That culture understood virginity and abstinence not as a mere rejection of something enjoyable--To what end?-- But as something naturally taken up by one whose life has been consecrated by the Lord's Spirit to be a vessel of salvation to His people. The intervening centuries of social, religious, and philosophical conditioning have made us suspicious of virginity and chastity in a way that no one in the Lord's time would have been.

Marian Types, Symbols, and Titles

Mary became the vessel for the Lord of Glory Himself, and bore in the flesh Him whom heaven and earth cannot contain. Would this not have been grounds to consider her life, including her body, as consecrated to God and God alone? Or it more plausible that she would shrug it all off and get on with keeping house in the usual fashion? Consider that the poetically parallel incident of the Lord's entry through the east gate of the Temple (in Ezekiel 43-44) prompts the call: "This gate shall be shut; it shall not be opened, and no one shall enter by it, for the Lord God of Israel has entered by it; therefore it shall be shut" (44:2).

And then there is Joseph's character to consider. Surely his wife's miraculous conception and birthgiving (confirmed by the angel in dream-visions) and the sight of God incarnate in the face of the child Christ would have been enough to convince him that his marriage was set apart from the norm. Within Mary's very body had dwelt the second Person of the Trinity. If touching the ark of the covenant had cost Uzzah his life, and if even the scrolls containing the Law, the Psalms, and the Prophets were venerated, certainly Joseph, man of God that he was, would neither have dared nor desired to approach Mary, the chosen of Israel, the throne of God, to request his "conjugal rights"![541]

The nuanced approach to virginity among the Hebrew people became a celebration of, and in some cases a preference for virginity over marriage within the early church. This approach became dogmatized by the early church councils. For example, the Capitula of the [Fifth Ecumenical] Council contains several statements regarding our Lady, styling her both Theotokos and Aeiparthenos: Mother of God and Ever-Virgin, and actually anathematizes those who reject the use of these terms. But notice the basis for this is not Mariology, but Christology.

II.

IF anyone shall not confess that the Word of God has two nativities, the one from all eternity of the Father, without time and without body; the other in these last days, coming down from heaven and being made flesh of the holy and glorious Mary, Mother of God and **always a virgin**, and born of her: let him be anathema.

VI.

IF anyone shall not call in a true acceptation, but only in a false acceptation, the holy, glorious, and ever-virgin Mary, the Mother of God, or shall call her so only in a relative sense, believing that she bare only a simple man and that God the word was not incarnate of her, but that the incarnation of God the Word resulted only from the fact that he united himself to that man who was born [of her]; if he shall calumniate the Holy Synod of Chalcedon as though it had asserted the Virgin to be Mother of God according to the impious sense of Theodore; or if anyone shall call her the mother of a man (ἀνθρωποτόκον) or the Mother of Christ (Χριστοτόκον), as if Christ were not God, and shall not confess that she is exactly and truly the Mother of God, because that God the Word who before all ages was begotten of the Father was in these last days made flesh and born of her, and if anyone shall not confess that in this sense the holy Synod of Chalcedon acknowledged her to be the Mother of God: let him be anathema.

XIV.

IF anyone shall defend that letter which Ibas is said to have written to Maris the Persian, in which he denies that the Word of God incarnate of Mary, the Holy Mother of God and ever-virgin, was made man, but says that a mere man was born of her, whom he styles a Temple, as though the Word of God was one Person and the man another person ... let him be anathema.[542]

Marian Types, Symbols, and Titles

The Seventh Ecumenical Council, when speaking of the Virgin Mary, first uses the term inviolate in its opening statement. In its subsequent doctrinal statements the Council reverted to using the term "ever-virgin". (The citations are quoted in the subsequent section entitled "Panagia, or All-Holy.") The use of both terms is quite interesting, and illumines Florovsky's statement that the two terms Theotokos and Aeiparthenos contain the whole of Mariology. It is one thing to state that Mary remained Ever-Virgin; it is another to say that she remained Inviolate. The use of both terms suggests that had she lost her virginity, it would have been a violation. But in what sense, exactly? We read that "Marriage is honourable in all, and the bed undefiled" (Heb 13:4). So it is not that sex is unclean or sinful; in fact, within marriage sex is honorable. But Mary's womb is the temple of the Lord; she is the Ark of the New Covenant. Once we come to a discussion of the temple furnishings and temple worship, we must needs remember that a priest was to abstain from sexual relations before serving in the temple, so as not to defile the temple through his ceremonial uncleanness (Lev 22:4; cf Lev 15:1-5).

Florovsky writes:

*[T]he mystery of the Incarnation was for her also the mystery of her own personal existence. Her existential situation was unique and peculiar. She had to be adequate to the unprecedented dignity of this situation. This is perhaps the very essence of her particular dignity, which is described as her "Ever-Virginity." She is **the Virgin**. Now virginity is not simply a bodily status or a physical feature as such. Above all it is a spiritual and inner attitude, and apart from that a bodily status would be altogether meaningless. The title of Ever-Virgin means surely much more than merely a "physiological" statement. It does not refer only to the Virgin Birth. It does not imply only an exclusion of any later marital intercourse (which would be utterly inconceivable if we really*

believe in the Virgin Birth and in the Divinity of Jesus). It excludes first of all any "erotic" involvement, any sensual and selfish desires or passions, any dissipation of the heart and mind. The bodily integrity or incorruption is but an outward sign of the internal purity. The main point is precisely the purity of the heart, that indispensable condition of "seeing God".[543]

Of virginity's essence, George Gabriel writes:

The fathers say that her maternity and her virginity were a condition of her whole person, not only of her body. "She was wholly united to God....Her soul and her body bore God." [John of Damascus, Second Encomium on the Dormition, ch 13.] Her sexuality was transformed into everlasting motherhood to God and, inseparably, into everlasting virginity. She became the Mother of God, not for nine months, not for thirty-three years, but forever. Jesus is forever God the Word. God the Word remains forever Jesus her Son and, therefore, she is forever the Unwedded Bride of the Father. Through her womb and motherhood she transmitted the nature of humanity to God, and He transmitted to her His kingdom, that is, the uncreated power or rule of God. Indeed, if "the kingdom of God is within you," [Luke 17:21], she became the very "Palace of the only King."[544] [First Ode, Canon of the Akathist Hymn.]

We shall let George Gabriel provide our summary to our discussion of the Aeiparthenos, or Ever-Virgin Mary. "Mary's permanent virginity ...was not a subject for the public Gospel. The Holy Spirit reserved it for the interior life and empirical dogmas in the Church."[545]

59: Panagia, or All-Holy

Closely related to the Perpetual Virginity of the Virgin Mary is the teaching that Mary was and remained sinless. Sergius Bulgakov writes: "The Mother of God was sinless, not a single attack of sin approached her most pure soul, the bearer of perfect virginity."[546] How can these things be, you may well ask. I have had more than a little trouble with the idea of the sinlessness of the Virgin Mary, as I find no explicit Scriptural evidence of this. As a former Protestant and relatively recent convert to Orthodoxy, I would be much more comfortable if there were some proof text for the sinlessness of Mary. However, is possible to make an argument from silence regarding the sinlessness of Mary.

The Christian scriptures are quite interesting in that they present its principle characters, warts and all. We see Zacharias doubting God, and a despondent John the Baptist asking if Jesus were really the promised one. We see the disciples demonstrating their lack of faith and their lack of constancy: we see them born up to the heights and quickly dashed to the ground; we see them for the sinners they are. We never see anything like this regarding Mary; we never see any evidence of Mary caught in sin. Some see in Mary some occasional doubts; however, doubt itself is not sin, but rather the weakness of the flesh. Moreover, the case can be made that Mary was never doubting, but merely ignorant of the whole plan of God, and acting from what understanding she had. I therefore admit the possibility that Mary was preserved from sin: I don't know how that might have happened, but given the treatment Mary is given in the Revelation, I suggest that we should consider the possibility — for no one else in scripture (apart from Christ Himself) is described likc the apostle John described Mary — both in his Gospel, and in the Revelation.

Panagia, or All-Holy

The Panagia and Original Sin

The Protestant problem with the sinlessness of Mary is principally derived from their understanding of Original Sin. What we think of as Protestants are actually divided into two main camps: one camp, known as Armenians, believes man is basically good, but corrupted by the fall; the other camp, generally known as the Reformed, believes that after the fall man's nature is basically evil. Generally, when a Protestant refers to Original Sin, he is referring to the guilt for Adam's sin that is transferred from parent to child. This differs from what the early church fathers called ancestral sin (Gr: *amartema*), the idea that sin is an alien corruption attached to human nature, and that each person is responsible for their own sin, not the sins of their fathers.[547]

In the anthropology of the Protestant Church (also known as the Doctrine of Man, and following the tradition of Augustine of Hippo, Anselm of Canterbury, and the Roman Catholic Church), humanity is defined by Original Sin, by the guilt for Adam's sin which is born by all humanity. The Presbyterian Confession of Faith provides the following definition of Original Sin:

> *Man, by his fall into a state of sin, hath wholly lost all ability of will to any spiritual good accompanying salvation; so as a natural man being altogether averse from that good, and dead in sin, is not able, by his own strength, to convert himself, or to prepare himself thereunto.*[548]

This simple definition is basically an argument against Pelagianism, the heresy that man can defeat sin by an act of the human will apart from Divine aid. However, as interpreted and expounded upon by R. L. Dabney, this anti-Pelagian statement becomes an argument for the imputed guilt of Adam's sin. Dabney argues for a state of sin, apart from the guild of personal sins, when he writes:

Marian Types, Symbols, and Titles

What we teach is that by the fall man's moral nature has undergone an utter change to sin, irreparable by himself. In this sense it is complete, decisive—or total. The state is as truly sinful as their actual transgressions, because it is as truly free and spontaneous.[549]

As I was taught growing up, when the Sacred Scriptures speak of Sin, it means the guilt of Adam's sin, our sinful condition; and when the Sacred Scriptures speak of Sins, it is speaking of the guilt of our personal sins. For example, see the following from the apostle John.

But if we walk in the light, as he is in the light, we have fellowship one with another, and the blood of Jesus Christ his Son cleanseth us from all sin. If we say that we have no sin, we deceive ourselves, and the truth is not in us. If we confess our sins, he is faithful and just to forgive us our sins, and to cleanse us from all unrighteousness. If we say that we have not sinned, we make him a liar, and his word is not in us. (1 Joh 1:7-10).

If we interpret this verse according the formula I was taught, the apostle John tells us we are kidding ourselves if we don't think we bear the guilt of Adam's sin, but that if we confess our personal sins, God not only forgives our own sins, but cleanses us from the guilt of Original Sin. This interpretation is plausible from within the Calvinist framework, but actually does violence to the text. The apostle John repeats himself in this passage, using the singular in one place and the plural in the other, making it clear there is no hidden distinction between "sin" and "sins". The apostle first writes: "if we say that we have no sin"; and then he writes: "If we say we have not sinned." The two phrases say the same thing.

However, this passage from the apostle John is important for our understanding of the Holiness of the Virgin Mary — especially in light of the apostle Paul's statement: "for all have sinned, and come short of the glory of God." How can we claim the Holiness of the Virgin Mary, while at the same time claim that all have sinned?

The concept of Original Sin may have been derived from Tertullian, but the term itself originated with Augustine.[550] However, even Blessed Augustine, in his dispute with the Pelagians, did not include the Virgin Mary with the rest of humanity. Augustine's position was that the sinlessness of Mary was by means of the abundance of grace accorded her so that she would merit the conception and parenting of our Lord.

We must except the holy Virgin Mary, concerning whom I wish to raise no question when it touches the subject of sins, out of honour to the Lord; for from Him we know what abundance of grace for overcoming sin in every particular was conferred upon her who had the merit to conceive and bear Him who undoubtedly had no sin.[551]

Augustine's term was taken in a different direction by the western Church, eventually becoming imbued with meanings Augustine never intended.

While the Greek appellation of Panagia, or All-Holy, was never formally applied to Mary by any of the Seven Ecumenical Councils, the doctrine underlying the term clearly has a conciliar and ecumenical basis. Among the Eastern Orthodox, this title denotes the doctrine that the Virgin Mary is free from actual sin, but as the Orthodox do not embrace the Augustinian doctrine of original sin, the doctrine stops there.[552] Among the Roman Catholics, this title of Panagia represents the dogma that the Virgin Mary is free from original sin, which then became the basis for the Roman Catholic dogma of the Immaculate Conception of the Virgin Mary.

Marian Types, Symbols, and Titles

Sacred Scripture seem to present a problem for those expressing a belief in the holiness of the Virgin Mary. Vladimir Lossky writes:

Some passages in the gospels, if viewed externally, from a point of view outside Church tradition, seem to contradict quite flagrantly the extreme glorification and unlimited veneration of the Theotokos, in the Church. Let us take two examples. Christ, when bearing witness to John the Baptist, calls him the greatest of them that are born of women. It is therefore to him, and not to Mary, that the highest position among human beings should belong (Matt. xi. 11, Luke vii.28). ...Another passage in the gospels shows us Christ publicly opposing the glorification of his Mother. He answers the exclamation of the woman in the crowd who crises out 'Blessed be the womb that bare thee, and the paps that thou hast sucked', by saying 'Yea, rather, Blessed are they that hear the Word of God, and keep it' (Luke xi. 27-28).[553]

As mentioned before, these passages are not always clear in their meaning. The Christian church, up until the time of the reformation, always explained these passages in a manner that supported the veneration of Mary, and even her holiness. By contrast, the churches of the Reformation have proposed (and imposed) alternate interpretations. Vladimir Lossky explains this as the result of their rejection of church tradition, which includes a particular interpretation of these passages. "Apart from Church tradition, theology would be dumb on this subject and unable to justify this astounding glorification. This is why Christian communities which reject the idea of tradition in every form are also alien to the cult of the Mother of God."[554]

However, it is possible to construct an alternate interpretation of the passages concerning John the Baptist. Remember the context; John the Baptist was in prison and was soon to be beheaded. He sent his disciples to Jesus to

Panagia, or All-Holy

ask if He was indeed the one who was to come, or if they should wait for another. After sending reassurances to John the Baptist, Jesus addressed the crowd.

What went ye out into the wilderness for to see? A reed shaken with the wind? But what went ye out for to see? A man clothed in soft raiment? Behold, they which are gorgeously apparelled, and live delicately, are in kings' courts. But what went ye out for to see? A prophet? Yea, I say unto you, and much more than a prophet. This is he, of whom it is written, Behold, I send my messenger before thy face, which shall prepare thy way before thee. For I say unto you, Among those that are born of women there is not a greater prophet than John the Baptist: but he that is least in the kingdom of God is greater than he (Luke 7:28).

It is important to note what Jesus is saying here. He is explicitly contrasting the prophets of the Old Covenant with those of the New. John the Baptist was the last and the greatest of the prophets of the Old Covenant. Jesus makes this clear by His closing statement: "He that is least in the kingdom of God is greater than he [meaning John the Baptist]." In this context we can understand how someone could be considered greater than John the Baptist, but we have not yet discovered how that concept applies to the Virgin Mary.

Once again we must consider the passage in the gospels where Jesus seems to be arguing against the veneration of Mary. "And it came to pass, as he spake these things, a certain woman of the company lifted up her voice, and said unto him, Blessed is the womb that bare thee, and the paps which thou hast sucked. But he said, Yea rather, blessed are they that hear the word of God, and keep it" (Luke 11: 27-28). I note first of all that it was a "woman of the company", by which is meant one of the women who travelled with and supported Jesus' ministry. Thus it is

345

reasonable to assume she was making an explicit reference to the Virgin Mary. It should also be noted the grounds upon which her glorification of the Blessed Virgin were purely fleshly — her being the Mother of God according to the flesh. Jesus assertion is totally in keeping with his other assertions concerning the relative unimportance of familial associations. Instead of her being blessed for having given birth to the man Jesus, who is the Christ, Mary is to be honored for hearing the Word of God, and keeping it.

And so we come, finally, to an understanding of how Mary could be both least in the Kingdom of God, and greater than John the Baptist. While John was the last and greatest of the prophets, Mary was and remains the least and therefore the first in the kingdom of heaven.

The Holiness of Mary and the Fathers of the Church

Hippolytus, third from the apostles (being the disciple of Irenaeus, who was the disciple of Polycarp, who was the disciple of the apostle John), may be one of the first of the church fathers to apply the appellations "all-holy" and "ever-virgin" to the Virgin Mary. It is clear Hippolytus was preserving the apostolic teachings, for not only was he not condemned as a heretic, but his works were valued enough to be laboriously copied by hand and distributed to various Christian churches, thereby being preserved for our benefit. Note that in the quote below, Hippolytus states (without apparent contradiction) that the personal holiness and perpetual virginity of Mary is the pious confession of believers, which confession is inextricably linked to the confession of Christ as both God and man of the Virgin Mary.

But the pious confession of the believer is that, with a view to our salvation, and in order to connect the universe with unchangeableness, the Creator of all things incorporated with Himself a rational soul and a sensible body from the all-

holy Mary, ever-virgin, by an undefiled conception, without conversion, and was made man in nature, but separate from wickedness.[555]

Serious questions exist regarding the sinlessness or personal holiness of the Virgin Mary. For most Protestants, this idea is connected with the Roman Catholic dogma of the Immaculate Conception. Of course some connection exists between the two concepts, but Protestants ought not dismiss the idea of the sinlessness of Mary on the basis of an animosity towards the Latins, or because of theological issues with the dogma of the Immaculate Conception of Mary.

The basic Eastern Orthodox understanding is: "Mary, as a human being, could indeed have sinned, but chose not to."[556] However, Protestants have scriptural arguments with the idea of the sinlessness of Mary, in that the Sacred Scriptures state that all have sinned and come short of the glory of God (Ro 3:23), and that there are none that doeth good, no not one (Ps 14:3; 53:3; Ro 3:10, 12). The Eastern Orthodox understanding is in some sense closer to the Protestants than one might imagine. Saint John (Maximovitch) of Shanghai & San Francisco writes the following in opposition to the Roman Catholic dogma of the Immaculate Conception.

The teaching of the complete sinlessness of the Mother of God (1) does not correspond to Sacred Scripture, where there is repeatedly mentioned the sinlessness of the One Mediator between God and man, the man Jesus Christ (I Tim. 2:5); and in Him is no sin (John 3:5); Who did no sin, neither was guile found in His mouth (I Peter 2:22); One that hath been in all points tempted like as we are, yet without sin (Heb. 4:15); Him Who knew no sin, He made to be sin on our behalf (II Cor. 5:2 1). But concerning the rest of men it is said, Who is pure of defilement? No one who has lived a single day

347

of his life on earth (Job 14:4). God commendeth His own love toward us in that, while we were yet sinners, Christ died for us. If, while we were enemies, we were reconciled to God through the death of His Son, much more, being reconciled, shall we be saved by His life (Rom. 5:8-10).[557]

Saint John (Maximovitch) also writes concerning the universality of Original Sin (by which the Orthodox mean ancestral sin, which means an inheritance of corruption attached to human nature instead of a corrupted nature and the guilt that comes with it):

This same Holy Father teaches concerning the universality of original sin, from which Christ alone is an exception. "Of all those born of women, there is not a single one who is perfectly holy, apart from the Lord Jesus Christ, Who in a special new way of immaculate birthgiving, did not experience earthly taint" (St. Ambrose, Commentary on Luke, ch. 2). "God alone is without sin. All born in the usual manner of woman and man, that is, of fleshly union, become guilty of sin. Consequently, He Who does not have sin was not conceived in this manner" (St. Ambrose, Ap. Aug. "Concerning Marriage and Concupiscence"). "One Man alone, the Intermediary between God and man, is free from the bonds of sinful birth, because He was born of a Virgin, and because in being born He did not experience the touch of sin."[558]

And finally, Saint John (Maximovitch) quotes St. Bernard, Abbot of Clairvaux[559] on this subject:

"I say that the Virgin Mary could not be sanctified before Her conception, inasmuch as She did not exist. If, all the more, She could not be sanctified in the moment of Her conception by reason of the sin which is inseparable from conception, then it remains to believe that She was sanctified after She was conceived in the womb of Her mother. This sanctification, if it annihilates sin, makes holy Her birth, but

not Her conception. No one is given the right to be conceived in sanctity; only the Lord Christ was conceived of the Holy Spirit, and He alone is holy from His very conception. Excluding Him, it is to all the descendants of Adam that must be referred that which one of them says of himself, both out of a feeling of humility and in acknowledgement of the truth: Behold I was conceived in iniquities (Ps. 50:7). How can one demand that this conception be holy, when it was not the work of the Holy Spirit, not to mention that it came from concupiscence? The Holy Virgin, of course, rejects that glory which, evidently, glorifies sin. She cannot in any way justify a novelty invented in spite of the teaching of the Church, a novelty which is the mother of imprudence, the sister of unbelief, and the daughter of lightmindedness" (Bernard, Epistle 174; cited, as were the references from Blessed Augustine, from Lebedev). The above-cited words clearly reveal both the novelty and the absurdity of the new dogma of the Roman church.[560]

I must confess that — perhaps as an artifact of my Protestant upbringing — I found the Protestant arguments compelling. However, the longer I study the issue, the more I find the sinlessness of Mary, as defined by Eastern Orthodoxy, to be consistent with Sacred Scripture and attested to by the church fathers.

Regarding the dogma of the Immaculate Conception of the Virgin Mary, Fr. Seraphim Rose draws an interesting connection to the Calvinist doctrines of Irresistible Grace and Predestination.

The teaching that the Mother of God was preserved from original sin, as likewise the teaching that She was preserved by God's grace from personal sins, makes God unmerciful and unjust; because if God could preserve Mary from sin and purify Her before Her birth, then why does He not purify other men before their birth, but rather leaves them in sin? It follows likewise that God saves men apart from their will, predetermining certain ones before their birth to salvation.[561]

This is an interesting argument, because it suggests a scholastic inconsistency in both Roman Catholicism & Protestantism. If God could save one from the guilt of Original Sin, then God could save all from sin. This lays the responsibility for sin back upon God, and makes God unjust, unmerciful, and capricious. Furthermore, if God could arrange the conception of one without sin, God could have accomplished the same for everyone. When connected with the western idea that the death of the Son of God pays the penalty for our sins, it also makes the death of God unnecessary, because one born without the guilt of Original Sin and supernaturally preserved from personal sin has committed no crime against God's law, and therefore has no need of a savior. If God had another option available, but chose the one that caused the death of His only-begotten Son, that makes God some kind of a monster to be feared, rather than the God who is love, and whom we love in return. There are some tortured arguments against this line of reasoning, but like the legend of Alexander the Great and the Gordian Knot, I prefer to cut through all the nonsense.

60: Mary as the New Eve

The apostle Paul writes comparing the first Adam and the last Adam, which is Christ. "For as by one man's disobedience many were made sinners, so by the obedience of one shall many be made righteous" (Rom 5:19). Paul explicitly references the obedience of Christ as opposed to the disobedience of Adam, through whom "sin entered the world, and death by sin" (Rom 5:12). The creedal phrase "born of the Virgin Mary" has in view not only the Nativity, but the Annunciation, and therefore includes Mary's statement of obedience: "Behold the handmaid of the Lord; be it unto me according to thy word" (Lu 1:38). By this statement the Virgin Mary accepted the Word of God, knowing that it would be the cause of much suffering on her part. She did not run away from the path set before her: despising the shame, she trusted in the messianic promises and was obedient to God's will. Thus the obedience of the Virgin Mary is a foretaste of the obedience of Jesus Christ.

The discussion of Jesus being the seed of the woman moves quite naturally into a discussion of Mary as being the new Eve (or the antitype of Eve, also called the doctrine of the spiritual motherhood of men),[562] for while Eve was deceived, Mary was obedient.

Jaroslav Pelikan points out that taken chronologically, the first New Testament book to reference Mary is Galatians; not only that, but Paul's interpretation of the Old Testament formed the basis for the understanding of Mary as the New Eve.

"When in the fullness of the time was come, God sent forth his Son, made of a woman, made under the law, to redeem them that were under the law, that we might receive the adoption of sons." [Gal 4:4-5] Most New Testament scholars would agree that "Made of a woman" did not mean or even imply "but not of a man" (although it also did not

exclude the idea of the virgin birth), but rather that it was a Semitic expression for "Human being," as in the statement "Man that is born of woman is of few days, and full of trouble." [Job 14:1] ...Thus the phrase in Galatians was taken from early times as a way of speaking about Jesus Christ as truly human. ...[A]ssociated with this New Testament point was one of the devices employed by the apostle Paul to make this same point about the true humanity of Christ, which he did on the basis of a special interpretation of the Old Testament. It was expressed in the verse "As by one man's disobedience many were made sinners, so by the obedience of one shall many be made righteous," [Rom 5:19] through the One to whom she gave birth. ...[B]ecause Mary, the Second Eve, was the heir of the history of Israel, the history of the First Eve could be — or, as the early Christians saw it, had to be — read as a biblical resource and a historical source for providing more information about her.[563]

Eve was the mother of all sinners, for all mankind was yet in her womb at the time of her disobedience, making her the Mother of all Sinners (for all have sinned). Mary became not only the Mother of God, but the mother of the sons of God — for the last Adam was Himself conceived by the Holy Spirit, yet born of the Virgin Mary. L. S. Thornton describes the "Eva-Ave" doctrine this way: "[It] is the teaching that the disobedience of Eve is reversed in the response of Mary to the message of the Archangel. For Latin writers the reversal with all its joyful consequences was symbolized in the replacement of Eva by the 'Ave' of the angelic salutation."[564] In this way we may say that Mary is the Mother of the Christian Race: of all who believe in the incarnate Son of God, who was crucified for our sins, was buried, and rose again on the third day.

The Pauline comparison between "one man's disobedience" and "the obedience of the one" is obviously a reference to the first and last Adam. But the phrase "the obedience of the one" also applies to the Virgin Mary. The obedience of the Virgin Mary, according to Irenaeus, is a parallel and recapitulation of the first disobedience of the virgin Eve. In this way the life of Mary is given a theological significance paralleling the first Adam/last Adam imagery used by the apostle Paul in I Cor 15.

That the Lord then was manifestly coming to His own things, and was sustaining them by means of that creation which is supported by Himself, and was making a recapitulation of that disobedience which had occurred in connection with a tree, through the obedience which was [exhibited by Himself when He hung] upon a tree, [the effects] also of that deception being done away with, by which that virgin Eve, who was already espoused to a man, was unhappily misled, — was happily announced, through means of the truth [spoken] by the angel to the Virgin Mary, who was [also espoused] to a man. For just as the former was led astray by the word of an angel, so that she fled from God when she had transgressed His word; so did the latter, by an angelic communication, receive the glad tidings that she should sustain (portaret) God, being obedient to His word. And if the former did disobey God, yet the latter was persuaded to be obedient to God, in order that the Virgin Mary might become the patroness (advocata) of the virgin Eve. And thus, as the human race fell into bondage to death by means of a virgin, so is it rescued by a virgin; virginal disobedience having been balanced in the opposite scale by virginal obedience. For in the same way the sin of the first created man (protoplasti) receives amendment by the correction of the First-begotten, and the coming of the serpent is conquered by the harmlessness of the dove, those bonds being unloosed by which we had been fast bound to death.[565, 566]

In his commentary on Luke, Dr. Just points to the "parallels between the corporate and individual promises", by which he means the corporate promises made to Israel and the individual promises made to Mary.[567] Based on these parallels, Dr. Just suggests Mary can be "seen as representing the new Israel, the church, the virgin bride of Christ." She is the "mother of God's Son, and of God's sons." Just also describes the connection between Eve and Mary: "As Eve contained in her whom all humanity that was doomed to sin, now Mary contains in her womb the new Adam who will father a new humanity by His grace (Rom 5:12-21)." Part of the Annunciation, Luke 1:31b -1:33, form a catechesis of the King and his kingdom. Therefore, "Mary is the mother of God, and also the first catechumen. She sets the pattern for all who will follow her."[568] Therefore we honor the Virgin Mary as the new Eve, through whose obedience our Lord was incarnate of the Holy Ghost by the Virgin Mary.

Jacob of Serug, in his Homily Concerning the Blessed Virgin, Mother of God, Mary, writes the following concerning the Annunciation and the overturning of Eve's legacy.

Maiden and Watcher met each other and conversed in argument on the matter
> *until they abolished the conflict between the Lord and Adam.*

That great strife which occurred amidst the trees came up for discussion,
> *and it all came to an end; there was peace.*

An earthly being and a heavenly one spoke with love;
> *the struggle between the two sides ceased, and they were at peace.*

The evil time which had killed Adam was changed;
> *another good time came in which he would be raised.*

Instead of that serpent, Gabriel arose to speak;

instead of Eve, Mary began to consent.
Instead of the treacherous one who brought death by the tale
he set forth,

> *the truthful one arose to announce life by the tidings*
> *which he brought.*

Instead of the mother who wrote among the trees what she
owed,

> *the daughter paid all the debts of Adam, her father.*

Eve and the serpent with the Watcher and Mary were
transmuted;

> *that affair was put right which had become distorted from*
> *the beginning.*

See how Eve's ear inclines and hearkens

> *to the voice of the deceiver when he hisses deceit to her.*

But come and see the Watcher instilling salvation into Mary's
ear

> *and removing the insinuation of the serpent from her and*
> *consoling her.*

The building which the serpent pulled down, Gabriel built up;

> *Mary rebuilt the foundation which Eve broke down in*
> *Eden.*[569]

The correspondence of Eve and the Virgin Mary is also connected with paradise lost and paradise regained; of virginity lost and virginity regained. In this context, virginity is ontological, not merely physical. The writings of Paul Evdokimov serve to close out this discussion.

Eve's virginity was but a condition she lost, and, as Jacom Böhme says, "Virginity flew away to heaven, leaving behind "bad femininity." [570] *With the Theotokos, Virginity has returned to earth; ontologically, Virginity is ready to contain in its depths the One who cannot be contained. The dogma of the Perpetual Virginity in, during, and after giving birth (ante partum, in partu, et post partum) states this precisely while also presenting the Virgin as eternally Mother.*[571]

Eve was deceived, and made a false choice; Adam was not deceived, but sinned freely. As the new Eve, Mary was not deceived and made the correct choice; as the last Adam, Jesus did not sin, but freely chose the way of the cross. When we confess the Nicene Creed we not only confess the triune God, but we confess the part the Virgin Mary played in our redemption. Mary did not redeem us, but her obedience made possible our redemption. For that we must needs venerate Mary as Mother of God and the spiritual Mother of the Christian Race.

61: Queen of Heaven

In Revelation chapter 12 we see a picture of Mary, clothed with the sun, which is the glory of God (Luke 1:35); [572] crowned with twelve stars, which are likely the apostles (the 24 elders in Revelations are likely the twelve sons of Jacob and the twelve apostles); giving birth to Jesus, who is caught up into heaven before the great dragon (Satan) can destroy him. We see a battle in heaven where Satan is thrown down; and we see a battle on earth, where the dragon pursues Mary. Then, in Rev 12:17 we see that the dragon makes war with the woman *and her seed*. Because Jesus is both head of the church and of the seed of Mary, we too are her seed. Therefore Mary is given the title "Mother of the Christian Race" (or in the parlance of the Latins, the "Mother of the Church"), for she is the mother of all who believe. This passage is also of primary importance for the Marian title "Queen of Heaven".

It is important that we interpret Revelation in light of Scripture; therefore, let us turn to Psalms 44(45):11-18, which is perhaps the most extensive reference to the Virgin Mary in the Old Testament. Psalm 44(45) is one of the so-called Messianic psalms. We see Mary addressed as the daughter (vs. 10, 11, 14); then as the one whose beauty the King desires (v. 12), and whose beauty is from within (v. 14). We see the virgins and neighbors being brought both to her (v. 15), and brought before the King (v. 15-16). As we have discussed this psalm before in the chapter entitled *Hail, Full of Grace*, we shall not delve deeply into it again. It is enough to note that this psalm has typological significance; that "daughter of Tyre" is the type for which the Virgin Mary is the antitype.

We have previously mentioned that in Israel, queens were not the wives of kings, but their mothers. In Jeremiah we have the following: "Say unto the king and to the queen,

Humble yourselves, sit down: for your principalities shall come down, even the crown of your glory." Interestingly, the word for used for queen (הריבג, gebiyrah) actually means queen-mother. We see an example of this in the story of Athaliah, Queen Mother of Ahaziah, who ruled in her son's stead after his death (2 Kings 11:1-20). The paradigmatic example of this is found in the relationship between Bathsheba and her son, King Solomon. Adonijah, who had attempted to usurp the throne of David, yet whose life was spared by Solomon, attempted to usurp the throne through trickery by means of a request made to Bathsheba; it was assumed that Solomon would grant Adonijah's request for the virgin widow of his father David, thereby sealing Adonijah's claim to the throne. Interestingly, in this story the king says he will not say no to his mother, yet ultimately denies the request of Adonijah (1 Kin 2:12-25).

The following illustration helps our understanding. There is a man in a sinking boat with his mother, his wife, and his daughter, and he can save only one of them. Who does he choose? In the East the answer is clearly the mother, because while a man may get married again, and may father a daughter again, he only has one mother. By this we come to an understanding of the Scriptural perspective on the Queen as the mother of King, and how Mary has come to be termed the Queen of Heaven.

We should be remiss if we did not acknowledge that the term queen of heaven is sometimes used in a pejorative sense in Sacred Scripture, as Steven Robinson and Bill Gould described in the program notes to their radio show, before pointing out that scripture can use a term in more than one way.

In Jeremiah we see the term used to refer to a pagan deity. Based on these passages some argue that Mary, who is also called the Queen of Heaven, is a replacement for the pagan goddess and to worship her is to fall into idolatry and be destroyed as Israel was:

1) "Seest thou not what they do in the cities of Judah and in the streets of Jerusalem? The children gather wood, and the fathers kindle the fire, and the women knead their dough, to make cakes to the queen of heaven, and to pour out drink offerings unto other gods, that they may provoke me to anger." [Jeremiah 7:17-18]

2) "As for the word that thou hast spoken unto us in the name of the LORD, we will not hearken unto thee. But we will certainly do whatsoever thing goeth forth out of our own mouth, to burn incense unto the queen of heaven, and to pour out drink offerings unto her, as we have done, we, and our fathers, our kings, and our princes, in the cities of Judah, and in the streets of Jerusalem: for then had we plenty of victuals, and were well, and saw no evil. And when we burned incense to the queen of heaven, and poured out drink offerings unto her, did we make her cakes to worship her, and pour out drink offerings unto her, without our men?" [Jeremiah 44:16-17)

3) "Thus saith the LORD of hosts, the God of Israel, saying; Ye and your wives have both spoken with your mouths, and fulfilled with your hand, saying, We will surely perform our vows that we have vowed, to burn incense to the queen of heaven, and to pour out drink offerings unto her: ye will surely accomplish your vows, and surely perform your vows." [Jeremiah 44:25] God is telling Israel why He is about to destroy them as a nation He is saying that this worship of the Queen of Heaven is "provoking" Him to wrath.

The fact that a particular title is idolatrously used in one context doesn't preclude it being non-idolatrously used in another. The fact that the Devil (or the wicked King of Babylon, depending on your interpretation) is called "the morning star" in Isaiah 14:12 does not mean we cannot use the same title to refer to Jesus, as in 2 Peter 1:19 and Revelation 22:16.

Marian Types, Symbols, and Titles

Pagan myths of dying and rising gods abound: Dionysius, Osiris, Adonis, etc. Parallels can certainly be drawn between them and the Christian doctrines of the Incarnation and Redemption. But such parallels prove nothing — certainly they do not prove that Jesus Christ is just one more dying god myth.[573]

As you may remember from our previous discussion, symbols are polysemic, meaning they have a variety of related meanings. Symbols can refer to multiple things, just as things can be referenced by multiple symbols. In addition, words are often multivalent; they often have a variety of different values or meanings, even within the same context, which values and meanings are inherent in the original language and culture. Therefore, it would help to think of Sacred Scripture as more akin to poetry than prose. In prose, as in the quote often attributed to Sigmund Freud, "Sometimes a cigar is just a cigar". In poetry, however, a cigar is more often than not representative of something else. Given this, we should anticipate that in scripture, the term queen would mean different things in different contexts.

In Psalm 44(45) we see the Mary as both daughter and bride become Queen, which we have just determined to be the Hebrew title for the mother of the king. Thus we arrive at derivation of the title "Queen of Heaven". Paul Evdokimov draws the following relationship: "As the predestined manifestation of God's Wisdom, *Sophia*, she is 'the Gate of Paradise,' she is Jacob's ladder extended, she changes heaven and earth. She gives birth to the divine form on earth, and to the human form in heaven (this is the very specific meaning of the liturgical expression, 'Queen of heaven and earth'."[574]

St. Gregory Palamas, waxed eloquent on this topic.

To which angel were those words ever said, which were addressed to her while still an infant, "The king shall greatly desire thy beauty" (Ps. 45: 11)? Did the angels not rather desire, according to the Scripture, to look into the things bestowed on us through her (cf. 1 Pet. 1: 12)? Isaiah writes concerning the highest angelic orders, "And seraphims stood round about him" (Isa. 6: 2 Lxx), whereas David, again, says of her, "Upon thy right hand did stand the queen" (Ps. 45: 9). Do you see how they stand in different places? Learn from this the distinction between their ranks. The seraphim are round about God, but only the Queen of all is beside Him, she who is admired and extolled even by God Himself, who, as it were, proclaims her to the powers surrounding Him, saying, as it tells us in the Song of Songs, "How fair is my companion?" (cf. Song of Songs 4: 1 Lxx). She is more radiant than light, richer in flowers than paradise, more beautifully adorned than the whole visible and invisible world. She is not just next to God, but, as is fitting, on His right hand. For where Christ took His seat in heaven, "on the right hand of the Majesty on high" (Heb. 1: 3), she stands too, not just because she longs for Him, and is longed for in return, more than all others, even according to the dictates of nature, but because she is truly His throne. And where the King sits, there stands the throne. Isaiah saw this throne in the midst of the choir of cherubim and said it was "high and lifted up" (Isa. 6: 1), showing that the Mother of God is far exalted above the heavenly powers.

That is why the prophet presents the angels themselves glorifying God on her account, saying: "Blessed be the glory of the Lord from his throne" (cf. Ezek. 3: 12). Elsewhere David, uniting in himself the masses of those being saved, and using the different voices of the various races, brought into harmony by her, strikes up that song so appropriate as a hymn, saying: "I will make thy name to be remembered in all generations: therefore shall the people praise thee for ever and ever" (Ps. 45: 17).[575]

We see then that the idea of Mary as the Queen of Heaven is not only derived from Sacred Scripture, but has a very particular meaning, one that is foreign to the western notion of Queen as either the wife of the King, or the ruler in her own right (as we see in Western Europe).

62: Mother of the Christian Race

The subject of the Virgin Mary as the Mother of the Christian Race has previously been discussed in a variety of contexts. Ordinarily it is not considered good practice to repeat oneself; yet because people should expect a central exposition of this topic, I've taken the liberty to pull quotes from other chapters of the book. You can go back and read them in their specific contexts, if you like.

If Mary is the Mother of God (because the Christ child contained in His one person both a divine and a human nature), then Mary could be said to be the mother of all who believe, just as Abraham was called "the father of all them that believe" (Rom 4:16). Mary, as the Mother of God, has become the mother of all who believe in her Son. From there it is but a simple step to call her the Mother of the Christian Race.

Jaroslav Pelikan, in his book *Mary Through the Centuries,* writes:

[Abraham] was what Romans called him, "the father of all them that believe." But if there were to be a "mother of all them that believe," the prime candidate would have to be Mary, just as Eve was identified in the Book of Genesis as "the mother of all living." The key statement by which Mary qualified for such a title was her response to the angel Gabriel and through the angel to the God whose messenger Gabriel was: "Be it unto me according to thy word." For without invoking the word "faith" explicitly, these words put into action the identification of faith with obedience, and by describing her obedience to the word of God made of her the model of faith. Indeed, beginning with Mary and moving backward through the history of Israel, it would be possible to devise a roll call of female saints — Eve and Sarah, Esther and Ruth, and many more — of whom she was an exemplar, just as it would be possible to begin with Mary and construct

a similar roster of female saints since the New Testament era. And by its emphasis on faith such a roster could commend itself even to those heirs of the Protestant Reformation who have traditionally regarded with profound suspicion any such elitism among believers.[576]

In our discussion of the Johannine Witness, we provided the following information. "As Origen notes, this correspondence relates to the identification of each believer with Christ, and Mary's identification as the Mother of the Christian Race."

"We might dare say, then, that the Gospels are the firstfruits of all Scriptures, but that the firstfruits of the Gospels is that according to John, whose meaning no one can understand who has not leaned on Jesus' breast nor received Mary from Jesus to be his mother also. But he who would be another John must also become such as John, to be shown to be Jesus, so to speak. For if Mary had no son except Jesus, in accordance with those who hold a sound opinion of her, and Jesus says to his mother, "Behold your son," and not, "Behold, this man also is your son," he has said equally, "Behold, this is Jesus whom you bore." For indeed everyone who has been perfected "no longer lives, but Christ lives in him," [Gal 2:20] and since "Christ lives" in him, it is said of him to Mary, "Behold your son," the Christ."[577]

Jaroslav Pelikan discusses the meaning behind two short statements of Jesus from the cross.

Among these seven words [of Christ from the cross], John provided the one most directly relevant here: "Woman, behold thy son! Behold thy mother!" Homiletically if not theologically, "Behold thy mother" could easily become the charter for entrusting to the maternal care of Mary not only "the disciple who Jesus loved," identified by the tradition though not by present-day scholarship as John the evangelist, but all the disciples who Jesus loved in all periods of history, therefore the entire church past and present.[578]

And now we see (in part), the importance of the perpetual virginity of Mary. If she had other sons after the flesh, then as Origen makes clear, the statement of Jesus to his mother was merely temporal, not spiritual. But why then would that statement not be in the Gospel of Luke, which is the most historical Gospel, rather than in the Gospel of John, the theological Gospel? If Mary is not ever-virgin, is not *Semper Virgo*, then according to Origin, Pelikan would be incorrect in his assessment — neither homiletically nor theologically can Mary be considered the Mother of the Christian Race.

Now in our discussion of Mary as the New Eve, we made the following statement(s): "Eve contained in her womb all sinners, and is the mother of all sinners. By contrast, Mary contained within her womb Immanuel, God with us, and so became the Mother of the Christian Race, of all who believe." This is an important scriptural point. The God who is with us was first with and within Mary. She bore him, suckled him, cleaned his diapers, dressed him, and raised him into adulthood. There is no indication that Jesus ever lived apart from Mary until He began his ministry. There was no one Jesus was closer to than His mother. She was His first disciple, His first catechumen, and one of His most important witnesses. Some even consider the first two chapters of Luke to be virtually the memoirs of the Virgin Mary.[579] Thus she is not just our exemplar, but she is an evangelist in her own right.

And so we come to our second quote from our discussion of Mary as the New Eve: "When we confess the Creed we not only confess the triune God, but we confess the part the Virgin Mary played in our redemption. Mary did not redeem us, but her obedience made possible our redemption. For that we must needs venerate Mary as

Marian Types, Symbols, and Titles

Mother of God and the spiritual Mother of the Christian Race."

Now the Latins speak of Mary as the mother of the Church,[580] which title is inexact, as Mary is part of the church; thus, Mother of the Christian Race — as opposed to Eve, the mother of all sinners — is more precise. Karl Barth noted the problem as follows:

In the doctrine and worship of Mary there is disclosed the one heresy of the Roman Catholic Church which explains all the rest. The 'mother of God' of Roman Catholic Marian dogma is quite simply the principle, type and essence of the human creature co-operating servantlike (ministerialiter) in its own redemption on the basis of prevenient grace, and that extent the principle, type and essence of the church.[581]

Karl Barth goes on to describe how this too close of an identification of Mary with the Church, and the Church with Mary, led to the promulgation of various problematic dogmas.

Mater ecclesiae is one of the honorific titles ascribed to Mary by Catholic dogmatics. This does not only mean what is obvious because of her mediation of grace, the fact that she is "the mother of all believers" (cf. for this Grosche, op. cit. p. 35f.). It does not only mean that Mary is the heart of Christ's mystical body (Scheeben, op. cit. p. 514). But it means the relation — Scheeben (op. cit. p. 618) speaks of a perichoresis — between her motherhood and the motherhood of the Church. It means an "inner link and resemblance" between the two, so great "that either of the two can be known perfectly only in and with the other." As we must speak of a motherhood of Mary to the redeemed, so, in relation to the eucharistic Christ, we must speak of a motherhood of the Church to Christ. To that extent it holds quite generally and strictly that in Mary "the Church is pictured as the mediatorial principle for applying redemptive grace in respect of her dignity, power and efficacy" (p. 455), "and it is altogether to the point when a Protestant scholar opined that in Mary Catholics glorified and maintained their mystical conception of the Church as the mother and mediatrix of grace" (p. 456). Here, too, the tertium comparationis [common platform of comparison] is clear. Like Mary (and like the pardoned human creature in general) the Church also possesses a relatively independent place and function in the redemptive process. It, too, vies with Christ, in the infinite distance, it is true, between creature and Creator, yet in such a way that not only is it born of Christ but, particularly in the eucharistic centre of its life, Christ is also born of it. Not only does it need Christ, but in all seriousness Christ also needs it. As Mary inevitably co-operates in man's redemption as an "intercessory power," so does the Church in consummating the sacraments. As, therefore, Mary acquires the dignity that distinguishes her from all other creatures, as her existence from her procreation to her death is inevitably an only slightly weaker parallel to the existence of Christ Himself, so, too, within the creaturely limit there may be ascribed to the Church a dignity, authority and omnipotence, whose independence is only too insufficiently relative. Utterly logical was the connexion in the life-work of Pius IX between the proclamation of the immaculata conceptio [Immaculate Conception of Mary] in 1854 and that of papal infallibility in 1870.[582]

Barth begins (with what for us will begin our summation) by announcing: "We reject Mariology, (1) because it is an arbitrary innovation in the face of Scripture and the early Church, and (2) because this innovation consists essentially in a falsification of Christian truth."[583] It is important to note that this section of his *Church Dogmatics* is entirely devoted to refuting the 19th century's new Roman Catholic dogma. Barth can be interpreted as saying "Mariology is simply an outgrowth of Christology which must be pruned away."[584] But as we have already noted, Mariology actually protects Christology; a Christology without Mariology inevitably leaves room for doctrinal error. What Karl Barth is actually denouncing is the 19th century dogmatic declarations of the Immaculate Conception of Mary, and Papal Infallibility; he is actually declaring that these innovations must be pruned away to protect Christology, without actually discussing the Mariological doctrine of the Ecumenical Councils and the Creed.

Therefore, by means of the free choice of the Blessed Virgin, she was found to be with child by the Holy Spirit, and gave birth to the one through whom we receive the adoption of sons, and through whom we can be called sons of God. As we have previously stated, Mary, as the Mother of God, has become the mother of all believers, which makes her the Mother of the Christian Race; and, as we are to judge angels (1 Cor 6:3), she has become higher than the cherubim, and more honorable than the seraphim.

It Is Truly Meet

It is very meet and right to call thee blessed,
Who didst bring forth God,
Ever blessed and most pure
And the Mother of our God.
More honorable than the cherubim,
More glorious than the seraphim,
Who without spot didst bear the Eternal Word,
Thee, very Mother of God,
We laud and magnify.
Glory be to the Father, and the Son, and the Holy Spirit,
Both now and ever, and unto the ages of Ages. Amen.

O Pure Virgin

Refrain: O Rejoice Bride unwedded.
O Virgin pure, immaculate, O Lady Theotokos. (Refrain)
O fleece bedewed with every grace. O Virgin Queen and

Mother of the Christian Race

Mother.(Refrain)
More radiant that the rays of the sun, and higher than the
heavens. (Refrain)
O joy of virgin choruses, superior to the angels. (Refrain)
O brighter than the firmament and purer that the sun's light.
(Refrain)
More holy than the multitude of all the heavenly armies.
(Refrain)

O ever virgin Mary of all the world, the Lady.(Refrain)
O Bride all pure immaculate, O Lady Panagia. (Refrain)
O Mary Bride and Queen of all, the cause of our rejoicing.
(Refrain)
O noble Maiden, gracious Queen,
supremely holy Mother. (Refrain)
More honored than the Cherubim,
beyond compare more glorious(Refrain)
Than the unbodied Seraphim, transcending the angelic
Thrones. (Refrain)

Rejoice, the song of Cherubim rejoice,
the hymn of angels
Rejoice the ode of Seraphim; the joy of the archangels.
Rejoice, O peace and happiness and cause of our rejoicing.
O sacred chamber of the Word, the flower of incorruption.
Rejoice, delightful Paradise of blessed life eternal.
Rejoice O sacred Tree of life and fount of immortality.

I supplicate you, Lady now, I fervently entreat you.
O Queen of all, I earnestly implore and seek your favor.
O gracious Maiden, spotless one, O Lady Panagia.
I call upon you ardently , O holy hallowed Temple.
O help me and deliver me protect me from the enemy.
And make me an inheritor of blessed life eternal.

Epilogue: Why Mary Matters

Mary matters, because the Virgin Mary is the one in whom is best manifest our Lord.[585,586] Over the course of this book I have attempted to unpack this statement, to explain its many nuances, and to place the Virgin Mary within the context of Christology where she belongs. And yet I am afraid that my feeble talents are no match for the glory of the subject matter.

Mary is the Mother of God, the means by which God became flesh. Her free choice, made possible Christ's victory over sin, death, and the devil. She is intimately connected to the life and work of her Son, Jesus Christ. She was present at His death, burial, resurrection, and ascension, and the only person named at Pentecost.

St. Gregory Palamas sums up the importance of Mary in this manner:

> She alone forms the boundary between created and uncreated nature, and no one can come to God except through her and the mediator born of her, and none of God's gifts can be bestowed on angels or men except through her. As in the case with lamps on earth constructed of glass or some other transparent material, it is impossible to look at the light or enjoy its rays except through the lamp, so it is beyond the reach of all to look upwards to God or be helped by Him to make progress in any direction, except through the Ever-Virgin, this God-bearing lamp who is truly radiant with divine brightness. "God is in the midst of her", it says, "she shall not be moved" (Ps. 46: 5).[587]

Church tradition records a number of events in Mary's life, including her travelling to Cyprus where she presented Lazarus, the first bishop of Kition (present-day Larnaka) with his Omophor,[588] which she had woven herself. In the absence of evidence to the contrary, it is perhaps best to accept these as true. It is evident that Mary played a vital role in the spread of the early church.

As we have shown, Mary is likely the source for the early chapters of Luke's gospel, and is represented theologically in John's gospel. She is hinted at in Paul's epistles. She is portrayed in John's apocalypse in a manner unlike anyone else apart from her son, and plays a central role in the story of the devil's defeat.

The scriptures are not silent on the importance of the Virgin Mary. The typological significance of the Virgin Mary is found throughout the Old Testament, but always in connection with her Son. That is indeed the function of the Virgin Mary — she is the Hodegetria, "She who shows the way". This is her true significance, which is Why Mary Matters.

Glossary

Adoptionism: the idea that Jesus was adopted as the Son of God at his baptism, resurrection, or ascension.

Aeiparthenos: Ever-Virgin

Ante Nicene: the period from the Apostolic Age through to the First Council of Nicaea in 325 A.D.

Anthropology: the study of humanity

Antipathy: a deeply rooted dislike or aversion

Apollinarians: followers of Apollinaris of Laodicea, who proposed that Jesus had a human body and emotions, but a divine mind, thus making Jesus neither fully God, nor fully man.

Archimandrite: in Greek usage, an abbot of a large or important monestary; in Slavic usage, a rank given to a celibate priest, ranked just below a bishop.

Arianism: the belief that the Father is a superior and distinct being to the Son (there was a time when the Son was not), and the Son is a superior and distinct being to the Holy Spirit

Catechesis: instruction in the faith

Chiaroscuro: an artistic technique using strong contrasts between light and dark

Chimera: a hybrid creature

Christological: a field of study concerned with the nature and person of Jesus Christ

Cosmology: the nature of the universe

Dispensationalism: a system whereby God's revelation proceeds through a series of stages, or dispensations. Dispensationalism rejects the idea that the Christian Church is the spiritual Israel, but maintains that God has one plan for the Jews, and another for the Gentiles.

Docetists: believed that Christ's manhood and passion were unreal, a phantasm, an illusion.

Dormition: The falling asleep (death) of the Virgin Mary

Ebionites: believed that Jesus was the Messiah, but denied the virgin birth and the divinity of Christ.

Eschatology: the branch of theology dealing with death, judgment, and the end of the world.

Eschaton: the age to come

Eucharist: another term for Holy Communion

Evangelical: a designation for Protestant Christians who believe in the authority of the bible, ones personal conversion by faith in Jesus Christ, and one's salvation from sin or hell, and the preaching of these beliefs to others

Ex nihilo: creation "out of nothing"

Gnostics: believers in secret knowledge, and that salvation was a matter of gaining that knowledge. Gnostics were also dualists, believing that matter was evil and spirit was good; therefore, the human spirit is a divine spark trapped in body of flesh.

Hebraism: the use of a Hebrew idiom in the Greek text

Heresy: the denial or deformation of dogma, or something essential to the faith.

Hypostatic unity: The humanity and divinity of Christ, united in one hypostasis, one individual existence, one person.

Irruption: a violent incursion, invasion, or breaking in

Juridical theology: the idea that the relationship between God and man is primarily related to judicial proceedings and the rule of law, with God the Father as the Judge, Satan as the accuser of the brethren, and Jesus Christ as our advocate. As our advocate, Jesus Christ points to the infinite punishment He bore on our behalf.

Kenosis: emptiness or emptying, as in the self-emptying of the Son of God when He became man

Manichaeism: a pre-Christian, syncretistic sect that attempted to blend all known religious traditions. Like the Gnostics, the Manichees were dualistic, believing matter to be evil and the spiritual to be good.

Mediatrix: in ancient Christian tradition, this refers to Mary's role as the preeminent intercessor with her Son, Jesus Christ. In Roman Catholic dogma (see the "Lumen gentium"), this refers to Mary's role as a mediator of the redemption won by her Son, Jesus Christ, and as the bestower of divine graces.

Monophysites: Christ was not only a single person, but had a single blended nature.

Nestorians: believed that Mary was the Mother of Christ, but not of God.

Ontological: having to do with the nature of being, the basic categories of being, and their relations

Passim: used in bibliographical references for material scattered throughout the work in question.

Plerosis: fullness, fulfilling, or (in some cases) regeneration

Polysemic; a sign or symbol having multiple meanings, interpretations, or applications

Protoevangelium: the first proclamation of the Gospel; see Genesis 3:15

Sabellianism: the belief that Father, Son, and Holy Ghost are roles God takes in his interactions with humanity, and ways humanity perceives and experiences God

Sovereignty of God: the teaching that all things are under God's rule and control, and that nothing happens without His direction or permission. (theopedia.com) To put it another way, this is an argument against and a denial of free will.

Teleological: an idea that existence tends toward definite ends.

Telos: end

Theolegoumenon: a theological opinion that is neither part of church dogma, nor in line with the general consensus of the church fathers (as in St Gregory the Theologian's concept of the eventual restoration of all things to God, known as universalism

Theotokian: Hymn to the Virgin Mary

Glossary

Theotokos: God-bearer, Mother of God

Tropological: a type of biblical interpretation that stresses the use of metaphor and, in particular, the moral meaning of the metaphor

Typology: the interpretation of the Old Testament in light of the New, where something in the O.T. prefigures something in the N.T. (i.e. Joseph is a type of Christ)

Valentinians: a particular Gnostic sect

Veneration: to honor someone or something, as in the veneration displayed at the Tomb of the Unknown Soldier

Viscera: internal organs; blood and guts

Bibliography

Ahmad, Mirza Tahir. "The Sonship of Jesus Christ." *Al Islam Online.* n.d. http://www.alislam.org/library/books/christianity_f acts_to_fiction/chapter_1.html (accessed June 18, 2011).

Alfeyev, Hilarion. *Orthodox Christianity: Doctrine and Teaching of the Orthodox Church.* Translated by Andrew Smith. Vol. 2. 2 vols. Yonkers: St Vladimir's Seminary Press, 2012.

—. "Prayer and Monasticism in Orthodox Tradition." *Bishop Hilarion Alfeyev.* October 24, 2008. http://en.hilarion.orthodoxia.org/6_21 (accessed February 1, 2011).

Alter, Robert. *The Book of Psalms: A Translation with Commentary.* New York: W. W. Norton & Company, Inc., 2007.

Ambrose of Milan. "Ambrose of Milan, On the holy mysteries." *Monachos.net.* n.d. http://www.monachos.net/content/patristics/patris tictexts/648-ambrose-milan-on-the-holy-mysteries (accessed November 20, 2010).

—. "Letter XLII." In *The Letters of S. Ambrose, Bishop Of Milan,* by Ambrose, translated by H. Walford, 282-287. London, Oxford, & Cambridge: James Parker And Co., And Rivingtons, 1881.

Anonymous. "The Gospel of Philip." *The Gnostic Society Library.* 1990. http://www.gnosis.org/naghamm/gop.html (accessed July 28, 2014).

Arakaki, Robert. *Why Evangelicals Need Mary.* May 20, 2012. http://orthodoxbridge.com/why-evangelicals-need-mary/ (accessed January 23, 2013).

Bibliography

Arndt, W. F. *The Gospel According to St. Luke.* St. Louis: Concordia Publishing House, 1956.

Aulén, Gustaf. *The Faith of the Christian Church.* Philadelphia: Fortress Press, 1960.

Baker, Benedict. "Vitae Patrum." *Vitae Patrum: Lives of the Desert Fathers.* July 12, 2004. http://www.vitae-patrum.org.uk/ (accessed August 2010, 21).

Balthasar, Hans Urs von, and Cardinal Joseph Ratzinger. *Mary: The Church at the Source.* San Francisco: Ignatius Press, 1979.

Barth, Karl. *Church Dogmatics I.1: The Doctrine of the Word of God.* New York: T&T Clark Ltd, 2009.

—. *Church Dogmatics The Doctrine of the Word of God, Volume 1, Part 2: The Revelation of God; Holy Scripture: The Proclamation of the Church.* New York: T&T Clark Ltd, 1956.

Beckett, Wendy. *Encounters With God: In Quest of the Ancient Icons of Mary.* Maryknoll: Orbis Books, 2009.

Behr-Sigel, Elisabeth. *Discerning the Signs of the Times.* Edited by Michael Plekon and Sara E. Hinlicky. Translated by Lyn Breck, Michael Plekon, Deno Takles and Rachel Mortimer. Crestwood: St Vladimir's Seminary Press, 2001.

Benedict XVI. "Meeting with Representatives of Oriental and Oriental Orthodox Churches." *Vatican: The Holy See.* September 24, 2011. http://www.vatican.va/holy_father/benedict_xvi/speeches/2011/september/documents/hf_ben-xvi_spe_20110924_orthodox-freiburg_en.html (accessed September 2011, 25).

Bishop Hilarion Alfeyev. "St. Isaac the Syrian: A Theologian of Love and Mercy." *World Apostolic Congress on Mercy.* April 4, 2008. http://www.worldapostoliccongressonmercy.org/IMG/pdf/Bishop_Hilarion_Alfeyev.pdf (accessed 08 30, 2012).

Böhme, Jacom. "Mysterium Magnum (part one)." *Gnosis research.* October 9, 2009. http://meuser.awardspace.com/Boehme/Jacob-Boehme-Mysterium-Magnum-part-one-free-electronic-text.pdf (accessed November 15, 2010).

Boyce, James Petigru. *Abstract of Systematic Theology.* Grand Rapids: Christian Classics Ethereal Library, 1887.

Boychuk, Jodie. "The Orthodox Christian Veneration of Mary." *Imperfectly Ordinary.* July 01, 2012. http://imperfectlyordinary.blogspot.com/ (accessed July 01, 2012).

Bransfield, J. Brian. *The Human Person According to John Paul II.* Boston: Pauline Books & Media, 2010.

Bratcher, Dennis. "The Five Articles of the Remonstrants (1610)." *CRI/Voice, Institute.* 2010. http://www.crivoice.org/creedremonstrants.html (accessed November 13, 2010).

Breck, John. *God With Us: Critical Issues in Christian Life and Faith.* Crestwood: St Vladimir's Seminary Press, 2003.

—. *Scripture in Tradition: The Bible and Its Interpretation in the Orthodox Church.* Crestwood: St Vladimir's Seminary Press, 2001.

Brighton, Louis. *Revelation.* St Louis: Concordia Publishing House, 1999.

Brunner, Emil. *The Mediator.* Philadelphia: Westminster Press, 1947.

Brunner, Peter. *Worship in the Name of Jesus.* Translated by M. H. Bertram. St Louis: Concordia Publishing House, 1968.

Bryan, William Jennings, and Francis Whiting Halsey, . "The World's Famous Orations." *Bartleby.com.* March 2003. http://www.bartleby.com/268/7/8.html (accessed June 4, 2013).

Bibliography

Bulgakov, Sergius. *The Burning Bush: On the Orthodox Veneration of the Mother of God.* Translated by Thomas Allan Smith. Grand Rapids: William B. Eerdmans Publishing Company, 2009.

Byantoro, Daniel. "Christ The Word Become Flesh." *Christ the Eternal Kalimat.* August 30, 2008.

Carlton, C. Clark. "The Temple That Held God: Byzantine Marian Hymnography and the Christ of Nestorius." *St Vladimir's Theological Seminary* (The Faculty of St Vladimir's Orthodox Theological Seminary) 50, no. 1-2 (2006): 99-125.

Catholic Church. *Catechism of the Catholic Church.* Washington DC: USCCB Publishing, 1997.

Chapman, Henry Palmer. "Didascalia Apostolorum." *Catholic Encyclopedia.* 1913. http://en.wikisource.org/wiki/Catholic_Encyclopedia_(1913)/Didascalia_Apostolorum (accessed June 9th, 2013).

Chemnitz, Martin. *The Two Natures In Christ.* Translated by J.A.O. Preus. Saint Louis: Concordia Publishing House, 1971.

Chesterton, G.K. *Orthodoxy.* San Francisco: Ignatius Press, 1995.

Constantinou, Eugenia Scarvelis. *Andrew of Caesaria and the Apocalypse of the Ancient Church of the East: Studies and Translation.* Quebec: Faculté de Théologie et des Sciences Religieuses Université Laval, 2008.

—. *Andrew of Caesarea And The Apocalypse in the Ancient Church of the East: Studies and Translation.* Translated by Eugenia Scarvelis Contantinou. Laval: Faculté des études supérieures de l'Université Laval, 2008.

Cortez, Marc. *Theological Anthropology: A Guide for the Perplexed.* New York: T&T Clark International, 2010.

Cox, John Bradley. "email message to author." May 18, 2013.

Croy, N. Clayton, and Alice E. Connor. "Mantic Mary? The Virgin Mother as Prophet in Luke 1.26-56 and the Early Church." *Journal for the Study of the New Testament* (Sage Publications) 34, no. 3 (2011): 254-276.

Cunneen, Sally. *In Search of Mary: The Woman and the Symbol.* New York: Ballantine Books, 1996.

Cunningham, Mary B. "All-Holy Infant: Byzantine and Western Views on the Conception of the Virgin Mary." *St Vladimir's Theological Quarterly* (The Faculty of St Vladimir's Orthodox Theological Seminary) 50, no. 102 (2006): 127-148.

—. *Wider Than Heaven: Eighth-century Homilies on the Mother of God.* Kindle Edition. Yonkers, New York: St Vladimir's Seminary Press, 2011.

Currie, David B. *Born Fundamentalist, Born Again Catholic.* San Francisco: Ignatius Press, 1996.

Dabney, R. L. "The Five Points of Calvinism." *An R. L. Dabney Anthology.* n.d. http://www.spurgeon.org/~phil/dabney/5points.htm (accessed January 28, 2014).

Damick, Andrew Stephen. "An Introduction to God: Encountering the Divine in Orthodox Christianity." *Roads From Emmaus.* Ancient Faith Radio, May 18, 2012.

—. *Orthodoxy and Heterodoxy: Exploring Belief Systems Through the Lens of the Ancient Christian Faith.* Kindle Edition. Chesterton, Indiana: Conciliar Press, 2011.

Dau, William H. T., and Gerhard F. Bente, . *Triglot Concordia: The Symbolical Books of the Ev. Lutheran Church.* St. Louis: Concordia Publishing House, 1921.

Bibliography

Durham, Edith. *High Albania.* Middlesex: Echo Library, 2009.

Ehrman, Bart D. *Misquoting Jesus: The Story Behind Who Changed the Bible and Why.* San Francisco: Harper San Francisco, 2005.

Elder Cleopa of Romania. *The Truth of Our Faith.* Edited by Peter Alban Heers. Translated by Peter Alban Heers. London: Uncut Mountain Press, 2007.

Engelder, Theo. "The Three Principles of the Reformation: Sola Scriptura, Sola Gratia, Sola Fides." In *Four Hundred Years: Commemorative Essays on the Reformation of Dr. Martin Luther and its Blessed Results.*, edited by W.H.T. Dau, 97-109. St. Louis: Concordia Publishing House, 1916.

Evdokimov, Paul. *In the World, of the Church: A Paul Evdokimov Reader.* Edited by Michael Plekon and Alexis Vinogradov. Translated by Michael Plekon and Alexis Vinogradov. Crestwood: St Vladimir's Seminary Press, 2001.

—. *Orthodoxy.* Translated by Jeremy Hummerstone and Callan Slipper. Hyde Park: New City Press, 2011.

—. *Woman and the Salvation of the World.* Translated by Anthony P. Gythiel. Crestwood: St. Vladimir's Seminary Press, 1994.

Fannon, Patrick. "The Protestant Approach to Mariology." *Irish Theological Quarterly*, no. 121 (1962): 121-135.

Flam, Faye. "Jesus and genetics:Thorny questions revolve around Christ's Y chromosome." *The Salt Lake Tribune.* November 12, 2005. http://www.sltrib.com/lifestyle/ci_3207769 (accessed June 18, 2011).

Fletcher, Elizabeth. *Bible Archaeology:Tombs and Catacombs:tomb where Jesus called Lazarus back from the dead,catacombs of St.Priscilla,St.Callixtus for the early Christians.* n.d. http://www.bible-archaeology.info/tombs_catacombs.htm   (accessed May 25, 2009).

Florovsky, Georges. *Creation and Redemption.* Belmont: Nordland Publishing Company, 1976.

Forde, Gerhard O. *On Being a Theologian of the Cross: Reflections on Luther's Heidelberg Disputation, 1518.* Grand Rapids: William B. Eerdmans Publishing Company, 1997.

Fr. Stephen Freeman. *In Accordance with the Scripture.* March 25, 2007. http://fatherstephen.wordpress.com/2007/03/25/in-accordance-with-the-scriptures-2/ (accessed January 16, 2010).

Fr. Touma (Bitar). "There's Doubt, and then there's Doubt." *Notes on Arab Orthodoxy.* April 22, 2012. http://araborthodoxy.blogspot.com/2012/04/fr-touma-bitar-theres-doubt-and-then.html (accessed April 28, 2012).

Gabriel, George S. *Mary: The Untrodden Portal of God.* Ridgewood: Zephyr Publishing, 2000.

Gambero, Luigi. *Mary and the Fathers of the Church: The Blessed Virgin Mary in Patristic Thought.* San Francisco: Ignatius Press, 1991.

Geisler, Norman. "Mary---Fully Human, or Nearly Divine?" *Ankerberg Theological Research Institute.* 1997. http://ankerberg.com/Articles/_PDFArchives/theological-dictionary/TD4W1299.pdf (accessed January 18, 2009).

Gillett, Lev. "The Veneration of the Blessed Virgin Mary, Mother of God." *The Mother of God: A Symposium.* Westminster: Dacre Press, 1949. 76-80.

Gillquist, Peter. *Becoming Orthodox: A Journey to the Ancient Christian Faith.* Third. Ben Lomond: Conciliar Press, 2009.

Graef, Hilda. *Mary: A History of Doctrine and Devotion.* Notre Dame: Ave Maria Press, 2009.

Bibliography

Gregory of Nazianzus. "Gregory of Nazianzus, Epistle 51, to Cledonius (First epistle against Apollinarius)." *Monachos.net - Orthodox Christianity through patristic, monastic, liturgical and ecclesiastical study.* n.d. http://www.monachos.net/content/patristics/patristictexts/158 (accessed July 18, 2010).

Guroian, Vigen. *The Melody of Faith: Theology in an Orthodox Key.* Grand Rapids: William B. Eerdmans Publishing Company, 2010.

Hahn, Scott, and Kimberly Hahn. "Mary, Ark of the Covenant." *Catholic Adult Education Program.* Trinity Communications. 1994. http://zuserver2.star.ucl.ac.uk/~vgg/rc/aplgtc/hahn/m4/ma.html (accessed December 22, 2008).

—. *Rome Sweet Home: Our Journey to Catholicism.* San Francisco: Ignatius Press, 1993.

Hainsworth, John. "The Ever-Virginity of the Mother of God." *Greek Orthodox Archdiocese of America.* 2004. http://www.goarch.org/ourfaith/ourfaith9174 (accessed August 12, 2010).

Halperin, David J. *Seeking Ezekiel: Text and Psychology.* University Park: Pennsylvania State University Press, 1993.

Harrison, Everett R. *Introduction to the New Testament.* Grand Rapids: Wm. B. Eerdmans Publishing Company, 1971.

Harrison, Nonna Verna. *God's Many-Splendored Image: Theological Anthropology for Christian Formation.* Grand Rapids: Baker Academic, 2010.

—. "The Entry of the Mother of God into the Temple." *St Vladimir's Theological Quarterly* (The Faculty of St Vladimir's Orthodox Theological Seminary) 50, no. 1-2 (2006): 149-160.

Henry, Matthew. "Commentary on the Whole Bible Volume IV (Isaiah to Malachi)." *Christian Classics Ethereal*

383

Library. Edited by Ernie Stefanik. Christian Classics Ethereal Library. 07 09, 2000. http://www.ccel.org/ccel/henry/mhc4.html (accessed December 30, 2009).

Hieromartyr Hilarion (Troitsky). "The Incarnation and Humility." *Pravmir.com.* January 3, 2012. http://www.pravmir.com/the-incarnation-and-humility/ (accessed January 27, 2012).

Hippolytus. "The Apostolic Tradition of Hippolytus of Rome." *Kevin P. Edgecomb.* July 8, 1997. http://www.bombaxo.com/hippolytus.html (accessed May 25, 2009).

Hislop, Alexander. *The Two Babylons: or the Papal Worship proved to be the Worship of Nimrod and his Wife.* 3rd. Neptune, New Jersey: Loizeaux Brothers, 1959.

Holton, Jeffrey. "Mary, how does your garden grow?: Mary, the Theotokos, part 2." *Examiner.com.* June 5, 2009. http://www.examiner.com/eastern-orthodoxy-in-san-francisco/mary-how-does-your-garden-grow-mary-the-theotokos-part-2 (accessed October 12, 2011).

Holy Apostles Convent. *The Orthodox New Testament.* Vol. 2. 2 vols. Buena Vista: Holy Apostles Convent, 2000.

Hopko, Thomas. "Radical Monogamy." *Ancient Faith Radio.* May 2, 2012. http://ancientfaith.com/podcasts/hopko/radical_monogamy (accessed May 7, 2012).

Howard, Robert. "Ark of the Covenant." *Wake Up America By Robert Howard.* n.d. http://www.theforbiddenknowledge.com/hardtruth/ark_of_the_covenant.htm (accessed June 18, 2011).

Howard, Thomas. *Evangelical is Not Enough: Worship of God in Liturgy and Sacrament.* San Francisco: Ignatius Press, 1984.

HP-Time.com. "What Mary Means to Protestants." *Time.* September 11, 1964.

Bibliography

http://www.time.com/time/magazine/article/0,917
1,830660,00.html (accessed December 24, 2008).

Hughes, Antony. "View of Sin in the Early Church: Ancestral
Versus Original Sin: An Overview with Implications
for Psychotherapy." *Antiochian Orthodox Christian
Archdiocese.*   n.d.
http://www.antiochian.org/assets/asset.php?type=a
ssetLink&id=2338 (accessed January 2, 2010).

Jacob of Serug. *On the Mother of God.* Translated by Mary
Hansbury. Crestwood: St Vladimir's Seminary Press,
1998.

Jahn, Curtis A. *Exegesis and Sermon Study of Luke 1:46-55
The Magnificat.* Essay, Mequon: Wisconson Lutheran
Seminary, 1997, 1-15.

Jenkins, Philip. *The new anti-Catholicism: the last
acceptable prejudice.* New York: Oxford University
Press, 2003.

John of Damascus. "John of Damascus, Homily 1 on the
Dormition of the Theotokos." *Monachos.net.* n.d.
http://www.monachos.net/content/patristics/patris
tictexts/680-john-damascus-homily-1-dormition
(accessed November 22, 2010).

—. "John of Damascus, Homily 2 on the Dormition of the
Theotokos."   *Monachos.net.*   n.d.
http://www.monachos.net/content/patristics/patris
tictexts/681 (accessed November 22, 2010).

John Paul II. *Man and Woman He Created Them: A Theology
of the Body.* Boston: Pauline Books & Media, 2006.

Josephus, Flavius. "The Wars of the Jews, Book 1." Chap. 7
in *The Works of Josephus: New Updated Edition*, by
Flavius Josephus, translated by William Whiston,
554-555. Peabody: Hendrickson Publishers, 1987.

Just Jr., Arthur A. *Heaven on Earth: The Gifts of Christ in
the Divine Service.* St. Louis: Concordia Publishing
House, 2008.

—. *Luke 1:1 - 9:50*. St. Louis: Concordia Publishing House, 1996.

Kelly, J.N.D. *Early Christian Creeds*. 3rd. Essex: Longman House, 1972.

Khan, Sarah. "Views of Women: Social and Gendered Instruction in Medieval and Early Modern European Preaching." *The Medieval History Journal*, no. 109 (2004): 109-135.

Khomyakov, Aleksei Stepanovich. "On the Western Confessions of Faith." In *Ultimate Questions: An Anthology of Modern Russian Religious Thought*, edited by Alexander Schmemann, translated by Asheleigh E. Moorhouse, 31-69. St. Vladimir's Seminary Press, 1977.

Kiefer, James. *The Apostle's Creed*. Edited by Phillip R. Johnson. 2001. http://www.spurgeon.org/~phil/creeds/apostles.htm (accessed July 20, 2011).

Kipling, Rudyard. *Kim*. Pleasantville: The Reader's Digest Association, Inc., 1990.

Kleinig, John. *Leviticus*. Saint Louis: Concordia Publishing House, 2003.

Klug, Eugene F. "The Doctrine of Man: Christian Anthropology." *Concordia Theological Quarterly* (Concordia Theological Seminary) 48, no. 2-3 (April-July 1984): 141-152.

Koblosh, Michael, interview by Kristofer Carlson. *Spiritual Brotherhood* (August 26, 2010).

Krauth, Charles Porterfield. "The Relations of the Lutheran Church to the Denominations around us." In *First Free Lutheran Diet in America, Philadelphia, December 27-28, 1877: The Essays, Debates and Proceedings*, by Henry Eyster Jacobs, 27-69. Philadelphia: J. Frederick Smith, Publisher, 1877.

Kreitzer, Beth. *Reforming Mary: Changing Images of the Virgin Mary in Lutheran Sermons of the Sixteengh Century.* New York: Oxford University Press, 2004.

Lane, Anthony N. "The Rationale and Significance of the Virgin Birth." *Vox Evangelica,* 1977: 48-64.

Leeming, Bernard. "Protestants and Our Lady." *Irish Theological Quarterly,* 1960: 91-110.

Lenski, R. C. H. *The Interpretation of Luke's Gospel.* Minneapolis: Augsburg Publishing House, 1946.

Letham, Robert. *Through Western Eyes.* Fearn: Christian Focus Publications, Ltd., 2007.

Lloyd-Moffett, Stephen R. *Beauty for Ashes: The Spiritual Transformation of a Modern Greek Community.* Crestwood: St Vladimir's Seminary Press, 2009.

Lossky, Vladimir. "Panagia." *The Mother of God: A Symposium.* Westminster: Dacre Press, 1949. 24-36.

—. "The Creation." In *Orthodox Theology: An Introduction,* by Vladimir Lossky, edited by Ian Kesarcodi-Watson and Ihita Kesarcodi-Watson, 51-78. Crestwood: St. Vladimir's Seminary Press, 1989.

—. *The Mystical Theology of the Eastern Church.* Crestwood: St. Vladimir's Seminary Press, 1958.

Louth, Andrew. "Father Sergii Bulgakov on the Mother of God." Edited by John Behr. *St Vladimir's Theological Quarterly* (The Faculty of St Vladimir's Orthodox Theological Seminary) 49, no. 1-2 (2005): 145-164.

Louth, Andrew, Marco Conti, and Thomas C. Oden. *Ancient Christian Commentary on Scripture: Old Testament I, Genesis 1-11.* Vol. 1. 28 vols. Westmont: InterVarsity Press, 2001.

Luther, Martin. *What Luther Says.* Edited by Ewald M. Plass. St. Louis: Concordia Publishing House, 2006.

Luther, Martin, and Joachim Karl Friedrich Knaake. *Weimarer Ausgabe.* Vol. 11. Weimar H. Böhlaus, 1883.

Maas, Anthony. *The Blessed Virgin Mary.* Vol. 15, in *The Catholic Encyclopedia.* New York: Robert Appleton Company, 1912.

Manelli, Stefano. *All Generations Shall Call Me Blessed.* New Bedford: Academy of the Immaculate, 2005.

Marlowe, Michael D. *The Semitic Style of the New Testament.* n.d. http://www.bible-researcher.com/hebraisms.html (accessed August 21, 2010).

Martin, James. "The Last Acceptable Prejudice?" *America Magazine.* March 25, 2000. http://americamagazine.org/content/article.cfm?article_id=606 (accessed December 30, 2011).

Mascall, Eric L. "The Dogmatic Theology of the Mother of God." *The Mother of God: A Symposium.* Westminster: Dacre Press, 1949. 37-50.

Mathewes-Green, Frederica. *The Lost Gospel of Mary: The Theotokos in Three Ancient Texts.* Brewster: Paraclete Press, 2007.

Matusiak, John. *Sinlessness of Mary.* n.d. http://www.oca.org/QA.asp?ID=116&SID=3 (accessed August 21, 2010).

Mauriello, Rev. Matthew R. *Mary, Mother of the Church.* January 1996. http://campus.udayton.edu/mary/meditations/Mchrch.html (accessed February 2011, 10).

Maximovitch, John. *The Orthodox Veneration of Mary the Birthgiver of God.* Platina: St. Herman of Alaska Brotherhood, 2004.

Maximus the Confessor. *Maximus Confessor: Selected Writings.* Translated by George C. Berthold. New York: Paulist Press, 1985.

McGuckin, John Anthony. *The Orthodox Church: An Introduction to its History, Doctrine, and Spiritual Culture.* West Sussex: Wiley-Blackwell, 2011.

Bibliography

McKnight, Scot. *The Real Mary: Why Evangelical Christians can Embrace the Mother of Jesus.* Brewster: Paraclete Press, 2007.

McLemee, Scot. "Opening of the Evangelical Mind?" *Inside Higher Ed.* November 23, 2011. http://www.insidehighered.com/views/2011/11/23/essay-new-book-evangelical-culture (accessed November 23, 2011).

"Menachem Mendel of Kotzk." *Wikiquote.* August 30, 2010. http://en.wikiquote.org/wiki/Menachem_Mendel_of_Kotzk (accessed May 21, 2012).

Mencken, H. L. *In Defense of Women.* New York: Alfred P. Knopf, 1922.

Metropolitan John of Pergamon. "Proprietors or Priests of Creation?" *OrthodoxyToday.org.* June 2, 2003. http://www.orthodoxytoday.org/articles2/MetJohnCreation.php (accessed January 4, 2010).

Meyendorff, John. *Christ in Eastern Christian Thought.* Translated by Fr. Yves Dubois. Crestwood: St. Vladimir's Seminary Press, 1975.

Moss, Vladimir. *The Theology of Eros.* Rollinsford: Orthodox Research Institute, 2010.

Myers, Phillip Van Ness. *Rome: its rise and fall.* 2nd. Boston: The Athenaeum Press, 1901.

Nelson, Lynn H. "The Rise of Monasticism." *The ORB: On-line Reference Book for Medieval Studies.* 1999. http://www.the-orb.net/textbooks/nelson/monasticism.html (accessed December 13, 2009).

O'Loughlin, Thomas. *The Didache: A Window on the Earliest Christians.* Grand Rapids: Baker Academic, 2010.

Olson, Jeanine E. *Deacons and Deaconesses Through the Centuries.* St. Louis: Concordia Publishing House, 1992.

Origen. *Commentary on the Gospel According to John Books 1-10.* Washington DC: The Catholic University of America Press, Inc, 1989.

Orthodox Metropolitanate of Hong Kong and Southeast Asia. "The Oldest Hymn to the Theotokos." *OMHKSEA.* August 10, 2011. http://www.omhksea.org/2011/08/the-oldest-hymn-to-the-theotokos/ (accessed February 12, 2012).

Pascal, Blaise. *Pensees.* Translated by William Finlayson Trotter. Forgotten Books, 2008.

Payton, James R. *Light from the Christian East: An Introduction to the Orthodox Tradition.* Kindle Edition. Downers Grove: IVP Academic, 2007.

Pelikan, Jaroslav. *Mary Through the Centuries: Her Place in the History of Culture.* New Haven: Yale University Press, 1996.

—. *The Riddle of Roman Catholicism.* Nashville: Abingdon Press, 1959.

Pennock, Dee. *Path to Sanity: Lessons from Ancient Holy Counselors on how to have a Sound Mind.* Minneapolis: Light and Life Publishing Company, 2010.

Pentecost, J. Dwight. *Things to Come: A Study in Biblical Eschatology.* Grand Rapids: Academie Books, 1958.

Perry, Tim. *Mary for Evangelicals.* Downer's Grove: IVP Academic Press, 2006.

Peter of Alexandria. "That Up to the Time of the Destruction of Jerusalem, the Jews Rightly Appointed the Fourteenth Day of the First Lunar Month." In *About ANF06. Fathers of the Third Century: Gregory Thaumaturgus, Dionysius the Great, Julius Africanus, Anatolius, and Minor Writers, Methodius, Arnobius,* by Phillip Schaff, 476-480. Grand Rapids: Christian Classics Ethereal Library, 2004.

Bibliography

Piepkorn, Arthur Carl. *Mary's Place Within the People of God According to Non-Roman Catholics.* Vol. 1, in *The Church: Selected Writings of Arthur Carl Piepkorn*, by Arthur Carl Piepkorn, edited by Michael P. Plekon and Willam S. Wiecher, 295-326. Delhi: American Lutheran Publicity Bureau, 2006.

Pliny the Younger. "EPISTULAE X.96." *The VRoma Project.* n.d. http://www.ancient-literature.com/rome_pliny_epistulae_X96.html (accessed July 28, 2014).

Pope Paul VI. "Gaudium et Spes: Pastoral Constitution on the Church in the Modern World." *Vatican: the Holy See.* December 7, 1965. http://www.vatican.va/archive/hist_councils/ii_vatican_council/documents/vat-ii_const_19651207_gaudium-et-spes_en.html (accessed January 31, 2009).

Preus, Robert. *Getting Into the Theology of Concord: A Study of the Book of Concord.* St. Louis: Concordia Publishing House, 1977.

Pseudo-Dionysius, the Areopagite. *Pseudo-Dionysius: The Complete Works.* Translated by Colm Luibheid. New York: Paulist Press, 1987.

Ratzinger, Cardinal Joseph. *Eschatology: Death and Eternal Life.* Washington, D.C.: The Catholic University of America Press, 1988.

—. "Hail, Full of Grace: Elements of Marian Piety According to the Bible." In *Mary, The Church at the Source*, by Cardinal Joseph Ratzinger and Hans Urs von Balthasar, translated by Adrian Walker, 61-79. San Francisco: Ignatius Press, 2005.

—. "Hail, Full of Grace: Elements of Marian Piety According to the Bible." In *Mary, The Church at the Source*, by Cardinal Joseph Ratzinger and Hans Urs von Balthasar, translated by Adrian Walker, 61-79. San Francisco: Ignatius Press, 2005.

—. "THE ECCLESIOLOGY OF THE CONSTITUTION ON THE CHURCH, VATICAN II, 'LUMEN GENTIUM'." *Global Catholic Television Network.* September 19, 2001. http://www.ewtn.com/library/curia/cdfeccl.htm (accessed June 18, 2011).

—. "The Sign of the Woman." In *Mary: The Church at the Source*, by Cardinal Joseph Ratzinger and Hans Urs von Balthasar, 37-60. San Francisco: Ignatius Press, 2005.

—. "Thoughts on the Place of Marian Doctrine and Piety in Faith and Theology as a Whole." In *Mary: The Church at the Source*, by Cardinal Joseph Ratzinger and Hans Urs von Balthasar, translated by Adrian Walker, 19-36. San Francisco: Ignatius Press, 2005.

Relevant Media Group. *RELEVANT Magazine - From the Mag: 7 Big Questions.* Jan/Feb 2007. http://www.relevantmagazine.com/features-reviews/god/1344-from-the-mag-7-big-questions (accessed March 14, 2009).

Rich, Tracey R. *Looking for Jesus?* n.d. http://www.jewfaq.org/looking4.htm (accessed January 16, 2010).

Robinson, Steven, and Bill Gould. "The Orthodox Church's Understanding of the Virgin Mary, Parts 2 and 3." *Our Life in Christ.* December 2004. http://www.ourlifeinchrist.com/Program%20Notes/mary2_121904.htm (accessed September 6, 2010).

Rodriguez, Rosa Salter. "James' version king." *The (Fort Wayne) Journal Gazette.* Fort Wayne, May 14, 2011.

Romanides, John S. *The Ancestral Sin.* Translated by George S. Gabriel. Ridgewood: Zephyr Publishing, 2008.

Sadedin, Suzanne. "War in the Womb." *Aeon Magazine.* August 4, 2014. http://aeon.co/magazine/nature-and-cosmos/pregnancy-is-a-battleground-between-mother-father-and-baby/ (accessed August 4, 2014).

Samples, Kenneth R. "What Think Ye of Rome? An Evangelical Appraisal of Contemporary Catholicism (Part One)." Edited by Elliot Miller. *Christian Research Journal*, no. Winter 1993 (1993): 32.

Scaer, David P. *Discourse in Matthew: Jesus Teaches the Church.* St. Louis: Concordia Publishing House, 2004.

—. "Semper Virgo: A Doctrine." *Logia: A Journal of Lutheran Theology*, 2010: 15-18.

Schaff, Philip. *ANF01 The Apostolic Fathers with Justin Martyr and Irenaeus.* Edited by Alexander Roberts and James Donaldson. Vol. 1. 10 vols. Grand Rapids: Wm. B. Eerdmans Publishing Company, 1884.

—. *ANF01 The Apostolic Fathers with Justin Martyr and Irenaeus.* Edited by Alexander Roberts and James Donaldson. Vol. 1. 10 vols. Grand Rapids: Wm. B. Eerdmans Publishing Company, 1884.

—. *ANF02 Fathers of the Second Century: Hermas, Tatian, Athenagoras, Theophilus, and Clement of Alexandria (Entire).* Edited by Phillip Schaff. Vol. 2. 10 vols. Grand Rapids: Christian Classics Ethereal Library, 2004.

—. *ANF03 Latin Christianity: Its Founder, Tertullian.* Vol. 3. 10 vols. Grand Rapids: Christian Classics Ethereal Library, 2006.

—. *ANF05 Fathers of the Third Century: Hippolytus, Cyprian, Caius, Novatian, Appendix.* Edited by Alexander Roberts, James Donaldson and A. Cleveland Coxe. Translated by S. D. F. Salmond. Vol. 5. 10 vols. Grand Rapids: Wm. B. Eerdmans Publishing Company, 2004.

—. *ANF06 Fathers of the Third Century: Gregory Thaumaturgus, Dionysius the Great, Julius Africanus, Anatolius, and Minor Writers, Methodius, Arnobius.*

Vol. 6. 10 vols. Grand Rapids: Christian Classics Ethereal Library, 2004.

—. *ANF06 Fathers of the Third Century: Gregory Thaumaturgus, Dionysius the Great, Julius Africanus, Anatolius, and Minor Writers, Methodius, Arnobius.* Vol. 6. 10 vols. Grand Rapids: Christian Classics Ethereal Library, 2005.

—. *ANF07 Fathers of the Third and Fourth Centuries: Lactantius, Venantius, Asterius, Victorinus, Dionysius, Apostolic Teaching and Constitutions, Homily, and Liturgies.* Edited by Philip Schaff. Vol. 7. 10 vols. Grand Rapids: Christian Classics Ethereal Library, 2004.

—. *History of the Christian Church, Volume I: Apostolic Christianity. A.D. 1-100.* Vol. 1. 3 vols. Edinburgh: T&T Clark, 1882.

—. *NPNF1-03 On the Holy Trinity; Doctrinal Treatises; Moral Treatises.* Edited by Phillip Schaff. Translated by H. Brown. Vol. 3. 14 vols. New York: The Christian Literature Publishing Company, 1890.

—. *NPNF1-05 St. Augustin: Anti-Pelagian Writings.* Translated by Peter Holmes, Robert Ernest Wallace and Benjamin B. Warfield. Vol. 5. 14 vols. New York: Christian Classics Ethereal Library, 1886.

—. *NPNF1-09 St. Chrysostom: On the Priesthood; Ascetic Treatises; Select Homilies and Letters; Homilies on the Statutes.* Edited by Philip Schaff. Translated by W. R. W. Stephens, T. P. Brandram and R. Blackburn. Vol. 9. 14 vols. Grand Rapids: Wm. B. Eerdmans Publishing Company, 1889.

—. *NPNF2-01 Eusebius Pamphilius: Church History, Life of Constantine, Oration in Praise of Constantine.* Edited by Philip Schaff and Henry Wace. Translated by Arthur C. McGiffert and Ernest C. Richardson. Vol. 1. 14 vols. Grand Rapids: Wm. B. Eerdmans Publishing Company, 1890.

Bibliography

—. *NPNF2-04 Athanasius: Select Works and Letters.* Edited by Philip Schaff. Vol. 4. 14 vols. Grand Rapids: Copyright Christian Classics Ethereal Library, 1892.

—. *NPNF2-06 Jerome: The Principal Works of St. Jerome.* Edited by Philip Schaff. Translated by W. H. Freemantle. Vol. 6. 14 vols. New York: Christian Literature Publishing Co., 1892.

—. *NPNF2-06 Jerome: The Principal Works of St. Jerome.* Edited by Philip Schaff. Translated by M A Freemantle. Vol. 6. 14 vols. Grand Rapids: Christian Classics Ethereal Library, 1892.

—. *NPNF2-09 Hilary of Poitiers, John of Damascus.* Vol. 9. 14 vols. Grand Rapids: Christian Classics Ethereal Library, 2004.

—. *NPNF2-11 Sulpitius Severus, Vincent of Lerins, John Cassian.* Edited by Phillip Schaff and Henry Wace. Vol. 11. 14 vols. Grand Rapids: Christian Classics Ethereal Library, 2004.

—. *NPNF2-14 The Seven Ecumenical Councils.* Vol. 14. 14 vols. Grand Rapids: Christian Classics Ethereal Library, 2005.

—. *NPNF2-14 The Seven Ecumenical Councils.* Grand Rapids: Christian Classics Ethereal Library, 2005.

Schlink, Edmund. *Theology of the Lutheran Confessions.* Translated by Paul F Koehneke and Herbert J.A. Bouman. St. Louis: Condordia Publishing House, 1961.

Schmemann, Alexander. *Introduction to Liturgical Theology.* Translated by Asheleigh E. Moorehouse. Crestwood, New York: St. Vladimir's Seminary Press, 1996.

—. *The Eucharist.* Translated by Paul Kachur. Crestwood: St Vladimir's Seminary Press, 1988.

—. *The Historical Road of Eastern Orthodoxy.* Translated by Lydia W. Kesich. Crestwood: St Vladimir's Seminary Press, 2003.

—. *The Virgin Mary: Celebration of Faith.* Translated by John A. Jillians. Vol. 3. Crestwood: St Vladimir's Seminary Press, 1995.

Scofield, C. I. *The Scofield Reference Bible.* New York: Oxford University Press, 1917.

Sheikh Muzaffer Ozak Al-Jerrahi. *Blessed Virgin Mary.* Translated by Muhtar Holland. Westpory: Pir Publications, 1991.

Shilakar, Purna Lal. "The King Has Come." *Bhaktivani: Text and Context in Dialogue.* n.d. http://www.bhaktivani.com/book/5.%20The%20Pri est%20of%20God.pdf (accessed August 5, 2008).

Shoemaker, Stephen J. "Death and the Maiden." *St Vladimir's Theological Quarterly* (The Faculty of St Vladimir's Orthodox Theological Seminary) 50, no. 1-2 (2006): 59-97.

Skarsaune, Oskar. *In the Shadow of the Temple: Jewish Influences on Early Christianity.* Downers Grove: IVP Academic, 2002.

Skobtsova, Maria. *Mother Maria Skobtsova: Essential Writings.* Edited by Robert Ellsberg. Translated by Richard Pevear and Larissa Volokhonsky. Maryknoll: Orbis Books, 2003.

Smith, William. *A Dictionary of Greek and Roman Antiquities.* Third American Edition. New York: American Book Company, 1843.

Souvay, Charles. "Elias." *The Catholic Encyclopedia.* Robert Appleton Company. 1909. http://www.newadvent.org/cathen/05381b.htm (accessed October 24, 2008).

Spurgeon, Charles Haddon. *The Treasury of David.* Mclean: MacDonald Publishing Company, 1988.

St Athanasius. *On the Incarnation.* Crestwood: St Vladimir's Theological Seminary, 1993.

St Augustine. *The Confessions of Saint Augustine.* New Kensington: Whitaker House, 1996.

Bibliography

St Basil the Great. *On the Holy Spirit.* Kindle. Edited by John Behr. Translated by Stephen Hildebrand. Yonkers: St Vladimir's Seminary Press, 2011.

—. *On the Human Condition.* Translated by Nonna Verna Harrison. Crestwood: St Vladimir's Seminary Press, 2005.

St Ephrem the Syrian. "Commentary on Genesis." *Scribd.com.* n.d. http://www.scribd.com/doc/56174298/St-Ephraim-the-Syrian-Commentary-on-Genesis (accessed June 9, 2013).

—. *Hymns on Paradise.* Translated by Sebastion Brock. Crestwood: St Vladimir's Seminary Press, 1989.

St Gregory Nazianzen. "Oration 38." In *NPNF2-07. Cyril of Jerusalem, Gregory Nazianzen,* by Phillip Schaff, 624-637. Grand Rapids: Christian Classics Ethereal Library, 1893.

St Gregory Palamas. *Mary the Mother of God: Sermons by Saint Gregory Palamas.* Edited by Christopher Veniamin. Dalton, PA: Mount Thabor Publishing, 2013.

St John of Kronstadt. *My Life in Christ, or Moments of Spiritual Serenity and Contemplation, of Reverent Feeling, of Earnest SelfAmendment, and of Peace in God.* Edited by John Iliytch Sergieff. Translated by E. E. Goulaeff. Grand Rapids: Christian Classics Ethereal Library, 2010.

St John of Shanghai & San Francisco. *The Orthodox Veneration of Mary the Birthgiver of God.* Sep 7, 2005. http://www.stmaryofegypt.org/library/st_john_maximovich/on_veneration_of_the_theotokos.htm (accessed August 21, 2010).

St Nicolas Cabasilas. "Homily On The Annunciation." *Holy Synod In Resistance.* April 08, 2010.

http://www.synodinresistance.org/Theology_en/E3d
7050Cabasilas.pdf (accessed October 13, 2011).

St Nikodimos of the Holy Mountain and St Makarios of
Corinth. *The Philokalia, Vol II*. Edited by G.E.H.
Palmer, Philip Sherrard and Kallistos Ware.
Translated by G.E.H. Palmer, Philip Sherrard and
Kallistos Ware. Vol. 2. 4 vols. London: Faber and
Faber Limited, 1981.

—. *The Philokalia, Vol III*. Edited by G. E. H. Palmer, Philip
Sherrard and Kallistos Ware. Translated by G. E. H.
Palmer, Philip Sherrard and Kallistos Ware. Vol. 3. 4
vols. London: Faber and Faber Limited, 1984.

—. *The Philokalia, Vol IV*. Edited by G. E. H. Palmer, Philip
Sherrard and Kallistos Ware. Translated by G. E. H.
Palmer, Philip Sherrard and Kallistos Ware. Vol. 4. 4
vols. London: Faber and Faber Limited, 1995.

St. Cyril of Jerusalem. *The Catechetical Lectures of St. Cyril
of Jerusalem*. Kindle Edition. Translated by Edwin
Hamilton Gifford. 2013.

Stakemeier, E. *De Mariologia et Oecumenismo*. Edited by K.
Balic. Rome: Academia Mariana Internationalis,
1962.

Staniloae, Dumitru. *The Experience of God: Revelation and
Knowledge of the Triune God*. Translated by Ioan
Ionita and Robert Barringer. Vol. 1. 6 vols.
Brookline: Holy Cross Orthodox Press, 1998.

—. *The Experience of God: The Person of Jesus Christ as God
and Savior*. Translated by Ioan Ionita. Vol. 3. 6 vols.
Brookline: Holy Cross Orthodox Press, 2011.

Stark, Rodney. *The Rise of Christianity*. New York:
HarperCollins Publishers, 1996.

Stark, Thom. *The Human Faces of God: What Scripture
Reveals When it Gets God Wrong (And Why Innerancy
Tries to Hide it)*. Eugene: Wipf & Stock, 2011.

Tacitus. *The Histories, Book V*. 109.

Bibliography

The Christian Apologetics Society. "Apologetics - The Perpetual Virginity of Mary." *Christian Apologetics Society.* 2007. http://christian-apologetics-society.blogspot.com/2008/03/apologetics-perpetual-virginity-of-mary.html (accessed January 1, 2010).

The Christian Expositor. "Why the rise in Ecumenism?" *The Christian Expositor.* n.d. http://www.thechristianexpositor.org/page101.html (accessed July 13, 2011).

Thomas, Derek. "Komodo Dragons and the Virgin Mary: a Belated Christmas Story." *Reformation 21.* December 2006. http://www.reformation21.org/counterpoints/derek-thomaskomodo-dragons-and-the.php (accessed June 18, 2011).

Thornton, L. S. "The Mother of God in Holy Scripture." Edited by E. L. Mascall. *The Mother of God.* Westminster: Dacre Press, 1949. 9-23.

Thunberg, Lars. *Man and the Cosmos: The Vision of St Maximus the Confessor.* Crestwood: St Vladimir's Seminary Press, 1985.

Toorn, Karel van der. *Scribal Culture and the Making of the Hebrew Bible.* Cambridge: Harvard University Press, 2007.

Tribe, Shawn, and Henri de Villiers. "The Sub Tuum Praesidium." *New Liturgical Movement.* February 3, 2011. http://www.newliturgicalmovement.org/2011/02/sub-tuum-praesidium.html (accessed February 12, 2012).

Unger, Merrill F. *Unger's Bible Dictionary.* Third Edition. Chicago: Moody Press, 1966.

Velimirovich, Nikolai. *Prayers by the Lake.* Grayslake: Diocese of New Grananica and Midwestern America, 2010.

Vitz, Rico, ed. *Turning East: Contemporary Philosophers and the Ancient Christian Faith.* Vol. 4. Yonkers: St Vladimir's Seminary Press, 2012.

Voelker, David J. "The Five Points of Calvinism (From the Synod of Dort, 1619)." *History Tools.org.* May 13, 2006. http://www.historytools.org/sources/dort-5-points-calvinism.pdf (accessed December 12, 2010).

Von Schenk, Berthold. *The Presence: An Approach to the Holy Communion.* New York: E. Kaufmann, Incorporated, 1945.

Wace. "Wace Introduction." *Early Christian Writings.* 2001. http://www.earlychristianwritings.com/info/didache-wace.html (accessed January 1, 2010).

Ware, Kallistos. *The Orthodox Way.* Crestwood: St. Vladimir's Seminary Press, 1979.

Ware, Timothy. *The Orthodox Church: New Edition.* London: Penguin Books, 1997.

Wesley, John. "Wesley's Notes on the Bible." *Christian Classics Ethereal Library.* n.d. http://www.ccel.org/ccel/wesley/notes.html (accessed December 30, 2009).

White, Carolinne. *Early Christian Lives.* New York: Penguin Books, 1998.

Whiteford, John. "Why is Mary Considered Ever Virgin." *Orthodox Information Center.* n.d. http://www.orthodoxinfo.com/inquirers/evervirgin.aspx (accessed August 5, 2008).

Willis, John R. *The Teachings of the Church Fathers.* San Francisco: Ignatius Press, 2002.

Yazykova, Irina. *Hidden and Triumphant: The Underground Struggle to Save Russian Iconography.* Translated by Paul Grenier. Brewster: Paraclete press, 2010.

Zwingli, Ulrich. *Zwingli Opera, Corpus Reformatorum.* Vol. 1. Berlin, 1905.

Index

Abraham 142, 163, 173, 363
Adam 29, 42, 43, 47, 49, 76, 77, 79, 83, 93, 95, 96, 101, 102, 107, 108, 111, 112, 113, 125, 170, 180, 184, 215, 283, 286, 303, 341, 349, 351, 352, 353, 354, 355, 356
Adoptionism 30, 43, 210
Alfeyev, Hilarion
 Metropolitan 154, 232
Allison, Dale C. 204
Alter, Robert 111
Ancestral sin 49, 341, 348
Andrew of Caesarea 312
Angel 16, 23, 39, 40, 110, 114, 137, 138, 155, 159, 170, 204, 211, 222, 231, 234, 237, 238, 239, 240, 242, 250, 252, 253, 260, 261, 271, 274, 286, 303, 311, 314, 331, 336, 353, 363
Annunciation ix, 6, 23, 47, 66, 103, 114, 116, 138, 142, 211, 216, 227, 228, 229, 230, 233, 235, 237, 253, 254, 256, 260, 263, 281, 316, 351, 354
Anthropology 61, 62, 63, 64, 65, 79, 81, 87, 89, 90, 91, 92, 93, 95, 97, 118, 135
Antichrist 136
Apollinarianism 31, 43, 89, 90, 320
Apollinarius 89
Apologetics 54
Apology to the Augsburg Confession 136
Arakaki, Robert 18, 19
Archangel 352
Archangel Gabriel 39, 40, 47, 114, 181, 190, 220, 222, 226, 227, 229, 231, 237, 238, 239, 240, 241, 242, 247, 252, 260, 261, 263, 264, 274, 303, 311, 314, 354, 355, 363
Archimandrite 39, 158
Arianism 43, 166, 210, 328
Aristotle 150
Ark (of the Covenant) 113, 148, 182, 187, 228, 231, 300, 311, 312, 313, 314, 315, 316, 336, 338
Arndt, William F., Dr. 227, 228
Augsburg Confession 136
Aulén, Gustaf 10, 62, 143

Axion estin...18, 19
Babylon 10, 359
Baker, Benedict...163
Balthasar, Hans Urs von 132
Baptist..133, 247, 256, 344, 345
Barth, Karl14, 29, 189, 278, 279, 280, 282, 283, 320, 366, 367, 368
Bathsheba..358
Behr-Sigel, Elisabeth 157
Bene esse 131
Benedict XVI, Pope..13, 63, 128, 241
Bethlehem....................................115, 116, 256, 287, 288
Böhme, Jacom...112, 355
Book of Concord 136
Boychuk, Jodie..148, 230
Bransfield, J. Brian 79
Breck, John, Fr.....................................36, 87, 97, 104, 189
Brighton, Louis, Dr..312, 321
Brunner, Emil 47
Brunner, Peter..68, 69
Bukharev, Alexander
   Archimandrite Feodor..157
Calvin, John....................................50, 189, 193, 320, 332
Calvinist 253, 255, 342, 349
Campenhausen, Hans von...51
Carlton, C. Clark 149
Carmen Christi..213
Catholic, Roman 2, 3, 4, 5, 8, 9, 10, 11, 13, 14, 19, 34, 45, 46, 49, 51, 63, 91, 127, 133, 134, 136, 139, 140, 193, 194, 195, 196, 230, 233, 247, 248, 278, 317, 324, 325, 327, 343, 347, 350, 366, 367, 419
Celibacy ...134, 150, 156, 157, 165, 170, 171, 190, 191, 192
Chalcedon*See* Ecumenical Council, *See* Ecumenical Council, *See* Ecumenical Council, *See* Ecumenical Council, *See* Ecumenical Council, *See* Ecumenical Council, *See* Ecumenical Council, *See* Ecumenical Council, *See* Ecumenical Council
Charis 238, 239
Charism 177
Charismatic..25

Chastity ...122, 156, 159, 165, 171, 173, 177, 275, 333, 335

Chemnitz, Martin...330, 331

Cherubim 19, 240, 369

Chesterton, G.K. 149, 150, 151, 171

Christ...419

Christian iv, 2, 9, 10, 11, 12, 13, 14, 22, 23, 24, 25, 26, 34, 36, 39, 40, 44, 45, 46, 47, 51, 54, 56, 59, 61, 62, 64, 66, 67, 68, 69, 74, 77, 81, 84, 87, 89, 92, 93, 95, 104, 118, 123, 127, 129, 133, 136, 139, 140, 141, 150, 157, 161, 162, 163, 165, 166, 167, 168, 170, 171, 185, 188, 192, 193, 208, 209, 215, 217, 221, 222, 226, 230, 238, 250, 257, 258, 271, 283, 292, 299, 309, 310, 318, 327, 328, 340, 344, 346, 352, 360, 367

Christianity 3, 5, 10, 13, 14, 23, 24, 29, 34, 35, 36, 37, 39, 41, 45, 51, 54, 61, 64, 65, 87, 89, 91, 123, 125, 127, 130, 140, 149, 150, 151, 159, 163, 166, 170, 188, 191, 192, 225, 226, 230, 309, 419

Christmas..2, 23, 186, 279

Christological 4, 17, 35, 36, 44, 50, 56, 57, 84, 89, 118, 225, 270, 271, 274, 296, 318, 320, 323, 325, 326, 329, 330

Christology 34, 35, 36, 46, 48, 61, 64, 69, 118, 124, 125, 215, 225, 226, 227, 271, 299, 317, 320, 325, 329, 334, 336, 367, 370, 419

Church

  Virgin Bride..108

Clarke, Dr. Neville 256

Communion of persons 94, 95, 96, 97, 101, 102, 103, 105, 108, 111, 113, 180, 181, 183, 250, 310

Connor, Alice E...263, 264

Constantinou, Eugenia Scarvelis 311

Cortez, Marc..71, 72

Cosmology 56, 57, 65, 66, 280

Cosmos..56, 57, 65, 290

Council of Trent...327

Covenant Theology 280

Cox, Fr. John 233

Creation 16, 27, 43, 47, 48, 57, 59, 60, 64, 65, 66, 68, 71, 72, 76, 77, 78, 79, 81, 84, 85, 89, 90, 93, 94, 95, 97, 99, 103, 106, 107, 108, 109, 110, 111, 115, 118, 124, 128,

129, 172, 179, 180, 215, 234, 253, 254, 267, 290, 303, 304, 307, 308, 353

Creed 327

Apostles...22, 327, 328

Athanasian...22, 327

Chalcedonian...22, 69, 327, 330

Nicene...................22, 69, 84, 87, 112, 328, 356

Croy, N. Clayton 263, 264

Crucifixion 211

Cunneen, Sally......................47, 193, 194, 221, 419

Currie, David B. 8, 9, 58

Cyril of Alexandria..317, 324

Damick, Andrew Stephen.............................26, 208, 251

Deification 88, 92, 99

Deity..58, 77, 328

Didache..123

Didascalia Apostolorum 123, 124

Dionysius the Areopagite 16

Pseudo-Dionysius..16, 58

Disciplina arcani...36, 37, 39, 41

Dispensationalism...2

Docetism 37, 43, 320

Dogma 11, 36, 44, 56, 58, 61, 66, 135, 137, 193, 209, 210, 280, 282, 325, 343, 347, 349, 355, 366, 367, 419

Dogmatics 14, 366

Dormition 3, 21, 276, 339

Driscoll, Rev. Mark 129, 130

Durham, Edith 195

Ebionites..43

Ecclesiology 48, 51, 130

Ecumenical 17, 50, 81, 225, 334, 343

Ecumenical Council 83, 317, 323, 324, 325, 329, 334, 336, 338

Eden..96, 192, 355

Egypt 161, 223, 232, 244, 308

Ehrman, Bart D...292

Elijah................21, 143, 145, 162, 163, 173, 175, 176, 177

Elisha..173, 176

Elizabeth 17, 40, 125, 142, 184, 220, 247, 250, 260, 261, 266, 313, 314, 318

Emperor Constantine 13, 141, 164, 165, 166

Emperor Constantius 166

Emperor Diocletian...162

Emperor Trajan 39

Emperor Valens...166

Enoch 21

Eschatological 96, 117, 118, 159, 165, 168, 179, 181, 183, 228, 258, 333

Eschatology 48, 51, 63

Eschaton 47, 59, 299

Essene 163

Eucharist....................................19, 26, 39, 108, 144, 257

   Communion 39

Eucharistic..92

Eusebius 200, 216

Evangelica...22

evangelical 10, 19, 22, 40, 45, 419

Evangelical 4, 8, 22, 35, 40, 45, 46, 58, 192, 211, 213

Evdokimov, Paul 17, 55, 56, 84, 85, 91, 93, 99, 102, 128, 149, 158, 159, 218, 252, 253, 254, 257, 258, 355, 360

Eve 21, 43, 47, 51, 77, 79, 93, 94, 96, 101, 102, 111, 113, 118, 125, 170, 180, 184, 210, 215, 227, 231, 274, 285, 286, 303, 351, 352, 353, 354, 355, 356, 363, 365, 366

   Mother of all Sinners 352

Exegesis 20, 326

Faith 11, 23, 233, 251, 290, 327

Fiat...See Free will

Florovsky, Georges 89, 90, 325, 329, 333, 338

Forde, Gerhard O. 106

Forefeast of the Nativity...20

Free will 66, 72, 103, 115, 130, 169, 236, 250, 251, 253, 255, 256, 258, 283, 368, 370

Freeman, Fr. Stephen...272

Fundamentalism..................................2, 8, 9, 13, 21, 22, 26

Gabriel, George S.48, 220, 237, 239, 276, 283, 286, 299, 314, 333, 339

Geisler, Norman...247, 248

Gentiles..372

Gillett, Lev...39

Gillquist, Peter...............9, 34, 143, 220, 221, 222, 224, 226

Gnostic...........................37, 38, 42, 43, 87, 327, 328, 331

God the Father 12, 20, 31, 32, 33, 47, 54, 55, 59, 60, 62, 78, 81, 82, 83, 84, 85, 86, 97, 99, 100, 116, 128, 156, 169, 173, 182, 192, 202, 203, 214, 220, 234, 255, 267, 276, 278, 302, 303, 310, 317, 323, 324, 327, 328, 329, 330, 337, 339, 368

God the Word 18, 82, 83, 234, 240, 323, 330, 337, 339

God-Man 17, 56, 59, 90, 256, 327

   theandric mystery 186

   Theanthropos...327

Grace.................75, 240, 248, 280, 303, 304, 310, 349, 357

Graef, Hilda 20, 26, 27, 36, 39, 332

Greek 49, 61, 64, 140, 194, 196, 200, 213, 215, 231, 232, 237, 238, 241, 248, 274, 302, 318, 334, 343

Gregory of Nazianzus 44, 77, 83, 322

Guroian, Vigen...20, 118, 290

Hahn, Scott & Kimberly...19

Hainsworth, John 148, 334, 335

Halperin, David J...292, 293

Harrison, Nonna Verna...67, 309

Hebraism...194, 199

Hebrew 63, 87, 111, 139, 175, 176, 194, 271, 272, 274, 275, 290, 318, 336, 360

Hebrew Scriptures 270, 274

Hegesippus..200, 201

Helvidius 184, 189, 204, 205, 206, 291, 332

Henry, Matthew..293

Heresy 30, 31, 35, 37, 56, 60, 61, 87, 89, 186, 225, 317, 366

Hermeneutic......................77, 116, 227, 233, 271, 272, 298

Hermeneutics 272

Hermits 162

Hieromartyr Hilarion (Troitsky) 20

High Priestly Prayer 99, 100, 214

Hinduism 13

Hippolytus 123, 161, 346

Hislop, Alexander 37

Hodegetria 133, 371

Holy Bible

   Sacred Scripture 2, 4, 5, 6, 13, 16, 22, 35, 36, 39, 41, 45, 48, 57, 77, 96, 112, 116, 122, 125, 138, 145, 175,

192, 199, 205, 208, 210, 216, 220, 233, 296, 298, 299, 344, 347, 349, 358, 360

Scripture 3, 12, 34, 46, 51, 60, 77, 78, 125, 136, 139, 153, 154, 175, 176, 182, 184, 194, 199, 204, 206, 208, 209, 233, 266, 299, 315, 325, 357, 367

Word of God 2, 13, 21, 44, 47, 234, 307, 318, 320, 324, 337, 344, 346, 351

Holy Spirit 8, 16, 23, 32, 40, 41, 43, 44, 45, 47, 55, 59, 60, 69, 84, 85, 97, 99, 101, 109, 114, 115, 116, 117, 131, 149, 153, 173, 181, 182, 185, 188, 220, 231, 234, 235, 250, 252, 255, 258, 260, 267, 275, 276, 277, 278, 286, 305, 309, 310, 311, 314, 316, 327, 328,331, 335, 339, 349, 352, 354, 368

Hopko, Thomas 160

Howard, Thomas 22, 23

Human being 27, 30, 69, 73, 89, 102, 108, 128, 162, 251, 283, 310, 326, 344, 352

Human nature 20, 30, 44, 68, 72, 76, 80, 82, 83, 84, 85, 100, 103, 108, 182, 225, 234, 255, 280, 281, 282, 325, 328, 330, 331, 341, 348, 363

Humanity 24, 30, 31, 32, 33, 37, 43, 44, 47, 55, 56, 58, 59, 60, 61, 62, 63, 64, 65, 68, 69, 72, 74, 75, 78, 79, 80, 81, 82, 83, 84, 85, 86, 89, 90, 91, 92, 94, 101, 102, 103, 105, 106, 108, 111, 112, 116, 118, 125, 135, 153, 186, 193, 202, 203, 215, 221, 242, 250, 253, 256, 271, 281, 290, 310, 317, 323, 328, 339, 343, 352, 354, 419

Hypostasis... 59

Hypostatic union 256

Ignatius of Antioch 34, 37, 38, 125, 173, 307

Image and likeness 42, 58, 59, 64, 66, 69, 71, 72, 75, 76, 77, 79, 80, 91, 97, 102, 108, 135

Image of God 66, 71, 72, 73, 74, 75, 76, 79, 80, 102, 104, 128, 157, 250, 253

Immaculate Conception 45, 63, 230, 248, 343, 347, 349, 367, 368

Immanence... 118, 267

Immanuel 18, 274, 278, 331, 365

Incarnation vi, vii, viii, 2, 8, 14, 16, 17, 18, 20, 21, 22, 23, 24, 25, 26, 27, 29, 30, 31, 32, 36, 37, 43, 44, 46, 47, 48, 51, 55, 56, 58, 59, 60, 62, 64, 65, 68, 69, 75, 77, 80, 81, 83, 84, 85, 87, 89, 90, 107, 108, 114, 115, 116, 117, 118,

169, 182, 183, 186, 187, 188, 189, 213, 215, 216, 222, 228, 230, 250, 251, 256, 258, 260, 263, 267, 271, 274, 277, 278, 279, 280, 282, 283, 299, 302, 305, 316, 320, 323, 324, 325, 329, 331, 335, 336, 337, 338, 352, 354, 360

Isaac 173
Isaiah 18, 27, 35, 39, 173, 177, 188, 189, 222, 224, 230, 243, 244, 274, 275, 277, 297, 307, 359
Islam 332
Israel 21, 27, 46, 68, 113, 115, 138, 145, 190, 205, 214, 228, 230, 232, 241, 242, 243, 245, 246, 257, 260, 261, 265, 275, 287, 288, 290, 291, 308, 318, 334, 335, 336, 352, 354, 357, 359, 363

Jacob 173
Jacob of Serug 229, 354
Jahn, Curtis A. 262, 263
James 195
James the Younger 200
Jephthah 122, 175, 182
   dreadful vow 122, 175
Jeremiah 173, 243, 245, 246, 248, 312, 357, 358, 359
Jesus 13, 16, 19, 21, 23, 27, 29, 30, 31, 32, 33, 37, 39, 40, 41, 42, 43, 45, 58, 59, 62, 68, 78, 79, 82, 86, 91, 96, 97, 99, 100, 110, 118, 125, 129, 130, 142, 143, 145, 154, 157, 159, 162, 172, 173, 176, 179, 180, 181, 182, 184, 185, 188, 189, 190, 191, 192, 193, 194, 195, 196, 198, 199, 200, 201, 202, 204, 205, 206, 212, 214, 215, 216, 217, 218, 219, 220, 226, 227, 228, 231, 232, 236, 238, 239, 242, 244, 250, 254, 258, 265, 267, 270, 271, 276, 277, 293, 296, 297, 298, 302, 305, 307, 311, 313, 315, 327, 328, 332, 334, 339, 340, 345, 348, 351, 356, 357, 359, 364, 365, 370, 419
   Lord 16, 17, 18, 20, 21, 22, 24, 29, 38, 40, 43, 47, 49, 59, 69, 81, 82, 84, 85, 89, 104, 117, 144, 153, 156, 158, 159, 169, 182, 184, 185, 188, 201, 202, 206, 213, 215, 217, 224, 229, 231, 233, 239, 258, 272, 274, 277, 280, 283, 303, 304, 305, 309, 322, 323, 327, 328, 329, 330, 343, 354, 370
   Son of God 20, 25, 26, 27, 30, 31, 32, 33, 36, 39, 43, 48, 55, 57, 58, 59, 68, 69, 80, 82, 84, 107, 116, 117, 118,

125, 213, 215, 216, 231, 234, 235, 250, 255, 267, 278, 282, 286, 305, 323, 327, 330, 331, 350, 352

Jesus Christ 2, 12, 16, 19, 21, 22, 30, 31, 32, 33, 35, 37, 38, 41, 42, 43, 44, 45, 46, 48, 49, 51, 55, 56, 57, 61, 62, 68, 69, 75, 80, 81, 82, 83, 85, 87, 89, 90, 96, 97, 99, 101, 107, 108, 109, 110, 112, 116, 117, 118, 124, 126, 127, 128, 129, 133, 134, 136, 141, 143, 144, 145, 150, 153, 154, 155, 156, 157, 158, 163, 166, 168, 170, 173, 181, 182, 183, 185, 186, 187, 188, 189, 190, 192, 193, 194, 195, 197, 198, 202, 205, 213, 215, 218, 221, 224, 230, 244, 246, 251, 255, 256, 257, 258, 271, 275, 276, 277, 278, 281, 283, 285, 286, 288, 291, 292, 293, 296, 298, 299, 302, 304, 307, 309, 310, 311, 312, 315, 316, 318, 320, 321, 322, 323, 326, 327, 328, 329, 330, 331, 332, 333, 334, 336, 340, 344, 346, 347, 348, 349, 351, 352, 354, 360, 363, 364, 366, 370, 419

fiat 255

Messiah.....................35, 43, 247, 260, 281, 287, 288, 315

seed of the woman............21, 56, 117, 215, 285, 286, 351

John Paul II 79, 93, 98, 101, 180

John Rylands Papyrus 470...139

John the Baptist 21, 173, 176, 216, 228, 248, 255, 258, 340, 344, 345, 346

fiat 255

Joseph of Arimathea...185

Joseph, putative Father of Jesus 31, 32, 33, 116, 148, 173, 182, 184, 185, 191, 196, 198, 199, 200, 201, 204, 205, 211, 247, 274, 314, 334, 335, 336

Josephus, Flavius...176

Joshua 173

Judaism 87, 270, 290

Just Jr., Arthur A. 228, 264, 354

Justification 137, 256

Kecharitomene..237, 238, 239

Kerygma 318, 326

Khomyakov, Aleksei...11

Klug, Dr. Eugene F. 76, 77

Koblosh, Fr. Michael..167

Kotzer Rebbe 251

Kotzker Rebbe 251

Kreitzer, Beth 50, 221

Lane, Anthony 31

Lazarus 21, 42, 91, 142, 370

Leeming, Bernard 49, 189, 256, 278, 320, 321

Lenski, R. C. H. 227, 228, 237, 239

Letham, Robert 225

Libanius 170

Likeness of God 66, 72, 75, 79

Lloyd-Moffett, Stephen R. 131

Logos 17, 32, 59, 75, 89, 103, 330, 331

LORD God 79, 91, 250, 252, 260, 285, 312, 335, 336

Lossky, Vladimir 35, 44, 209, 271, 344

Luther, Martin 12, 25, 49, 50, 136, 137, 139, 173, 189, 193, 275, 302, 303, 320, 332

Lutheran 2, 4, 5, 10, 26, 34, 49, 50, 68, 76, 106, 133, 136, 137, 143, 144, 145, 173, 182, 191, 208, 209, 217, 223, 237, 238, 239, 253, 255, 256, 312, 320, 330

Machan, J. Gresham 49, 189

Magnificatix, 175, 216, 217, 226, 227, 228, 245, 260, 262, 263, 264, 266

Manelli, Fr. Stefano M 238, 273, 288

Manicheans 328

Marcion 43, 87

Marcionites 328

Mariology 2, 3, 4, 5, 8, 10, 13, 26, 34, 35, 36, 45, 54, 61, 64, 117, 118, 122, 124, 125, 127, 130, 133, 134, 138, 210, 215, 216, 220, 274, 299, 311, 321, 325, 329, 336, 338, 367, 368

Marian doctrine 3, 4, 5, 6, 41, 46, 49, 50, 54, 124, 125, 193, 194, 228, 229

Marriage 92, 122, 148, 174, 179, 274, 338, 348

Martyrdom 125, 158, 159, 166, 168, 191, 201, 255, 322

Mary Magdalene 199, 200

Mary, the wife of Clopas 200

Mascall, Eric 21

Masoretic text 275

Material realm 43, 56, 57, 58, 60, 77, 94, 327

Maximovitch, St. John 198, 205, 347, 348

McGuckin, Fr. John Andrew 326

McGuckin, Fr. John Anthony 20, 54, 59, 211, 260, 334

McKnight, Scot 35

Melanchthon, Philip 136

Melchizedek...173

Mencken, H.L. 128, 134, 135

Metropolitan John of Pergamon 106

Miriam...142, 175

Mohammed 225

Monasticism 149, 154, 158, 161, 163, 165, 166, 167, 168, 173

Monk John, Presbyter of Euboea 315

Monogamy 149, 160, 170

Monophysites 43, 82

Moses 21, 27, 42, 85, 95, 142, 143, 145, 162, 172, 175, 190, 202, 204, 272, 285, 296, 302, 303, 304, 309, 312, 315, 335

Moss, Vladimir 101

Mother Maria Skobtsova..11

Mother of Christ 43, 225, 317, 321, 323, 329, 337

Muhammad ....*See* Mohammed

Myers, Philip Van Ness 161, 165

Mystery 13, 17, 34, 36, 37, 43, 54, 55, 56, 58, 81, 108, 124, 132, 149, 169, 170, 181, 187, 188, 229, 253, 279, 282, 283, 291, 299, 318, 338

natus ex virgine.................*See* Virgin Birth, *See* Virgin Birth

Nelson, Lynn H...161

Nestorian 225, 226, 321, 323, 325

Nestorianism.............................36, 43, 225, 299, 323, 331

Nestorius 186, 226, 317, 322, 324

New Testament 4, 22, 35, 43, 46, 103, 122, 127, 142, 155, 185, 193, 194, 197, 211, 220, 233, 238, 239, 245, 272, 280, 297, 309, 313, 318, 334, 351, 352, 364

Nicea........*See* Ecumenical Council, *See* Ecumenical Council

Nicodemus 277

Nimrod 13

Oecumenius the heretic...321

Oecumenius the heretic...312

Old Testament 4, 20, 26, 27, 35, 39, 43, 87, 138, 158, 163, 175, 177, 190, 194, 203, 211, 224, 230, 232, 233, 241, 242, 243, 245, 270, 271, 272, 275, 284, 285, 287, 290, 296, 297, 313, 351, 352, 357, 371

opus Dei..252, 256

Origen...216, 218, 364, 365
Original Sin 29, 62, 278, 282, 341, 343, 348, 349, 350
Orthodox, Eastern 2, 3, 4, 5, 8, 16, 17, 18, 19, 20, 26, 29,
    35, 40, 48, 54, 67, 91, 92, 97, 99, 109, 127, 129, 136,
    140, 141, 158, 159, 167, 196, 209, 220, 233, 240, 282,
    290, 317, 327, 331, 334, 343, 347, 348, 349
Orthodoxy, Eastern 334
Outler, Dr. Albert 127
Paganism 13, 14, 21, 32, 36, 37, 57, 68, 141, 150, 161,
    166, 170, 171, 255, 358, 359
    heathen religion 280
Panagia...338, 343, 369
Papist 136, 256
Paradise 93, 112, 282, 300, 360, 369
Pascal, Blaise 254
Pater Potestas..214
Pelagians...343
Pelikan, Jaroslav Jan 117, 185, 189, 238, 318, 320, 351,
    363, 364, 365
Pentecost.................................209, 211, 216, 258, 293, 370
Pentecostal...25
Perry, Professor Tim...............................213, 215
Peter of Alexandria 332
Pharisees 96, 172, 180
Philo...163, 335
Philosophy...89
Pietism 25
Pliny the Younger 39
Polycarp 125, 346
Pope John Paul II 13, 95
Pope Paul VI..94
Pope Pius IX 367
Presbyterian 16, 133, 293
Preus, Robert 209
Protestant 2, 3, 4, 5, 8, 9, 10, 11, 13, 18, 19, 21, 23, 34, 40,
    41, 42, 43, 45, 48, 49, 50, 51, 54, 55, 58, 63, 76, 77, 115,
    116, 117, 118, 122, 130, 133, 134, 136, 137, 139, 145,
    146, 148, 169, 170, 179, 184, 189, 190, 193, 197, 208,
    209, 220, 221, 224, 227, 228, 229, 230, 233, 237, 253,

262, 270, 271, 278, 283, 293, 294, 298, 317, 320, 324, 328, 329, 331, 340, 341, 347, 349, 364, 367, 419

Protanstantism5, 9, 10, 11, 13, 22, 34, 45, 51, 127, 184, 299, 350

Protoevangelium 55, 117, 191, 215, 227, 273, 285, 288

Psilanthropism 43

Rabbi Menachem Mendel Morgensztern .....See Kotzer Rebbe

Ratzinger, Cardinal Joseph..13, 63, 128, 130, 132, 241, 242

Recapitulation 43, 103, 107, 125, 250, 353

Recrudescence 13

Reformation 9, 25, 26, 49, 50, 51, 127, 193, 208, 329, 344, 364

Magisterial 25

Radical..25, 26

Reformed................................208, 225, 253, 280, 282, 320

Resurrection..23, 292

Revivalism..25

Azusa Street..25

Romanides, John..49, 66

Rose, Fr. Seraphim..349

Ruach Elohim..See Holy Spirit

Rublev, Andre..99

Russia..167

Sabellianism..210

Sacrament 34, 108, 109, 149

Sadducees 142, 179, 181, 182

Saint Paul 24

Salvation 11, 17, 26, 36, 40, 42, 49, 50, 51, 56, 61, 65, 68, 69, 70, 82, 83, 84, 85, 89, 90, 104, 105, 109, 137, 145, 157, 169, 227, 235, 236, 254, 256, 258, 265, 270, 271, 283, 302, 318, 323, 326, 330, 335, 346, 350, 355

Samples, Kenneth R. 9, 45

Sanctification 70, 72, 104, 166, 258, 283, 349

Sanjuanist Triangle..98, 99, 250

Santeria 13

Satan..56, 285, 357

serpent.................227, 285, 286, 288, 307, 353, 354, 355

Scaer, Dr. David 190, 191, 192, 193, 195, 196, 199, 204

Schaff, Philip 170, 291

Schenk, Berthold Von..144

Schmemann, Fr. Alexander 5, 41, 61, 108, 161, 163, 165, 166, 167

Scripture Alone...26, 35, 317
  Sola Scriptura 41, 208, 263
Sebolt, Roland A..45
Septuagint...241, 274, 275
Seraphim 240, 368, 369
Shekinah...233, 289, 310
  overshadowing........47, 114, 231, 233, 235, 250, 286, 311
Shepherd of Hermas...151
Shoemaker, Stephen J...50
Skydsgaard, Professor K. E. 49, 320
Smalcald Articles...136
Smith, William...213
Solomon.................................39, 224, 244, 300, 312, 358
Son of God 20, 25, 26, 27, 30, 31, 32, 33, 36, 39, 41, 43, 47, 48, 54, 55, 57, 58, 59, 62, 68, 69, 78, 80, 81, 82, 84, 85, 97, 99, 100, 107, 115, 116, 117, 118, 125, 143, 144, 156, 202, 203, 213, 215, 216, 220, 231, 232, 234, 235, 240, 250, 255, 256, 267, 275, 278, 280, 282, 285, 286, 296, 304, 305, 309, 310, 317, 318, 323, 326, 327, 328, 329, 330, 331, 339, 348, 350, 351, 352, 354, 363, 368, 370, 371
Son of Man 36, 118, 125, 296
Sovereignty of God...66, 255
Spiritual realm...56, 57, 58, 309
Spurgeon, Charles Haddon...244
St. Ambrose of Milan.....................................275, 277, 348
St. Andrew of Crete...315, 316
St. Anthony 167
St. Athanasius 65, 83, 158, 186, 332
St. Augustine 8, 50, 62, 129, 166, 254, 275, 276, 277, 343, 349
St. Basil the Great 73, 74, 75
St. Bernard of Clairvaux 348
St. Ephrem the Syrian 112
St. Epiphanius of Cyprus...198
St. Gregory of Nazianzus...77, 78
St. Gregory Palamas 74, 105, 151, 152, 153, 154, 155, 156, 360, 370

St. Hilary of Poitiers...235
St. Ignatius of Antioch 34
St. Irenaeus...353
St. Irenaeus of Lyon...42, 71, 75
St. John Chrysostom 39, 112, 170, 181
St. John Damascene ....See St. John of Damascus
St. John of Damascus 266, 276, 327, 333, 339
St. John of Kronstadt 24, 71, 105, 141, 142, 146, 286
St. Justin Martyr 125, 286
St. Leo the Great 275
St. Luke 262
St. Maximus the Confessor........17, 47, 75, 76, 81, 169, 187
St. Nikolai Velimirovich 41
St. Peter of Damascus 266
St. Theodore the Studite 220
St. Theodotus of Ancyra..292
Staniloae, Dumitru 29, 44, 102, 103
Syria...27, 116, 123, 162
Teleology 70
The Fall of Man 48, 49, 51, 59, 63, 66, 75, 76, 77, 102, 107,
    108, 113, 153, 193, 282, 283, 341
The spiritual motherhood of men 351
Theolegoumenon...191, 192, 193
Theology of the body 93, 98, 180
Theotokian 18
Theotokos 18, 36, 43, 139, 140, 189, 220, 224, 225, 240,
    271, 276, 299, 304, 315, 316, 317, 318, 319, 320, 322,
    324, 325, 326, 327, 330, 331, 333, 336, 338, 344, 355,
    368
Thornton, L. S................................209, 227, 230, 231, 352
Thunberg, Lars...75
Touma, Fr. (Bitar)..251
Transcendence 17, 43, 58, 115, 116, 117, 118, 257, 267,
    293, 315
Transfiguration 109, 143, 231, 233, 311
Trinity 32, 47, 48, 69, 72, 92, 99, 101, 111, 116, 180, 181,
    183, 192, 209, 226, 267
    Triune God 48, 224
Tropological...375
Typology...............................271, 272, 296, 297, 299, 313

antitype............................245, 274, 296, 297, 305, 351, 357
archetype........21, 103, 182, 187, 189, 211, 276, 297, 304
type 85, 103, 187, 190, 245, 276, 290, 292, 296, 297,
    312, 313, 357, 366
Unger, Merrill F. 190, 193
Valentinians 419
Vatican II...46, 127
Veneration..375
Vincentian Canon...133
Virgin Birth vii, viii, 23, 29, 30, 31, 32, 33, 43, 49, 51, 183,
    186, 188, 189, 215, 263, 273, 277, 278, 279, 280, 282,
    285, 293, 332, 338, 352
Virgin Mary 2, 3, 4, 8, 13, 16, 17, 18, 19, 20, 21, 23, 24, 26,
    27, 30, 31, 32, 34, 35, 36, 37, 38, 39, 40, 41, 42, 43, 44,
    45, 46, 47, 48, 49, 50, 51, 54, 55, 56, 61, 62, 63, 66, 69,
    80, 82, 84, 85, 89, 90, 103, 108, 110, 115, 116, 117, 118,
    119, 124, 125, 127, 128,133, 136, 138, 139, 140, 143,
    144, 148, 153, 169, 170, 171, 175, 181, 182, 183, 184,
    185, 186, 187, 188, 189, 190, 191, 193, 194, 195, 196,
    198, 199, 201, 202, 203, 204, 205, 206, 208, 209, 210,
    211, 213, 215, 216, 217, 218, 219, 220, 221, 222, 224,
    225, 226, 227, 228, 229, 230, 231, 232, 233, 234, 235,
    236, 237, 238, 239, 240, 242, 245, 246, 247, 248, 249,
    250, 251, 252, 253, 254, 255, 256, 257, 258, 260, 261,
    265, 266, 267, 270, 271, 273, 274, 275, 276, 277, 280,
    281, 283, 285, 286, 287, 288, 290, 291, 292, 294, 299,
    302, 303, 304, 305, 306, 310, 311, 312, 313, 314, 315,
    317, 318, 319, 320, 321, 322, 323, 326, 327, 328, 329,
    330, 331, 332, 333, 334, 335, 336, 337, 338, 339, 340,
    341, 343, 344, 345, 346, 347, 348, 349, 351, 352, 353,
    354, 355, 356, 357, 358, 360, 363, 364, 365, 366, 367,
    368, 369, 370, 371, 419
    Aeiparthenos 122, 185, 333, 334, 336, 338, 339
    Blessed Virgin 5, 16, 20, 37, 39, 47, 49, 54, 63, 89, 103,
        108, 115, 144, 145, 184, 206, 211, 217, 229, 236,
        240, 255, 259, 272, 286, 293, 329, 333, 334, 346,
        354, 368
    daughter of Zion...................241, 242, 243, 244, 245, 246
    Ever-Virgin 122, 140, 148, 185, 199, 204, 220, 286, 322,
        332, 333, 334, 336, 337, 338, 339, 346, 347, 365,
        369
    fiat 103, 250, 252, 253, 254, 255, 256, 257, 258

Free Choice 271

Holy Mother.. 198, 337

Holy Virgin 36, 85, 211, 324

Mother of God 16, 18, 35, 43, 44, 45, 50, 82, 108, 117, 125, 140, 141, 142, 184, 209, 225, 226, 229, 233, 236, 266, 271, 286, 304, 305, 310, 315, 317, 318, 320, 321, 322, 323, 324, 326, 327, 329, 330, 331, 332, 333, 336, 337, 339, 344, 346, 347, 349, 352, 354, 356, 363, 366, 368, 370

Mother of the Christian Race 21, 108, 218, 219, 274, 352, 356, 357, 363, 364, 365, 366, 368

Panagia 369

Perpetual Virginity 3, 50, 183, 184, 186, 188, 189, 190, 191, 193, 194, 199, 204, 205, 206, 215, 219, 273, 291, 293, 294, 305, 314, 334, 340, 346, 355, 365

Queen of all Saints 45

Queen of Heaven 45, 145, 224, 357, 358, 359, 360, 368, 369

Semper Virgo 184, 185, 186, 191, 192, 196, 365

the sealed gate 203, 290, 291, 292, 294, 305

veneration of 2, 13, 35, 36, 37, 39, 40, 41, 43, 54, 55, 133, 217, 258, 259, 260, 306, 344, 345

woman in travail 246, 287, 288, 289

Virginity 32, 34, 39, 92, 122, 148, 149, 150, 151, 153, 154, 155, 156, 159, 160, 168, 169, 171, 172, 173, 175, 176, 177, 179, 181, 182, 183, 187, 189, 191, 206, 235, 274, 276, 281, 294, 333, 334, 335, 336, 338, 339, 355

Visitation, the.................................. 125, 216, 227, 260, 313

Vulgate 238, 248

Waldstein, Michael 98

White, Carolinne 165, 166

Yazykova, Irina 93

Zacharias 142, 184, 235, 247, 261, 314, 340

Zechariah 137, 138

Zwingli, Ulrich................................. 50, 193, 208, 320, 332

Endnotes

[1] (Krauth 1877, 33)

[2] I am embarrassed to admit this, as it shows how far I had strayed from ancient Christianity. In the second century, Irenaeus argued against this concept in his polemic against the Valentinians. "There are also some who maintain that he also produced Christ as his own proper son, but of an animal nature, and that mention was made of him by the prophets. This Christ passed through Mary just as water flows through a tube." (Schaff, ANF01 1884, 532) This passage describes how the body of Jesus was not derived from Mary, which is not what Protestants believe. However, what is of note here is the separation of the person of Jesus from that of His mother, a separation which is a *de facto* denial of the humanity of Christ.

[3] An argument can be made that the Latins go too far, abandoning analysis for speculation, then codifying speculation into infallible dogma. We are a long way from speaking of those excesses, however.

[4] There are Catholics who disagree with this assessment. Catholic author Sally Cunneen, in attempting to discover the real Mary, makes the following statement: "What is striking in the Gospel stories how seldom Mary is mentioned." (Cunneen 1996, 31)

[5] Christology is the study of the beliefs and doctrines concerning Christ.

[6] A common way of describing ourselves is as follows. "The Orthodox Church is evangelical, but not Protestant. It is orthodox, but not Jewish. It is catholic, but not Roman. It isn't non-denominational - it is pre-denominational. It has believed, taught, preserved, defended and died for the Faith of the Apostles since the Day of Pentecost 2000 years ago." In our liturgy we sing: "We have found the true faith, we have received the Holy Spirit, worshiping the undivided trinity, who has saved us."

[7] (Schmemann, The Virgin Mary: Celebration of Faith 1995, 12)

[8] In an article celebrating the 400th anniversary of the King James Bible, Christian bookstore owner Martha Hoepnner

notes: "The Bible isn't like other books. You don't get a Bible and say, 'Here, read it.' The Bible is something you're taught." (Rodriguez 2011) One is taught from within one's own tradition, which augments their system of hermeneutics by guiding and to some extent predetermining one's theological conclusions.

[9] (Martin 2000)

[10] (Jenkins 2003, 23)

[11] (Currie 1996, 155-156)

[12] Many evangelicals lump Eastern Orthodoxy together with Roman Catholicism, and thus dismiss them both, along with whatever doctrines and practices seem to distinguish Roman Catholics from Evangelicals. And since most Protestant churches continue to react against the papal pronouncements of the Immaculate Conception of the Virgin Mary, it is perhaps not surprising that the superficial resemblance of the Orthodox honor paid to the Virgin Mary should appear to link the Orthodox and the Catholic communions together. (Payton 2007, Loc 465)

[13] (Currie 1996, 13)

[14] (Gillquist 2009, 51)

[15] (Samples 1993)

[16] (Aulén 1960, 310-311)

[17] (Khomyakov 1977, 40-41)

[18] (Skobtsova 2003, 62, 65)

[19] (The World's Famous Orations 2003)

[20] A recrudescence is the reappearance of a disease after a quiescent period. Therefore, the term fits, for Protestants often think of Roman Catholicism as the reappearance of paganism in Christian garb.

[21] (Ratzinger, The Sign of the Woman 2005, 43)

[22] (Hislop 1959, passim)

[23] (The Christian Expositor n.d.)

[24] (Barth, Church Dogmatics The Doctrine of the Word of God, Volume 1, Part 2 1956, 143)

²⁵ (Evdokimov, In the World, of the Church: A Paul Evdokimov Reader 2001, 120)

²⁶ Paul Evdokimov (of blessed memory) is writing in the context of a larger discussion about the Virgin Mary, and quotes Maximus the Confessor's definition of "mystical" as "the one in whom is best manifest the birth of the Lord." Unfortunately, Evdokimov does not source this quote, and I've been unable to find an English language translation approximating the quote. I expect that is because Evdokimov was reading the original Greek, translating it in his head into Russian, then writing it in French, and I'm now quoting the English translation. In the context of Evdokimov's writing, I suspect he would agree with my modest alteration of his quotation, and its direct application to the Virgin Mary.

²⁷ (Holton 2009)

²⁸ (Schaff, NPNF2-11 2004, 209)

²⁹ (Pseudo-Dionysius, the Areopagite 1987, 65-66)

³⁰ (St Nikodimos of the Holy Mountain and St Makarios of Corinth 1981, 127)

³¹ (Evdokimov, Orthodoxy 2011, 187)

³² David Bradshaw, chair of the Department of Philosophy at the University of Kentucky, writes concerning certain scriptural passages that rarely discussed during his time as a Protestant. "Needless to say, the Magnificat was wholly off limits. I actually read this passage out loud once in a devotional session, when we each had been invited to read a passage to 'edify the brethren.' The result was a pained and embarrassed silence." (Vitz 2012, 21)

³³ (Arakaki 2012)

³⁴ (Arakaki 2012)

³⁵ (Hahn and Hahn, Rome Sweet Home: Our Journey to Catholicism. 1993, 145)

³⁶ (McGuckin 2011, 212)

³⁷ (Hieromartyr Hilarion (Troitsky) 2012)

³⁸ The Irmos (the first troparion) of the canon read during Compline on the day of the Forefeast of the Nativity.

[39] (Guroian 2010, 65)

[40] Chiaroscuro is an artistic technique using strong contrasts between light and dark. It creates a sense of space and volume; it both hides and reveals the subject.

[41] (Graef 2009, 25)

[42] (Mascall 1949, 41)

[43] Scott McLemee writes: "It might be a good moment to clarify the distinction between evangelical and fundamentalist Christianity, which are not the same thing even though the labels are often taken as synonymous. The evangelical Christian has had a transformative inner experience ... and then communicates the message of the gospels to others. The fundamentalist regards the scriptures as literally and timelessly true. The Bible was dictated by God in plain terms requiring no interpretation at all, except in a very few places where He has laid the symbolism on so thick (beasts, crowns, horsemen with names like War and Famine, etc.) that nobody can miss it. "Someone can be both evangelical and fundamentalist, of course. Each perspective plunges a believer right into the absolute. But they are ultimately distinct. To put it one way, the evangelical stance is ethical (it defines a way of living) while the fundamentalist claim is not just about interpretation but about access to knowledge (which is certain, unchanging, and immediately available)." (McLemee 2011) Ken Samples defines Fundamentalist as follows: "This term, like 'evangelical,' suffers from ambiguity, and has changed much in meaning since its first usage early in this century. Fundamentalists have always stood in opposition to liberalism within the church. But today the term conveys certain additional characteristics which set fundamentalists apart from other evangelicals, including: a general suspicion of scholarship, a separatist mentality which includes a rejection of the entire ecumenical movement, an anti-historical (anti-creedal) or restorational view of the church, and a rigid approach to what constitutes appropriate Christian conduct." (Samples 1993)

[44] (T. Howard 1984, 1)

[45] (T. Howard 1984, 3)

[46] (T. Howard 1984, 3-4)

[47] Perhaps you might think the implication is unfair—the implication that for Protestants, their interest in the Incarnation is merely sentimental. The explanation for this is likely more than can be explained in a footnote. The Incarnation embodies the reality that God became man, becoming one with both man and matter. He assumed into Himself the nature of createdness, thereby transforming it. Thus spirituality (of necessity) must have a physical dimension to it. You may argue from the Gospel of John: "God is a Spirit: and they that worship him must worship him in spirit and in truth." (John 4:24) But you divorce that from the accompanying verses: "The woman saith unto him, I know that Messias cometh, which is called Christ: when he is come, he will tell us all things. Jesus saith unto her, I that speak unto thee am he." (John 4:25-26) In other words, Jesus (in his physical body) expected worship "in spirit and in truth". You will recall that the word "worship" in Hebrew denotes the physical act of prostration; Jesus fully expected the Samaritan woman to prostrate herself before Him. You will also recall that Old Testament worship was intensely physical, being tied to a specific place, with specific physical acts being performed, acts that were laden with spiritual portent (Col 2:17). And so the idea that Christian worship is purely spiritual, with no specific physical forms, or acts, or physical representations, is not only foreign to the scriptures, but is ultimately a denial of the reality of the Word made flesh.

[48] (T. Howard 1984, 82)

[49] (St John of Kronstadt 2010, Kindle Locations 2856-2862)

[50] (Damick, Orthodoxy and Heterodoxy 2011, Kindle Locations 1761-1767)

[51] (Graef 2009)

[52] (Graef 2009, 4-5)

[53] (Bishop Hilarion Alfeyev 2008, 8)

[54] (Barth, Church Dogmatics The Doctrine of the Word of God, Volume 1, Part 2 1956, 176)

[55] (Lane 1977, 48)

[56] A materialistic understanding of the necessity of the

Virgin Birth has the following non-comprehensive list of problems.

- It presumes original sin is passed through the paternal line.
- It encourages a materialistic understanding of the Holy Spirit's overshadowing the Virgin Mary, implying the fertilization of Mary's egg by some sort of divine sperm. In which case, what is the difference between this view and the pagan view of gods impregnating human women?
- Since maleness is a large part of human existence, this implies the material world is somehow evil, which leads to the pagan philosophy of dualism

[57] (Staniloae, The Experience of God: The Person of Jesus Christ as God and Savior 2011, 61-62)

[58] (Lane 1977, 50)

[59] (Lane 1977, 50-51)

[60] The word "catholic" with a little "c" is a reference to that which has been believed everywhere, in every place, and by all, or what is sometimes called the church catholic. With a capital "C", Catholic is a shorthand reference to the Roman Catholic church.

[61] (Schaff, ANF01 1884, 87, 95-96)

[62] Lutherans retained a semblance of sacramental theology, but redefine them and limit them in a manner unacceptable to non-Protestant Christians. With the Catholics, they number the sacraments; unlike the Catholics, they only accept two sacraments—baptism and the Lord's Supper.

[63] (Schaff, ANF01 1884, 96)

[64] (Gillquist 2009, 97)

[65] (McKnight 2007, 3)

[66] (Lossky, Panagia 1949, 25)

[67] (Lossky, Panagia 1949, 24)

[68] St. Basil the Great writes: "Of the dogmas and proclamations [kerygma] that are guarded in the Church, we hold some from the teaching of the Scriptures, and

others we have received in mystery as the teachings of the tradition of the apostles." (St Basil the Great 2011, Kindle Location 1657) Metropolitan Hilarion Alfeyev notes that St. Basil the Great is speaking "chiefly of traditions of a liturgical or ceremonial character, passed down by word of mouth and thereby entering into church practice." (Alfeyev, Orthodox Christianity 2012, 16)

[69] (Breck, Scripture in Tradition 2001, 143)

[70] (Graef 2009, 25-26)

[71] (Hislop 1959, passim)

[72] (Schaff, ANF01 1884, 86)

[73] (Anonymous 1990)

[74] (Graef 2009, 27-28)

[75] (Pliny the Younger n.d.)

[76] The term "Archimandrite" can refer to a superior abbot who is given authority over several ordinary abbots and monasteries. However, it is more commonly used as an honorific, bestowed upon certain clergy out of respect, often out of gratitude for a special service to the church. This term is applied only to celibate clergy; married clergy receive the honorific of "archpriest".

[77] (Gillett 1949, 76)

[78] (Gillett 1949, 76)

[79] (Gillett 1949, 77)

[80] (Velimirovich 2010, 40)

[81] (Schmemann, The Virgin Mary: Celebration of Faith 1995, 12)

[82] (Schaff, ANF01 1884, 756-757)

[83] (Kelly 1972, 115)

[84] (Kelly 1972, 141)

[85] Part of this was a due to differences between the Greek language of Chalcedon, and its translation into Semitic languages which do not differentiate between person and nature (much like most languages do not differentiate between house and home). Another part of this was due to

political differences between the Eastern Roman Empire and Christian nations outside the empire, who did not consider being part of the Eastern Roman Empire to be a Christian.

[86] (Gregory of Nazianzus n.d.)

[87] (Staniloae, The Experience of God: Revelation and Knowledge of the Triune God 1998, 25)

[88] (Lossky, Panagia 1949, 26)

[89] This famous hermeneutical principle was developed by St. Jerome in his treatise against Helvidius, entitled *The Perpetual Virginity of the Virgin Mary*. He writes: "But as we do not deny what is written, so we do reject what is not written. We believe that God was born of the Virgin, because we read it. That Mary was married after she brought forth, we do not believe, because we do not read it." (Schaff, NPNF2-06 1892, 662) Jerome also stated that we do not adopt possibilities as the standard of judgment, but stick solely to the Word of God, which is a very Protestant understanding. Which is itself curious, because although we do not read that Mary was married after she brought forth, yet Protestants typically believe she was. The alternative position is expressed in the Akathist Hymn to the Virgin Mary, composed in the fifth or sixth century, whose odd-numbered strophes end with a phrase that may be literally translated: "Hail, Virgin and unmarried bride", but which Fr. Vincent McNabb translates as: "Hail! Bride Unbrided." (Gambero 1991, 339)

[90] Space does not allow for a fuller discussion regarding theological traditions and their impact on scriptural interpretation. For now, let us simply state that Protestants are inconsistent in their rejection of tradition. It is tradition — rather than any explicit scriptural evidence — that tells us that the calling of the first seven deacons is found in Acts chapter 6. Search the scriptures, and you will not find the term deacon used of any of these seven men; yet Protestants accept the witness of tradition in this area. To use Aleksei Khomyakov's terminology, Protestants selectively accept the living tradition of dogma in some areas, but not in others.

[91] (Piepkorn 2006, 313)

[92] (Leeming 1960, 91)

[93] (Samples 1993)

94 (E. Brunner 1947, 286)

95 This does not constitute an antimony in Orthodox thought, which makes a distinction between the essence of God, and his uncreated energies. It is unfortunate, but this topic is outside the scope of this book. For more information, I refer you to Gregory Palamas and his *Declaration of the Holy Mountain in Defence of Those who Devoutly Practice a Life of Stillness*, found in the Philokalia, volume 4. The footnotes to that text suggest other areas of exploration.

96 Fr. Daniel Byantoro, in comparing Christianity to Islam, notes that for Islam, the Quran is the Word made text (the Quran), while for Christians the Word became flesh. To carry this one step further, Mohammed is the means through whom the Word made Text was revealed, while for Christianity Mary is the means through whom the Word made Flesh was revealed. Thus, Christians venerate Mary in the same way and for much the same reason as Muslims venerate Mohammed. (Byantoro 2008)

97 The eschaton is the end of this world; eschatology is in part the study of the eschaton; to immanentize the eschaton is to attempt to either trigger the eschaton, or to bring to pass the conditions of the afterlife within the conditions of the here and now.

98 (Cunneen 1996, xviii)

99 (Maximus the Confessor 1985, 103)

100 (Gabriel 2000, 19)

101 (Romanides 2008, 32-33)

102 (Leeming 1960, 91)

103 (Leeming 1960, 95)

104 (Leeming 1960, 100)

105 (Zwingli 1905, 424)

106 See Phillip Cary's article in Pro Ecclesia, Vol. XIV, No. 4, entitled "Why Luther is Not Quite Protestant."

107 (Kreitzer 2004, 111)

108 This view of Mary as modeling traditional female roles is not exclusively Lutheran, nor even Protestant. Roman

Author Sally Cunneen cites a Catholic in her fifties with a rather negative view of Mary's example for women: "I can't separate her from the church's treatment of women as second-class citizens, good for cleaning churches, and taking care of priests and husbands, but not really equal." (Cunneen 1996, 12) Sara Khan notes that the Virgin Mary was preached as an example for women of their proper roles in society; daughter, wife, and mother. The contrast between the fallen Eve and the virtuous Mary was used to reinforce cultural norms. (Khan 2004, 121, 127-134)

[109] (Kreitzer 2004, 140)

[110] (Shoemaker 2006, 96-97)

[111] Eve at least argued with Satan, and was deceived. Adam didn't even bother to argue, but sinned willfully. This is why the phrase "in Adam" is descriptive of the fall, and of sinners in general: Eve was deceived, but Adam intentionally sinned.

[112] (McGuckin 2011, 210)

[113] (Evdokimov, Orthodoxy 2011, 157)

[114] (St Nicolas Cabasilas 2010)

[115] The arguments that the woman in the protoevangelium refers to anyone other than Mary are puerile at best, a conclusion in search of a rationale.

[116] (Evdokimov, Orthodoxy 2011, 187)

[117] The unknown author who wrote under the pseudonym Dionysius the Areopagite, in his writings on "The Celestial Hierarchy" (drawing from Platonic terminology) uses the terms intelligible and perceptible to describe the spiritual and material realms. In this work, he describes how figures of the perceptible realm, such as the "wheels within wheels" in Ezekiel's vision, lift us up from the physical to the transcendent; and from the transcendent to the contemplation of God. (Pseudo-Dionysius, the Areopagite 1987, 147-152) But Pseudo-Dionysius also makes clear in this and other writings that God in His essence remains beyond our comprehension. In that sense we are like the angels, for whom God remains a mystery, as even in the divine economy there are "things the angels desire to look into" (1 Pet 1:12). And although we are currently "a little

lower than the angels" (Heb 2:7), yet "we shall judge angels" (1 Cor 6:3), "for we be like him, for we shall see him as he is" (1 Jo 3:2).

[118] (Pseudo-Dionysius, the Areopagite 1987, 156)

[119] (Currie 1996, 143-144)

[120] (McGuckin 2011, 125)

[121] (Schmemann, The Virgin Mary: Celebration of Faith 1995, 45)

[122] (Meyendorff 1975, 11)

[123] (Schmemann, The Virgin Mary: Celebration of Faith 1995, 46)

[124] (Aulén 1960, 195-196)

[125] There are numerous attempts to rationalize the genetic basis of Jesus birth. One proposal has been parthenogenesis, or reproduction from a female alone. This is known to occur amongst various animals, and science has been able to stimulate cell division in unfertilized eggs of higher order animals. Some propose this is what the Holy Spirit did. (Flam 2005) (Thomas 2006) Another idea is that Jesus had 24 chromosomes; the 23 provided by Mary, plus a Y chromosome provided by the Holy Spirit. (R. Howard n.d.) This attempt to rationalize a mystery is one of the Islamic arguments against the Virgin Birth. (Ahmad n.d.)

[126] (Ratzinger, Eschatology: Death and Eternal Life 1988)

[127] (St Athanasius 1993, 29)

[128] (St Athanasius 1993, 30)

[129] (Romanides 2008, 51)

[130] (N. V. Harrison, God's Many-Splendored Image: Theological Anthropology for Christian Formation 2010, 3)

[131] (P. Brunner 1968, 35)

[132] I note that even in this, one of the more profound discussions of the Incarnation in Protestant literature, I find no reference to the Virgin Mary's connection with the Incarnation.

[133] Teleology has to do with the *telos*, the end (purpose, object, or goal) of existence. Teleology is a philosophical

concept, whereas eschatology (last things) is specific to theology. Teleology is concerned with the *why* of things, whereas eschatology is concerned with the *what* and *when* of the last things (death and judgment, heaven and hell).

[134] (St John of Kronstadt 2010, Kindle Edition, Locations 1692-1695)

[135] (Cortez 2010, Kindle Locations 204-206)

[136] (Lossky, The Mystical Theology of the Eastern Church 1958, 120-121)

[137] (Cortez 2010, Kindle Locations 219-225)

[138] (St Basil the Great 2005, 35-36)

[139] (St Gregory Palamas 2013, Kindle Locations 917-920)

[140] (St Basil the Great 2005, Kindle Locations 620-626)

[141] Tropological has to do with a type of biblical interpretation that stresses the use of metaphor and, in particular, the moral meaning of the metaphor.

[142] (Thunberg 1985, 55)

[143] (Klug 1984, 146)

[144] (Klug 1984, 146)

[145] (St Gregory Nazianzen 1893, 630)

[146] (St Gregory Nazianzen 1893, 630)

[147] (Romanides 2008, 65)

[148] (Bransfield 2010, 84)

[149] The misandrist joke that God created Adam first, then corrected his errors when he made Eve, is not only a poor joke, it is poor theology. Eve is made of the same stuff as Adam, which is why Adam could say: "This is now bone of my bones, and flesh of my flesh" (Ge 2:23). Thus, the orders of creation do not support the inherent superiority or inferiority of either gender. In particular, the misogynist conception of the superordination of men and the subordination or subjugation of women does not exist by divine degree, but is rather a consequence of our fallen state, which means that the curse is the result of our choices and actions rather than the will or decree of God. Nonna Harrison comments: "In early Christian times, this

Scripture was usually interpreted in a way opposite to the misogynistic joker's interpretation. For one thing, the word translated "rib" also means "side" in Hebrew and Greek. So in effect, the verse means that man is one "side" of humankind while woman is the other. (N. V. Harrison, God's Many-Splendored Image: Theological Anthropology for Christian Formation 2010, 96)

150 (St Athanasius 1993, 93)

151 (St Nikodimos of the Holy Mountain and St Makarios of Corinth 1981, 250)

152 (Schaff, NPNF2-14 2005)

153 Part of this problem was due to language differences: Greek has one word for nature, and another for person, while the native languages of the monophysites used the same word for both nature and person. Another problem was political; the monophysites wanted to be Christian without being part of the Eastern Roman (or Byzantine) Empire, and a theological rupture was the only political way to be Christian and maintain their political independence.

154 (Schmemann, The Historical Road of Eastern Orthodoxy 2003, 173)

155 (Schaff, NPNF2-14 2005)

156 (Gregory of Nazianzus n.d.)

157 (Evdokimov, Woman and the Salvation of the World 1994, 221)

158 (Evdokimov, Woman and the Salvation of the World 1994, 221-222)

159 (Skarsaune 2002, 243-244)

160 (Skarsaune 2002, 244, 246, 254-255)

161 (Breck, God With Us: Critical Issues in Christian Life and Faith 2003, 41)

162 (Florovsky 1976, 31)

163 The idea of the flesh as the prison of the soul is sometimes expressed at the death of a believer when it is said they have gone to a better place, as though the sundering of body and spirit was not a tragedy great enough to cause even our Lord to shed bitter tears (Jn 11:35).

[164] This is why the worship of God is not merely spiritual, but also bodily. In Sacred Scripture, worship is a bodily action, a bowing down, a prostration. The psalmist sings: "in thy name will I lift up my hands" (Ps 62(63):4). The apostle tells us to "Glorify God in your body and in your spirit, which are God's" (1 Cor 6:20). And again the apostle tells us to "pray everywhere, lifting up holy hands without wrath and doubting" (1 Tim 2:8). This is the anthropological reason why most Christians have no difficulty crossing themselves, for they recognize that what we do in the body affects the soul. It can be argued that God "is [not] worshipped with men's hands, as though he needed anything" (Acts 17:25). Likewise, "God is a Spirit, and they that worship Him must worship Him in spirit and in truth." Elder Cleopa of Romania explains these passages for us. "The first passage...tells us only that we should not worship God with the toil of our hands as we would someone who is our superior. God doesn't have need of that kind of service. ...The second passage concerns other, completely different matters. Specifically it said that soon there will begin another age in which the worship of God will be true and perfect, internal and spiritual, and not as it had existed—all but conventional (external and material)." (Elder Cleopa of Romania 2007, 121)

[165] (Evdokimov, Woman and the Salvation of the World 1994, 72)

[166] (Evdokimov, Woman and the Salvation of the World 1994, 72-73)

[167] (Pennock 2010, 10)

[168] (John Paul II 2006, 146-156)

[169] (Yazykova 2010, 13)

[170] (Evdokimov, Woman and the Salvation of the World 1994, 39)

[171] (Pope Paul VI 1965, 12)

[172] This passage comes in the midst of a discussion of ordinances delivered to the Corinthian church; specifically, head coverings. Paul says men should pray with their heads uncovered, but women with their heads covered, because of the angels. Paul's meaning is unclear. There are some who say that women should pray with heads covered because

they bear the shame of Eve. Others say that women cover their heads so that the angels, who have no gender, may differentiate between men and women. However, there are others who say that women veil themselves because of the glory with which they are clothed on account of the Virgin Mary. The apostle seems to argue against the first interpretation when he discusses the interdependence of men and women, and their mutual dependence upon God. The sin of Adam and the shame of Eve have been blotted out in and through Christ, making the first void.

[173] (John Paul II 2006, 163)

[174] (John Paul II 2006, 167)

[175] Much could be said here about the nature of gender and sexual distinctions before the fall, and whether those distinctions were given in prevision of and preparation for the fall. This is not the place to delve into this discussion, but I refer those interested in such matters to "Eros in the Beginning", which is chapter one of Vladimir Moss's book *The Theology of Eros.* (Moss 2010). Although it does not address those matters directly, I would also direct your attention to Nonna Harrison's book *God's Many-Splendored Image.* (N. V. Harrison, God's Many-Splendored Image: Theological Anthropology for Christian Formation 2010)

[176] (Breck, God With Us: Critical Issues in Christian Life and Faith 2003, 29)

[177] (Evdokimov, Orthodoxy 2011, 240)

[178] (John Paul II 2006, 24)

[179] (Moss 2010, 18-19)

[180] (Moss 2010, 25)

[181] (Evdokimov, Woman and the Salvation of the World 1994, 152, 184)

[182] Note that Evdokimov's use of the phrase "gift of self" predates the writing and publication of John Paul II's study, *Man and Woman He Created Them.*

[183] (Staniloae, The Experience of God: Revelation and Knowledge of the Triune God 1998, 12)

[184] (Staniloae, The Experience of God: The Person of Jesus Christ as God and Savior 2011, 23)

[185] (Breck, God With Us: Critical Issues in Christian Life and Faith 2003, 31)

[186] (St John of Kronstadt 2010, 7)

[187] (St Gregory Palamas 2013, Kindle Locations 880-884, 887-888)

[188] (Forde 1997, 58)

[189] Unfortunately, this passage from Gerhard Forde describes the Lutheran view of humanity before the fall, and is part of a longer passage describing the Lutheran concept of the active and the passive will. Lutherans believe that even before the fall, mankind has only a passive capacity for good; after the fall, God will is active and working through His gifting of faith to mankind. (Forde's description of the Edenic state is remarkably close to the Orthodox view of anthropology, with the exception that Lutheran theology tends to focus too much on the fall, and not enough on the humanity as the image and likeness of God.) Forde notes that after the fall, the natural man is spiritually dead on account of original sin; the will of unregenerate man is only active in lower things, not in higher things. The will is active in higher things only when acted upon from the outside, through the gifting of faith. (Forde 1997, 56-58)

[190] (Metropolitan John of Pergamon 2003)

[191] (Lossky, The Mystical Theology of the Eastern Church 1958, 121-134)

[192] (Schmemann, The Eucharist 1988, 33-34)

[193] On the nature of the sign and the thing signified, Karl Barth notes: "Sign and thing signified, the outward and the inward, are, as a rule, strictly distinguished in the Bible, and certainly in other connexions we cannot lay sufficient stress upon the distinction. But they are never separated in such a ("liberal") way that according to preference the one may be easily retained without the other." (Barth, Church Dogmatics The Doctrine of the Word of God, Volume 1, Part 2 1956, 179) In other words, the sign always points to the thing signified. However, if we believe in the thing signified, we have to accept the sign as well—as, for example, with the virgin birth being the sign of the Incarnation (Isa 7:14).

[194] (John Paul II 2006, 163)

[195] The Lord is my light and my rescue.

Whom should I fear?

The Lord is my life's stronghold.

Of whom should I be afraid?

Ps 27:1, Robert Alter's translation (Alter 2007, xxv-xxvi; 91)

[196] (Alter 2007, xxviii)

[197] (St Ephrem the Syrian n.d., 99, 106)

[198] (Louth, Conti and Oden, Ancient Christian Commentary on Scripture: Old Testament I, Genesis 1-11 2001, 72)

[199] (Böhme 2009)

[200] (St Ephrem the Syrian 1989, 87)

[201] (Lossky, The Creation 1989, 77)

[202] (Pelikan, The Riddle of Roman Catholicism 1959, 134)

[203] While thinking about this, I noticed the title to the Wim Winders' movie "Faraway, So Close", the sequel to his movie "Wings of Desire". The central conceit of these two movies is that angels are always present, listening to us and providing comfort, yet separated by a seemingly unbridgeable gulf — just as for us God sometimes seems so far away, yet remains so close.

[204] Theories of inspiration come into play regarding later additions to the scriptures, such as the *Pericope Adulterae* (John 7:53-8:11). The issue is quite clear in John, where the original text appears to end at chapter 20; chapter 21 appears to have been added later, although Fr. John Breck provides an alternate and compelling explanation for this anomaly. (Breck, Scripture in Tradition 2001, 105-124) Another well-known issue exists in the gospel of Mark, where an entirely new ending (Mark 16:9-20) was appended to the original text. These additions were not written by the original authors, but added by disciples and copyists. If we emphasis the divine origin of scripture too much, we have to either 1) find a forced explanation for these passages, or 2) argue that they are not scripture. If we emphasis the human

origin of scripture too much, we end up arguing 1) that they merely "contain" the Word of God, 2) that the scriptures contain error and cannot be trusted, or 3) losing our faith altogether. A proper Mariology gives us a handle to properly understand inspiration, to understand scripture both as human creation and as holy writ.

[205] (Pelikan, The Riddle of Roman Catholicism 1959, 134)

[206] (Guroian 2010, 72)

[207] It was Christians who first began cutting scrolls into pages, sewing the four gospels together to form a Codex, the predecessor of our modern books. Even so, the Bible was still known as a collection of scrolls and codices—a library, and not a single book.

[208] A study by William Harris indicates "literacy rates were rarely higher than 10-15 percent of the population." (Ehrman 2005, 37)

[209] (O'Loughlin 2010, 26)

[210] Clement of Alexandria, writing in the 2nd century, quotes directly from the Didache as though it were scripture. In the Stromata, or Miscellanies, Book 1, chapter 20, he says: "he who appropriates what belongs to the barbarians, and vaunts it is his own, does wrong, increasing his own glory, and falsifying the truth. It is such an one that is by Scripture called a 'thief.' It is therefore said, 'Son, be not a liar; for falsehood leads to theft.' (Schaff, ANF02 2004, 529) This is a direct quote from the Didache 3:5, also known as The Teaching of the Twelve Apostles: "My child, be not a liar, since a lie leadeth the way to theft". (Schaff, ANF07 2004, 561) Irenaeus, also writing in the 2nd century, may mention the Didache in fragment 37, as discussed by Henry Wace: "In one of the fragments, published by Pfaff, as from Irenaeus, we read: 'Those who have followed the *Second Ordinances of the Apostles (οι ταις δευτεραις των αποστολων διαταξεσι παρηκολουθηκοτες)* know that our Lord instituted a new offering in the New Covenant according to the saying of Malachi the prophet, 'From the rising of the sun to the going down, my name has been glorified in the Gentiles; and in every place incense is offered to my name and a pure offering." This passage is quoted in the *Didaché* with reference to the Eucharist [Didache XIV:3-4]; not, however, textually, as in the fragment, but very loosely. We can only

say then that it is *possible* the *Didaché* may be the *Second Ordinances of the Apostles* referred to here." (Wace 2001)

[211] (Schaff, ANF07 2004)

[212] (Hippolytus 1997)

[213] (Chapman 1913)

[214] (Schaff, ANF07 2004)

[215] (Bulgakov 2009, Kindle Location 266)

[216] (Fletcher n.d., Beckett 2009, 30-31)

[217] (Beckett 2009, 31-32)

[218] (Beckett 2009, 31-33)

[219] (Beckett 2009, 33-34)

[220] (Gambero 1991, 29-32)

[221] (Gambero 1991, 44-47)

[222] (HP-Time.com 1964)

[223] (Balthasar and Ratzinger 1979, 16)

[224] (Evdokimov, Woman and the Salvation of the World 1994, 152-153)

[225] A *Schafskopf* is a German pejorative term meaning blockhead, dolt, or numskull.

[226] The Aurochs was the (now extinct) ancestor of domesticated cattle, and was much larger than modern breeds, standing nearly seven feet tall at the shoulder, and weighing well over 2,000 lbs.

[227] (Mencken 1922, 7)

[228] (Relevant Media Group 2007)

[229] *Kenosis* is an emptying; *plerosis* is a fullness or a filling up. Thus the seeming kenosis or emptying of Christ is actually His self-fulfillment.

[230] (K. Ware 1979, 82)

[231] (Balthasar and Ratzinger 1979, 16-17, 25-26)

[232] (Lloyd-Moffett 2009, 188-189)

[233] (Balthasar and Ratzinger 1979, 25)

[234] Pope Benedict XVI states: "[Mary is] the Hodegetria, the "Guide along the Way", who is also venerated in the West under the title "Our Lady of the Way". The Most Holy Trinity has given the Virgin Mother Mary to mankind, that she might guide us through history with her intercession and point out to us the way towards fulfillment." (Benedict XVI 2011)

[235] Mencken here is referring to the late Mediaeval identification of Mary Magdalene as being the penitent prostitute who washed Jesus's feet with her hair. There is no scriptural or historical support for this view.

[236] Mencken refers to the common theological misunderstandings of the apostle Paul. For example, when Paul says women should pray with their heads covered "because of the angels", it is often assumed this is a reference to Eve's shame. However, it is actually a reference to the glory they share with, through, and by virtue of the Virgin Mary; the "veiling" is similar to that of Moses having come down from the mount (Ex 34:32 – 35; 2 Cor 3:13).

[237] (Mencken 1922, 162-163)

[238] (Dau and Bente 1921, SA II, 26-28)

[239] (Tribe and Villiers 2011)

[240] (Orthodox Metropolitanate of Hong Kong and Southeast Asia 2011)

[241] (Mathewes-Green 2007, 85-86)

[242] (Tribe and Villiers 2011)

[243] This is an excerpt from the diary of St. John of Kronstadt. As such it lacks the theological precision one might otherwise expect. Theologically, we honor or venerate Mary and the saints, but reserve worship for God alone.

[244] (St John of Kronstadt 2010, Kindle Locations 3050-3059)

[245] (St John of Kronstadt 2010, Location 63-68)

[246] (Gillquist 2009, 101)

[247] (Aulén 1960, 310)

[248] (Von Schenk 1945)

[249] Scandinavian Lutheran churches often have a semi-

circular altar rail; the other half of the circle is in heaven, and reserved for the departed saints who celebrate their heavenly liturgy with us.

[250] (St John of Kronstadt 2010, Kindle Location 4056)

[251] (Hainsworth 2004)

[252] (Boychuk 2012)

[253] (Evdokimov, Orthodoxy 2011, 299)

[254] (Carlton 2006, 113)

[255] (Chesterton 1995, 95)

[256] (Chesterton 1995, 99)

[257] (Chesterton 1995, 103-104)

[258] To demonstrate the fluidity of the canon in the primitive Christian Church, it should be noted that Irenaeus, in his work "Against Heresies", refers to the Shepherd of Hermas as Scripture.

Truly, then, the Scripture declared, which says, "First of all believe that there is one God, who has established all things, and completed them, and having caused that from what had no being, all things should come into existence. He who contains all things, and is Himself contained by no one." [4.20.2] (Schaff, ANF01 1884, 815)

[259] (Schaff, ANF02 2004, 34)

[260] (St Nikodimos of the Holy Mountain and St Makarios of Corinth 1995, 300)

[261] (St Nikodimos of the Holy Mountain and St Makarios of Corinth 1995, 301)

[262] (St Nikodimos of the Holy Mountain and St Makarios of Corinth 1995, 289)

[263] (Alfeyev, Prayer and Monasticism in Orthodox Tradition 2008)

[264] (St Nikodimos of the Holy Mountain and St Makarios of Corinth 1995, 301-302)

[265] (St Nikodimos of the Holy Mountain and St Makarios of Corinth 1995, 328)

[266] (St. Cyril of Jerusalem 2013, Kindle Locations 3435-

3443)

267 (Behr-Sigel 2001, 59-60)

268 (T. Ware 1997, 15)

269 (Evdokimov, Orthodoxy 2011, 107)

270 Troparian of virgin martyrs.

271 (Evdokimov, Orthodoxy 2011, 28-29)

272 Interestingly, Islam has the same concept of the meaning of virginity. Nur al-Jerrahi writes: "Virginity is not primarily a biological condition but a spiritual state. To be a virgin, male or female, is to give oneself entirely to God, only to the living Truth." (Sheikh Muzaffer Ozak Al-Jerrahi 1991, i)

273 (Hopko 2012)

274 (Myers 1901, 541)

275 (Schmemann, Introduction to Liturgical Theology 1996, 131)

276 These are: pimp, sculptor, painter, actor, teacher, charioteer, gladiator, priest or attendant of idols, soldier, military authority, military governor, ruler of a city, prostitute, wanton man, man who castrates himself, one who does that which may not be mentioned (a homosexual?), sorcerer, enchanter, diviner of dreams, maker of amulets, and a man who has a concubine. (Hippolytus 1997)

277 (Schmemann, Introduction to Liturgical Theology 1996, 95)

278 (Nelson 1999)

279 (Baker 2004)

280 (Schmemann, Introduction to Liturgical Theology 1996, 68-89, passim)

281 (White 1998, xv)

282 (Myers 1901, 541)

283 (Schmemann, Introduction to Liturgical Theology 1996, 132)

284 (White 1998, xiii)

[285] (Schmemann, Introduction to Liturgical Theology 1996, 133)

[286] (Schmemann, Introduction to Liturgical Theology 1996, 133)

[287] (Koblosh 2010)

[288] (Maximus the Confessor 1985, 104)

[289] I note again that the reference to women praying with their heads covered is often interpreted as a sign of women's subordination to men. This is not the apostle's intent; his entire line of reasoning is typological, and we are meant to ponder the Eve-Ava mystery as we read.

[290] (Schaff, History of the Christian Church, Volume I: Apostolic Christianity. A.D. 1-100. 1882, 316-317)

[291] (Schaff, ANF01 1884, 133)

[292] (John Paul II 2006, 428)

[293] For additional information I recommend St. Gregory of Nyssa's treatise *On Virginity*, available in NPNF2-05.

[294] (Kreitzer 2004, 98)

[295] Some argue that Jephthah did indeed sacrifice his daughter as a burnt offering. This would seem to violate Scripture itself: Abraham was spared from actually sacrificing his son Isaac (Ge 22:9-14); the Hebrews were sent into captivity for, among other things, sacrificing their children to Molloch (Am 5:26); and parents were known to have delivered their children over to be raised by the priests at the temple (1 Sam 1). Since human sacrifice was forbidden, it is reasonable to assume Jephthah's daughter was given over (sacrificed) to the Lord. However, there is another argument which can be made, which is that the prohibition against human sacrifice is a rather late development in Judaism. (T. Stark 2011, Kindle Locations 3029-3049)

[296] (Souvay 1909)

[297] The first book of Moses says to "be fruitful, and multiply, and fill the earth", and records God's promise to Abraham that his offspring would be "as the stars of the heaven, and as the sand which *is* upon the sea shore" (Ge 1:28; 22:17). Procreation was not only a religious obligation, but had

almost a sacramental significance for the Jews. Moreover, the fifth book of Moses says that a person "that is wounded in the stones ...shall not enter into the congregation of the Lord. The forced castration of their best and brightest sons is one reason why the psalmist writes: "O daughter of Babylon, who art to be destroyed; happy shall he be, that rewardeth thee as thou hast served us. Happy shall he be, that taketh and dasheth thy little ones against the stones" (Ps 137: 8-9). By castrating their best and brightest, the Babylonians had cut their sons off from the congregation; according to the law of Moses, their sons had been denied the possibility of procreation, and thereby denied the blessing of the Lord.

[298] (John Paul II 2006, 423)

[299] Because a marriage is a sign and symbol of the relationship the trinity has with itself, and also because marriage is a sign and symbol of the relationship between Christ and the church, a marriage without children is not only valid, but still serves its ultimate purpose.

[300] (Schaff, NPNF1-09 1889, 294-295)

[301] (Luther and Knaake, Weimarer Ausgabe 1883, v11, 319-320)

[302] (Schaff, NPNF2-06 1892)

[303] (Pelikan, Mary Through the Centuries: Her Place in the History of Culture 1996, 29-30)

[304] (Cunningham, All-Holy Infant: Byzantine and Western Views on the Conception of the Virgin Mary 2006, 127)

[305] (Schaff, NPNF2-04 1892, 223)

[306] (St Nikodimos of the Holy Mountain and St Makarios of Corinth 1981, 166)

[307] (The Christian Apologetics Society 2007)

[308] This was written in 1960, well before Jaroslav Pelikan's conversion from Lutheranism to Orthodoxy in 1998.

[309] (Leeming 1960, 99-100)

[310] Prolepsis is that which is anachronistically present before its proper time. Thus we could say that the angel Gabriel was proleptically present in the person of Moses at

the dividing of the waters; and that the Virgin Birth and Mary's perpetual virginity were proleptically present in the crossing of the Red Sea.

311 (Breck, Scripture in Tradition 2001, 64-65)

312 (Unger 1966, 702)

313 (Scaer, Semper Virgo: A Doctrine 2010, 15)

314 The attempt to "revive the faith of a pristine church" is the functional definition of repristination. In Lutheran history, repristination was an attempt to restore historical Lutheranism over and against the Prussian Union, which attempted to unify the Lutheran and Reformed churches in Germany. Although the founder of the Lutheran Church-Missouri Synod (C.F.W. Walther) is historically identified as part of this movement, today the term is generally used in a pejorative sense, for a romantic attachment to a golden age. Dr. Scaer is careful not to use the term, but the thoughtful theologian will see it there nonetheless.

315The statement "*Et homo factus est*" comes from the Nicene Creed. It is translated "And became man."

316 (Scaer, Semper Virgo: A Doctrine 2010, 16)

317 (Cunneen 1996, 35)

318 It is possible that some of the biblical authors wrote through an amanuensis, a person who takes dictation. Dr. David Scaer (Chairman of Systematic Theology at Concordia Theological Seminary), in his book *Discourses in Matthew*, describes how an author would create at least two copies of a writing—one for himself and his congregation, and one (or more) to be sent out. (Scaer, Discourse in Matthew: Jesus Teaches the Church 2004, 102-105) Often an amanuensis would be employed to translate what the author said into another language—Rudyard Kipling has his protagonist employing this process in his book *Kim*; the letter writer would ask which language the letter was to be written in, and would then translate it on the fly. (Kipling 1990) Thus it is possible the biblical authors actually spoke in Aramaic, and the author's wrote it down in Greek—which could account for some of the curious Hebraisms in scripture. (Marlowe n.d.)

319 (Durham 2009, 21)

Endnotes

[320] (Scaer, Semper Virgo: A Doctrine 2010, 15)

[321] The Johannine account of Jesus committing his Mother to the care of the apostle John, and the apostle John to the care of His mother, is theologically significant because Mary is the Mother of the Christian Race. (See chapter 62.) She is our Mother, and we are her children.

[322] The reader should know that I do not consider Dr. Scaer and others to be disingenuous, nor to be poor scholars. Far from it; Dr. Scaer is one of the most brilliant scholars I've ever met. Instead, I consider Dr. Scaer and others to be under the sway of their particular traditions — traditions that will not allow them to accept or even properly evaluate alternative positions.

[323] This list is not comprehensive. I left off some specialized usages which required prefixes, and I did not include all the references. For example, W.E. Vine assumes that references to Jesus' brethren are either male children of the same parents or male children of the same mother. Since our argument is against this interpretation, it seemed valid to let the reader decide for him or herself.

[324] (The Christian Apologetics Society 2007)

[325] In Christian usage, the term 'brother' is similar to the way our Lord used the term 'neighbor'. In Sacred Scripture, the term neighbor (πλησιον, plesion) can mean neighbor, friend, a member of the Hebrew nation, or simply one's fellow man. In Luke chapter 10, a lawyer quotes the law to Jesus: "Thou shalt love the Lord thy God with all thy heart, and with all thy soul, and with all thy strength, and with all thy mind; and thy neighbour as thyself"; the lawyer then asks: "Who is my neighbor?" (Lu 10:27, 29). Jesus then tells the parable of the Good Samaritan regarding two men who passed by a wounded and dying, and a third—a foreigner—who dressed the man's wounds, carried him to lodging, and then paid for everything. Jesus then asks: "Which now of these three, thinkest thou, was neighbour unto him that fell among the thieves?" Upon hearing the answer, our Lord then says the lawyer (and to us): "Go, and do thou likewise." Therefore, all humanity are our brothers and sisters; we are called to be neighbors to every person we come in contact with—to bind their wounds, to heal their hurts, to take on their debts—for they are our brethren.

[326] (St John of Shanghai & San Francisco 2005)

[327] (Schaff, NPNF2-01 1890, 248)

[328] (Schaff, NPNF2-01 1890, 380)

[329] (Scaer, Semper Virgo: A Doctrine 2010, 17)

[330] (Maximovitch 2004, 32)

[331] Church traditional tells us the so-called brothers and sisters of our Lord are Joseph's children by a wife who died before he was betrothed to Mary. However, with Protestants it is better to make the case from the text of Scripture rather than from tradition.

[332] (Schaff, NPNF2-06 1892, 646)

[333] (Damick, Orthodoxy and Heterodoxy 2011, Kindle Locations 1089-1091)

[334] (Damick, Orthodoxy and Heterodoxy 2011, Kindle Locations 1102-1106)

[335] (Thornton 1949, 9)

[336] (Lossky, Panagia 1949, 24)

[337] (Preus 1977, 22)

[338] Adoptionism is the belief that Jesus was an ordinary man who became the Christ and the Son of God at His baptism; Sebellianism is the belief that Father, Son, and Holy Ghost are roles God takes in his interactions with humanity, and ways humanity perceives and experiences God. Arianism is the belief that the Father is a superior and distinct being to the Son, and the Son is a superior and distinct being to the Holy Spirit; in other words, that Father, Son, and Holy Spirit are distinct from each other in their essence, and exist in a superior/subordinate relationship with each other.

[339] (Thornton 1949, 9-10)

[340] (McGuckin 2011, 211)

[341] (Perry 2006, 22-24)

[342] (Smith 1843, 741)

[343] (Smith 1843, 741)

[344] (Perry 2006, 25)

[345] It is beyond the scope of this book, but the Immaculate Conception of Mary is a late Catholic doctrine designed to protest the dogma of Original Sin, a concept which is alien to Christianity prior to Augustine, was never expressed by any ecumenical council, and was promulgated in the west only.

[346] By contrast, apart from a brief conversation with an Angel, Joseph is silent—which is theologically significant and sociologically surprising.

[347] (Evdokimov, Woman and the Salvation of the World 1994, 213)

[348] Everett F. Harrison, Professor of New Testament Studies at Fuller Theological Seminary, dismisses the Pauline influence of Luke's Gospel. "The idea that when Paul referred to 'my gospel' (Rom 2:16) he had in mind the Gospel account drawn up by Luke, was widely current among the Fathers. This notion will not stand examination in the light of the Prologue, where the testimony of eyewitnesses is made the basis of the materials used. Paul does not qualify as an eyewitness." (E. R. Harrison 1971, 195) What Harrison fails to mention is that in the ancient world, the authority of a document was more important than its authorship. (Toorn 2007, 27ff) What this means is that Paul, at the very least, lent his authority to Luke's Gospel.

[349] (Schaff, ANF01 1884, 685)

[350] (Schaff, NPNF2-01 1890, 571)

[351] See also the Anti-Marcionite prologue to the Gospel of Luke which backs up much of what was said by Origen and Eusebius. The Greek and Latin texts, along with their English translation, are available from TextExcavation.com: http://www.textexcavation.com/latinprologues.html#monar chian.

[352] (Schaff, NPNF2-01 1890, 225-226)

[353] Origen writes: "Now it is possible to introduce evidence from Paul's words on our point that the whole New Testament is the gospel when he writes somewhere, 'according to my gospel.' [Rom 2:16] For among Paul's writings we do not have a book called a 'gospel' in the usual sense, but everything which he preached and said was the gospel. And the things which he preached and said he also

wrote. What he wrote, therefore, was 'gospel.'" Origen then proceeds to define the term Gospel to exclude any but the four books commonly spoken of as gospels. (Origen 1989, 38ff)

[354] The Gloria In Excelsis: Luke 2:14; The Sanctus: Luke 13:35; The Nunc Dimittis: Luke 2:29-32

[355] Writing of the Magnificat, Martin Luther says: "In it she really sings sweetly about the fear of God, what sort of Lord He is, and especially what His dealings are with those of low and high degree. ...It is a find custom, too, that this canticle is sung in all the churches daily at vespers, and in a special and appropriate setting that sets it apart from the other chants." (LW 21:298)

[356] Paul Evdokimov attributes this to Origen's *Commentary on the Gospel according to John*. However, he does not provide a citation. I was unable to find a specific statement by Origen to this effect, but it is possible to extrapolate Evdokimov's citation from Origen's remarks concerning the Holy Spirit. (Origen 1989, 113ff) It should also be noted that although Origen was condemned as a heretic at the Fifth Ecumenical Council, he was not condemned on the basis of these writings.

[357] (Origen 1989, 38)

[358] (Gabriel 2000, 17)

[359] Kyriotokos: Mother of our Lord

[360] (Gabriel 2000, 17-18)

[361] (Gillquist 2009, 98)

[362] (Kreitzer 2004, 29)

[363] (Kreitzer 2004, 62)

[364] (Cunneen 1996, 20)

[365] (Gillquist 2009, 100)

[366] (Gillquist 2009, 101)

[367] (Kleinig 2003, 5)

[368] (Cunningham, Wider Than Heaven 2011, Kindle Location 5809)

[369] (Letham 2007, 44)

[370] (Thornton 1949)

[371] (Arndt 1956, 50)

[372] (Lenski 1946)

[373] (Arndt 1956, 63)

[374] (Just Jr., Luke 1:1 - 9:50 1996, 62)

[375] (Just Jr., Luke 1:1 - 9:50 1996, 63)

[376] (Just Jr., Luke 1:1 - 9:50 1996, 75)

[377] (Just Jr., Luke 1:1 - 9:50 1996, 64)

[378] (Just Jr., Heaven on Earth 2008, 64)

[379] (Jacob of Serug 1998, 23, 27)

[380] (Boychuk 2012)

[381] (Thornton 1949, 11)

[382] (Thornton 1949, 11-12)

[383] (Thornton 1949, 12)

[384] (Alfeyev, Orthodox Christianity 2012, 71)

[385] Fr. John Cox, email conversation, May 2013

[386] (Schaff, NPNF2-09 2004, 574-575)

[387] (Schaff, NPNF2-09 2004, 208-209)

[388] Unfortunately, I am not a Greek scholar, so I rely heavily upon those who are.

[389] (Lenski 1946, 62)

[390] (Manelli 2005, 162)

[391] Lutheran scholar Jaroslav Pelikan wrote *Mary Through the Centuries* in 1996. Two years later, at the age of 75, Jaroslav Pelikan and his wife were received into the Eastern Orthodox church.

[392] (Pelikan, Mary Through the Centuries: Her Place in the History of Culture 1996, 13)

[393] (Manelli 2005, 163)

[394] (Lenski 1946)

[395] This hymn is sung at Matins, at Vespers, and at all the

services of the hours.

[396] Veneration is not worship: Veneration is the translation for *dulia*, which is the respect given to saints and angels; while Adoration is the translation for *latria*, the worship due God alone. It must be said that while the two terms are different theologically, the distinction is difficult to observe or maintain in practice. (Pelikan, The Riddle of Roman Catholicism 1959, 134-135)

[397] (Ratzinger, Hail, Full of Grace 2005, 64)

[398] (Ratzinger, Hail, Full of Grace: Elements of Marian Piety According to the Bible 2005, 64-65)

[399] (Scofield 1917)

[400] Epithalamium: a song or poem to the bride and bridegroom at their wedding.

[401] (Spurgeon 1988, 315)

[402] (Ratzinger, Thoughts on the Place of Marian Doctrine and Piety in Faith and Theology as a Whole 2005, 30)

[403] This is the normal meaning of the present indicative sense (γινωσκω), and this understanding is confirmed by the context.

[404] (Geisler 1997)

[405] (Geisler 1997)

[406] (Menachem Mendel of Kotzk 2010)

[407] (Damick, An Introduction to God: Encountering the Divine in Orthodox Christianity 2012)

[408] (Fr. Touma (Bitar) 2012)

[409] (Evdokimov, Woman and the Salvation of the World 1994, 50)

[410] (Evdokimov, Orthodoxy 2011, 82)

[411] Lutherans believe that the human person is active in lower (temporal) things, but passive in higher (spiritual) things. (Schlink 1961, 258) Thus, the human person must be acted upon by God to come to saving faith. (Lutherans, along with other Protestants, are basically dualists, in that the essential part of man is flesh rather than spirit—in that the fall caused the loss of the image of God, but not the loss

of what was essential to humanity.) (Schlink 1961, 258) Calvinists, (which includes the Reformed), believe in the total depravity of humanity, that the image of God was totally lost in the Fall, and that God chooses who will be saved and who will not. The Reformed are Calvinist, but not all Calvinist are Reformed; Reformed theology is also known as Covenant Theology, structured around the three covenants of Redemption, Works, and Grace. There are some bodies which are pseudo-Calvinists, in that they are not five-point Calvinists, meaning they do not accept the five points of the Synod of Dort: 1) Total Depravity, 2) Unconditional Election, 3) Limited Atonement (meaning Christ died only for the Elect), 4) Irresistible Grace (meaning no free will), & 5) Perseverance of the Saints. (Voelker 2006) Protestants from an Armenian background have a somewhat higher view of the human will, in that we can choose to resist God's grace; however, the ability to choose *for* God is not part of their theology. (Bratcher 2010)

[412] (Evdokimov, Orthodoxy 2011, 89)

[413] (St Augustine 1996, 11)

[414] Pascal's original quote from is as follows: What else does this craving, and this helplessness, proclaim but that there was once in man a true happiness, of which all that now remains is the empty print and trace? This he tries in vain to fill with everything around him, seeking in things that are not there the help he cannot find in those that are, though none can help, since this infinite abyss can be filled only with an infinite and immutable object; in other words by God himself. (Pascal 2008)

[415] (Evdokimov, Woman and the Salvation of the World 1994, 193)

[416] (Evdokimov, Woman and the Salvation of the World 1994, 212-213)

[417] Please note that Jesus was born of woman, without the biological seed of a man. If woman was and is inferior, either in her body or by virtue of a share in Eve's guilt, Jesus would share in that inferiority and guilt through Mary. That this is not the case demonstrates that men and women are coequal members of humanity.

[418] (Leeming 1960, 100)

[419] (Leeming 1960, 100-101)

[420] (Leeming 1960, 101)

[421] (Evdokimov, Woman and the Salvation of the World 1994, 51)

[422] (Evdokimov, Woman and the Salvation of the World 1994, 52-53)

[423] (Evdokimov, Orthodoxy 2011)

[424] (McGuckin 2011, 211)

[425] The apparent citation of Judith by Elizabeth, as recorded in Luke's gospel, has important canonical implications, not the least of which is that Martin Luther may have been wrong by separating the Apocrypha from the Jewish scriptures. One of the more common arguments for the removal of the "Apocrypha" from the Old Testament is that the New Testament never (or rarely) quotes from it. The Lutheran author Oskar Skarsaune states: "All the canonical books are quoted or alluded to as Scripture, except Esther. Only one non-canonical book is verbally quoted—and once only, and not explicitly as Scripture (1 Enoch 1:9 in Jude 14-15." (Skarsaune 2002) This argument is demonstrably false; we have already made mention of the citation of Judith. Other "Apocryphal" books either alluded to or directly quoted are 1st & 2nd Maccabees, Baruch, Daniel 13, Judith, Sirach, Tobit, and the Wisdom of Solomon. This suggests the basis for the restrictions made to the Protestant canon of the Old Testament may be faulty, which means Protestants may be using an incomplete canon of Scripture.

[426] (Shilakar n.d.)

[427] (Jahn 1997, 2)

[428] (Jahn 1997, 3)

[429] Rev. Curtis A. Jahn demonstrates a misunderstanding of the Old Testament prophetic ministry and its relationship to their inspired prophecies. There is often an overlap between the prophets and their ministries, such that it is possible for the younger prophet to have known and learned from the elder. The Old Testament also records the existence of the school of the prophets (1 Sam 10:5-6; 2 Kings 2:3,15). Thus, the prophets often restated and/or added to what they

learned from their elders. To imply Mary's words were not inspired because the Bible doesn't state they are inspired, and because she was simply restating what others had said, is faulty thinking. We must also consider the possibility of misogyny as the underlying motivation.

[430] From the Gospels, the book of Acts, and from the Epistles, we know that women played an important part in the ministry of Christ and the ministry of the early Church. (Olson 1992, 21, 25-27, 29, 35) Historically, we know that Christianity elevated the status of women, something that contributed to the growth of the Church. (R. Stark 1996, 95-128)

[431] (Croy and Connor 2011, 255-256)

[432] (Croy and Connor 2011, 256)

[433] *Various persons in early Christianity are called 'slaves of God', including prophets. In Rev. 10.7 προφηται [prophet] and δουλοι [servant] stand in apposition, and in Rev. 11.18 the servants of God comprise the prophets, the saints and those who fear God's name. The Old Testament seems to treat the prophets as the Lord's slaves par excellence, the appositional construction being quite common: 2 Kgs 9.7; 17.13, 23; 21.10; 24.2; Ezra 9.11; Amos 3.7; Zech 1.6; Jer 7.25; 25.4; Ezek. 38.17; Dan. 9.6, 10. In addition, individual prophets are dubbed the slave of the Lord: Moses (2 Kgs 18.12; Dan. 9.11), Joshua (Josh. 24.29), and Jonah (Jon. 1.9 LXX). As mentioned earlier, Mary is twice called the δουλη [slave girl] of God/the Lord in Luke's infancy narrative (1.38, 48). While this expression is not necessarily a synonym for prophet, its application to Mary may evoke the prophets as the quintessential δουλοι [servant] of God in the Old Testament. (Croy and Connor 2011, 260)*

[434] (Croy and Connor 2011, 260)

[435] Croy and Conner cite Eusebius, Theodoret, Basil of Cesarea, Didymus of Alexandria, Epiphanius, and Cyril of Alexandria. (Croy and Connor 2011, 268-269)

[436] (Just Jr., Luke 1.1 - 9:50 1996, 81)

[437] (Just Jr., Luke 1:1 - 9:50 1996, 81)

[438] In Mark 6:3 Jesus is called the son of Mary, rather than the son of Joseph. This likely indicates that Joseph was dead by this time.

[439] (St Nikodimos of the Holy Mountain and St Makarios of Corinth 1984, 122)

[440] This is generally applicable — but in specific and generally academic circles, the situation is much different. Bernard Leeming writes: "Protestants are making serious studies in Mariology (though they dislike the term). Barth cites, among Catholic authors, Scheeben, F. Diekamp, B. Bertmann, E. Przywara, R. Grosche, K. Adam, and Gertrud von le Fort; and others quote, also, Balthasar, K. Rahner, Graber, F. M. Hocht, M. Schmaus, B. Altener, M. Jugie, M. J. Congar, Guardini, E. Dhanis, and Donald Attwarer. ...Protestants do quote various declarations of the Popes, scrutinize the petitions for the definitions of the Assumption, review the history of Fatima and analyze diverse Catholic prayers to our Lady (Leeming 1960, 94-95)

[441] I use the term literalistic instead of literal. When speaking of literal interpretation, we have to ask what type of literature the Bible is and interpret it accordingly. But those who claim to use a literal interpretation rarely if ever treat that question with the rigor it deserves. Yes there are historical books, but what type of history is it? It is in fact a history with a point of view, which is the only type of history practiced at that time. Moreover, it is Deuteronomic History, explicating a single theme: disobedience of the law producing judgment, and repentance bringing reconciliation. The biblical authors do not discuss sociological, economic, technological, or meteorological factors independently, but instead use them in the service of their point of view. Failing to recognize the reasons for which the scriptures were written is not to be literal, but merely literalistic.

[442] Interestingly, and beginning with the Lutheran reformation, Protestants have generally adopted the same method of interpretation used by our Jewish brethren to deny that Jesus is the Christ.

[443] (Rich n.d.)

[444] (Lossky, Panagia 1949, 29)

[445] (Fr. Stephen Freeman 2007)

[446] (Fr. Stephen Freeman 2007)

[447] (Manelli 2005, passim)

[448] (Manelli 2005, 39)

[449] We know the Jews altered their text as part of their argument with Christianity, and in particular Christianity's use of the Septuagint as its own Sacred Scriptures. This change in the Hebrew Scriptures began in the mid-2nd century, as demonstrated by Justin Martyr in his Dialogue with Trypho the Jew. (Schaff, ANF01 1884, Chapters LXXI and LXXII)

[450] (Ambrose of Milan 1881, 284)

[451] (Schaff, NPNF1-03 1890, 483)

[452] (Willis 2002, 359)

[453] WA 6:510

[454] (Luther, What Luther Says 2006, 1257)

[455] (Willis 2002, 360)

[456] (John of Damascus n.d.)

[457] (John of Damascus n.d.)

[458] (Ambrose of Milan n.d., 9.59)

[459] (Leeming 1960, 98)

[460] (Barth, Church Dogmatics I.1: The Doctrine of the Word of God 2009, 179-180)

[461] (Barth, Church Dogmatics I.1: The Doctrine of the Word of God 2009, 187)

[462] Covenant Theology sees the eternal plan of God as working through the two covenants of works and grace. Covenant Theology is a distinctly Calvinist way of providing an overview of and framework for understanding the Bible. As such, it serves as an organizing principle for theology. Covenant Theology shares a similarity to the Lutheran understanding of Law and Gospel, in that it presents a

logical choice: this category or the other, but rarely both.

[463] In our previous discussion of Christian Anthropology, we mentioned that the Orthodox understanding of the fall is much different from the typical Protestant understanding. Barth's thinking is an outgrowth of that difference, which is itself an outgrowth of the Roman Catholic doctrines of original sin and inherited guilt. This is one example of how the Roman and Protestant communions ask the same questions, but provide different answers.

[464] (Barth, Church Dogmatics The Doctrine of the Word of God, Volume 1, Part 2 1956, 188)

[465] (Barth, Church Dogmatics The Doctrine of the Word of God, Volume 1, Part 2 1956, 188)

[466] (Gabriel 2000, 27-28)

[467] (Schaff, ANF01 1884, 404-405)

[468] In this quote, St. John of Kronstadt is explicitly tying together the term mediatress with the function of intercessory prayer. For St. John the term mediatress and the title Mediatrix have nothing to do with the doctrines of Justification or Atonement.

[469] (St John of Kronstadt 2010, Location 325-326)

[470] (Manelli 2005, 56-57)

[471] (Guroian 2010, 3)

[472] (Pentecost 1958, 514)

[473] (Schaff, NPNF2-06 1892, 864-865)

[474] (Schaff, NPNF2-06 1892)

[475] (Gambero 1991, 265)

[476] (Halperin 1993, 228)

[477] (Wesley n.d., 1847)

[478] (Henry 2000, 1534)

[479] (Pentecost 1958, 513)

[480] (Gabriel 2000, 19-20)

[481] (Engelder 1916, 103)

[482] Our Lord took His flesh of the Virgin Mary. In the

process of gestation, the fetus attempts to take over the mother's body. Suzanne Sadedin writes: "Cells from the invading placenta digest their way through the endometrial surface, puncturing the mother's arteries, swarming inside and remodelling them to suit the foetus. ...These foetal cells are so invasive that colonies of them often persist in the mother for the rest of her life, having migrated to her liver, brain and other organs. There's something they rarely tell you about motherhood: it turns women into genetic chimeras." And so we have a physical basis for our understanding that the holiness of God became part of the Blessed Virgin. (Sadedin 2014)

[483] (Louth, Father Sergii Bulgakov on the Mother of God 2005)

[484] (Schaff, ANF01 1884, 135)

[485] The seven pillars of the Church are understood to be the Holy Spirit, what the apostle John calls "the seven Spirits of God" (Rev 3:1). These are the seven spirits (or graces) which rest upon our Lord, which are described by the prophet Isaiah: "And the spirit of the Lord shall rest upon him: the spirit of wisdom, and of understanding, the spirit of counsel, and of fortitude, the spirit of knowledge, and of godliness. And he shall be filled with the spirit of the fear of the Lord" (Isa 11:2-3). These are the seven pillars by which Christ supports His Church.

[486] In the post-enlightment era, a distinction is made between the natural and the supernatural. This distinction is foreign to Sacred Scripture. God did not leave his creation void; no, just as the Spirit brooded over the primeval waters, so God remains involved with His creation. The created order contains both the natural and spiritual realms, with human beings serving to link the two realms.

[487] (N. V. Harrison, The Entry of the Mother of God into the Temple 2006, 159)

[488] (Just Jr., Heaven on Earth 2008, 95)

[489] (Just Jr., Heaven on Earth 2008, 94)

[490] The Ark of the Covenant appears to have been lost to history, perhaps destroyed during the Babylonian Captivity. What is known is that the second temple contained no Ark. The Roman General Pompey, after taking Jerusalem in 63

B.C., entered into the Holy of Holies and declared it was empty. (Tacitus 109); (Josephus 1987)

[491] (Contantinou 2008, 125)

[492] Oikoumenios is a late sixth century author of the first extant Greek commentary on the book of Revelation. It appears that Oikoumenios was a non-Chalcedonian and a Monophysite, making his commentary the work of a heretic, and therefore unacceptable to the prevailing Christian orthodoxy. (Constantinou 2008, 17ff) That this is so is evidenced by the pressure put upon Andrew of Ceasarea to produce his own commentary, which was acceptable to the community, as evidenced by the numerous copies that were made. In contrast, the commentary of Oikoumenios exists in very few copies, and was only discovered in 1901. (Constantinou 2008, 13)

[493] (Brighton 1999, 310-311)

[494] (Just Jr., Heaven on Earth 2008, 95)

[495] (Hahn and Hahn, Mary, Ark of the Covenant 1994)

[496] Mary's statement may provide a way of understanding the involvement of a human being in salvation. Certainly Mary accepted the angel Gabriel's word, with all its physical and spiritual portent. Her acceptance was necessary—God is not a rapist. Yet the Incarnation of the Son by the Holy Spirit of the Virgin Mary was accomplished with no action on the part of Mary, apart from her voluntary acceptance of and submission to the will of God.

[497] (Whiteford n.d.)

[498] (Cunningham, Wider Than Heaven 2011, Kindle Locations 2309-2314)

[499] (Cunningham, Wider Than Heaven: Eighth-century Homilies on the Mother of God 2011, Kindle Locations 4077-4082)

[500] (Cunningham, Wider Than Heaven: Eighth-century Homilies on the Mother of God 2011, Kindle Locations 4725-4728)

[501] (McGuckin 2011, 214)

[502] (Pelikan, Mary Through the Centuries: Her Place in the History of Culture 1996, 16)

[503] (Leeming 1960, 95)

[504] (Leeming 1960, 97-98)

[505] (Brighton 1999, 327)

[506] (Brighton 1999, 327)

[507] (Brighton 1999, 332)

[508] (Peter of Alexandria 2004, 476)

[509] (Schaff, ANF06 2004, 450)

[510] (Schaff, ANF06 2005, 495-496)

[511] (Florovsky 1976, 172)

[512] (Schaff, ANF01 1884, 887-888)

[513] (T. Ware 1997, 258)

[514] (Schaff, NPNF2-14 2005, 373-374)

[515] (Schaff, NPNF2-14 The Seven Ecumenical Councils 2005, 303)

[516] (Schaff, NPNF2-14 2005, 314)

[517] (Florovsky 1976, 172)

[518] (McGuckin 2011, 216-217)

[519] The Formula of Chalcedon is a product of the 4th Ecumenical Council (451 A.D.). It was intended to resolve theological conflicts as to the manner in which both the Son of God and the man Jesus could be united in the one Christ. (Meyendorff 1975, Ch 1, passim) The formula did not entirely resolve the issues—for reasons both theological and political, certain churches did not subscribe to the Formula, churches known today as the Coptic and Oriental Orthodox churches. (Certain countries objected to the assertion that to be Christian was to be Byzantine.) (Schmemann, The Historical Road of Eastern Orthodoxy 2003, 138-142) In the western churches, the formula of Chalcedon became the basis for the Athanasian Creed.

[520] (Meyendorff 1975)

[521] (Florovsky 1976, 174)

[522] (Guroian 2010, 65)

[523] This is the most common way of citing this phrase. In

the Nicene and Post-Nicene Fathers collection, the quotation is broken into two sentences which maintain the same sense, but not the same force: "Hence it is with justice and truth that we call the holy Mary the Mother of God. For this name embraces the whole mystery of the dispensation." (Schaff, NPNF2-09 2004, 592)

[524] (Kiefer 2001)

[525] (Florovsky 1976, 172-173)

[526] (Schaff, NPNF2-14 2005, 388)

[527] *Si Martinus non fuisset, Martinus vix stetisset* ("If Martin [Chemnitz] had not come along, Martin [Luther] would hardly have survived")

[528] (Chemnitz 1971, 209-210)

[529] (Chemnitz 1971, 101)

[530] (Luther and Knaake, Weimarer Ausgabe 1883, v11, 319-320)

[531] (Leeming 1960, 100)

[532] (Stakemeier 1962, 456)

[533] (The Christian Apologetics Society 2007)

[534] (Graef 2009, 37)

[535] (Schaff, ANF06 2004, 478)

[536] (Gabriel 2000, 41)

[537] (Florovsky 1976, 171)

[538] (T. Ware 1997, 258)

[539] (McGuckin 2011, 214)

[540] (Hainsworth 2004)

[541] (Hainsworth 2004)

[542] (Schaff, NPNF2-14 2005, 453-454, 458)

[543] (Florovsky 1976, 184)

[544] (Gabriel 2000, 42)

[545] (Gabriel 2000, 45)

[546] (Bulgakov 2009, Kindle Locations 316-317)

[547] (Hughes n.d., 3-4)

[548] (Dabney n.d.)

[549] (Dabney n.d.)

[550] (Hughes n.d., 4)

[551] (Schaff, NPNF1-05 1886, 316)

[552] Sergei Bulgakov notes:

Original sin consists in choosing life in and for the world. ...Two dimensions of original sin are transmitted by Adam to all human beings: the infirmity of nature, expressed most clearly in the process and fact of death, and sinfulness. While the first is a constant, shared without exception by all human beings, the second is a variable and may by the power of grace be entirely suppressed. This is true of the Virgin Mary in an exceptional way, but is also true of John the Forerunner and other holy persons whose feats are recorded in scripture. (Bulgakov 2009, Kindle Locations 224-228)

[553] (Lossky, Panagia 1949, 25-26)

[554] (Lossky, Panagia 1949, 26)

[555] (Schaff, ANF05 2004, 419)

[556] (Matusiak n.d.)

[557] (St John of Shanghai & San Francisco 2005, 57-58)

[558] (St John of Shanghai & San Francisco 2005, 55)

[559] St. Bernard, Abbot of Clairvaux (a.k.a. Bernard of Clairvaux) is the author of hymns much beloved in the protestant church, such as *Oh Sacred Head Now Wounded*, *Jesus the Very Thought of Thee*, and *Jesus, Thou Joy of Loving Hearts*.

[560] (St John of Shanghai & San Francisco 2005, 57)

[561] (St John of Shanghai & San Francisco 2005)

[562] (Maas 1912)

[563] (Pelikan, Mary Through the Centuries: Her Place in the History of Culture 1996, 15-16)

[564] (Thornton 1949, 9)

[565] (Schaff, ANF01 1884, 919)

566 Tertullian writes much the same in "On the Flesh of Christ, Chapter XVII." (Schaff and Menzies, ANF03 2006, 939-940)

567 The parallels between the corporate promises to Israel and the individual promises to Mary are too numerous to mention here.

568 (Just Jr., Luke 1:1 - 9:50 1996, 65-70)

569 (Jacob of Serug 1998, 29-30)

570 The phrase "bad femininity" is an unfortunate turn of phrase from this 17th century mystic and theologian. It likely has a cultural rather than a theological foundation. Theologically, we should think of this as referring to Eve's state after the fall — of both Eve and Adam having lost their state of original righteousness, of which virginity was the sign.

571 (Evdokimov, Woman and the Salvation of the World 1994, 222)

572 In the Annunciation the angel Gabriel tells Mary "the power of the Highest shall overshadow thee" (Lu 1:35). Compare this with Rev 12:1 where we see the woman (Mary) "clothed with the sun."

573 (Robinson and Gould 2004)

574 (Evdokimov, Woman and the Salvation of the World 1994, 207)

575 (St Gregory Palamas 2013, Kindle Locations 693-705, 710-714)

576 (Pelikan, Mary Through the Centuries: Her Place in the History of Culture 1996, 20)

577 (Origen 1989, 38)

578 (Pelikan, Mary Through the Centuries: Her Place in the History of Culture 1996, 19)

579 (Pelikan, Mary Through the Centuries: Her Place in the History of Culture 1996, 18)

580 Edward Schillebeeckx points out that the Dogmatic Constitution on the Church (a.k.a. *Lumen Gentium*), places Mary in the context of "ecclesiology" rather than "Christology and redemption". (Breck, Scripture in Tradition

2001, 230) This is not an entirely fair assessment; since the *Lumen Gentium* is discussing dogma as it relates to the church, it could be said with equal vigor that the *Lumen Gentium* places Christ Himself in the context of "ecclesiology" rather than "Christology and redemption". However, it could also be argued that when Vatican II decided to include Mary within the *Lumen Gentium* rather than as a separate document, it expressly connected Mary with ecclesiology instead of Christology. (Ratzinger, THE ECCLESIOLOGY OF THE CONSTITUTION ON THE CHURCH, VATICAN II, 'LUMEN GENTIUM' 2001) The title of "Mother of the Church" is a Mariological innovation that serves to separate Mary from the Church and consider her apart from her Son. This innovation first occurs in 1125 (not long after the great schism of 1054), and the title was formally ascribed to Mary by Pope Paul VI at the conclusion of the Third Session of Vatican II in 1964. (Mauriello 1996) Moreover, although the Catechism of the Catholic Church gives more space to Mary in the context of Christology than it does to Ecclesiology, the section on Ecclesiology refers to Mary's "saving office" as expressed by the titles "Advocate, Helper, Benefactress, and Mediatrix". (Catholic Church 1997, 252) Thus it could well be argued that the Latin Church today does indeed place more emphasis on Mary in the context of ecclesiology than it does on Christology.

[581] (Barth, Church Dogmatics The Doctrine of the Word of God, Volume 1, Part 2 1956, 143)

[582] (Barth, Church Dogmatics The Doctrine of the Word of God, Volume 1, Part 2 1956, 145-146)

[583] (Barth, Church Dogmatics The Doctrine of the Word of God, Volume 1, Part 2 1956, 143)

[584] (Fannon 1962, 126)

[585] (Evdokimov, In the World, of the Church: A Paul Evdokimov Reader 2001, 120)

[586] Paul Evdokimov (of blessed memory) is writing in the context of a larger discussion about the Virgin Mary, and quotes Maximus the Confessor's definition of "mystical" as "the one in whom is best manifest the birth of the Lord." Unfortunately, Evdokimov does not source this quote, and I've been unable to find an English language translation approximating the quote. I expect that is because

Evdokimov was reading the original Greek, translating it in his head into Russian, then writing it in French, and I'm now quoting the English translation. In the context of Evdokimov's writing, I suspect he would agree with my modest alteration of his quotation, and its direct application to the Virgin Mary.

[587] (St Gregory Palamas 2013, Kindle Locations 723-728)

[588] The Omophor is part of an Orthodox bishop's vestments, distinguishing the bishop from other clerical orders. The Omophor is similar to a stole, although shorter, and is worn about the neck and shoulders.

www.ingramcontent.com/pod-product-compliance
Lightning Source LLC
Chambersburg PA
CBHW021350090426
42742CB00009B/805